The Meaning of Paul for Today

A LIVING AGE BOOK

THE
MEANING
OF
PAUL
FOR TODAY

by C. H. DODD

Meridian Books
THE WORLD PUBLISHING COMPANY
Cleveland and New York

C. H. Dodd

Charles Harold Dodd was born in England in 1884 and educated at Oxford. After studying theology at Mansfield College, he was ordained in 1912 and became minister of the Congregational Church at Warwick. From 1915 to 1930 he was Yates Lecturer in New Testament Greek and Exegesis at Mansfield College. He was a lecturer in New Testament Studies at Oxford from 1927 to 1930. At Manchester from 1930 to 1935 he was Rylands Professor of Biblical Criticism and Exegesis. He was Norris-Hulse Professor of Divinity at Cambridge from 1935 to 1949. Since then he has lectured at Columbia University, Princeton Theological Seminary, and Union Theological Seminary. His other publications include *The Gospel in the New Testament* (1926), *The Authority of the Bible* (1928), *The Bible and Its Background* (1931), *The Bible and the Greeks* (1935), *Parables of the Kingdom* (1935), *History and the Gospel* (1937), *The Bible Today* (1946), *The Coming of Christ* (1951), *Gospel and Law* (1951), *Christianity and the Reconciliation of the Nations* (1952), *The Interpretation of the Fourth Gospel* (1953), and *New Testament Studies* (1953).

M

A LIVING AGE BOOK (MERIDIAN)
Published by The World Publishing Company
2231 West 110 Street, Cleveland 2, Ohio
First printing January 1957
Fourth printing August 1961

Library of Congress Catalog Card Number: 57-6677
Manufactured in the United States of America

PARENTIBUS PRIMITIAS

Contents

. . . But the big courage is the cold-blooded kind, the kind that never lets go even when you're feeling empty inside, and your blood's thin, and there's no kind of fun or profit to be had, and the trouble's not over in an hour or two but lasts for months and years. One of the men here was speaking about that kind, and he called it 'Fortitude.' I reckon fortitude's the biggest thing a man can have—just to go on enduring when there's no guts or heart left in you. Billy had it when he trekked solitary from Garungoze to the Limpopo with fever and a broken arm just to show the Portugooses that he wouldn't be downed by them. But the head man at the job was the Apostle Paul . . ."

Peter Pienaar speaking in *Mr. Standfast*
by JOHN BUCHAN

PREFACE

"These that have turned the world upside down are come hither also." So the people of ancient Salonica judged two men who came proclaiming the Christian Way to a pagan society. By happy fortune, one of the two revolutionaries has survived in his writings, and we are in a position to learn at first-hand how Paul of Tarsus, artisan, scholar, traveller, leader of men, carried out into that imperial world the gospel that had transformed his own life, interpreting it in daring and vivid terms to the mind of his time. A gospel so deeply personal and so widely human can survive the intellectual vicissitudes of centuries, and bear reinterpretation for a new age without losing its vital force.

In this little book I have made some attempt to suggest the place of Paul in the history of religion; but I have been more particularly concerned to bring out what I conceive to be the permanent significance of the apostle's thought, in modern terms, and in relation to the general interests and problems which occupy the mind of our generation. I find in Paul a religious philosophy of life orientated throughout to the idea of a society or commonwealth of God. Such a philosophy finds ready contact with the dominant concerns of our own day.

The basis of this study is the Pauline epistles. There is now a very general agreement among students that in the First Epistle to the Thessalonians, in both epistles to the Corinthians, and in those to the Galatians, Romans, Colossians, to Philemon, and to the Philippians, we possess authentic letters from the hand of the great missionary himself. The order in which they are here named is probably the order of their composition. The remaining five epistles (for no one now supposes that Paul wrote "Hebrews") are still in dispute. Without entering into the dispute here, I may state my belief that the balance of probability is on the side of the genuineness of II Thessalonians and of Ephesians. The latter, however, was probably not written to Ephesus, or at least not exclusively to Ephesus. It may have been some kind of circular letter, written, as we must suppose, almost simultaneously with Colossians. Even if it could be shown not to be from the hand of Paul, it would still remain an important statement of the Pauline philosophy of life in its most developed form. Upon these ten letters I have based my exposition. On the other hand, I cannot persuade myself that the Epistles to Timothy and Titus are, at any rate in their present form, authentic letters of Paul, though they no doubt contain Pauline material. I have not used them as sources for Paul's thought. The Acts of the Apostles, which contain a valuable outline of the Apostle's missionary journeys from the pen of one of his companions, I have treated as only a secondary authority where his inner life and thought are concerned.

I have given quotations from the epistles in an English form which represents my own attempt to reproduce, sometimes by way of paraphrase rather than literal translation, the precise meaning of the original.

They may be compared with any other version that may be accessible. For those who do not read Greek a comparison of a number of different versions is perhaps the next best thing.

I may perhaps be permitted a word upon one aspect of the subject which is at the moment a matter of controversy. The view here taken of the religion from which Paul reacted is very different from the picture of first-century Pharisaism which has recently been set before us by Dr. Abrahams and Dr. C. G. Montefiore. I would observe that Paul himself leaves us in no doubt as to the general effect of the type of Judaism he once professed; and whether or not this type of Judaism was the orthodox Pharisaism of the time, matters little for our present purpose. It is a phase of religion which recurs in many periods, and not only within Judaism. But Paul unequivocally describes himself in his pre-Christian days as a Pharisee. Moreover, we have in the gospels an independent description of Pharisaic religion from a different point of view; and it appears to me that on this matter the gospels and the Pauline epistles explain and corroborate one another. The Jewish scholars I have mentioned have selected from the corpus of Rabbinic writings a set of sayings which give a very attractive picture of Judaism under the Law, and their method of selection seems more critical and discriminating than that pursued by scholars of a former generation—Weber, Schürer, Edersheim—who out of the same corpus produced a far less attractive picture. In any case, however, the evidence for the first century seems to be extracted with difficulty and some uncertainty from a mass of material committed to writing not earlier than the close of the second century. The gospels and the Pauline epistles, on the other hand, are contemporary evidence that in the first century a very strict and exclusive kind of legal puritanism did overshadow the religious life of a group of pious Jews:

that this group was for the time being dominant; and that this group, if not identical with the Pharisees, was at least included in that sect, and largely determined its main religious tendency. Both the gospels and the Pauline epistles give us hints of a more humane and spiritual tendency within Judaism and even within Pharisaism; and this tendency may be represented by the Rabbinic teaching to which Dr. Abrahams and Dr. Montefiore have introduced us. Paul, if Luke has reported him correctly, belonged to "the strictest sect."

To acknowledge my indebtedness to all books and teachers without whose help this little book could never have come into existence would be an endless task; nor is it part of my purpose to give a bibliography. But I cannot refrain from commending to others two books from which I learned very much about Paul: Heinrich Weinel's *S. Paul: the Man and his Work* (E.T. pub. Williams & Norgate 1906), and Adolf Deissmann's *S. Paul: a Study in Social and Religious History* (E.T. pub. Hodder & Stoughton 1912). I could wish that any whom this book may lead to further study of the apostle would read those two books. But above all, let them read the letters themselves— not lections from the letters, but each letter as a unit in itself—either in the original or in a good modern translation such as that of Professor Moffatt.

I am grateful to my colleague Dr. Buchanan Gray, to the Rev. John R. Coates, and to the Editor of this series for suggestions and advice while the book was in proof.

C.H.D.

Mansfield College, Oxford,
July 17, 1920.

The Meaning of Paul for Today

FROM JESUS TO PAUL

I

The story of the Gospels is an unfinished drama. Its historic interest is pivoted upon the conflict between the new liberating message of the Kingdom and the religious system represented by the Pharisees. In the narrative of Mark we watch the forces gather for the inevitable clash. Challenged on one issue after another—with a challenge not forced upon a reluctant situation but growing out of the nature of irreconcilable ideals—the supporters of the old order gradually rally for a battle royal on the whole front of man's religious destiny. More and more it becomes clear that no accommodation is possible. There is a clear issue: on the one hand the Way of the Nazarene, with His startling assertions and denials; on the other hand all that the piety of the time prized as the essentials of a revealed religion. The plot thickens, until in the dim morning light of the fatal Passover the antagonists stand face to face—a nation on one side, the rejected Prophet on the other. The clash comes, and when the earthquake and the eclipse are past, the Established Order remains supreme. The gospel of emancipation has been added to the limbo of shattered illusions, and Pharisaism is triumphant.

That is the crisis of the movement. The situation holds all the elements of real tragedy: a conflict of passionate human interests in which ancient good, becoming uncouth, overcomes the better that might be, and the stirrings of the human spirit after freedom are baffled by historic necessity. But it is evident that the plot is not finished. The whole development has pointed forward, to this situation certainly, but not to this as conclusion. And indeed the gospels themselves obscure the tragedy in a sudden blaze of supernatural light. In the intoxicating joy of Easter morning the defeat is forgotten, and the divine Victor holds the stage. But the faith of the Resurrection is so far a matter of personal religious experience: it is not, as yet, history. As a *dénouement* of the tangled plot it is scarcely even relevant. It is the supreme appearance of the *Deus ex machina*. The risen Christ is Victor indeed over Death; but He is not Victor over the Pharisees. For all the raptures of the disciples, the great system of Pharisaic Judaism stands, as imposing, as self-sufficient, as ever. The tragic conflict is not yet resolved.

Various hands have essayed the construction of a convincing Last Act. For the "realist" school the illusion of the Resurrection is but the deepest note in a final and irredeemable catastrophe. The President of the Immortals has finished His sport with the Nazarene. This is, however, to abandon the data of the plot; for the drama is cast not for disaster but for joy. For the school of romantic melodrama there must be a vindication of poetic justice; and the Risen Christ takes His sword of vengeance and sees His desire upon His enemies. It matters here little whether the *mise en scène* is a Michelangelesque Last Day, or whether, the venue being removed to solid earth, Christ is shown triumphing over the ruins of Jerusa-

lem in the fatal year of Titus's victory.[1] Such a dé-
nouement is a denial of the central motive of the
drama. The character of the Hero must be consistent
with itself; and the triumph of a vengeful Messiah is
not the triumph of the Victim of Calvary. It is therefore no resolution of the tragic knot.

For a convincing *dénouement* the Hero of the
drama—the Speaker of the Sermon on the Mount, the
Prisoner of the Sanhedrin, the Bearer of the curse of
the Law on Golgotha,—must emerge, He and no
other, as the conqueror, the conqueror by His own
weapons and by no other, of that unchanged Pharisaism, so noble in its stuff, so pernicious in the final
issue of its spirit, which had by an inner necessity of
its being destroyed Him. In His victory the Cross
must have its indispensable part, and the Resurrection
must be shown to be not only an imaginative truth of
the supernal world, where the baffled spirit takes
refuge from intractable facts, but an active force in
real life. Then, and not till then, shall we rest satisfied
that the whole dramatic situation has been adequately dealt with and the tragic conflict reconciled.
This is the *dénouement* which History has written.
The beginning of it can be told in a few words: "A
Hebrew of Hebrews, in regard to the Law a Pharisee
. . . I was laid hold of by Christ Jesus . . . I am
crucified with Christ, and yet I am alive—not I, but
Christ is alive in me." [2] Was revenge ever more complete? Imagine this man (as we may well imagine
him, for he was there in spirit at least) among those
fanatical Jews who would not enter Pilate's hall "lest
they should be defiled," yet stood without clamouring
for the death of the Carpenter-Prophet who had
dared affront the majesty of their hoary Law. And
then see him yielding utterly to the spell of the Cross
upon which he or his like had fastened the Rejected.
That is real conquest. It is the method of the Christian
Revolution.

Here we get the clue to the unity of the New Testament. The Epistles are often opposed to the Gospels
as though they contained "rival philosophies." If in
the story of the Prodigal Son we have the heart of
Christ's message, where, it is asked, is this message to
be found amid the maze of speculation about Law,
Sin, and Sacrifice which fills the pages of the Epistles?
Those who ask that question have failed to notice that
the real problem of that immortal tale is the churl-
ish elder brother. "He was angry and would not go
in"; and in spite of the father's pleadings, there he is
left when the tale ends. Good reason for this: when
Jesus told the tale the elder brothers were fiercely refusing His invitations to renew fellowship with those
despised prodigals whom Jesus "came to seek and to
save." The epistles of Paul show us the elder brother
broken down by the Father's love and leaving home
and its secure delights to go into far countries and
seek out those brothers who still lingered among the
swine and the husks. If the language in which he tells
us how it came about is tortuous and difficult, we may
find in it a sign of the contortions of the spirit which
had to be straightened out before the elder brother
could put away his pride and prejudice and learn his
Father's mind.

In all this we are thinking of Paul not as an individual merely, but as the one mind through which we
can read from the inside what Christ's victorious assault on Pharisaism meant. Paul's letters reflect his
experience; and his experience was an epitome of the
revolution which Christ wrought in religion. There
was in Jewish religion a rich spiritual treasure, gathered through centuries of a history as strange as any
this world can show. But the treasure was not available for mankind, and the process which denied it to
the world made it useless or worse to its possessors.
"You Pharisees," said Jesus, "have taken away the
key of knowledge; you have not entered in yourselves,

and you hindered those who were trying to enter in." The task which He set Himself was not simply to teach new truth and leave it at that. He embraced the destiny of Messiahship. That meant a harder task. It meant gathering up the threads of the past and weaving them into the new design. He came, "not to destroy, but to fulfil." In particular it meant that He undertook the task of liberating the spiritual treasure of Israel's faith for humanity. Because He was faithful to that destiny He died on a Roman cross.[3] In Paul and in the work of his mission we see the task being accomplished. In Paul the devout passion for conduct which distinguished the Jewish religion is seen liberated, enlightened, made spiritual and personal, by what Paul found in Christ; and then impressed upon the life and thought of the wide world in terms which belong to that strangely composite state of mind where the mystical East met the Roman West through the humanizing medium of the great Hellenic tradition.

Because of this Paul is a great figure in the history of religion. Yet his thought has more than a merely historic interest. Religion is one of the determining factors in all history. Too often its organization becomes, as it had become in the time of Christ, an obstacle to the free progress of man. For this reason the reformer and the revolutionary are very ready to lose patience with religion and set it aside. Yet the dynamic of religion remains, for good or ill, the strongest of all human motives. Part of the work of Christ was that He redeemed religion itself for the saving of men. It is this side of His work which so powerfully affected Paul that he remains the classic exponent of the idea of freedom and universality in religion. While religion remains the problem, the peril, but also the one hope of human progress, his work has a contemporary interest.

II

A CITIZEN OF NO MEAN CITY

In the first century of our era Western civilization was coterminous with the Roman Empire. Augustus had set forward with some differences and with greater success the far-reaching policy of his brilliant uncle. He put an end to the evil political system, or want of system, which had made the Roman Republic in its later phases a menace to civilization. The constitution which he established worked at least in the direction of public order and peace. A tendency set in to make the provinces co-operative parts of a great commonwealth instead of the plunder of a narrow circle of aristocratic families.

Throughout the eastern provinces of the Empire Rome was the inheritor, and in a great measure the upholder, of an earlier system. From the time of Alexander the Great the countries bordering the Levant had come strongly within the circle of Greek civilization. The Greek language was current in most of the towns, even if native languages subsisted alongside them, as they did more especially in the country districts. The towns which had been founded, or transformed, by Greek monarchs in the period after Alexander possessed, and retained under Roman rule, a limited local autonomy which was the shadow of the proud independence of the old Greek city-state, though the encroachments of the central authority slowly sapped their vitality. In our period, however, this disintegrating process was not far advanced; and on the other hand the frequent elevation of these towns to full municipal rank, carrying with it the Roman citizenship for the municipal aristocracy, gave a very secure position to the city-state within the Empire. In these municipal communities the old keen intellectual life of Greece, fertilized by its new association with Oriental thought, flourished exceedingly. Alexandria, Ephesus, Antioch, and many other cities, had their schools of philosophy; but not only so: philosophy had come out of the schools, and was rapidly becoming a concern of the man in the street, who listened with at least that measure of interest which fashion decreed to the "preaching friars" of the Cynic or Stoic doctrines. His understanding of them might be exceedingly superficial, and he might listen only to find subjects for after-dinner talk; but at least he was not hopelessly at sea when he heard a philosophic term used in conversation. There was a large reading public, and books of a sort were plentiful and fairly cheap. Not philosophy alone, however, but religion too, was becoming a popular concern. Alongside the stately public rituals of the various cities were the more or less private and independent religious brotherhoods which tried to provide a religious atmosphere more fervent and more satisfying to the feelings of the ordinary man than those antiquated and formal rites could supply.

There was one very widely spread religion which combined the splendour of antiquity, the tenacity of a national faith, and the direct personal appeal of a religion of heart and life—the religion of the Jews. This strange people was already becoming cosmopolitan. Few towns of any size throughout the Eastern provinces of the Empire were without their Jewish colonies. In some of the greatest the Ghetto was an element of extreme significance in the corporate life of the place. The Jews had already embarked on that career for which they seem so singularly endowed by nature—the career of finance.[1] Their eminence in this walk of life, together with their fanatical nationalism and their queer religious customs, made them far from popular. Yet the attraction of Judaism was strongly felt, especially in those circles where men could not find satisfaction with the State religions. The Jewish communities, or synagogues—civil and reli-gious brotherhoods enjoying much liberty of self-gov-ernment—were almost everywhere a nucleus for a more or less loosely knit group of "God-fearers," to use the Jewish term, who adopted many of the beliefs and practices of their Hebrew neighbours without ac-tually becoming Jews.

The ancient city of Tarsus in Cilicia is a favourable example of the municipal city-state; Oriental in the background of its life and traditions, markedly Greek in its culture, and enjoying a secure position in the general order of the Empire. It had its school of philos-ophy, in which a succession of able teachers had given a pre-eminence to the Stoic sect. Its commerce pros-pered. Doubtless the important Jewish colony was in-timately associated with this side of the city's life. Among them was at least one family possessed of the Roman citizenship, which implies, probably, member-ship of the order from which the local magistrates were drawn, and at any rate some social standing in the town. It is with a son of this family that we have to do.[2] The boy had the old Hebrew name of Sha'ul, famous in history as the name of the first King of Israel, whose tribe, that of Benjamin, was also that of these Tarsian Jews. That, however, was only his home-name. To his fellow-citizens outside the syna-

vogue he was Paulus. He must, of course, have possessed a Roman family name and first name—we may
think of him as Gaius Julius Paulus, or Gnaeus Pom-
peius Paulus, if we wish to fit him into his natural
environment in the city of his birth. He learned to
speak and write Greek with ease. He could quote
Greek poets, and use the popular philosophical language of the time easily and naturally. With all this,
however, he was by no means a Greek. His family belonged to the Puritans of Judaism—nationalist in outlook, strict in religious observance. They spoke
Aramaic at home, even though they used Greek at
market or in the City Councilchamber.[3] The boy was,
in fact, sent to Jerusalem, the national capital, in
order that his education should be strong on the dis-
tinctively Jewish side. He made great strides in his
studies, and was probably preparing for the career of a
Rabbi, when events occurred which disturbed the
tenor of his life.[4]

A new sect had appeared within Judaism. It was
composed of the followers of a Galilaean craftsman,
who without any apparent authority had set up for a
Rabbi, and had scandalized the religious leaders by his
bold appeal to the common people and his intensely
critical attitude to the Law and the Temple. He had
fallen into their hands, and they had secured his condemnation at the hands of the Roman Governor on
the charge of being a claimant to the throne of Judaea
—a preposterous charge which nevertheless seemed to
have some foundation in his well-attested claim to
be the "Messiah." The execution had not fulfilled its
purpose to any considerable extent; for the followers
of the Galilaean asserted that he was still alive, and
apparently got people to believe this extraordinary
statement; for the sect was growing with alarming
rapidity. The young Paul saw here a vocation which
commanded his ardent devotion. He would be the instrument of the God of his fathers in putting down

this pestilent and blasphemous heresy. After some
very effective work to this end in the city and its neigh-
bourhood, he obtained a commission from the religious
authorities to extend the good work. He set out for
Damascus with instructions to the local synagogue
there to accept his direction in rooting out the Gali-
læans.⁵

On the way something happened. Paul arrived at
the city of Damascus in sorry plight—nervously shaken
and half blind. As he recovered, instead of carrying
out his commission he commenced a vigorous campaign on behalf of the faith he had set out to de-
stroy.⁶ From this time on his whole life was given to
the propagation of Christianity. His activities were by
no means always pleasing to the older Christians, and
especially to their leaders, but after a time he succeeded in establishing some sort of a concordat with
the principal men of the Christian community at
Jerusalem, which left him a free hand in his mission
to the populations of the Roman provinces outside
Judæa, including the non-Jewish elements in those
populations.⁷ Indeed, as time went on, the non-Jewish
elements in the Christian communities he founded
greatly preponderated over the Jewish, and the type
of Christianity which prevailed among them was of a
broader, more cosmopolitan type than that of the
original community. It was above all a religion of
emancipation. "For liberty you were called," is the
watchword of Paul's great controversy. This liberty
rested upon a personal and inward relation to Christ,
replacing allegiance to laws and traditional institutions. The person of Christ was thus not less, but possibly more, central to the new Christians than even to
the first preachers of the faith; and Paul's mission was
an assertion of the completeness and independence
of the Christian faith. It meant that the new religion
had broken through the narrow limits of a mere Jewish sect, and set out to claim the world. Paul, Ro-

man citizen as he was, would seem to have conceived the idea—a wild idea it may well have appeared—of "the Empire for Christ." In pursuit of it he spent years in travelling up and down the Roman ways which had linked up the world of that age in so wonderful a fashion, and in navigating the Eastern Mediterranean in storm and shine.

It was an adventurous life he led—and a perilous. Robbers still haunted, in spite of Rome, the inland regions of Asia Minor; and the fleet which had swept the Levant of pirates could not control the Levantine storms, which at least four times brought the intrepid traveller to shipwreck, and once tossed him for twenty-four hours in open sea before rescue arrived. In addition there were the perils to which the propagator of unpopular doctrines exposes himself, even in an age so tolerant on the whole as the first century. It was no doubt something of a joke among Paul's friends that he had once outwitted his enemies by escaping from Damascus in a basket let down from a window, but it was no joke that he was three times scourged by local magistrates (in spite of his Roman citizenship), and no less than five times received the savage maximum penalty of "forty stripes save one" from the Jewish synagogue authorities. This penalty, it is said, was usually commuted or reduced on grounds of mere humanity, and the fact that Paul underwent it five times gives us a hint of the great physical strength which he must have possessed, in spite of his insignificant appearance and his recurrent attacks of a complaint which may have been malarial.[8]

Of his earlier preaching tours we have only the most meagre accounts. Later the record, partly in the form of a diary made at the time, which is generally attributed to his medical attendant Luke, is much more complete. We can trace his strategy. He would settle down in some central spot, preferably a Roman con-

ventus or assize town, such as Ephesus, Philippi, or Corinth. Very often he found a favourable starting-point in the local synagogue; and if the doors of the synagogue were closed to him when it was discovered how revolutionary his teaching really was, at least he had by that time made good his footing among the "God-fearer." Sometimes he spoke quite publicly, like the Cynic preachers, in the market-places. At Ephesus he hired a philosopher's lecture-hall after the morning session was over, and gave instruction there daily from 11 to 4.[8] Meanwhile he supported himself by his trade of tentmaking. At Corinth his trade was the means of winning him a footing among the Jews of the place, and of gaining for him one of his most permanent friendships. He found work with a Jew from the Black Sea and his wife, who apparently were in a somewhat large way in the tent-manufacturing business, and travelled between Rome and Ephesus. Prisca and Aquila (the lady is almost always mentioned first) became his trusted coadjutors in the mission; and the incident may suggest to us how the very mobile conditions of international trade and industry in that period lent themselves to the spread of new ideas.[10]

After preaching came the organization of the new Christians into communities, formed partly on the model of the Jewish synagogue with its traditions of self-government, and partly on the lines of the guilds and brotherhoods, which were so popular among the middle and lower classes of the Empire. The actual amount of organization was kept to a minimum, and free cooperation was the central idea. The members of these communities were mainly obscure persons, many of them poor persons, slaves or freedmen, some of them in business, or holding positions under the municipalities, or even in the imperial Civil Service. A few, but not many, persons of wealth, a few, but not many, highly educated persons, might be found in close fellowship with their poorer neighbours in the brotherhood of the Christian Church.11

With these scattered communities Paul kept in constant touch, partly through his own and his friends' continual travels, and partly by correspondence, of which we possess some valuable specimens. These letters are for the most part called forth by circumstances. They do not set out to be "literature," but to meet the occasion. One of them is a brief note to a personal friend, about a slave who had run away. Most of the others discuss matters of interest to the particular churches addressed. Two only, those to the Romans and to the Ephesians, make any attempt at a systematic and comprehensive statement of a line of thought. It is from these fragmentary materials that we have to reconstruct Paul's ideas. It is obvious that we cannot hope in such circumstances to attain great completeness or precision. But while there are disadvantages in possessing our materials in this casual form, there are advantages which more than compensate. The letters of Paul are intensely alive—alive as few documents are alive which have come down to us from so remote antiquity. They give us, not a mere scheme of thought, but a living man. We have the same intimate knowledge of Paul that we have, also through his letters, of Cicero, and of scarcely anyone else in those times.

He was a person of extraordinary versatility and variety. He was an enthusiast and a mystic, with powers of rapt contemplation beyond the common. He was also one who could apply the cold criticism of reason to his own dreams, and assess soberly the true value of the more abnormal phenomena of religion. This combination of enthusiasm with sanity is one of his most eminent marks of greatness. His thought is strong and soaring, adventurous rather than systematic. He had a hospitable mind, and a faculty for assimilating and using the ideas of others which is a great asset to anyone who has a new message to propagate: he could think in other people's terms. In it all he was dominated by a white-hot zeal for the truth of which he was convinced as he was convinced of his own existence; and more, by a personal devotion to "the Lord Jesus," as he habitually called the divine Person who, as he believed, had spoken to him first on the road to Damascus and never again left his side. That devotion was his religion, and it controlled his thought and his life. With this went a strong humanity, and a longing that others should enter into the free and joyous life that he had found. This longing was not the mere fervour of the religious bigot for his own creed. It was the passion of a man who loved men and had a genius for friendship. His was a warmly emotional nature, passionate in affection, passionate also in opposition when his hostility was aroused. He said and wrote things he was sorry for, when he wrote or spoke in heat; but it was always a generous heat, kindled by no selfish feelings. The most difficult lesson he had to learn from his Lord was that of tolerance and charity. We can see him again and again in his letters pulling the rein upon his passion lest it get out of control. It was perhaps partly a sense of the need to cultivate tolerance, partly a sense of strategy, which led him at times into ways of accommodation which were easily misunderstood, not only, perhaps, by opponents. He may have made mistakes in this direction, but we can hardly respect too highly the efforts of this naturally intolerant man to "become all things to all men"—to go to the very verge of compromise, and to risk misunderstanding, that he might assert the central and essential principle over against relatively unimportant accidents. That he was able to do so was the result of a sympathy—sufficiently rare in strong, self-confident natures—which could see very clearly the other man's point of view. This faculty sometimes makes difficulties for Paul's interpreters! To these qualities it is hardly necessary to add, so patent is it, that this man displayed an inflexible determination, a persistence that nothing could weary, and a courage that was not a mere constitutional audacity, but a steady fortitude prepared for anything except retreat.[12]

He fell a victim to the malice of his old associates, who could not forgive him for becoming the leader in a movement which had shaken their position to its foundations. On a visit to Jerusalem he was set upon by a mob, and rescued by the Roman officer in command of the garrison. The Jewish authorities preferred charges against him which he offered to answer, as was his privilege, before the Emperor's tribunal. The result of the appeal was that he attained, in strange fashion, his lifelong ambition of visiting Rome.[13] During a long imprisonment he continued his activities, both by intercourse with a wide circle in the City, and by a lively correspondence, which contains some of the most mature fruits of his thought. Towards the end, however, he found himself almost forsaken, and it was a lonely man whom we see dimly through the mists of tradition led to the Three Fountains by the Ostian Way to receive the swordstroke which was his last prerogative as a Roman. His tomb is beneath "St. Paul's without the Walls"; and in spite of the mighty impression he made in his own day, in spite of the veneration of his name, for the bulk of the Christian Church this passionate champion of a religion free, personal, and ethical remains "outside the walls." [14] It is for those who can never satisfy themselves with institutional or legal religion that he has in every age a message.

III

THE HOPE OF THE WORLD

How did the first great Christian missionary look upon the world he lived in, its condition and destiny? Paul has been regarded as a pessimist, and if optimism means the belief that this world as it stands is the best of all possible worlds, then it is difficult to clear him of the charge. He found the world deeply marked with failure and imperfection; but he never dreamed that it need remain so, or that it could ultimately remain so.[1] The whole universe, he says, is groaning and travailing in pain. It is full of suffering and it is a slave to decay—"subject to vanity." That word, echoing the haunting refrain of Ecclesiastes, the classic of pessimism, accurately calls up those suggestions of tiresome futility which the world of nature with its ceaseless round of change and decay brought to the mind of Paul as of many other observers, especially in the East. Man too is part of nature, and shares its heritage of pain and thwarted endeavour." "They were born; they were wretched; they died." So in an Eastern tale the Wise Man sums up the course of human history. So far the outlook of Paul does agree with the typical Oriental pessimism.

But for him that is not the whole story. Beside the groaning and travailing there is in the world an "eager expectation." The whole universe, with head outstretched and intense gaze, is waiting for something very glorious which shall finally deliver it from slavery to futility and give a meaning to all its pangs. It is a sorry world, but an expectant world, subject to vanity but saved in hope; travailing now, but destined to glory. It is a world, above all, with a real history; and that is what Oriental pessimism never allows. But the conception of a universe in which there is real movement and real development is very congenial to the modern mind. Indeed, we feel ourselves here very much at one with Paul in his view of the world. We, like him, dare not deny the miserable facts of pain and failure, in nature and in man as part of nature; but we would fain believe that the change and flux have a tendency, and that tendency an upward one. That the upward tendency is automatic and inevitable we are perhaps less sure than our fathers. Perhaps we feel, like Paul, that the universe—or at least this earth—is waiting for something. And perhaps, too, Paul was right in thinking that the key to its destiny was in the hand of man.

For us, even more definitely than for him, man is part of nature. In man the energy of the material world, the instinct of animal life, rises—precariously and incompletely, but really—into the sphere of consciousness and of will. In him the apparently blind impulse towards greater perfection working, as we believe, in the universe, attains a measure of freedom and self-direction. In him also instinct, become rational, can turn back upon the material world out of which he has partly emerged and actually control its changes, aid its advance, intercept its decay. Directly upon his body, indirectly upon other parts of the physical universe, the thought of man, and the action which is the outcome of his thought, works beneficently or destructively according to his choice. For the most part his action upon the world seems blundering and of doubtful value. The immense control of manner that man has gained—our so-called "progress"—is of very uncertain benefit to the universe conceived as a system aiming at perfection in every part after its kind. But if man himself could be different; if his own life were altered by the attainment of right relations with God and with his fellow-man, his role in the world in which he lives might be a more beneficent one than we can well imagine. The artist uses the material world as means to the expression of that love of beauty which is one aspect of the love of God, and thereby transfigures the material—delivers it, as Paul might say, from the bondage of decay into the liberty of glory. If we could all become artists over the whole of life, using our whole environment to express the highest spiritual relations within our reach, is it not possible that the influence of humanity upon the world might change its whole aspect? Paul at least thought that in some way the universe was waiting for man to attain right relations in the spiritual sphere—"waiting for the revealing of the sons of God."

A contemporary poem addresses "Everyman" in language which beautifully suggests a thought akin to Paul's:

All things search until they find
God through the gateway of thy mind.

Highest star and humblest clod
Turn home through thee to God.

When thou rejoicest in the rose
Blissful from earth to heaven she goes;

Upon thy bosom summer seas
Escape from their captivities;

Within thy sleep the sightless eyes
Of night revisage Paradise:

In thy soft awe yon mountain high
To his creator draweth nigh;

This lonely tarn, reflecting thee,
Returneth to eternity;

And thus in thee the circuit vast
Is rounded and complete at last,

And at last, through thee revealed
To God, what time and space concealed.

How Paul conceived the "emancipation" of the physical world we cannot tell. Many contemporary thinkers imagined a miraculous change of the very substance of things—a new heaven and a new earth in strict literalness. Paul may have shared the belief. But the important point seems to be that he conceived such a change as no accident, but directly connected with the working out of human relations. In attacking what was wrong with men he firmly believed that he was attacking the problem of the universe. Shall we put it in this way, that the problem of reality is at bottom a problem of personal relations? [3] No purely physical speculations will ever solve for us the problem of this tangled universe. Personality holds the clue; and the solution is personal and practical. The spiritual aspirations of man, faithfully followed, let us into the secret of evolution and give the only hint we can get of its purposes.

We turn, then, from the Apostle's philosophy of the world to his philosophy of human history. We shall expect to find it based upon a gloomy estimate of human life as it is, saved from pessimism by a tremendous faith in what it may become. He saw the world of men in two opposing groups—his own nation and pagan society, i.e. practically the pagan Græco-Roman Empire. His interest in that Empire, its ethical and social life and problems, was intense. It dated, doubtless, not from his conversion to Christian-

ity, but from his youth at Tarsus. Only the character
of that interest was changed from condemnation and
despair to hope when he looked afresh with the eyes
of Christ. The Empire indeed, as he saw it, was rot-
ten with vice and injustice. His picture of pagan
morals in the opening chapter of the Epistle to the
Romans is lurid, but most of it could be corroborated
from pagan sources. His judgment, however, was
not undiscriminating or blind. Even in the pagan he
recognized a natural knowledge of God, a conscience
bearing witness to a "law written on the heart," an
instinctive knowledge of right and wrong.[4] Its political system, he confessed, aimed at the vindication of
right and the suppression of wrong, and in its measure succeeded.[5] Its imperial law restrained the threatened outbreak of undiluted and anarchic evil.[6] And
yet he saw a monstrous perversion of the whole. A
mass of humanity, the offspring of God, had somehow
taken a wrong turn so decisive that at every step it
was farther from God. The light that was in it had
become darkness; and God had given it over to its
own unrestrained passions.

It is in this strain that Paul inveighs in his letter to
Rome against the corruption of the Pagan world; and
so far, we can imagine an audience of Pharisaic Jews
listening with applause. Suddenly Paul turns upon
them and drives home the charge that they have known
better but not done better. "You call yourself a Jew,
and rely upon your law, and boast of your God. . . .
You set up for a guide of the blind, a light to the
benighted, a trainer of the ignorant, a teacher of in-
fants. . . . You teach others, but do not teach yourself. You preach 'Do not steal,' and you are a thief!
You preach 'Do not commit adultery,' and you are an
adulterer! You abominate 'idols,' but you plunder
their temples! You, who boast about your law, by
breaking the law dishonour God!"[7] They are strong
words for a Jew to use to Jews. We can surely over-

hear in them the indignant shame of a high-minded Israelite who found that in the great cities of the pagans men of his own race had made the name of Jew to stink by their hypocrisy and baseness.

We must not forget that the darkness of this picture is relieved by a pagan here and there who "did by nature the things of the 'Law'" and by at least a faithful remnant among renegade Israel. But Paul found nowhere, neither in the pagan world nor yet among his own people, the moral power and stability which his sense of the divine holiness demanded of "sons of God." Out of the mass of weakness and corruption the universe awaited their revealing: where could they be found? To the inquiring mind, all history comes to be a search for the family of God, the Divine Commonwealth through which alone man and the world can attain emancipation. This Commonwealth of the sons of God can only be of God's own creation. Thus from the divine point of view history shows God seeking His sons among sinful humanity. Paul had inherited from his Pharisaic training a belief in divine predestination, though the Pharisees, we are told, somehow managed to preserve alongside of this doctrine a belief in human free will. The use, however, which Paul makes of the doctrine is most instructive. It is for him the means of asserting and maintaining the freedom and originality of God's personal dealings with men. The Pharisaic God was for practical purposes an Absentee. He had created the world; at a few points in the remote past He had definitely intervened; in the future He would once more intervene in Judgment; but in the present age the history of man was the mechanical working-out of an inexorable Law. The pagan mind, on the other hand, was haunted by fatalism. In that age philosophy tended to support with its authority the ancient popular superstition that a man's fate was controlled by his stars. You were born with a certain horoscope, and by that your fate was irrevocably fixed. That the dominion of the "world-rulers," the "elemental spirits," was broken[8] was a part of the message of primitive Christianity which scarcely appeals to us; but it came with the sense of a tremendous relief to the spirit-ridden mind of the first century, as it still comes to many in China and India. Over against the mechanical rule of law and the domination of the fatal star alike, Paul maintains that God always and in every age is free to deal personally with men.[9] He called Abraham to be His son, but He did not then leave natural heredity to produce His Divine Commonwealth. He chose Isaac; He chose Jacob; He called seven thousand in Elijah's day, who stood firm against the idolatry of their time; He chose the faithful remnant on whom Isaiah set his hope—the saving salt of a lost people. Last of all He ordained as His Son Jesus the son of David "according to the flesh," and through Him brought a multitude out of all nations into "adoptive sonship."[10] At every point a free, personal act of God. The doctrine of absolute and arbitrary divine sovereignty which accompanies this view of history seems to us destructive of human freedom in any real sense; but in the early preaching of the Gospel it served a purpose of the highest value. If you could believe that your destiny was not decided by the working of mechanical law, or determined by a ruthless fate, but that the divine vocation of which you were conscious in your own soul was an act of sovereign power on the part of a God present here and now to save you, it would surely give a new sense of assurance and stability in the face of all hostile forces. It is with that intent that Paul always makes use of the argument from predestination. "Those whom He foreknew He also predestined; and those whom He predestined He also called. . . . If God be for us, who can be against us?"[11] And any philosophy which admits a divine government of the universe must

leave a place for something like this Pauline theory
of a "selective purpose." [12] As Paul meant it, it is not
a doctrine of determinism, but rather a protest
against the prevalent determinism of his time by the
assertion that a real "fresh start" is possible at any
time where God comes into fresh touch with man.
So much for history viewed from the divine end.
From the human end it is the story of the progressive
response of sons of God to the calling of their Father,
and the resultant constitution of the People of God.
On man's part, simple trust in God gives play to the
divine purpose. The inevitable instance of such trust
in the past was Abraham: "Abraham trusted God."
[13] So soon as a man was
found to take that attitude to God, the People of God,
or the Divine Commonwealth, was already in existence, if only in germ. It was maintained and increased, Paul argued, by exactly the same means, by
the successive personal response of men in each generation to the calling of God. [14] Behind all the scholastic arguments of the Epistles to the Romans and the
Galatians lies the crucial question whether religion is
a matter of national inheritance and external tradition, or a matter of ever-fresh personal response to the
gracious dealing of God. In form, the nation founded
by Abraham was the People of God; but "the majority of them God did not choose," as was shown by the
fact that in spite of their participation in the ordi-
nances of the Covenant they "were unfaithful." [15] The
nation possessed the outward forms of a Divine Commonwealth or Kingdom of God or "Theocracy," but
it was only a minority in the heart of it that kept
hold of the reality. Elijah's Seven Thousand, Isaiah's
Remnant—these were the representatives of the true
People of God, the faithful Divine Commonwealth
hidden in the bosom of apostate Israel. [16] Not that
even they could be said to have attained perfect obedience to the precepts of the divine Will, or to be able

to claim God's favour on the basis of their own achievement, but their "faith" in God kept them true, amid doubts, uncertainties, failures, and imperfections, as they waited confidently for the next stage of His dealing. For the time being, this Divine Commonwealth was in "bondage." Like an heir in his minority "under tutors and guardians," it led a kind of provisional existence under the shadow of the Law, unable to win freedom of action or to become a power of salvation to the world.[17]

The upshot of past history, as Paul saw it, may be put in these terms: in the pagan world, a few isolated individuals doing, in some measure, the will of God as revealed in their consciences, but unable to form a real community;[18] in Israel, a Theocracy in form, but so bound and hedged about as to be unable to effect anything for God in the world at large. The prophets had always foreseen that this age must be succeeded by another, in which the free life of the Spirit should create a world-wide society or Kingdom of God. Now with the Resurrection of Christ, Paul held, this new age began. The heir had come of age; the dim light of an ever-deferred hope had given place to the clear dawning of the "The Day." [19] Out of Israel and out of the pagan world alike God was calling His sons into a real community-life through which the world should be saved. This is the "mystery" kept silent through agelong periods, but now revealed." [20] A "mystery" to Paul's Greek readers meant a dramatic spectacle which conveyed to those who had the key deep truths of the unseen world unsuspected by the "profane" mind, and not to be expressed in language. Even so the historic drama of Christ's death and resurrection had brought into clear light the hidden purposes of God, by uniting faithful men, out of all nations and classes, in one firm commonwealth free and powerful to do the will of God.

Thus the New Age had begun. That is a fundamental belief of all early Christians. They knew they were living at a crisis—at the crisis—of History. They were "children of The Day"—the day of God's self-revela-tion; they were inhabitants of a new world.[21] They were quite sure that fresh powers had entered into them, and that the divine purpose was forcing its way through their efforts into the world at large. And though they knew also that the time of crisis must bring sufferings which they must share, of which in-deed they must bear the brunt,[22] yet they were upheld and animated by a vivid hope to which nothing seemed too good to be true. That hope clothed itself in strange apocalyptic imagery. Paul, in his earlier letters, and no doubt in his earlier preaching, made free use of this imagery, though it is clear that he was all the time re-interpreting it. At first he certainly ex-pected that before long—at all events in his lifetime —Christ would visibly return and lead His people in an aggressive campaign against all evil;[23] that He would reign over a Kingdom which would come to include those Israelites who in the course of the "selec-tive purpose" had fallen out by the way, and, we may take it, those pagans also who had hitherto remained unrepentant, until the whole race should be gathered into one.[24] At the End of All, having put down all hostile or rival authority and power in heaven and on earth, He would offer us all to God, and God would be all and in all.[25]

Putting aside so far as we can what is (for us at least) merely figurative in this sketch of the future, we can at least see how for Paul the time in which he lived was the turning-point of history; before Christ, the disintegration of humanity, and the gradual selec-tion of a small remnant to carry on God's purpose; from the coming of Christ, the re-integration of the race, the inclusion, step by step, of the "rejected," and the attainment of final unity for all that is, in the perfected Sovereignty or Kingdom of God. As he grew older, the apocalyptic imagery of the earlier days tended to disappear at least from the foreground of his thought, and more and more his mind came to dwell upon the gradual growth and upbuilding of the Divine Commonwealth. He saw the Church going out into the world to save the world, ready to "fill up what was lacking of the sufferings of Christ" for the sake of mankind, and restlessly seeking out the sons of God in the name of their Father. He saw it impelled ever further and further in the quest, constrained by the love of Christ, reconciling, liberating, including in its universal fellowship Jew and Greek, barbarian, Scythian, slave, freeman, and so working out the divine purpose to "sum up all things in Christ." 26 If this is an idealized picture of what the Church has been even at its best, it gives the standard of what it might be, a perpetual rebuke and challenge to a Church which has fallen from its ideal.

IV

THE QUEST OF THE DIVINE COMMONWEALTH

An attempt has been made in the preceding chapter to sketch the philosophy of history which can be discovered in the writings of Paul. In its main outlines it is set forth in his letter to the Christians of Rome. That fact is not without significance. The Epistle to the Romans is the manifesto of Paul's missionary program written at the very height of his activity, in the near prospect of a visit to the imperial centre of the world. For the Romans, as for us, it was necessary to have some understanding of his philosophy of history if they were to appreciate what were his aims and principles in preaching the Christian Gospel throughout the Roman world. The hope of the world, as he saw it, lay in the "revelation of the sons of God"—the realization of the Divine Commonwealth. In his faith in Christ he held the key to the "mystery" of that Divine Commonwealth. He knew the secret of its realization. Hence he was a missionary.

In the circles in which Paul was brought up there was a perfectly definite theory about the Divine Commonwealth. He was a Jew, and the Jews believed

themselves to be in the most absolute sense God's
chosen people. The divine blessing was an estate en-
tailed upon the historic nation derived, as was believed, from Abraham, and preserved intact through
the centuries by its observance of the institutions
summed up in the Mosaic Code. The reverence and
enthusiasm with which these archaic institutions were
regarded are almost inconceivable. That they represented the eternal laws of all reality was held certain.
It was said that the Law was the pre-existent plan
according to which the world had been created, and
that the Deity spent eternity in its study.[1] The purport of such apparently hyperbolic expressions was
clearly to identify the particular set of rules for life
and thought contained in the Pentateuch with absolute truth and absolute right. With such a belief it is
no wonder that those who took it seriously had an
outlook upon the world which bears the appearance
of national arrogance run to an almost insane extreme. Strangely, and yet intelligibly enough, even
the Jew whose personal life and conduct had little
resemblance to the high ethical ideals of the Old Testament felt an exaltation of spirit as he thought that
his nation alone of all peoples of the earth possessed
the inmost secret of things. The rest of mankind was
there for Israel's sake[2]—to serve Israel or to chastise
Israel as might be Jehovah's inscrutable purpose, but
in any case to be subjugated or blotted out in the end,
when God should finally declare His judgment. The
Jewish people was the Divine Commonwealth.

The Pharisaic party which cherished these views
with deepest conviction was by no means indifferent
to the fate of the non-Jewish world. It is even
probable that this sect was prominent in the vigorous
Jewish propaganda which was going forward throughout the Mediterranean area at the time when Christianity appeared. But in the nature of things such
propaganda could only be a kind of spiritual im-

perialism. It rested on the assumption of the inherent and eternal superiority of one nation and one form of culture over all others. Individuals of other nations could be incorporated in the chosen people, but it was only as naturalized aliens that they could take their place. They were held at arm's length, admitted only grudgingly and by degrees to the spiritual privileges of Israel, and they could only be full members of the community by adopting all the peculiar, and in part barbarous, rites and observances of the Jewish religion, including the rite of circumcision, which was counted by Greeks and Romans as a degradation. It was no wonder that the civilized world of the time looked with scorn upon these pretensions, so opposed to the broad humanism of the Stoics with their gospel of Cosmopolis, the City of Zeus. For all that, Judaism had somewhere within it a moral passion and power of regeneration before which even Stoicism was impotent. Many an earnest soul was willing even to bow to the arrogant pretensions of the Jew for the sake of the ethical reality he stood for, so strangely high and pure in spite of the meanness of its earthly vessels.

In such a position of affairs we can see the peril to the future of humanity. It is not good that men should submit themselves to the dictation of any one people, whether in politics or in religion. It is not good that the highest personal morality should be associated with a corporate egotism. All imperialisms are a denial of the fundamental unity of mankind, however bright their fallacious promise of such a unity. The propaganda of Imperialism is a propaganda against the brotherhood of man, and if missions to the "heathen" or to the "lower classes" are inspired by the national or class egotism which believes that "our sort" must be right and everybody else must accept our direction, then they are a form of spiritual imperialism. "Woe to you, scribes and Pharisees, play-actors!" Jesus is reported to have said; "you traverse sea and land to make one convert, and when he is there, you make him twice as much a child of Gehenna as yourselves." [3] It sounds severe, even unfair, but religious propaganda which rests on sectional pride always runs this risk.

Paul the Jew had to suffer the shattering of his deepest beliefs before he came through to a new conception of a missionary's work. He had to learn that there was no distinction of Jew and Gentile. It needs some effort of the imagination to realize what this surrender cost him. Perhaps it was like an American of the South being obliged to admit that he must sit at the feet of the negro, or an Australian asked to view with equanimity, even to further, the spread of "yellow" civilization. As a young man he had heard the humanistic talk of popular Stoicism at Tarsus, and his religious instincts revolted against what seemed an obliteration of profound moral distinctions. Now he must capitulate. The Stoics were right: God had made of one stock all nations on earth.[4] Of all He made the same demands, to all the same offer on the same terms. In the present corruption of the world no one nation could stand aloof and say, "This is the wickedness of other people." If humanity was cursed by sin, all had sinned, whether Jew or pagan, and all had missed the divine splendour of ideal humanity.[5] God alone could make good what was amiss, and He could do it only with men who abandoned all self-confidence (all "glorying in the flesh," as our translation of Paul has it). How this new creation was to take place we must presently inquire. For the moment we are concerned to see this man as the pioneer of a new method of establishing the Divine Commonwealth. He saw it growing like a body, cell to cell; or built like a temple, stone to stone, through the sharing of a common life, the surrender to a common purpose. The union of mankind he saw taking place at a level of common humanity deeper than all the ramifications of nationality, culture, sex or status. He asked only that each should confess his part in the general wrong, and trust God to put him right in God's own way—not the way of his preference ("not my own righteousness, but the righteousness which comes from God through trusting Him"). On that common basis he saw a unity growing out of the very diversity of men's minds and gifts—many members, but one body; diversity of gifts, but one spirit.[6] On these terms he appealed to the devout Pharisee of the Jewish synagogue, to the philosophers of Athens, the civil servants of the Empire at Rome, the traders of Corinth, the artisans of Ephesus, the slaves and "riff-raff" of the seaport towns, the half-Greek inhabitants of Asiatic cities, and the barbarians of Malta and the Lycaonian highlands. With this demand he stood before kings and proconsuls, and with the same offer he won the rascal fugitive slave Onesimus, and made him "a brother beloved."

It has already been indicated that ideas of a universal commonwealth were present in the pagan world. Rome, largely inspired by the sublime ideals of Stoicism (which in Paul's time gave a Prime Minister to the Empire, and in the next century ascended the throne itself), was consciously aiming at its establishment. Paul, himself a Roman, was stirred by the thought of what Rome was doing. Imperial Rome is the background of his greatest epistle, and the writing of it was largely inspired by the thrilling prospect of setting up the standard of Christ on its ancient Seven Hills. And yet he knew that Rome must fail. The Roman Empire could never become the Kingdom of God. It lacked the moral foundation. Even its philosophic instructors were content to compromise with institutions which oppressed men and superstitions which degraded them. The Empire was founded on violence: Rome "made a solitude and called it peace." It transcended national boundaries, but it ruled by an upper class of the privileged and showed its contempt for the poor by giving them "bread and circuses." Its blossoming might be the fine flower of humane culture, but its roots were in the degradation of slavery. And it demanded the abject worship of an autocrat, which meant bondage, not of the body alone, but of the spirit. The failure, in the end, of this magnificent attempt to unify the human race justified Paul's judgment on it. He sought its best ends, by means which did not kill but made alive the individual spirit. Rome crushed the individual to glorify the State. In the end it destroyed itself by strangling or crippling every institution of local government and every guild or corporation through which free co-operation was possible. It was characteristic of Paul's mission that wherever he worked there sprang up live, vigorous local communities, free and democratic, where individual initiative was prized and individual gifts found play. Each of these communities felt itself to be a living embodiment of that City of God whose ultimate reality was eternal in the heavens. "Your citizenship is in heaven"—you are a colony of the Divine Commonwealth—Paul wrote to the Christians of the Roman colony of Philippi.[7] This was because in each individual member the great change had taken place whereby the "life of the (New) Age"[8] became a personal experience.

There is nothing which in the last resort can unite mankind but the free contagion of this life. It is a current view today that economic interdependence will unify mankind. It is questionable. Nor indeed can political organization attain that end, as we are learning every day, unless the spirits of men be made one. We see rather a forecast of the true process when the vision of the artist or the rapture of the musician draws men together across the barriers, for they too have touched life at a point deeper than our transient divisions. But there is something deeper and more universal than art or music, and of that Paul speaks. Man is born to be a son of God, and only in "the liberty of the splendour of the sons of God" can the commonwealth of man be founded. The missionary enterprise of Christianity, in its ideal and largely in its practice, is an indication of the true method of building the brotherhood of man in which the Kingdom of God may find expression. When the missionary enterprise enters, as it has sometimes done, into an unnatural alliance with national ascendancies and all the superstitions of Empire, it stultifies itself. But when the missionary goes out, not as a European or an American, but as a Christian simply, a son of God seeking brotherly fellowship with sons of God waiting to be revealed in all nations—when he makes his appeal to the simply human in men, speaking the word of reconciliation which unites us to God and to each other—then he is the truest servant of the coming Kingdom that the world can show. Such was Paul the Missionary.

It was not to be expected that Jewish patriotism would acquiesce in this treason to the national idea. The tradition of privilege was too strong. Even any loftier souls who may have given up the dream of political domination yet clung tenaciously to their spiritual ascendancy. Jerusalem might never become another Rome, but Jerusalem was the only conceivable spiritual metropolis of the world. To them Paul declared that their Jerusalem was a slave city, bound hand and foot to an obsolete tradition: "Jerusalem above is free, which is our Mother!" [9] The unifying patriotism of the City of God—that "city within whose walls the souls of the whole world may assemble" [10]— was in that watchword pitted against the divisive patriotism of the tribal State and tribal religion. That is the inner meaning of the fight which Paul waged all his life against his old associates.

There can be little doubt that in principle the question of "universalism" was decided for Paul in the fact of his conversion, even though it remains highly probable that both his theory of the matter and his practice underwent development. The Christianity with which he had come into direct conflict was not the timid "right wing" which under James the Lord's brother sought a quiet *modus vivendi* with national Judaism, but the militant radical section which the martyred Stephen had led into the most decisive break with the national and legal tradition.[11] It was to this radical Christianity that he was converted. From the beginning he had against him the organized force of the Jerusalem Sanhedrin and the synagogues. The main count in their indictment was that he was a traitor to the Law and a confederate of Gentiles. "It is the Jews," he wrote bitterly from Corinth in the first letter of his that has survived, "who killed the Lord Jesus and the prophets and drove us out, who never obey God, who are the enemies of all mankind, and *who try to prevent us from speaking to the pagans for their salvation."* [12] The turn of phrase shows how Paul felt about it.

But he had also against him the conservative right wing of the Church, which included some at least of the original disciples, though we may believe that converts from the sect of the Pharisees formed the backbone of the party.[13] So far as the more moderate leaders are concerned, we can understand and respect their position. They were cautious in the presence of an untried venture. They saw, and perhaps report exaggerated, the perils of Paul's bold propaganda. Some of the language he used about freedom from law had a dangerous suggestion of anarchy. They did not know to what subversive doctrines he might commit the Christian movement. Moreover, they felt, and not unreasonably, that they were likely to know the mind of their Master better than this new-comer who had never heard Him speak, and they could not think that He wished the door quite so widely opened. It is not the only time in history that the nearest followers of a great leader have failed to understand his secret, even while they died for his cause.

Nevertheless, Peter, generous and impulsive as ever, had, without thinking much of what was implied, early taken steps in the direction of a liberal attitude to pagans. It was perhaps his influence which led to the concordat under which Paul worked for some time with the concurrence of the "pillars" of the Church at Jerusalem, and according to the Acts of the Apostles it was he who persuaded the Council of Jerusalem to sanction a liberal missionary policy in Syria and Cilicia.[14] And indeed when he visited Paul and his friends at Antioch, he was quite carried away by the enthusiasm of the forward movement. The controversy had come to hinge upon the question of eating at table with converts from paganism who had not been adopted into the community with the recognized Jewish ceremonies, especially circumcision. Large questions do sometimes turn upon small points. This point, however, was not so small as it might seem. It is not a small thing to-day for an Indian Brahmin to break caste by eating with a pariah. Moreover, the Christian brotherhood had from the first made its life centre about the common table. To refuse to break bread with a fellow-Christian was to deny that he had any part in Christ, at whose table the brotherhood met. Peter, however, sat at table with these half-Greek Syrians in the friendliest way, and the difficulty seemed over. Then came members of the extreme "right wing"—adherents of James, but no doubt *plus royalistes que le roi*. Peter, frightened, drew back. Even Paul's old friend and leader, Barnabas, gave way. The dispute culminated in a regrettable public quarrel between Peter and Paul, the echoes of which, perhaps, were to be heard later even in the Pauline churches.[15] Peace, however, seems to have been restored, as between the leaders. Peter and John probably took in the end the liberal view, and even James kept on friendly terms with Paul, and it was not by any ill-will of his, but quite the contrary, that his ill-calculated tactics ultimately contributed to Paul's arrest and imprisonment.[16]

But the extreme conservatives pursued him everywhere with unabated zeal. They opened war by a powerful mission to Galatia, where they all but succeeded in winning to a Judaic Christianity the churches Paul had founded.[17] From that time he had to count "perils from false brethren" among the difficulties of his work.[18] During most of his active life he was a nonconformist and a free-lance, regarded with cool and rather suspicious tolerance by some of the most respected leaders of the Church, and with horror by the "ultra-orthodox" right wing. We need not impugn their motives, as Paul did in the heat of controversy. They were honest men and zealous servants of the Gospel as they understood it. Paul made mistakes, and some bad ones, in the course of the struggle. But Paul was right and his opponents were wrong on the main issue.

It was the controversy with the Jewish National Party in the Church that drove Paul to formulate and defend the principles underlying his Gospel. The laboured argument which fills large sections of the letters to Rome and Galatia—and which has often been treated as almost the only valuable element in the Pauline writings—is to be regarded as apologetic directed against Pharisaic Judaism (which he knew by early training from top to bottom) and its revival within the Christian Church. This apologetic is almost accidental; it does not represent his missionary preaching; it represents the theoretical justification of its principles against those who denied his right so to preach at all in the name of Christ. Much of it is *argumentum ad hominem* and of temporary validity only as addressed to those particular adversaries. The very success he gained antiquated his polemic. But concealed beneath these temporary forms of thought is his permanent contribution to the philosophy of religion. His victory, indeed, was less complete than it seemed. By other channels than that of the Judaistic propaganda the old spirit of Pharisaism entered into the Church: its narrowness, its formalism, its bondage to tradition, its proneness to national and class prejudice. We shall not fight it today, in ourselves or in the Church, with the precise weapons which Paul used; but if we can read his essential thought out of its obsolete forms into the living language of today we shall at least know how to deal with that undying Pharisee whom most of us carry beneath our hats. But, also we shall have learned what Christianity is, from the man who, though he knew not Christ after the flesh, divined better than any what Christ stood and stands for.

V

THE ANCIENT WRONG

We have seen how Paul saw humanity in evil case, and how he devoted himself to its rescue from this evil case by "the revealing of the sons of God" as a closely knit Divine Commonwealth. More precisely, he saw mankind enslaved, and lived for its emancipation; and he saw it alienated, and lived for its reconciliation. Those are the two great words of the Pauline gospel: "redemption," "atonement." By this time they have become wholly theological terms, with their meaning confused by centuries of dogmatic definition. "Redemption" was the process by which a slave obtained his freedom. Thousands of Jews taken prisoners in the wars had been sold into slavery in the Roman dominions, and it was a popular work of benevolence for wealthy Jews to "redeem" them into liberty. That is the source of the metaphor. We shall therefore do well to use the term "emancipation" as the nearest equivalent of the Pauline expression. "Atonement" is an old English word meaning the restoration of unity ("at-one") between persons who are estranged. In *Richard II* Shakespeare makes the king say to the rival noblemen, Mowbray and Bolingbroke,

"Since we cannot atone you, we shall see
Justice design the victor's chivalry."

The secondary meanings which the word has acquired
are foreign to the language of Paul. In the Authorized
Version of the New Testament "atonement" is the
translation of a perfectly ordinary Greek word for the
reconciliation of estranged persons. Paul saw men
divided into hostile camps "biting and devouring one
another." [1] Behind that internecine strife he saw the
hostility of men to God their common Father. Get rid
of the enmity toward God, and the divisions of men
may be overcome. "While we were enemies we were
reconciled to God through the death of His Son":
"He is our peace, who made both one, and broke
down that dividing wall, our enmity." [2] "Reconciliation," then, of the estranged, "emancipation" of the
enslaved, are the cardinal points of Paul's Gospel.

We have now to ask, What is the enslaving force,
and what is the cause of the alienation? To those
questions, Paul gives one answer, Sin. That word too,
however, he used in a sense different from that in
which it has come to be used in modern theology and
ethics. To understand his view of sin we must make
our way through some rather tangled metaphysics.

Paul conceived reality in a dualistic way. There are
two planes of being, the one eternal, the other temporal; the one visible, the other invisible. [3] The visible
world is in some sort a revelation of the invisible,
but an imperfect revelation, for it is entangled in a
mesh of decay ("corruption"). Decay is, in fact, so in-
separable a property of the visible world that Paul
gives us no other general term for its material substance. He simply calls it "decay," describing it by its
most evident property rather than defining it. Similarly, he describes the substance, if we may so call it,
of the invisible world as "splendour" ("glory"), and

he may have conceived it, with many Greek thinkers, as akin to light and fire.

The cosmical aspect of the question, however, is
only vaguely touched upon. It is only in man that
Paul shows us anything approaching a complete
scheme of the relations of the two planes. For man
belongs, at least potentially, to both. His bodily existence partakes of the nature of the temporal and visible: "he wears the image of the earthy." In him the
visible substance is "flesh," material, and inevitably
subject to decay. The flesh is temporarily animated
by the *psyché* (if we use the word "soul" we are suggesting false implications), which is the principle of
conscious life, including even intellectual processes,
but not belonging to the heavenly or eternal order. On
the other hand is the "inner man," whose nature is
different. About the inner man in the non-Christian,
Paul is somewhat vague; but it appears that the
"reason" by which God is known to all men, and the
"heart" upon which His law is written, partake of
the nature of the invisible and eternal world.[4] The
non-Christian is, however, to Paul's mind an imperfect,
immature specimen of Man. It is in the Christian that
we must study human nature in its developed form.
Here the inner man is definitely described as "spirit"
(*pneuma* as distinct from *psyché*). Like "flesh,"
spirit is a *continuum*; it is the form of being of God
Himself and of the risen and glorified Christ, but it is
also the form of being of the believer's own "inner
man." Not that "spirit" is to be considered as if it
were, like "flesh," mere substance. It is essentially
power, energy, and as such is "life-giving" ("quicken-
ing"). "Spirit" is therefore not properly a term of individual psychology. Every man, so far as he has attained to truly mature life, partakes both of flesh and
of spirit.

The principle of individuality is the "organism"

("body.") This does not mean to Paul the structure of bone, flesh, and blood to which we give the name of body. It is the pure organic form which subsists through all changes of material particles. The physical organ which I possess today is different in all or most of its material particles from that which I possessed eight years ago. In so far as it has an organic identity and continuity it is my body none the less. Thus for Paul the identity of the "organism" or "body" was in nowise affected by any change in its substance. The "flesh" might pass away, and "splendour" or light-substance be substituted, and the organism remain intact and self-identical. Thus Paul's insistence on the resurrection of the "body" is meant to assert the continuity of individual identity, as distinguished from the persistence of some impalpable shade or "soul" which was not in any real sense the identical man. Paul could not have talked of "saving souls"; it was the "emancipation of the body" that interested him, i.e. of the individual, self-identical, organic whole. The phrase in the Apostles' Creed, "the resurrection of the flesh," would have horrified him. He neither expected nor wished the "flesh" to rise again; he wished the "body" to be emancipated from the bonds of the "flesh." [5] It is probably on this analogy that we are meant to interpret the "emancipation of the creation." It, too, has somehow a "body" which can be redeemed from decay and clothed with splendour in the eternal world.[6]

The metaphysical distinction of two planes of being does not precisely correspond to ethical distinctions. It is often stated that Paul accepted a current view of his time, that spirit alone is good and matter essentially evil. He did not accept any such view. On the one hand there are "spiritual forces of wickedness";[7] and on the other hand what is wrong with the material world is not its moral evil, but its subjection to the futility of a perpetual flux of birth and decay.

That subjection is traced not, as in some contemporary theories, to the sin of Adam, for whose sake the earth was believed to have been "cursed," but vaguely to the will of God, i.e. it is in the nature of things as they are, though not of necessity permanent.[8]

In man, however, the case is complicated. By some means the "flesh" of mankind (which carries with it the *psyché*) has fallen under the dominion of sin, thus becoming not merely morally indifferent, though perishable matter, but "flesh of sin." This Sin is a mysterious power, not native to man or to the material world, but intruding into human nature on its lower side. Paul speaks of it in personal terms: it lives, reigns, holds us in slavery; it is condemned and overcome. Whether he was consciously personifying an abstraction, or whether Sin was for him really a personal power, like the Devil of popular mythology, is not clear. At all events it is not an inherent taint in matter, but rather one of the "spiritual forces of wickedness." [9]

How Sin came into human nature is a question which Paul does not answer very satisfactorily. He sometimes traces it to an historic transgression of a human ancestor in the remote past. This was the common account given in contemporary Judaism.[10] But in other passages he suggests a different origin. In the background of his world stand the "world-rulers" or "elemental spirits." They have some special relation to the material world, and it does not appear that in relation to it they are necessarily evil. But if man becomes subject to them, then he is fallen to a state of unnatural slavery. The process appears to be after this fashion: the reason of man, being a spark of the divine, knew God and read His law written on the heart; but instead of worshipping God and doing His will, it stooped to adore material forms, and thereby fell under the dominion of the elemental powers. The elevation of the material to the place of God led to the perversion of man's naturally right instincts. Reason itself became "reprobate" and the whole life of mankind was thrown into disorder.[11] If the transmitted sin of Adam is the characteristically Jewish doctrine, the theory of elemental spirits starts rather from Greek ideas. Neither can satisfy us, though each has hints of truth: on the one hand, the solidarity of humanity and the incalculable effects of individual transgression; on the other, the peril of exalting the physical and material to a dominance which is not in accord with man's real nature.

What might have been the relations of flesh and spirit had not sin intervened is a question on which Paul does not speculate. Taking things as they are, he scans history and sees that everywhere the power of evil has degraded man from the high estate he should hold, making even the "inner man," the reason which knew God, the conscience which witnessed to His law, slave to the material part and share in its fate of decay and futility. In the "flesh" sin has its seat. Reason may bow to the "flesh" and thereby fall under the dominion of sin and decay, but its nature remains alien from sin. "Flesh," on the other hand, has assimilated itself to the evil power, and the taint passes to the *psyché* or "soul" of which it is the organ, so that "the desires of the flesh and of the intellect" stand for the evil tendency in man. "The Flesh" therefore, in a moral sense, does not mean matter as evil in itself, but man's emotional and intellectual nature as perverted by sin and enslaved to material forces.[12]

It will be evident from this that "sin" is not for Paul identical with actual moral transgression of which the individual is fully conscious and for which he is fully responsible. That is the sense in which the word has been generally used by subsequent writers; but if it is taken in that sense, then Paul is inevitably misunderstood. The actual Greek word used (*hamartia*), like its equivalent in the Hebrew of the Old Testament, originally meant "missing the mark," or as we might say, "going wrong." Now whatever subtleties may complicate the discussion of such questions as moral responsibility and degrees of merit, at least it is plain that there is something wrong with mankind. There is a racial, a corporate, a social wrongness of which we are made in some sense partakers by the mere fact of our being born into human society. That is the meaning of "original sin," as the theologians call it. It is not the figment of an inherited guilt; how could anything so individual as guilty responsibility be inherited? It is a corporate wrongness in which we are involved by being men in this world. The purport of Paul's rather clumsy metaphysics is to show how the problem of evil in man is more than the problem of a series of sinful acts, which of his own free will he can stop if he makes up his mind to it. To some minds this distinction will seem artificial. They will agree with the child who refused to repeat the prayer "God make me a good girl," with the remark, "I wouldn't trouble God about a little thing like that: I can be good by myself if I want to." But a majority, perhaps, of those who take life seriously find that the trouble lies deeper. There is a deep-grained wrongness about human life as it is. The preoccupation with that wrongness as the primary interest of the religious life is certainly morbid; but no matter how freely and fully we recognize the wonderful potentialities of that human nature which we share, it remains true that there is a flaw somewhere, which defies simple treatment.

The monstrous development of the doctrine of "total depravity" and the reaction against it, have partly blinded us to the reality of what Paul called "sin in the flesh." That blindness has been partly connected with a fuller appreciation of individuality and individual responsibility than Paul had attained. But have we not placed an exaggerated emphasis upon individual responsibility? And is not that partly why the whole idea of sin (in the sense in which evangelical theology has used the term) has seemed to be invalidated by the modern re-discovery of solidarity, and the recognition of the influence of heredity and social environment? It would indeed be difficult to say definitely of any particular wrong act that its perpetrator was absolutely and exclusively responsible for it. When we have said that, it is often thought that the whole Christian doctrine of sin is disproved. It does not touch that doctrine as taught by Paul. He thought of the "flesh," or lower nature of man, as a *continuum* in which we all partake; and of that "flesh" as having acquired by some means an impulse towards what is wrong. We should set aside his terminology, and seek some other explanation of the fact; but on the fact we must surely agree with Paul, that there is something common, something racial about sin in his sense of the term. It is a tendency transmitted by heredity and deepened by environment, and its issues, like its sources, are not individual merely, but racial. No one of us can disown his part in the complicated evils in which society is entangled. We are wrong, and we need to be put right. No casuistry explaining away the measure of individual responsibility makes much difference here: the fact of wrongness remains. Our problem is Paul's problem. Indeed, with the modern emphasis on solidarity, and our rebelliousness against social evil in the world, the problem is pressing on us with a peculiar urgency. Perhaps, therefore, we may give ear afresh to a teacher out of that ancient imperial world when he sets before us his thoughts upon its solution. As we shall see, he finds the point of attack upon this gigantic force of wrong in the individual, though not in the individual as an isolated unit.

For the moment, however, we are concerned to pursue the trail of corporate wrong. For it brings disastrous consequences which also are corporate as well as individual. Human history is a moral order, in which it is impossible to be wrong without incurring disaster. This disaster Paul calls, in traditional language, "The Wrath," or much more rarely, "The Wrath of God." It has been supposed that Paul thought of God as a vengeful despot, angry with men whom nevertheless He had Himself created with the liability to err, even if He did not create them to be damned for His greater glory. That is a mere caricature of Paul's view. There are, indeed, many indications in his use of language that "The Wrath of God" is not being thought of as a passion of anger in the mind of God. It is not without significance that there are no more than three or possibly four passages where the expression "The Wrath of God" (or "His Wrath") appears at all, while the phrase "The Wrath" is constantly used in a curiously impersonal way. Paul carefully avoids ever making God the subject of the verb "to be angry." Once he speaks of God as "applying the Wrath"—a strange way of saying that God made His anger felt, if anger was thought of as a passion in the divine mind. It suggests rather a process directed or controlled by a person.[13] Even in the passage which has about it most of the sterner colours of Pharisaic theology the "vessels of Wrath" are the objects of God's forbearance; a statement which, if it does not rule out the idea that God is angry with the persons on whom at the same time He shows mercy, at least gives a startling paradox if Paul is supposed to have the thought of an angry God in mind.[14]

Let us, then, consider the one passage where "The Wrath of God" is spoken of in more than an allusive way. "The Wrath of God is being revealed," he says to the Romans: it is to be seen at work in contemporary history. How, then? In earthquake, fire and brimstone? "God gave them up in the lusts of their own hearts to impurity"; "God gave them up to disgraceful passions"; "God gave them up to their reprobate reason." "The Wrath of God," therefore, as seen in actual operation, consists in leaving sinful human nature to "stew in its own juice." [15] This is a sufficiently terrible conception, but if we believe, as Paul did, in any measure of human free will, what else is to happen if men choose steadfastly to ignore God? Are they not self-condemned to the reaping of the harvest of their sinful deeds, which is "a reprobate reason"—a disordered moral being, where the very instincts that should have led to good are perverted to the service of wrong? "If the light that is in thee be darkness, how great is that darkness!" And this "reprobation," be it observed, is the consequence of the rejection of that knowledge of God which is native to man. "The Wrath," then, is revealed before our eyes as the increasing horror of sin working out its hideous law of cause and effect. "The judgment" which overtakes sin is the growing perversion of the whole moral atmosphere of human society, which cannot but affect to a greater or less degree every individual born into it. Meanwhile, the characteristic personal activity of God is not wrath but "kindness," "long-suffering," rooted in His love and ready to display itself in "grace." [16] That is why "The Wrath" is not the last word of the moral order for Paul. The "wages of sin" is real and terrible; it is moral decay and death for the race. But that is not a complete account of the moral universe. "God justifies the ungodly." [17] To this matter we shall presently turn. The intention of this chapter is to set forth the problem of sin as Paul faced it, and to suggest how close to reality he was when he placed his finger on the point that sin is a racial and social fact, in which every individual is implicated, and that if the moral order is nothing more than a law of retribution, there is nothing before sinful man but greater sin and moral disaster.[18]

The whole of this is only preparatory to a decisive declaration of the way out of apparently desperate conditions. Even so, does it give too gloomy a view? We like to think that humanity left to itself would grow better. But would it? Is it not true that whole nations and societies of men have sunk lower and lower out of sheer inner rottenness, often bringing other peoples down with them in their fall, since there is a solidarity of mankind? And is such a future for our species as the ghastly imaginings of Mr. Wells's "Time Machine" wholly inconceivable? But Jesus Christ, we are told, whom Paul professed to follow, took no such gloomy view of human nature and its prospects. It may be granted at once that there is a difference of emphasis between the Master and His disciple. There was a good reason for this. Jesus worked among the Jews, where the dominant theology took a gloomy enough view of the nature of all men except a very few. It was therefore His first and chief care to give hope to those who seemed hopeless and to assure them of the glorious possibilities open to them in the love of the Father in heaven. Paul worked among the pagans, where real downright evil was readily condoned and glozed over, and its inevitable consequences explained away, while none the less the rottenness of sin was eating into the heart of that corrupt civilization, despite all the efforts of moralists and legislators. "The Wrath" that follows sin was actually being revealed; and it was part of Paul's task to open the eyes of the pagan world to it, that they might be willing to seek the better way. But we cannot quote Jesus against Paul as giving an easy and cheerfully optimistic view of the actual state of human society. On the contrary, there is enough in His teaching to show that He too saw the society of His day "rushing down a steep place into the sea," with no hope of its redemption save in the "Sovereignty of God." [19] Therein Paul was His true interpreter to the wider world.

VI

THE TYRANNY OF AN IDEA

We have now to approach that region of our subject where Paul's contribution is perhaps most original and characteristic, and where at the same time it is most cumbered with temporary elements: his treatment of the idea of Law. The enormous importance which attached to that idea in contemporary Judaism, and particularly in the Pharisaic branch of it to which Paul belonged, has already been indicated. Paul's attitude to the historic Law of Moses is curiously contradictory on the surface. On the one hand it reflects for him that inexorable moral order which is in the nature of things. The nature of things is the will of God, and the law which reflects it must be of God, and therefore holy, spiritual, just and good.[1] On the other hand he detests this law as the supreme instrument of slavery (why, we shall see presently). It is not unfair to regard this deep paradox in his thought as the penalty of a false upbringing, which had implanted almost a morbid *idée fixe* that he never threw off. His training and prepossessions made it for ever impossible for him to take a detached view of the Law in which he had been taught to see the eternal will of

God. He might reasonably have attacked its mixing upon equal terms of ritual trivialities and awful moral principles. He did not do so. His training made it impossible. The Law was a vast and indivisible system which must somehow be accounted for as a whole. His entire mental background made things peculiarly hard for him at this point. But it was not without advantage that Christian thought was thus led to face with the utmost definition the conflict which underlay the attack that Jesus Christ had made upon the organized religion of His day.

The attitude of Jesus to the Jewish Law was singularly free and unembarrassed. He made full use of it as an impressive statement of high ethical ideals. Even its ritual practices He treated with perfect tolerance where they did not conflict with fundamental moral obligations. From Pharisaic formalism He appealed to the relative simplicity of the venerable written law. But again from the written law itself He appealed to the basic rights and duties of humanity: the Sabbath was made for man, not man for the Sabbath; the Law might permit the dissolution of marriage, but there was something more deeply rooted in the nature of things which forbade it; the *lex talionis,* the central principle of legal justice, must go overboard in the interests of the holy impulse to love your neighbour not merely as yourself, but as God has loved you. Such free-handed dealing meant that the whole notion of morality as a code of rules with sanctions of reward and punishment was abandoned. But the average Christian was slow to see this implication. For instance, Jesus had taken fasting out of the class of meritorious acts, and given it a place only as the fitting and spontaneous expression of certain spiritual states. This is what an early authoritative catechism of the Church made of His teaching: "Let not your fasts be with the hypocrites, for they fast on Monday and Thursday; ye therefore shall fast on Wednesday and Friday." [2] It sounds ludicrous, but we may ask, Was it not on some very similar principle that the Church did actually carry through its reconstruction of "religious observance"? And a Church which so perverted Christ's treatment of the ritual law proved itself almost equally incapable of understanding His drastic revision of the moral law.

It was therefore of the utmost importance that one who knew from the inside the system which Jesus attacked should, through being compelled to confront his own exaggerated legalism with His Master's independence, point the way to the more fundamental implications of what Jesus had done. Paul found himself driven to reconsider, not this precept or that, but the whole nature of law as such; and it is a mark of his real greatness that he did so on the basis, not of theory merely, but of experience. In its elements, moreover, the experience on which he founded was wider than that of a Pharisaic Jew. For it is not of any peculiarly Jewish experience that he speaks. For himself, no doubt, whether as Jew or as Christian, the so-called Law of Moses was absolute law. Within the sphere of law there was nothing higher or more perfect. Yet the identical principle appeared also among the pagans. The pagan sense of right and wrong was God's law written on the heart—the same law as that delivered on Sinai, Paul would have said, though more doubtfully, obscurely, and imperfectly revealed. He had sympathy enough to perceive that the Stoic too must fall upon this problem of a law which he could not but acknowledge as divine, which yet condemned him without giving him strength to do better. There are passages in Stoic writers tinged with a melancholy which recalls the moving transcript from Paul's experience in the seventh chapter of his Epistle to the Romans. It is at bottom a human problem, and not a specifically Jewish one, that he is facing, but his own bitter experience in Pharisaic Judaism lent a cutting edge to his analysis.

The education of the youthful Paul in his Jewish home at Tarsus must have been a very rigorous one. We may compare it with the strictest kind of Puritan training which in England, and still more perhaps in Scotland and Wales, moulded the lives of a former generation. He was early drilled into a very high standard of personal purity and probity. As he grew up he found that his food and clothes, the way he washed his hands, the way he had his hair cut, and all the simplest operations of a boy's daily life were rigidly prescribed,[3] and were so distinct from those of other Tarsian boys that he was bound to ask, Why? He was told, Because the God of our fathers has commanded it in His law, as He has also commanded us not to kill or steal; and if we do otherwise, the wrath of God will come upon us. So he came to think of this God as very strong and holy, but also very stern and jealous. He was a merciful God too, but His mercy was chiefly shown in the inestimable gift of the Law to Israel, His darling people.[4] Through that gift they knew, and only they, the eternal rule of life by which alone happiness could be attained. "See, I set before you this day a blessing and a curse": so the young Paul learned to recite out of Deuteronomy. To know the Law and keep it in its entirety was the assured way to perfect blessedness. To infringe the least of its precepts was to bring down the vengeance of a justly incensed God, "an eye for an eye, and a tooth for a tooth." Such was the eternal justice, which God must vindicate, because He was God.[5] And the Law itself in all its precepts was a pattern for human life framed upon this eternal justice, with its root principle of reciprocity or retribution. This Law had been given, in the inscrutable providence of God, to His chosen people as the supreme mark of His favour.

So Paul was taught at home; and as he looked upon the Greek boys he passed in the street, he was proud to think that he had a secret denied to them all—he knew the Law. Its possession undoubtedly brought to an earnest-minded Jew a real moral elevation. Such writings as the hundred and nineteenth Psalm show with what enthusiasm a pious Jew could contemplate this great gift of God to his race. "Oh, how I love Thy law! It is my meditation all the day." We may think of Paul as sharing in such emotions in his study of the Law, especially from the time when, aiming at the Rabbinate, he devoted himself wholly to it. Out of this concentration upon the Law grew on the one side an intense national pride, on the other an overwhelming sense of the moral order with its awful principle of retribution. Both were affronted by the discovery in Palestine, when he went there, of those renegade Jews the Nazarenes, whose leader had set himself up against the Law and denounced its authorized inter-preters, and had at last been cast out of the commonwealth of Israel for blasphemy against God's Temple and His Holy Name. It was a grim enthusiasm for the moral order which made Paul a persecutor, as it has made many another. "Saul, Saul, why persecutest thou Me?" Paul might have thought he had his answer ready: "Because the moral order must be vindicated and the law-breaker punished." Yet when the question was actually pressed home he found he had no answer.

For while outwardly Paul was the proud, irreproachable champion of the Law, inward struggles plunged his soul in darkness and confusion. The weakness of his human nature had revealed itself in conflict with the absolute claims of the moral law. The sense of impotence and despair that took hold upon him is reflected in one of the most moving passages of his writings, the seventh chapter of the Epistle to the Romans. It is not without significance that the ex-

ample he there uses to illustrate his point is the one
commandment in the Decalogue which is concerned
with thought and not with overt word or act. "Thou
shalt not covet," said the Law. We may recall that
covetousness is noted in the Gospels as a special snare
of the pious Pharisee. From his Pharisaic days Paul
was well aware that morality must cover the inner
life of feeling, thought, motive, and desire. "He is not
a Jew who is such only outwardly" [6] is a sentence he
might have written at any time in his life. Now, it appears, he found that even though he might conform
his outward actions to the requirements of the Law he
could not control his thoughts and desires. But the
Law was a single whole; to break one precept was to
renounce all.[7] He was as honest and strict with himself
as he was severe with others, and he fell under the
scourge of self-condemnation. He loved the Law, con-
sented to it as good, rejoiced in it "after the inner
man," as he says, but he could not keep it. "The good
I would, I do not, and the evil I would not, that I
do . . . when I would do good, evil is present with
me."

It is at this point that Paul's experience as a Pharisee falls in with the common experience of men. It
was not a Jew who wrote *"Video meliora proboque,
deteriora sequor."* The moral incompetence of human
nature in the presence of an acknowledged ideal is
no private discovery. A man may perceive the
ideal clearly, and contemplate it with a keen æsthetic
delight, and yet desires and impulses which contradict
it may be so much more real to him that his actual
conduct is a perpetual denial of the ideal. This divided state of the personality is a state of miserable
impotence, in which the freedom of the will is a mere
illusion. "The freedom of the will," writes a modern
psychologist,[8] "may be a doctrine which holds true of
the healthy, and indeed the exercise of will and determination is the normal way in which to summon the

resources of power; but the doctrine that the will alone is the way to power is a most woebegone theory for the relief of the morally sick—and who of us is whole? Freedom to choose? Yes! But what if, when we choose, we have no power to perform? We open the sluice-gates, but the channels are dry; we pull the lever, but nothing happens; we try by our will to summon up our strength, but no strength comes." No wonder Paul described such a condition as a state of slavery.

Most of us know something about this condition, though few of us are reduced to the depths of despair to which Paul came. We pacify a not very exacting conscience with a rough approximation. But the question may be raised, whether this half-conscious tolerance of a real though unacknowledged rift between ideal and practice is not a form of "suppressed complex" which works more injury than we commonly imagine. Worse certainly is the state of the person who is sentimental enough to think that to admire what is noble is a sufficient substitute for doing it. Worst of all is the actual hypocrisy of pretending to ourselves that by great rigour in practices we find easy we can tip the balance even, and

> *Compound for sins that we're inclined to*
> *By damning those we have no mind to.*

Such hypocrisy is often a form of instinctive self-protection, and it is most common where moral ideals have been reduced to the most precise and comprehensive rules of life. That is probably why the Puritan of literature is so often a hypocrite, and likewise the Pharisee of the Gospels, whose religion was discipline pressed to an even more logical extreme. Paul was not that kind of Pharisee. He was earnest, clear-sighted, and absolutely honest with himself. He could find no way out of the *impasse*. He could not keep the Law, especially in its most inward and spiritual precepts, which sought to rule the thoughts and motives. But law must be upheld. It was in the nature of things, and God must needs vindicate it. Where then was any door of hope for Paul the sinner?

We now come to the turning-point in Paul's career. He set out for Damascus, the fierce avenger of an outraged Law; but in his heart he felt that the Law had broken him, and hope was almost gone. "Who will rescue me from the clutch of this dead body?" is his bitter cry. . . . Time passes, and we meet a new Paul. The terror of the Law has passed from his soul, with all the miserable sense of moral impotence: "There is now no condemnation"; "I can do anything in Him who gives me strength." And he has now no further thought of inflicting the terrors of the Law upon others. He who once "breathed out threatenings and slaughter" is now content if he may bear his share of the sufferings by which others may be saved: "I am glad of my sufferings for you; I am making up in my own flesh the deficit of Christ's sufferings for His Body, which is the Community"; "I am crucified with Christ." [9] What we observe in all this is that the preoccupation with law, and more precisely with its principle of retribution, has slipped away; and in the freedom and peace of mind that ensues Paul has gained the "heart at leisure from itself" and open to all tides of human sympathy. He has discovered some new secret of life. What is it?

"God who said 'Light shall flash out of darkness' flashed upon our hearts and enlightened us with a knowledge of the splendour of God in the face of Christ." [10] It was a new perception of God that had come to Paul. The God of Pharisaism was like the God of the Deists. He stood aloof from the world He had made, and let law take its course. He did not here and now deal with individual sinful men. Paul lets us see how new and wonderful was the experience, when God "flashed on his heart" in personal dealing with him. He had not suspected that God was like that. His theological studies had told him that God was loving and merciful; but he had thought this love and mercy were expressed once and for all in the arrangements he had made for Israel's blessedness— "the plan of salvation." It was a new thing to be assured by an inward experience admitting of no further question that God loved him, and that the eternal mercy was a Father's free forgiveness of His erring child. This was the experience that Christ had brought him: he had seen the splendour of God's own love in the face of "the Son of God, who loved me and gave Himself for me." [11] What knowledge of Jesus Christ and His teaching lay behind the flash of enlightenment it is now impossible for us to say; but it is clear that the God whom Paul met was the "Father" of Jesus' own Gospel parables, the "Shepherd" who goes after the one sheep until He finds it. It was the God, in fact, whom the whole of the life of Jesus set forth, to the astonishment of those among whom He moved. Living still, He brought God to men in the same unmistakable way. The divine love that through Jesus had found Zacchæus the publican had now through the risen Jesus found Paul the Pharisee. Henceforward the central facts of life for Paul were that while he was yet a sinner God had found and forgiven him, and that this was the work of Jesus Christ in whose love the love of God had become plain. About those two *foci* in experience his theology revolves.[12]

In order to establish against those who impugned it the validity of his new experience of God, Paul set out to discover in what were to him and to his critics indisputable facts, the proof of his assertion. The interest of these discussions for us is limited to the extent to which they illuminate on various sides the new conception of God and His dealings which had come to Paul in experience. His argument comes to

this, that while the Law had a place of its own in the
providential order, it never did and never could ex-
haust the whole truth about God and man. Law
worked wholly within the sphere of reciprocity or
recompense. But history showed that such reciprocity
was at least very irregular and incomplete in its operation. In the first place, his critics must grant
that in God's dealings with the ancestors of the
"Chosen people" there was an element of free choice
on God's part, altogether out of relation to the deserts
of the objects of that choice. Abraham was called
even before he had taken upon him the rite of circumcision. Jacob was loved by God, as the Scripture
showed, before he had done either good or ill. That
indicated a freedom of choice on God's part which
was incompatible with the strict working of law.[13]
Such freedom of choice, however, raises a new difficulty—the case of the "rejects." They are left in sin,
and must on the principles of law pay the inexorable
penalty of sin in ever greater and greater sin until
complete moral disaster and death is the result. But
what actually happens? "What if God, with all His
will to exhibit His wrath and make known His power,
bore very patiently with 'vessels of wrath,' fit only
for destruction?" [14] There is a flaw, that is, in the working of the system of recompense. "In this, O Lord," exclaims a contemporary Pharisaic writer, "shall Thy
righteousness and goodness be declared, if Thou wilt
compassionate them that have no wealth of good
works." [15] The writer of these words is clearly very
uncertain whether God's compassion does actually
reach so far. Paul, like most Pharisees, is sure that in
all ages a remnant at least has found unmerited mercy
of God, even though His normal principle was retribution. In other words, forgiveness is, and always has
been, a fact verifiable in the experience of some men
at least. But it is wholly inconsistent with the law
of retribution. "Do you make light," Paul wrote, "of

the wealth of His kindness and tolerance and patience? Do you not know that the kindness of God is trying to lead you to repentance?" [16] In practice, that is to say, the Law as an absolute system of recompense has wrecked itself upon the character of God as loving and pitiful. But this very fact that God has passed over, or "winked at," sin in spite of the Law, indicates the logical necessity for some different principle to be disclosed.[17]

Next, and arguing still from facts which would be admitted by his Pharisaic opponents to facts which they were attempting to deny, Paul showed that within the Jewish system itself a principle different from the legal principle was to be found. This seems so obvious to us, to whom the prophetic element is the heart of the Old Testament, as hardly to need labouring. But to the Pharisees the Law was the foundation of all, the prophets merely commentary. In effect, Paul challenged them to interpret the Law by the prophets, and to find, even in the books of the Law itself, statements suggesting a personal relation to God over and above the merely legal relation to Him as governor of the universe. In effect he says to his critics, *"You* cannot find a place for these sayings: *I* can." And so he shows that the Christian revelation of God is the fulfilment of a logical necessity in the heart of the old religion.[18]

But further, the system of legal retribution was fitted, Paul argued, to exhibit God's wrath, but *not,* in the full sense, His righteousness. That is a startling statement addressed to any Jewish public of the first century—or for that matter to the bulk of "Christian" opinion today. Yet it was a thought not unfamiliar to the prophets, that God's righteousness is shown in making His people righteous.[19] God must show Himself, says Paul, at once "just and justifier." [20] For all the scholastic language, there is here a very vital truth: that righteousness, or justice, is a bigger thing than mere reciprocity.[21] It is the point which Jesus Christ made when He drily observed that a man's field gets sun and rain whether he has deserved these good things or not, and when He likened God to an employer so lost to all sense of justice as to pay a day's wage for an hour's work.[22] God must, by an inner necessity of His nature, do good to men: His "property is to have mercy and to forgive." But within the sphere of law there is no place for forgiveness. If righteousness or justice is retribution, as law assumes, then forgiveness is unrighteous. Once more there is a logical necessity for the revelation of something other than law.

The real dilemma, therefore, which Paul places before his opponents is this: If you are once agreed that the ethical is the basis of all relation of God to man, then you are bound to deal with the moral law of retribution. It appears to be the very foundation of morality, and yet it conflicts with the religious instinct which says, "God is not like that." Until you can clear scores with the principle of retribution, you will be haunted by it in all your attempts to give play to the grace of God. As we have seen, some of Paul's Jewish compatriots, even of his fellow-Pharisees, found themselves able in some measure to hold to the legal principle and yet to find a "little door" for the grace of God. But if you are taking morality seriously, this position cannot be stable, and indeed Christianity itself, failing to understand or follow Paul, has given proof how if you persist in identifying righteousness with retributive justice, and then insist that God must be righteous or just before He is merciful, you cannot let the character of God have that effective power in the religious and moral life which belongs to it.

Yet law serves a purpose. After all, the moral order of retribution which it embodies is a real fact, though it is not the only relevant fact, nor the final and decisive fact. If Paul had worked with the idea of development or "evolution," he might have explained the place of law as a necessary stage in that development. Indeed he comes very near to doing so. "The Law," he says, "was our 'pedagogue,' until Christ should come." Those words have been interpreted as though they described the Law as a preparatory education, continued at a higher stage by Christ. That, however, is not quite what Paul meant. The "pedagogue" in Greek society was not a "schoolmaster." He did not give lessons (at least that was not his natural function). He was a slave who accompanied a boy to school, and both waited upon him and also exercised a supervision which interfered with the boy's freedom of action. He is, in fact, a figure in the little allegory which Paul gives us to illustrate the position of the People of God before Christ came. There was a boy left heir to a great estate. He was a minor, and so must have guardians and trustees. He was as helpless in their hands as if he had been a slave. He must live on the allowance they gave him, and follow their wishes from day to day. They gave him a "pedagogue" to keep him out of mischief. He could not please himself, or realize his own purposes and ambitions. Yet all the time he was the heir; the estate was his and no one else's. Just so the People of God, the Divine Commonwealth, was cramped and fettered by ignorance and evil times. It remained in uneasy expectation of one day coming into active existence. At last the heir came of age: guardians and trustees abdicated their powers, and the grown man possessed in full realization all that was his. So now the fettered life of the Divine Commonwealth bursts its bonds and comes into active existence.

The law therefore appears as a necessary but transitory stage of discipline. It was not fundamental to God's dealings with His sons. In the same passage

Paul points out, in his scholastic fashion, that historically the Law came four hundred years after the "promise" had been given to "faithful Abraham"; and the "testament" by which God devised His blessing upon Abraham could not be reversed by a codicil added four hundred years later! [23] In other words, the intervention of law was not a reversal of God's original and eternal purpose of pure love and grace towards men: it only subserved that purpose, while it seemed to contradict it, just as the presence of the "pedagogue" might seem to the high-spirited young heir quite contrary to the rights secured to him by his father's will.

How then did the Law subserve the purpose realized in Christ? Paul's answer is so startling that his commentators have been reluctant to take his words in their plain meaning. "The Law," he says, "came in, by a side wind, in order that there might be more transgression"! [24] If Paul often talked like that, we can understand how he shocked the good folk at Jerusalem, Jews and Christians alike! Yet there is no great difficulty in resolving the paradox. The Law came in, not to increase "sin," of course, but to increase *transgression*. We have seen that for Paul "sin" is a state of the Race, in which things have gone wrong, quite apart from any consideration of a conscious or deliberate wrongdoing on the part of any individual. "Before law came, sin was in the world, but sin is not imputed where there is no law." [25] The knowledge of the moral law confronts the sinful state with a rule of goodness, and by the contrast brings home the wrong to the conscience as guilt.

An examination of the seventh chapter of Romans makes this clear. We have already treated that chapter as an index to Paul's state of mind just before his conversion. But the passage is ideal biography rather than a strict transcript "from the life." It starts with the description of an "age of innocence," which for the individual as for the race is an inference of reason or a figment of the imagination rather than strict history. There never was a time when Paul, or when the human race, was self-conscious without also being in some rudimentary way conscious of moral obligation. Yet by comparison with later stages we may use as a working concept the notion of an "age of innocence." By that is meant, not that one did no wrong, but that one had no sense of any contrast between what one actually did and what one ought to have done. "Once I lived my own life, without any law," Paul puts it. But while that stage remained there was no chance of better things. The establishment of a clear distinction between right and wrong was essential. Yet it is probably true that in every normal case this distinction emerged in conscience as the sense of having done wrong, the sense of guilt or shame, essentially humiliating and painful. "Law came to life—and I died." Then follows the phase of struggle and defeat, with which we have already dealt.

It is necessary here to distinguish between two counts which Paul brings against law. He found that the knowledge that a thing was wrong provoked him to seek it, so that to that degree law actually increased "sin." The fact is sufficiently attested in proverbial lore—"stolen fruits are pleasant!"—to stand as a widespread experience. But it is not so important or perhaps so universal as Paul seems to have thought; or at least it is scarcely so important universally as it appears to have been for him. In any case it rather obscures his main point, which is this: Every individual of the human race is so entangled in the general "wrongness" that he has no power, left to himself, to avoid committing constantly acts which, whether he knows it or not, add to the sum of the wrong. To know that these acts are wrong does not prevent him from doing them, for "the law is weak through the flesh";[26]

but it does imprint upon his conscience in the indelible characters of shame and guilt the contrast of good and evil. It brings "sin" home, from being a general state of the human race, to be a conscious burden upon the mind of the individual. It is no longer "sin" merely; it is "transgression."

We may compare the condition which Aristotle describes as "incontinence," [27] the essence of which is that the individual now knows, as he did not at a lower stage, that the things he is doing are wrong, and yet cannot keep himself from them. Aristotle makes this state the natural approach to the next higher, that of "continence," in which the things known to be wrong are through struggle and effort gradually discarded. Similarly, Paul sees that it is a great advance to have discovered sin in one's own heart as guilt. Only the man who is conscious of his guilt can be saved from the sin of which he is guilty. Only as the individual acknowledges such guilt can the racial wrongness be successfully attacked. In this sense, the function of law as "increasing guilt" can be regarded as part of a beneficent divine plan. But only if there is something else to follow. Otherwise we may give up all hope. Paul's charge against the Judaism in which he was brought up was that its view of the world went no further than the merely legal stage. Perhaps his statement of the case was sometimes too sweeping. Surely he would have admitted that at all times it was *possible* even within Judaism for men to transcend the purely legal attitude, and that as a matter of fact many saints of the old order had done so. This is, indeed, implied in his references to Elijah's Seven Thousand and Isaiah's Remnant. But in the main the highest moralists of his time did actually see no further than a system which attempted to build the moral life of man exclusively upon that principle of reciprocity which they discerned in the nature of things, and allowed no real place for a fresh, direct, personal act of the loving, gracious God whom yet they professed to worship. Paul held that this God had indeed framed a universe in which the principle of retribution was at work: for he never denied that the Law largely answered to real facts, and certainly he never doubted that evil is ultimately disastrous and good ultimately blessed. The conception of a right which should be defeated at the end of the day did not dawn upon his mind: that was left for Mr. Bertrand Russell. But this whole universe, with all its complex reactions, he held to have been constituted by God to the end that through it man might rise to a higher order, that of the "sons of God." At that point the "pedagogue" must step aside, and God's heir claim his freedom.

VII

THE SON OF GOD

"What the law could not do, because it was powerless through our lower nature, that God did, by sending His own Son." [1] From what has already been said it should be clear that the problem before Paul was not "How can a just God forgive sin?" but "Granted that God is by His nature both 'just and justifier,' i.e. that because He is righteous He must forgive sin and impact righteousness, how is that righteousness to be made available for man?" It is therefore not a problem of the adjustment of abstract principles of justice and mercy, but of the relations of God and man on the personal plane. Man must discover himself as a son of God. With this in view, "When the full time had arrived, God sent out His Son, born of a woman, born in subjection to law, in order that He might emancipate those who were subject to law, i.e. that we might receive adoption into sonship." [2]

It is not here proposed to attempt any discussion in detail of what is called the "Christology" of Paul. It is a highly speculative structure of thought, making use of a difficult philosophical vocabulary. As a philosophy it is compounded of various elements, not easily disentangled. First, already in pre-Christian times there was a highly elaborated body of Jewish doctrine concerning the Messiah. Implying at one time no more than an ideal Hebrew prince of the dynasty of David, the conception had attracted to itself some of the most mystical elements in Jewish religious thought. At the beginning of the Christian era the Messiah was widely thought of as an eternal Being, called "The Son of Man," or "The Man," as though He were the type or representative of humanity, abiding with God from all eternity, partly revealed in vision and mystical experience to saints of all ages, such as Enoch and Ezra, but destined "in the fulness of time" to be openly manifested for the consummation of human history.[3] It may now be taken as certain that Jesus believed Himself to be Messiah, and shaped His life and went to His death in conviction. The only question is to what extent He shared various forms of contemporary belief about the Messiah, and in what ways He re-shaped the idea. It seems at least highly probable that He was the first to link the thought of the Messiah with that of the ideal "Servant of Jehovah" in the prophecies of the "Second Isaiah"—the Servant who would suffer and die that others might know God. Without further discussion, it will be plain that Paul was from the outset within the sphere of Messianic ideas, both in their traditional form in Pharisaic Judaism, and in the form in which from the life and teaching of Jesus they had passed into early Christian circles.

Further, Messianic beliefs had already, to some degree, become fused in certain types of Jewish thought with the idea of the "Wisdom" of God, by which He made the world, and by which He reveals Himself to man. And this in turn had been brought in contact with the Greek doctrine of the "Logos" or eternal Reason—the rational order of the universe, and the divine spark in man. Although Paul never actually identifies Christ with the "Logos," as the author of the Fourth Gospel does, yet in his attempt to understand the position of Christ in relation to man and his world he owes much to Logos speculation; and he does call Christ "The Wisdom of God," in so many words.[4]

In the world outside Judaism, the most living religions of the time generally centered in faith in a "Saviour-God," who was often believed to have lived, died, and risen again, and with whom the believer could win fellowship through certain rites. These were the so-called "mystery-religions." Their origins were various, their rites were sometimes wild and licentious, and in most the superstitions of magic and astrology played a part; but at best their offer of fellowship with a Saviour-God ministered to a real religious need of the time. The view has been put forward that Paul reacted from Judaism practically to a mystery-religion of the ordinary type, with Jesus Christ as its mythical Saviour-God. One need not be committed to any such paradoxical opinion, if one holds that he was influenced both in thought and language by these cults—probably not from personal knowledge, but because that sort of thing was "in the air" of the religious world at the time. His audience in the pagan world had not the background of Judaism. It did not know what he was talking about when he spoke of "the Christ" ("Messiah"); but when he spoke of "the Lord, the Saviour," the phrase at least conveyed some idea to their minds. Their highest religious experience had hitherto been associated with language of that kind, and it expressed an idea which could be filled in from the abundant material supplied by Christian experience and by the life and teaching of Jesus Himself. The Christian missionary in India, say, today, follows a not very different plan.

From such sources are the terms of Paul's "Christology" derived. But it cannot be too emphatically repeated that the thing he is talking about in these terms is not a speculative idea, but a piece of real experience. That he had met Christ face to face he never doubted; it was a part of his actual history. "It pleased God to reveal His Son in me"; "last of all, He was seen of me also"; "henceforth I am alive, and yet not I, but Christ is alive in me; and the life which I now live under physical conditions I live by virtue of my trust in the Son of God, who loved me and gave Himself for me." [5] This is the authentic language of personal experience. Mr. H. G. Wells has told us that what he means by "God" has a close resemblance to what Paul meant by "Christ." [6] He is so far right that each of these men is telling us of a personal meeting with an unseen Friend and Leader, who is known at once, intuitively, to be the Leader of humanity, and the Friend of all who have yielded themselves to the divine call sounding in the heart of man. So far as one can judge, the chief specific differences in the experience of the two men are that Paul's "Christ" bears the definite ethical lineaments of the historic Jesus, and that, unlike Mr. Wells's "Invisible King," He has a real and intimate relation to the whole universe and its Creator. He is, in fact, the "Son of God"—the eternal type of all the relationship between personal beings and the personal Centre of reality. What Paul saw in the vision that changed his life was "the splendour of God in the face of Christ." The Christ he met is the "Wisdom of God" by which the worlds were framed; that is, as we might put it, the ultimate meaning of all reality is no other than the meaning of the life and character of Christ. But, like the "Invisible King," Paul's Christ has had a history entwined with the history of man. Man was made "in the image of God": that "image" of God is Christ.[7] There is in men a life derived from their natural progenitor, whom Paul calls by the Hebrew word for man, "Adam." But there is in men also a higher life, by which they are linked with God and the eternal order. "The first man Adam became a living *psyché,* the last Adam, a life-giving Spirit. . . . The first man is earthy, of clay; the second Man is from Heaven." This second Adam or heavenly Man-in-men is Christ.[8] The people of God in their ancient pilgrimage "drank of the spiritual rock that followed them, and that rock is Christ";[9] or, as we might put it, the perpetual springs of the spiritual life of the Race are found in Him.

If we now recall what was said above of the dealings of God in history for the founding of the Divine Commonwealth, we shall see that in Paul's view every step in that direction was in some sense an act of Christ within humanity. And every such step led forward to some decisive act in which what was before obscure and halting should become definite and effective. Then at last "in the fulness of time," Christ came. By a gracious act of God, His Son was "sent forth"; or, to put the same thing in another way, by His own act of will, in absolute unity with the purpose of His Father, "He made Himself of no consequence, accepted the standing of a slave, and was born in human form; and so, presenting the appearance of a man, He stooped to a subordinate position, and persevered in it till death—a death on the gallows!" In other words, He who is always and everywhere the Man-in-men became *a man,* a Jew, a crucified criminal.[10]

So stated, the thought is by admission a difficult one. But there are certain points which need to be observed. The question in Paul's mind is not a question of the scarcely thinkable combination in one person of the contradictory attributes of transcendent Deity on the one hand and of a purely "natural" and non-divine humanity on the other. Humanity itself *means* Christ, and has no proper meaning without Him. Unless a man is a "son of God," he is so far less than man: he has yet to grow "to a mature man, i.e.

to the measure of the full stature of Christ." [11] The
history of man is the story of the course by which mankind is becoming fully human. The controlling Mind
in this history—the "life-giving Spirit" of the whole
process—Paul conceives as a real personality, standing
already in that relation to God in which alone man is
fully human; already, and eternally, Son of God.

The emphasis, implied in Paul's teaching, upon the
absolute importance of the entry of this Son of God
into human history as an individual may be regarded
as a part of the general movement of thought by which
during these centuries the individual was for the first
time being discovered, simultaneously with the transition from national or tribal to universal conceptions
of human history. In the center of this movement
stands the personality of Jesus Christ, intensely individual, and yet wonderfully universal—an individual
who consciously gathered up in His hands the threads
of history, and who has proved Himself through following ages to have a direct affinity with the most
diverse types of man in all peoples. We can yet discern in Him a continuity with the universal higher
impulses of humanity, and a personal command of
men who are brought in touch with Him; and these
are essentially the facts lying at the base of Paul's conception of the Son of God who became a man "in the
fulness of time." To this, however, we have to add,
what we shall presently consider, the definite achievement which Paul saw to have issued from the life and
death of Jesus, and which stands as a solid part of
history. It is on the ground of what He achieved historically that Paul identified Jesus with the Son of
God who is the "life-giving Spirit" of humanity. This,
it may be suggested, is a firmer ground for the building
of a "Christology" than minute psychological analysis
of the meager data concerning the self-consciousness
of Jesus in the Gospels. Not that psychology is of no
importance here; for the investigation of phenomena

of personality which seem to lie beyond the threshold of ordinary individual consciousness may well lead us nearer to an understanding of the greatest difficulty in which Paul's teaching about Christ after all leaves us—the union of the universal and the individual in one personality.

In any case we must set it down as a very suggestive element in Paul's thought, that he regards the whole of the individual life of Jesus as a working-out of one supra-historic act of self-sacrifice, in which we may see the gathering-up of the whole impulse of self-sacrifice to be found in the history of mankind. It is the "life-giving Spirit" from whom all this comes, and there was one human life which was entirely an expression of it, in that intense, purposive and deliberate form which is proper only to individuality.[12] According to Paul, not only had that life of self-sacrifice decisive results for all men, but it marked a crisis also in the life-history of Christ. By that humiliation He actually attained a new relation to humanity and to God, for "God highly exalted Him" to be Lord of the Race.[13] Henceforward having by His earthly ministry and death pioneered a highway for Himself into the hearts of men, He dwells spiritually in conscious communion with all those who are conformed to the image of His dying, so that their life is hidden with Christ in God, and on earth they form His body, "until He come." [14] For a day is yet to come when Christ will be "revealed" in a new and fuller way, and with Him all who share His life. And in a figurative or mythological form Paul shows us Christ as the Captain of His redeemed, smiting His foes to the ground: and the last of them is death. Then, Lord of a redeemed and deathless universe, He makes the last sacrifice. As in the hour of His humiliation He rendered up His body and soul to God for the redemption of the world, so now, its victorious King, He yields up the Body His Spirit has created "that God may be all and in all." [15]

Such is in rough outline Paul's conception of the "historic Christ"—a Christ who has a history of His own, intimately connected at every stage with the history of Man from start to finish; and who appears as an individual to share man's life at a point historically determined by His own working as hidden Spirit in humanity. That appearance on earth as an individual is the crisis in the history both of Christ Himself and of the humanity He saves and leads. The ministry of Jesus, therefore, culminating in His death, is essential to Paul's whole thought. If in certain aspects of his theology it is the death that bulks most largely—because it seemed to him to be the purest and most moving expression of what the whole life meant—he is quite aware that the ethical impulse given by the example and teaching of Jesus is of the very stuff of the Christian life. He alludes to the Gospel story but sparingly, but those who study his teaching most closely become aware that he is himself acting and speaking all through under the impulse of the life and teaching of Jesus. If he refuses to "know Christ after the flesh," [16] it means that he will not risk a harking-back to the temporary conditions of the Galilæan ministry when the Spirit of Christ is clearly leading out into new fields. The issues of that ministry have been gathered up in the new experience of "Christ in me," and that experience gives a living Christ, who leads ever onward those who will adventure with Him, and not a prophet of the past, whose words might pass into a dead tradition.

At the same time, the indwelling Christ is continuous with the Man who died; and Paul clearly assumes a knowledge of the Jesus of the Gospels in his correspondents. It is probable, in fact, that our earliest Gospel took form to meet the needs of the new Churches of the Gentile Mission, and that the Gospel according to Luke represents the picture of Jesus Christ which was given to the Pauline Churches by one who had worked for years under Paul's own direction. At the same time, we must say that Paul's service to Christianity might have been even greater than it was if he had given clear expression to the *direct* religious value of the life that Jesus lived. One of the tasks still awaiting Christian thought is the filling out of the categories of Pauline theology from the content of the human life of Jesus. The Christian of this generation, to which modern scholarship has given a clearer picture, perhaps, of Jesus of Nazareth than has been possessed by men since the earliest ages of Christianity, should steep his mind in the stories and sayings of the Gospels, until the Figure of Jesus stands before him in the colours of life, and then turn anew to the glowing language in which Paul tells what that Figure meant for him and means for all men. So we shall miss neither the vivid humanity of the Gospel story nor the splendid universality of Paul's vision of Christ—the unseen Companion of humanity on its long pilgrimage, who for the accomplishment of His high mission wrought in a human life the critical act of deliverance.

To the consideration of that act of deliverance we must now turn.

VIII

THE DECISIVE BATTLE

It will be well at this point to recall the view which Paul sets before us of the situation with which Christ came to deal. Humanity was fighting a losing battle against Sin. For Sin had laid claim to the whole range of man's physical and psychical existence. The "inner man" maintained a feeble protest, especially where it was fortified by a clear knowledge of Right as expressed in law. But that protest did not make itself effective in action, for knowledge of the Law could not of itself overcome the weakness of the "flesh." So complete was the social and racial degradation of mankind that no individual born could escape partaking in the general wrongness, consciously or unconsciously. In either case the wrong way of life must lead to disaster—"The Wrath," or inevitable Nemesis of Sin in a moral universe. To meet the need, a way must be found to break the power of Sin and secure for man a new moral competence, and at the same time to replace the revelation of Right in terms of law by one which should establish personal relations congruous with the real character of God. There will therefore be two sides to the work of Christ, a negative or backward-looking, and a positive or forward-looking. On the one hand He must defeat Sin and clear scores with Law. On the other hand He must bring man moral power and create in him a principle of self-determined goodness. These two aspects of the matter cannot always be clearly distinguished, for they are complementary at every stage; but we may say roughly that the one side is represented by what is called the doctrine of Justification by Faith, the other by the even more important Pauline teaching about life "in Christ." We consider first the former aspect of the matter.

In order to understand Paul's teaching here it is necessary to give full weight to his belief in the solidarity of man. On the one side that solidarity is considered as "forensic," i.e. mankind is regarded as a real corporation which acts and suffers in the person of its representative. In primitive society the "personality" of the tribe or other community is so much more clearly defined than that of the individuals composing it that the whole community naturally suffers for any crime of one of its members. If an Achan breaks *tabu*, his whole kin must perish. If a Macdonald of Glencoe delays to take the oath of allegiance, his whole clan must be massacred. It is only an extension of that idea when Paul thinks of the human race as a corporation represented on the natural plane by "Adam," the hypothetical ancestor, whose act of sin involves the whole Race; but capable also of being represented by Christ, and sharing likewise in His "act of righteousness." [1] On the other hand the solidarity is considered as metaphysical. "Flesh," or the lower part of human nature, is thought of as a *continuum*, in which all individual men share. It is a tainted heritage which comes to each man burdened with the results of racial sin. Thus a blow struck at Sin by any human being who partakes of the "flesh" is struck on behalf of all.

On this double idea of human solidarity rests the

theoretical exposition of Paul's thought about the work of Christ. It is clear that for the purpose of his doctrine the reality of Christ's human life is absolutely demanded. Only a real man of flesh and blood could strike the blow for all men. God, says Paul, sent His Son "in the form of sinful flesh." The word "form" is not to be taken as expressing any unreality. By taking "flesh," Christ occupied the post of danger, for Sin was lord of the flesh, and claimed Him as its slave. That He successfully resisted that claim is the gift He gave to all men who are partakers with Him of our common nature. He was not a sinner in His own person; but "God made Him sin for us." That is said from the point of view rather of the "forensic" doctrine of solidarity. Jesus was made the representative of sinful man, and so before the law was responsible for sin. We have now an elaborate metaphor of a law-suit. Sin (personified) claimed its slave, but the verdict was given against the plaintiff. That, and not merely the moral censure of sin, is meant by the strange phrase that "God condemned Sin in the flesh." The claim of Sin upon Christ was disallowed, and therefore the claim of Sin upon all men who are identified with Christ was disallowed. His death, which might seem a victory for Sin, is shown by the following resurrection not to be such a victory. Death had not touched Christ's real self; it had become, instead of final defeat, a passage out of the bondage of "flesh" into the "liberty of the Spirit." "The death He died, He died in relation to Sin, once for all; the life that He lives, He lives in relation to God." [2]

In all this, Christ is the representative of a corporation which potentially includes all humanity. Those who are made one with Christ by that act of "faith," which we shall presently consider more particularly, enter at once into the benefits of this emancipation from Sin and this liberty of the Spirit. It is very clearly to be observed that Christ's action is throughout strictly representative. He acts for us, but not in a sense which excludes us from the act, but rather includes us in it. "One died for all; therefore all died," says Paul quite clearly. And when he comes to expound the matter in more detail, he shows that this co-operation in the act, however "forensically" it is conceived, is to be interpreted in a very practical way. "He died for all, so that those who live should no longer live for themselves." In fact, Christ's action becomes available for men exactly in proportion as His representation of them becomes a real thing, that is in proportion as they accept its implications, and make them the guiding principles of their own lives.[3]

It is surely in a similar sense that we must understand the metaphor of sacrifice, which has been pressed so exclusively in much Christian theology, though so far as Paul is concerned it is less akin to his habitual ways of thought than the metaphor of the lawsuit. The practice of sacrifice is in one form or another characteristic of all religions in their earlier stages of development. The meanings given to it are various, but almost all depend upon the idea of solidarity in some sense. The victim is often considered as one with the Deity, and the worshippers by partaking in the sacrifice are admitted to the same unity. The sacrificing priest acts in a completely representative capacity: his act is the act of the body of worshippers, and the benefits of the act accrue to them all. Again, in many forms of ancient sacrifice the priest so represented the Deity that he was considered as identical with the Deity, and so also with the victim he offered. Deity, victim, priest, and worshippers formed in the act of sacrifice an organic whole. Just how much of this complex of ideas lay explicitly in the minds of the people to whom Paul wrote it is impossible to say; but such is the background of the most universal element in the religions of his time. It has indeed been well observed that to the ancients it seemed that they had told the inmost secret of a matter when they had expressed it in terms of sacrifice, whereas for us it is just there that the difficulty begins.

We may find a clue to the idea which for Paul was most regulative of the meaning of sacrifice in the exhortation which he addressed to his correspondents at Rome: "Offer your bodies as a living sacrifice, holy and fit for God's acceptance, for this is the worship which reason renders." [4] To give the sentence its proper tone we may recall that by "body" Paul meant the whole personality, and not merely the structure of flesh and blood. Sacrifice is therefore first of all the dedication to God of all that one has and is. It is surely of this sacrifice that he speaks when he uses that old-world expression "the blood of Christ." For to the ancient mind "the life thereof is the blood thereof." [5] The shedding of blood meant the laying down of the life. And this laying down of the life derives its full significance from the thought of solidarity. An ancient prophet had drawn from the thought of solidarity the splendid conception of an ideal Servant of the Lord who would surrender his life in all manner of humiliation and suffering that others might live. "Thou shalt make his life an offering for sin. . . . By his knowledge shall My righteous Servant justify many." [6] It seems to have been in that thought that Jesus went to His death. Paul did not regard this self-sacrifice of Christ as being altogether different in kind from the self-sacrifice to which all Christian people are called in their way. He professed himself ready "to make up the deficit of Christ's sufferings on behalf of His Body, the Community." [7] But there was a completeness about the self-dedication of Christ which, like everything about Him, pointed to a unique relation to the universal action and eternal purpose of God for and in man, and which certainly proved itself decisive in its historical results. The sacrifice of Jesus Christ takes its unique significance from what He was. The ethical basis of it all is most clearly brought out by Paul. "Just as the transgression of a single individual issued in condemnation for all men, so the *righteous act* of a single individual issued for all men in a setting-right ('justification'), which brought (new) life. For as through the disobedience of one man the multitude of men were set wrong, so by the *obedience* of the one the multitude will be set right." [8]

In the light of all this we may read the passage in which Paul most explicitly sets forth the work of Christ in sacrificial terms:

All went wrong and missed the divine splendour; and all are set right by God's free grace through the emancipation worked in the person of Jesus Christ. God set Him forth as a means of annulling sin, through the trust (of men), in virtue of the laying-down of His life. This God did to show His righteousness, because of His passing-over of former wrongdoings while He held His hand—with a view to showing His righteousness at the present time, so that He might be at once righteous and the Setter-right of those who take their stand upon trust in Jesus.[9]

On this difficult passage two comments in particular must be made. First, the word which our familiar version gives as "propitiation" does not mean propitiation, which is properly the soothing of an angry person. The noun *hilasterion* is derived from the verb *hilaskesthai,* and means an instrument or means for the accomplishment of the action indicated by the verb. The original meaning of *hilaskesthai* is "to soothe an angry person." [10] In the Greek Old Testament, for example, it is so used for Jacob's propitiation of Esau. But while pagan usage frequently makes God the object of such an act, this idea is suggested in the Old Testament by only three passages out of some scores, and nowhere in the New Testament.[11] On the other hand, the meaning "to expiate or annul sin or defilement," which is also found in the pagan use of the term, becomes the regular meaning in the Old Testament. The subject may be a man (such as a priest), or God. In the former case the reference may be to sacrifice, or to ritual washing, or to any such act by which it was believed in ancient times that uncleanness could be removed. In the latter case, the meaning is equivalent to "forgive." [12] In our present passage, though God is not actually made the subject of the verb "to expiate," yet He is said to have "set forth a means of expiation," or of dealing with sin. The means is shown to be thought of in sacrificial terms by the following mention of "blood," in the sense of life laid down. So far, therefore, from the sacrifice of Christ being thought of as a means of soothing an angry Deity, it is represented as an act of God Himself to cope with the sin which was devastating human life.

The other comment is upon the latter part of the passage, and may be made more shortly by a reference to what has been said above (p. 76). "The passing-over of former wrong-doings" means the exhibition, in religious experience, of a principle of the divine healing which is inconsistent with strict law. Under the old régime, as Paul sees it, there were two different principles at work, the principle of retribution embodied in the scheme of things, and the principle of mercy discerned in the personal dealings of God with men. What was called for was a new revelation in which one single principle of righteousness should be displayed, and God's character be fully shown forth in dealing with human sin.[13] This was accomplished in God's gift of Christ, and in that act of self-dedication to which His "obedience" to God led him.

There is nothing here about a penalty borne by Christ as a substitute for guilty man. The nearest Paul comes to such a suggestion is in a passage in the

Epistle to the Galatians where he uses the metaphor of the "curse." [14] To the thought of the ancient world the curse was a real force launched upon the world and destined ultimately to work itself out. Such was the curse that lay upon the House of Atreus in Greek legend, and such the curse pronounced upon Babylon by the Hebrew prophets. Now the Law pronounced a curse upon all who should break it. Such a curse must fulfil itself, quite mechanically. It is a good *argumentum ad hominem,* at least, when Paul, writing to the half-Greek, half-Anatolian, and wholly superstitious people of the Galatian province, bids them think of Christ as having exhausted in His own person the venom of the ancient curse—somewhat as Orestes in the Greek legend exhausted the curse of the House of Atreus and finally "reconciled" the Furies who pursued the family. The teachers who were seeking to bring Paul's converts back into the allegiance of the Jewish Law said that unless they complied at least with certain minimum requirements, the Law still had power to condemn them. Paul replies: "Even supposing the sentence of the Law to have all the inevitable potency you attribute to a solemn curse, yet such a curse can be exhausted. Now Christ bore that curse; for He was crucified, and the Law expressly puts under a curse the crucified person. Yet He survived it, and came out victorious. He must therefore have broken the power of the curse, and you need fear the Law no more." In so far as this is more than metaphor, it is meaningless to us, for we do not believe that a curse is a substantive force working inevitably. But we do believe, because we see it actually happen, that there are circumstances in which, by defying the consequences, a person may so endure the pain of corporate wrongdoing as to win power to lead his fellows out of it. In that sense the comparison throws a real light upon the work of Christ. It is, however, only a passing illustration which occurred to Paul in the midst of that particular controversy, and he does not return to it in later letters.

More might be said of the various figures and forms of thought in which Paul embodies his conviction of the decisive value of the work of Christ. To our ways of thought his whole construction is not very satisfactory, if it be treated in any sense as a system of theology. But by the flashes of light he throws here and there we can partly re-read what he tries to portray. Jesus Christ took the full risk of the human fight against wrong. He accepted honestly and fearlessly all the conditions of human nature, and in the wilderness, on the mountain, in the garden, and in those countless "temptations" of which He spoke to His disciples, he faced the common foe. He faced it as one "born of woman," having in his human nature the conditions which in us all make for sin. He faced it as one "born under the Law," that is as a Jew of His time, whose temptations took the specific forms proper to His age and country. What is more, He faced it as one who deliberately threw in His lot with the sinful and weak. He did not withdraw Himself or stand aloof, but was content to be known as the companion of disreputable characters. All this we know to be true of the actual life of Jesus Christ. And facing in this way our common battle, He won victory all along the line. He accepted life in a spirit of utter self-dedication—of what Paul calls a "living sacrifice"—and He carried it right through to death; death with every circumstance of horror, and with every chance of escaping it almost to the very end, at the cost of the smallest unfaithfulness.

But what has all this ancient history to do with us? We should scarcely accept Paul's ways of stating solidarity. We do know, however, that solidarity is very real. We are in large measure the product for good and ill of the racial history which lies behind us, and of the social environment into which we are born. The mystery of heredity is not yet solved; but certainly since man had a mental life or "psychology," that psychology has been social as well as individual, and it comprises factors, present in the individual, which are due to the experience of the race, and most of all to the achievements of its leaders. The champions of a nation's liberties, to take an example, bequeath to their nation more than the actual constitutional liberties they secure in black and white: they form a psychology of liberty into which every member of that nation is born. He must do something with it; he may disown and struggle against it, but he cannot divorce his life from its influence. The same is true of the great witnesses to truth, and the great lovers of men—the poets and artists in life, to whose music the chords of every individual soul within their corporate tradition are strung, whether they are played upon or not. So it is that on a universal human scale what Christ did He did for us. His great fight and victory are part of the spiritual history of the Race, into which we are all born. We react one way or another to those decisive facts. They happened, and they exist today as an indelible part of the psychological heritage of man. The world in which Christ died is not a world in which one can live without meeting at all points, in oneself and in one's environment, the moral challenge and the moral possibilities which that event mingled in the stuff of our history. We may react differently to them. One will accept Christ's way, thereby laying himself open to all the divine forces, working within humanity, which Christ released. Another will reject His way, and thereby make himself an alien from this main stream of spiritual progress. In either case, the acceptance or rejection is not a theoretical attitude to a dim past, but a daily reaction to forces "in the air" of the world in which we move from day to day. Society is still a tangle of conflicting forces; we throw our lives into the sphere of *these* forces or of *those*. To be a Christian is to fling oneself without reserve into the stream of forces issuing from Christ's supreme moral achievement.

When we take this point of view, there are certain elements in the life and death of Jesus Christ which are seen at once to be decisive for us all. He greeted God as Father and Friend in everything and at every point. His life was that of a Son, and it was as a Son of God that He made His sacrifice of self-dedication to the Father. Towards His fellows a love such as He discerned in God was the perpetual motive power of action—a love generous, impartial, uncalculating, passionate to save—a love that put active, unceasing beneficence to the "neighbor" in the central place, and met wrong with an overplus of good. In such a life, the principle of sonship and of freedom from retributive Law is made manifest, and so the possibility of a new kind of life is communicated to man.

A word should here be spoken upon the significance which Paul attaches to the resurrection of Christ as the consummation of His work. It is true that for him, and certainly for us, the resurrection is vastly more important as the condition of that permanent communion with Christ which is the center of the new life. Of this much more will be said presently. But Paul also sees in it the conclusive proof of His victory over Sin. For us it can hardly take the same place it took for him in precisely this relation, if only because bodily death has not for us the same intimate connection with Sin that Paul had been taught to attribute to it.[15] We see in death something quite natural, and not necessarily horrible. Yet in the fact that death had, manifestly, no power to quench the living activity of Jesus Christ we may see a pledge that the natural order itself is subordinate to the ends of the spiritual life. In that order the death of the body is an episode, of much interest and significance indeed, but still only an episode, for those who stand for what Christ stood for—which is in the end what the Universe stands for. Putting it negatively, we might say: Suppose Christ, having lived as He did live and died as He did die, had then simply gone under. Suppose no one had henceforward had any sense of dealing with Him. Suppose in particular that that great wave of spiritual experience had not passed over the primitive Christians, assuring them that their Lord was in their midst, and making a Church possible. Suppose all this to be true: it would not necessarily destroy the validity of what Christ stood for; but it might leave us asking whether perhaps He was a mere rebel against a universe which, on the whole, stood for something quite different. There are many who do think so. They are our allies in the great fight, but they are apt to be depressing allies. If, on the other hand, we hold the continued personal existence and activity of Jesus Christ to be an assured fact, then we know that what He wrought on our behalf is also wrought into the very fabric of the universe in which we live; and we are at home in it, even while we rebel against its wrongs.

IX

EMANCIPATION

The death of Jesus Christ, then, we shall consider as a decisive fact not only in past history, but in the present constitution of man's world of thought and action, a fact towards which we must needs take up an attitude positive or negative. It was the crisis of a great conflict. The forces of evil gathered themselves for a decisive assault upon the moral integrity of the Son of God. They drove Him through the horror of failure, scorn, agony of mind and body, dereliction of soul, and death in darkness. For all the storm He never bent or broke. It did not change His perfect self-surrender to God, or the purity of His love to those who wrought the wrong. Therein was the proof of His victory. Such is the fact to which we have to orientate ourselves. We may decline to accept for ourselves what Christ did; we may refuse the principle which His life and death carried to victory. If so, then we assert against Christ the contrary principle, the principle which slew Him. "Saul, Saul, why persecutest thou Me?" is the protest which Christ utters against our action. On the other hand, we may accept the principle of what Christ did. We may accept it, not as those who believe themselves fit and "able to drink of that cup, and with that baptism to be baptized," but as those who are willing that the act and mind of God so revealed should be the principle of their own lives, and will leave the shaping of those lives to Him. This is what Paul calls "faith."

This conception is of such fundamental importance in Paul's teaching that we must try to understand it more particularly. In the theological constructions which have been based upon Paul the term "faith" has suffered such twistings and turnings that it has almost lost definition of meaning. Indeed, even in Paul's own use of the word there is very great complexity. Perhaps, however, we may get a clue from his use of the familiar words "faith to remove mountains." The expression echoes a saying of Jesus Christ; and we shall not go far wrong in starting from the use Jesus made of the word. "Have faith in God" was the one condition He propounded to those who sought His help.[1] By that is clearly meant trust, confidence directed towards God as the Father and Friend of men. This is the meaning of the word to Paul.[2] As it is Christ who not only shows us the God in whom we trust, but who has also Himself cleared away obstacles and made such trust possible, faith is alternatively described as "the faith of Christ," or "faith towards Christ."[3] That, however, is for Paul in no way different from faith in God. God is in the last resort the object of faith, for "God is trustworthy." That is the fundamental postulate of Paul's belief: God is worthy of our trust.[4] It remains for us to trust Him sufficiently to let Him act. It is wrong to suppose that for Paul faith is a meritorious act on man's part, which wins salvation, or even, in a more modern way of speech, a creative moral principle in itself. Paul does not, in fact, speak when he is using language strictly, of "justification *by* faith," but of "justification by grace through faith," or "on the ground of faith." [5] This is not mere verbal subtlety. It means that the "righteousness of God" becomes ours, not by the assertion of the individual will as such, but by the willingness to let God work. The critical moment in the religious life, according to Paul, is the moment when one is willing to "stand still and see the salvation of God." We can see how he came upon that thought. Paul had supposed that he was securing "righteousness" by a life of feverish activity, self-assertive, competitive, violent. It all did nothing but involve him more deeply in moral impotence. Then he was struck down. "Lord, what wilt Thou have me to do?" was the confession of surrender, the word of "faith."

Naked I wait Thy love's uplifted stroke.
My armour piece by piece Thou hast hewed from me.
  I am defenceless utterly.

Such is the tone of saving faith in God. It is surrender. As related to Jesus Christ, it is expressed in the saying "I am crucified with Christ"—or at least that is part of the meaning of those pregnant words. For the cross of Christ manifests utter self-abandonment to the will of God. When Paul sought to recall his Galatian converts to the full meaning of their faith, he reminded them how he had "depicted Christ crucified before their eyes," and that had inspired their surrender to God.[6]

This trust in God is, Paul says, the ground of our "justification," or "setting-right." The word is in the first place a term of the law-courts. Much as we are said to "justify" a course of action when we show it to be the right course, a judge was said to "justify" a man when he pronounced him, upon the evidence, innocent of any crime laid to his charge, and so restored him to his rights as a citizen. Here, therefore, we have one of a whole series of religious and ethical terms which were inherited from Judaism with its legal outlook. For the later Jews morality was a legal obligation to be met; sin was a "debt," forgiveness a "remission" of the legal penalty. Along with these terms goes the word "justification," meaning the acquittal of an accused person. It must first be understood in its proper legal sense, with the help of the entire setting of the law-court, and then as the whole of ethics is translated out of legal into personal terms, "justification" will be translated with the rest. Paul's whole work is a standing challenge to make such a translation complete.

Here then we have the human soul a prisoner at the bar of ideal righteousness—its own thoughts accusing and defending, as Paul says.[7] The verdict on the facts must be "Guilty": there can be no other. No soul is clear from personal participation in the moral evil of the race. That verdict carries with it the sentence to go on sinning till moral disaster ensues; for the Wrath or Nemesis of sin is that man is left to his own evil propensities. The sin we have admitted into our life is self-propagating, for "what a man sows, he reaps." [8] But now the prisoner makes his appeal: "I confess myself guilty, a slave of sinful habit. Nevertheless I disown this sinful self. I accept the act of Christ, as representing me. He died to sin; I make His act mine. I am crucified with Christ, and I throw myself in trust upon the God whom Christ has shown me."

> "I bind unto myself to-day . . .
>   By power of faith, Christ's incarnation . . '
>   His death on Cross for my salvation,
>   His rising from the spiced tomb,
>   His riding up the heavenly way." [9]

On that basis the prisoner is acquitted. The process cannot be understood apart from the antique idea of solidarity which has already been explained. The accused is acquitted, not by virtue of a righteousness individually achieved by him, but by virtue of the righteousness of his representative which he accepts as his own in the act of faith. "The righteous act of one issues in justification for all . . . through the obedience of one the multitude are set right." [10] There is no thought of a penalty borne by a substitute, but only of a righteousness achieved by a representative.

So far it would seem that the transaction is a legal fiction. To an ancient, indeed, its fictitious character would scarcely be obvious, since for him representation was a fact, and not a fiction. For us, however, if this is all there is to be said, then the doctrine of justification is unreal. But this is not all. We now approach the translation from legal into personal terms. What is the actual state of mind of the "justified" person? He has disowned, not merely certain evil practices, but his own guilty self. That is implied in the act of faith in Christ. He is crucified with Christ. So far as the whole intention of his mind is concerned, that guilty self is dead and done with. The controlling factor in the situation is the power and love of God as revealed in Christ and His "righteous act." That is the center about which the man's whole being moves in the moment of "faith." Outwardly, he is the same man he was, open still to his neighbors' harsh judgment, liable still to condemnation under a law which balances achievement against shortcoming. But really the man is changed through and through by that act of self-committal, self-abandonment to God. Before God he is indeed dead to sin and alive in a quite new way to righteousness. In fact, he is righteous, in a fresh sense of the word; in a sense in which righteousness is no longer, so to say, quantitative, but qualitative; in which it consists not in a preponderant balance of good deeds achieved,[11] but in a comprehensive attitude of mind and will. If our highest values are personal values, then at bottom a man is right or wrong according to his relation with

the personal center of reality, which is God. There is
only one such relation which is right, and that is the
relation of trusting surrender to God. A man who is in
that relation to God is right. He is justified, in no fictitious way, but by the verdict of reality. He possesses
righteousness—"not a righteousness of my own, resting
upon law, but the righteousness which comes through
trust in Christ, (or to put it differently) the righteousness which comes from God on the condition of
trust." [12]

There is a real moral and religious revolution here.
A legal religion lays all the emphasis on what a man
does, or wills to do. The power of the will, the self-
assertive element in us, is brought into the foreground. In direct contrast to this is the religion which
says that not what we do, but what God does, is the
root of the matter. "It is not a matter of deeds done,
lest anyone should boast." [13] Righteousness is not the
offering of sacrifice, the doing of good deeds, the entertaining of right opinions, or any of the things
whereby the self is asserted. It is the quiet acceptance
of that working of God whereby we are saved. "It is
good that a man should both trust and quietly wait for
the Lord." The immense energy of the religious life is
rooted in a moment of passivity in which God acts.
There is, in fact, no ultimate deliverance from sin
apart from this. If every man started his course with
a clean sheet and a perfectly free will, things might
be different. But none of us do so start. Our best efforts at self-reform are tainted and misdirected by the
evil that is in us. That is why so often the most sincere efforts of religious men have produced the most
disastrous results. The more fervour and energy they
throw into their endeavours, the worse for society. The
author of Ecclesiastes had this kind of righteousness
in mind when he gave the caution "Be not righteous
overmuch." Paul knew about it, for he had, in the
fervour of his religious zeal, been a persecutor. But

on the Damascus road he came to a standstill; and in that moment a new creation was effected. The weight of past evil was gone: a new life, God-directed, began.

How immense the moral task which this new creation imposes we shall presently see. For the moment let us contemplate the significance of this revolution in religion. The higher faiths call their followers to strenuous moral effort. Such effort is likely to be arduous and painful in proportion to the height of the ideal, desperate in proportion to the sensitiveness of the conscience. A morbid scrupulousness besets the morally serious soul. It is anxious and troubled, afraid of evil, haunted by the memory of failure. The best of the Pharisees tended in this direction, and no less the best of the Stoics. And so little has Christianity been understood that the popular idea of a serious Christian is modelled upon the same type of character. There is little joy about such a religion; and as any psychologist can tell us, the concern about evil magnifies its power. The ascetic believed that because he was becoming so holy the Devil was permitted special liberties with him, and found in his increasing agony of effort a token of divine approval. Not along this track lies the path of moral progress. Christianity says: Face the evil once for all, and disown it. Then quiet the spirit in the presence of God. Let His perfections fill the field of vision. In particular let the concrete embodiment of the goodness of God in Christ attract and absorb the gaze of the soul. Here is righteousness, not as a fixed and abstract ideal, but in a living human person. The righteousness of Christ is a real achievement of God's own Spirit in man. It is a permanent and growing possession of humanity. It is historic and integral to our world. Let that righteousness be the center of attention, and the only movement of the soul a full consent to God from whom it all proceeds. When that is so, the morbid cleft between the soul and its ideal is bridged; the insidious haunting presence of sin is banished; new powers invade the soul. "It is God who is at work in us, both in act and in will." [14]

It is perhaps worth while to add that modern psychologists recognize the importance of passivity or self-surrender as the means to a renewal of life and energy. "Weakness results from the wastage caused by restlessness of mind; Power comes from a condition of mental quietude," says one of them, adding that "several of the greatest psychologists . . . have tended towards the view that the source of power is to be regarded as some impulse that works through us, and is not of our own making." [15] Another observes that "to exercise the personal will is still to live in the region where the imperfect self is the thing most emphasized. Where, on the contrary, the subconscious forces take the lead, it is more probably the better self *in posse* that directs the operation." Accordingly a person "must relax, that is, he must fall back on the larger Power that makes for righteousness.[16]

We must now observe that this experience of "justification" assumes a different aspect according as the point of view is specifically religious or specifically ethical. Religious experience has about it something which is timeless or eternal. In the moment of the soul's touch with God the time process disappears. Hence "justification" as a pure religious experience of the grace of God is complete in itself and eternal in its value. Paul can speak of it historically as if for the Christian it was an event finished once for all.[17] But, on the other hand, no one has more cogently than he presented the tremendous moral endeavour to live out the righteousness of God. From this ethical point of view, to which the time-process is all-important, righteousness is a gradual attainment. Almost at the very end of his life Paul could write, "It is not as though I had already won, or become perfect; I am pressing on in the hope that I may lay hold of that for which Christ Jesus laid hold of me. My brothers, I do not reckon that I have laid hold of it yet; but there is one thing—I do forget all that lies behind, and stretch out to what lies before, and I press on towards the mark, for the prize of God's upward call in Christ Jesus." [18] One who spoke in that way can hardly be accused of neglecting the progressive element in morality. Yet Paul is never far from the thought of that finished work from which all human endeavour flows. "Work out your own salvation, *because* it is God who is at work in you." [19]

There is a difficulty here for us, as it proved a difficulty for his first converts. It may be that the peculiar character of his own conversion—its suddenness and completeness—may have led him into too unqualified statements of the "once-for-all-ness" of justification. In any case it is clear that he was misunderstood on this point by converted pagans who took in unintelligent literalness his strong assertion that "we have been cleansed, justified, sanctified." We cannot, however, escape from the difficulty by any short cut. There *is* a finality in that religious experience which Paul calls justification, while there is none the less a moral process. For most of us there must be a repeated harking back to the moment of surrender. After failure and fall we must enter once more into the "secret place of the Most High" to renew our abnegation of the guilty self and our acceptance of the righteousness of God in Christ. Paul perhaps allows too little for this necessity, explicitly at least. But for all that, it is of vital importance that he told us so plainly that everything depends on an act of God, eternal and single, in the soul, renewable indeed by acts of faith, but in its essence the one abiding fountain of all such acts, as of all moral endeavour.

"God justifies the ungodly." [20] That is the watchword of the Pauline Gospel. It states in a dogmatic phrase the truth which the life of Jesus declared. To the paralytic He pronounced forgiveness, there and then, before any amendment or reparation of wrong had taken place, simply on the ground of faith. The woman who was a sinner He accepted as forgiven, finding the proof of it in the love she showed. He received disreputable characters. No Pharisee would have objected, one supposes, if He had first made them respectable and then consorted with them. The Pharisees could do not away with this restoration to full rights as children of God on the sole ground of a simple faith. To forgive the paralytic was "blasphemy"; to receive sinners was a scandal. But Jesus told a story of two men who went to pray. The disreputable tax-collector threw himself on the mercy of God in simple trust. He went home "justified." The Pharisee thanked God for the righteousness he had attained—as Paul would say, "he gloried before God on the ground of works." But he was not justified. One Pharisee at least awoke to the truth, and he has told us what it meant. It took a Pharisee to see all that Christ's action implied. Paul the Pharisee put it into the crabbed theological terms he had been taught, but transcended those terms in the statement.

It will help towards the appreciation of what Paul meant by the forensic term "justification" if we consider other figures which he uses to describe the same experience. It is emancipation, deliverance from the yoke of an external moral standard and from the tyranny of evil habit. The justified man is like a slave freed from his master's power; or like a widow whom her husband's death has emancipated from the absolute dominion (*potestas*) into which Roman Law gave the married woman; or like the heir who on attaining his majority bids farewell to guardians and trustees, and becomes master in his own house.[21] It is no mere change of status of which Paul speaks in such metaphors. It is a real deliverance from something which denies free play to the human will to good. Yet it is not the attainment of that "unchartered freedom" which means bondage to "chance desires." [22] On the other side, it means entering into a new allegiance. Once Paul describes it, apologizing for the boldness of the metaphor, as "servitude" towards God. And indeed his perpetual use of the appellation "slave of Jesus Christ," which is directly correlative to the title "Lord," preserves always the sense of a very binding allegiance. The immediate antecedents of language of that kind are probably to be found in the religious terminology of the time. The members of a religious cult, bound sacramentally to one another and to their patron God, addressed Him as their "Lord." The Emperor was addressed as "Lord" when he was regarded as a divine object of worship. It was because the Christian would not give the Emperor the divine honour which he retained for Jesus alone, that the Church came into deadly conflict with the Empire. Thus Paul thought of the Christian life as freedom within a very absolute allegiance.

The more pregnant term, however, for this relation to God is "sanctification." In religious language "holy" means devoted to the Deity. The sanctification of the Christian means that he is entirely devoted to God; he is as truly and exclusively dedicated to the service of God as any temple or priest in the older religions. The distinction which theology has made between justification as the momentary act of deliverance and sanctification as the process of attaining perfection is not to be found in Paul. For him they are only different aspects of the same act.[23] By the same act of grace that justifies we are also sanctified; and as the righteousness attributed to us by the act of justification is to be appropriated through a course of moral endeavour, so is the sanctity imparted to us by the same act to be worked out in the moral life. God justifies the ungodly, and in the same sense He sanctifies the unholy. He claims us as entirely His own; and in proportion as we admit that claim steadily in all the changing experiences of life, it establishes itself in a character bearing the manifest stamp of God.

We are already at the point of transition from what has been called the negative or backward-looking aspect of Christ's work for us to the positive or forward-looking. The two aspects are combined by Paul in one striking and comprehensive metaphor, that of dying and rising again. Here he makes use of the symbolism of baptism, which in the East was performed by the complete immersion of the believer in water. "We were buried with Christ through our baptism (and so entered) into a state of death, in order that, just as Christ was raised from the dead through the splendour of the Father, we too might walk in the newness which belongs to (real) life." [24] To the rite as such Paul did not attach overwhelming importance. "Christ," he says, "did not send me to baptize, but to preach the Gospel." [25] But to his pagan converts it appealed as a sacrament parallel to those of the Greek mysteries. The governing idea of all mysteries was that by the performance of physical acts spiritual effects could be attained. And principally, such sacramental acts united the worshipper with his dying and rising Saviour-God. In some cults such a union seems to have been regarded as a real dying and rising of the worshipper, in the sense that through the sacrament he acquired from the God an immortal essence. In a similar way Paul's pagan converts thought of baptism. Paul recognized in the idea a most suggestive figure for the change wrought by faith in Christ. He found it necessary to guard against the crude sacramentalism which found in the mere physical process as such the actual impartation of new life, quite apart from anything taking place in the realm of inward experience. The Israelites in the wilderness, he pointed out in a curious argument, received baptism in the Red Sea and in the cloud which overshadowed them; and yet they were disobedient, "the majority of them God did not choose," and they perished miserably.²⁶ The inference is plain. No sacramental act achieves anything unless it is an outward symbol of what really happens inwardly in experience. The test of that is the reality of the new life as exhibited in its ethical consequences. "How can we who are dead to sin live any longer in sin?" If baptism is a real dying and rising again, then it is indeed a profound revolution in the personal life, a revolution which is simply bound to show itself in a new moral character.

It is in this sense that Paul appeals to the baptism of the Christian—the act by which he entered into the Christian communion. If that rite means anything, he says, it means that you share with Christ His dying to sin and His rising to new life.

The death He died, He died in relation to sin, once for all; the life He lives, He lives in relation to God. In the same way you must reckon yourselves as dead in relation to sin, and alive in relation to God in (communion with) Christ Jesus. And so Sin must not reign in your mortal body (i.e. in the physical part of the individual organism, in which, according to Paul, Sin had become firmly entrenched) so that you obey its desires. Do not make over your bodily organs to Sin, as implements of unrighteousness, but make yourselves over to God, as persons raised to life from the dead, and your bodily organs as implements of righteousness to Him. For Sin shall not be your lord, since you are not under Law, but under (God's) grace.²⁷

In reading the passage we are aware that Paul is speaking of something profoundly real in his own experience. We have left now the region of *mere* metaphor, and entered into a sphere where spiritual realities are described in terms not indeed adequate to them, but coming as near as may be to direct expression. The "death" spoken of is a real deadening of certain sides of the nature, a real privation of life and energy on the part of evil propensities. "I am crucified to the world." The crucified person—the man with the hangman's rope about his neck, shall we say?—has done with this world, its interests and concerns. It is all over. The mind has become detached. Even so Paul found that in the moment of his conversion he had become detached from much which had before dominated him. That obstinate "covetousness" which the contemplation of law had seemed only to strengthen —the ambition, egoism, perhaps lust, which are summed up in that word—was dried up from its springs. He cared no more about the very things which had been his greatest pride. "The things which used to be gain to me," he wrote, "I have now reckoned so much loss because of Christ. In fact, I reckon everything mere loss, because the knowledge of Christ Jesus my Lord so far exceeds them all. On His account I have actually suffered the loss of everything, and I reckon it all mere refuse—so that I may gain Christ." [28]

It is apparent that, stated in its absolute form, this "death and resurrection" was not true of many of his pagan converts. To them the "death" was ceremonial, the "resurrection" a theoretical inference from it, and the moral change had taken place only partially. That is why, instead of the positive statement which would seem to be required logically, he sometimes gives an exhortation. "Let not Sin reign . . . Do not make your bodies implements of unrighteousness." He seems, indeed, to have found by experience the necessity for greater emphasis on the *process*. "I have been crucified with Christ," he wrote to the Galatians in the height of his mission. It has been pointed out that crucifixion is in any case a lingering death. But in what is possibly his last letter he speaks of "getting conformed to His death"—a process not yet complete. Yet he knew always that everything was involved in that decisive moment. He died to sin once.

Thenceforward he "carried about in the body the dying of the Lord Jesus," and the course of life as it came day by day made the death more and more a reality in the workaday world.[29] More and more in those later days he was conscious that the real life he lived was a hidden life. "You died," he wrote to the Colossians from his Roman prison, "and your life lies hidden with Christ in God. When Christ, who is our life, is manifested, then we too shall be manifested with Him in splendour." [30] The "self behind the frontage," it has been observed, is in all of us something greater than the self of the shop-window which all the world can see.[31] For the Christian that secret self is perpetually nourished into greatness by inward communion with God in Christ.

> *As torrents in summer,*
> *Half-dried in their channels,*
> *Suddenly rise, tho' the*
> *Sky is still cloudless,*
> *For rain has been falling*
> *Far off at their fountains—*
> *So hearts that are fainting*
> *Grow full to o'erflowing,*
> *And they that behold it*
> *Marvel, and know not*
> *That God at their fountains*
> *Far off has been raining.*[32]

The faithful endeavour to keep open all the avenues between this hidden world and the world of every day is the way to what Paul means by "getting conformed to the death of Christ" and "knowing the power of His resurrection."

X

THE LORD THE SPIRIT

"God gives proof of His love for us in the fact that while we were still in the wrong Christ died for us. Much more then, now that we have been set right by means of His self-sacrifice, shall we be saved from the Wrath through Him. For if while we were enemies we were reconciled to God through the death of His Son, much more now that we are reconciled shall we be saved by means of His life." [1] In that repeated "much more" is much virtue. Theology has often represented Paul as though he were supremely or even solely interested in the death of Christ on the cross and the "Atonement" thereby effected. This is a somewhat ironical fate for one who showed so clearly that his eyes were set upon the risen Christ, and his thought returned gladly again and again to the wonder of the new life He gave. That positive gospel of the resurrection-life in Christ was an even greater thing to Paul than the doctrine of justification, important as this was in clearing the ground of all that cumbered the course. "If you are risen with Christ, seek the things that are above, where Christ is, on the right hand of God." Paul is always exultantly aware that as a Christian he is a new man, living in a new age. With Christ's resurrection the limits of the old order have been broken through. It is an age of miracle, in which nothing is too good to be true. The hope of the new age had often associated itself with a belief in the emancipation of the body from the limitations of physical existence. Manifestly this had not come about for the Christians of the first century: they still looked for it to come at the Lord's appearing. But Paul held that in principle the Christian, whose real self was hid with Christ in God, was already delivered from the "flesh" and living in an age of "glory." The "flesh" might indeed be "an unconscionable time a-dying," but the actual experience of the new life showed that the moral powers of "eternal life" were at work.

Now in this Paul met half-way a characteristic belief of the pagan religious world. It was held possible, by the performance of certain rites, or the acquisition of certain secret knowledge, to become immortal while in the body. There was an inward "deification" which ensured everlasting life for the initiate after death. Paul made use of this idea, while correcting its exclusively metaphysical and sacramental bias. For the Greek—as indeed in large measure for later Christian theology as formed by the Greek mind—the essential thing was a change of "substance" or metaphysical nature; its means, a rite or an esoteric doctrine; and its aim and end the assurance of life beyond the grave. For Paul the essential thing was a new moral character, as the only real evidence of a life akin to the life of God, and its means was the receiving of Christ, not by any magical rite, nor by assent to a system of doctrine, but in the moral fellowship of "faith." The risen life is in the first place a life whose fruits are ethical. Prolonged into the future it means immortality, because life of that kind, made ethically valuable through a personal fellowship, cannot be ended by the death of the body.

Moral conduct and immortality alike are represented as the harvest of an indwelling Spirit. "The fruit of the Spirit is love, joy, peace, patience, kindness, goodness, loyalty, self-control"; "he who sows into the Spirit will reap out of the Spirit eternal life." Otherwise expressed, the Spirit is "the first instalment of our inheritance." All that man hopes for as the corporate perfection of life is given in principle by that Spirit whose moral efficacy is a matter of daily experience to the Christian.[2] This idea of the Spirit is so vital to Paul's teaching that it will be well to make some attempt to see it in its historical context of thought.

In Jewish apocalyptic thought, the expectation of "the life of the coming age," or the Kingdom of God, was associated with the idea of the possession of men by the divine, or holy, Spirit, which had moved the ancient prophets and saints. The possession of the Spirit was conceived as bringing a miraculous heightening of the normal powers—the ability to see things invisible, to hear divine voices, to speak mysterious and prophetic words, to heal disease, and to dominate the world of matter. After the death of Jesus there broke out among His followers phenomena such as have frequently been observed in periods of religious exaltation or "revival." Persons fell into trances in which they heard unutterable words spoken, or saw visions of Christ and of heavenly beings. The powers of suggestion and of suggestibility were greatly intensified, so that morbid cases of divided personality ("demon possession") yielded to the suggestions of sanity; and even physical ailments of the limbs and bodily organs proved amenable to treatment by mental processes. In public gatherings men would be moved by a storm of intense feeling to utter cries which, though inarticulate, were held to be full of deep meaning, perhaps even to be the "tongues of angels." On a higher level they had moments of exceptional insight into truth, which they attempted to express in words of "prophecy." [3] None of these phenomena were unparalleled or in the strict sense miraculous, but to the early Christians it seemed that these were the literal fulfilment of the miraculous expectations of Apocalyptic. They were valued accordingly, as the manifestation of the Messianic Spirit, the gift of the new age. The simple followers of Jesus to whom these strange things happened were elated by the sense of power they brought. They scarcely realized that the real miracle was something deeper and greater than all this. Beneath the froth of "revivalism" flowed the steady stream of moral life renewed through the inspiration of Jesus Christ in His life and death.

The Gospel went out into the pagan world, where the moral background of the original Christian community was lacking. The volatile converts of Anatolia and Greece hailed with avidity the most exciting and spectacular effects of the "revival" fervour. The magical and occult has always a fascination. There was grave danger that the Gospel would evaporate in a burst of sensationalism. This danger Paul had to face, and in facing it he was driven to apply the cold light of a searching criticism to these emotional phenomena in which he himself fully shared. The faculty of self-criticism is rare enough anywhere. It is particularly rare in enthusiasts. Paul possessed it, and for that reason he was able to give to the Christian community such a sympathetic and convincing estimate of spiritual values that the whole idea of the Spirit became a new thing. He never thought of denying that there was a real value in the visions of glory and the inspired utterances which men attributed to the Spirit; but he pointed out that these were mere symptoms, and symptoms of varying value. For instance, "speaking with tongues," or the utterance of emotional cries of no clear meaning, was, though more surprising, far less valuable than the clear insight into truth which expressed itself in prophecy. But greater than all was the moral renewal that the Spirit brought. The reality behind all was that sharing of the risen life of Christ which reproduced in the believer the character of his Lord.

We have seen that Paul believed in a "life-giving Spirit" who all through the ages was the fountain of life to men, and was manifested at last in an individual human person, Jesus Christ. In accordance with this belief he held the Spirit, which the early Church believed it possessed, to be no other than Christ Himself, now liberated from the necessary limitations of His human life, and entering by direct fellowship into the Christian. This did not mean, as has been said, "a certain de-personalizing" of Christ. On the contrary, it meant the elevation of the idea of Spirit from the category of substance to that of personality. To have the Spirit does not mean, as it used to mean, that some mysterious stream of divine essence is passing into the human organism. It means being in the most intimate conceivable touch with a Person. There are two sides to Christian experience as Paul knows it. On the one side it is a life of trust and love towards "the Son of God, who loved me and gave Himself for me"; on the other side it is a life renewed from within by an immanent Spirit. Yet the Lord we trust is none other than the indwelling Spirit that is the inspirer of our thoughts, our prayers, and our moral acts.[4] Christ without, our Saviour, Friend, and Guide; Christ within, the power by which we live.

There lies here a deep mystical experience only partially capable of description in words. But is there not a partly analogous duality in our deepest relations with one another? You have a friend, dear as your own soul, the very embodiment of that which you admire and aspire to. Now you may sit in the room and converse with your friend, and his spoken word, or act, or look, may exert upon you the influence of his personality. Or you may be apart and he may exert that influence by letter. Or without letter you may recall him so vividly that the memory serves as a potent source of influence. All this is still the friend without. But when once the influence is established, there is a somewhat abiding in the central places of your own mind which is yet not yours but your friend's. You may even be unconscious of it, but it shows itself in countless ways. Some one will remark, "I seemed to hear X. in what you said just now"; or "The way you did that was so exactly X. that I could have fancied him here." In some strange way your friend has become a part of yourself—*animæ dimidium tuæ*. There is more here than we can readily express; and perhaps it is not altgether different from the double relation of Christ to the faithful soul. Paul converses with the Lord as a man converses with his friend: "Thrice I besought the Lord . . . and He said . . ." But at other times "The Spirit of Jesus suffered him not."⁵

The Gospel used to be presented as an appeal to believe in the Saviour who "did it all for me long ago," and then retired to a remote heaven where He receives the homage of believers till He come again to inaugurate the Millennium. The mind of our generation, having little comprehension or taste for such a message, is usually content to try and discover "the Jesus of history," conceived as a human example and teacher of a distant past. Meanwhile there exists always alongside all forms of religious belief the great tradition of mystical experience. The mystic knows that whatever be the truth about an historic act or person there is a Spirit dwelling in man. In our time even natural science abates its arrogant denials and admits the possibility of such immanence. The most deeply religious spirits of our time tend to take refuge from the uncertainties of belief in an inward sense

of communion with the divine, which is too widely
attested in human experience to be easily set aside;
and they report that they have no need of an historic
Christ at all. The weak point of mysticism, as seen at
least by a matter-of-fact person, is that it is apt to be
so nebulous ethically. What the Immanent is, those
who claim most traffic with It can often tell us least.
Is It a power making for righteousness, or is It a
higher synthesis of good and evil? Or is It not a moral
—that is to say, not a personal—Being at all? Does
It work "by rapt æsthetic rote," "like a knitter
drowsed"? [6] The raising of these questions is not intended to throw any doubt upon the validity of
mystical experience as such; but we have a right to
ask what content is given in the experience. Paul was
a mystic, but all his mystical experience had a personal object. It was Jesus Christ, a real, living person
—historic, yet not of the past alone; divine, yet not
alien from humanity. The Spirit within was for him
continuous with the Spirit of Jesus Christ, and recognized by His lineaments. To express this fact, Paul
coined a new phrase. The primitive Christians were
accustomed to speak, in language which was older
than Christianity, of being "in the Spirit," as though
Spirit were an ethereal atmosphere surrounding the
soul, and breathed in as the body breathes the air.
Paul, too, used this expression, but he placed alongside it a parallel form of words, "in Christ," or "in
Christ Jesus." Where we find those words used we are
being reminded of the intimate union with Christ
which makes the Christian life an eternal life lived
in the midst of time. The deeper shade of meaning
would often be conveyed to our minds if we translated the phrase "in communion with Christ."

Thus the Imitation of Christ is not an attempt to
copy His recorded acts and ways of life—an attempt
which can scarcely expect much success, where the
conditions of life are so different. It means to be "in

Christ," to give heed to the Christ within, who seeks to propagate in other men the truly human life which He once lived in Galilee and Jerusalem. The Christ of Nazareth had one life only to live between the manger and the cross—the life of Carpenter, Teacher, and rejected Messiah of the Jews. He must live again in countless human lives before He is fully Messiah of mankind, in the lives of modern men and women placed in a world so different from that which spread itself around His village home in ancient Galilee. To express this in a satisfying theology is a baffling task: to make it a reality in life is a problem solved in surprisingly large measure by many simple Christians in all ages, who could say with Paul, "For me to live is Christ." The truly Christian life is a life not transcribed from the pages of the Gospels, but continuous with the divinely human life there portrayed, because the genius of the same Artist is at work on the new canvas. "We all reflecting as in a mirror the splendour of the Lord, are being transformed into the same image (of God), from splendour to splendour, as by the working of the Lord the Spirit." [7]

We can trace how in Paul's writings this thought of "the Lord the Spirit" dominated the whole range of Christian experience. The initiation into the Christian life—the baptism by which we die and rise again with Christ—is "baptism in the Spirit," the steeping of the whole being in the Spirit of Christ.[8] This is the true baptism, of which the immersion in water is only the effectual sign. It means the implanting within our human nature of a divine element, present indeed in germ and in potentiality before, but woefully obscured and frustrated by our participation in the wrongness which infects all human society as it is. This divine element, freed now and brought to conscious life, salutes the Lord and Giver of Life with the acclamation "Abba, Father!" For the Spirit we have received is the Spirit of the Son of God, and we possessing it are God's sons too, and "that of God in us" leaps out towards the God who is the source of it. The Spirit of Jesus within us moves us to prayer: indeed, prayer is just that moving of God's Son in us towards the Father. Though we are burdened with the greatness of our need, so that our prayers are not even articulate, yet in such "inarticulate sighs" the Spirit "intercedes for us." This gives us the true character of all Christian worship. It is an expression of our "partnership with God's Son." [9] Whatever outward forms it may use—or shun—Christian worship is the reciprocal fellowship of God and His sons. He gives the Spirit, which then returns to Him in prayer and adoration. The norm and prototype is Christ the Son of God. The lonely prayers on Galilæan hills by night, the "exultation in the Spirit" when He cried "I thank Thee, Father, Lord of heaven and earth," the agonizing supplications of Gethsemane—"Abba, Father, Thy will be done!"—these are re-enacted in His brethren in whom the Spirit prays.

Therewith comes also a new possibility of knowledge of God. There is indeed a natural knowledge of God innate in man, but it is, in experience at least, dim and lacking in conviction, being mediated by His works.[10] But to share Christ's Spirit is to be admitted to the secrets of God. Perhaps one of the most striking features of the early Christian movement was the re-appearance of a confidence that man can know God immediately. Judaism had become traditional: the word of the Lord, the Rabbis held, came to the prophets of old, but *we* can only preserve and interpret the truth they handed down. Jesus Christ, with a confidence that to the timid traditionalism of His time appeared blasphemous, asserted that He knew the Father and was prepared to let others into that knowledge. He did so, not by handing down a new tradition about God, but by making others sharers in His own attitude to God. This is what Paul means by "having the mind of Christ." Having that mind, we do know God. It was this clear, unquestioning conviction that gave Paul his power as a missionary: but he expected it also in his converts. To them too "the word of knowledge" came "by the same Spirit." He prayed that God would give them a spirit of wisdom and revelation in the knowledge of Him. Such knowledge is, as Paul freely grants, only partial, but it is real, personal, undeniable knowledge.[11] In friendship between men there is a mutual knowledge which is never complete or free from mystery: yet you can know with a certainty nothing could shake that your friend is "not the man to do such a thing," or that such and such a thing that you have heard is "just like him." You have a real knowledge which gives you a criterion. Such is the knowledge the Christian has of his Father.

This knowledge of God gives a new ground for the ethical life. We have seen that for Paul the "conscience," or consciousness of oneself as a moral being, is the court of moral judgment. Now when a man has received the Spirit of Christ, that Spirit enters and inhabits the central place of his self-consciousness:[12] he is conscious of himself, not as a man merely, but as a son of God, standing in a special relation to Jesus Christ. When a moral question arises, it takes the form, not "Is this unworthy of myself? Does it hurt my self-respect?" but "Does this hurt my relation to Jesus Christ? Is it unworthy of Him?" Not that Jesus is referred to as an outside standard: it is "Christ living in me" who is the judge. In this way the Christian approaches all practical problems of ethics: he brings the mind of Christ to bear on it. This, of course, he cannot do unless the mind of Christ is his mind too. That is to say, the Christian solution of any difficulty cannot be reached by one who disinterestedly and externally examines and compares the evidence, without being committed to the result of his examination. It is revealed to him who lets Christ's mind dominate him day by day, and then sees things as they appear to that mind. He has thus his ethical standard within himself. Here is the real secret of moral emancipation. In the Gospels we see Jesus taking up a wonderfully detached attitude to traditional morality, picking and choosing, rejecting and sanctioning, in a way which must have appeared bewildering to his contemporaries—in a way, indeed, which few of His followers really understood. Paul grasped the secret of it. Jesus dealt in this sovereign way with the moral law because the Spirit of God who gave the law was His Spirit: because the inward impulse that shaped His own life was the very central impulse of all true morality. He was God's Son, and lived in His Father's house; and the law of the family of God was His very nature. In all this the Christian is a "partner of the Son of God." "He who has the Spirit judges all things, and is judged by no one." The principle of moral autonomy could not be more strenuously asserted.[13] And Paul's willingness to trust the autonomy of others is often really touching,[14] though we need not seek to excuse his occasional attempts at a dictation which was really not consistent with his principles.

Here we have Paul's sufficient justification against those who accused him of antinomianism or a relaxing of moral standards. The moral demand of letting Christ's Spirit rule you in everything is far more searching than the demand of any code, and at the same time it carries with it the promise of indefinite growth and development. It means that every Christian is a centre of fermentation where the morally revolutionary Spirit of Christ attacks the dead mass of the world. Ethical originality is the prerogative of the Christian whose conscience is the seat of Christ's indwelling: and such originality is imperative for a world which is "saved in hope," a world which needs progress. The seeming extreme individualism of this doctrine is corrected by the doctrine of the Body to which we shall come presently: but for the moment let us do full justice to Paul's claim of autonomy for the Christ-inspired conscience. It is a claim we must press with all our might in a world where belief in regimentation is strong and growing. In relation to the existing world-orders, in so far as they are based on the violent assertion of authority, serious Christianity is anarchism. It does indeed reverence authority in so far as that authority is "an agent of God for good," but it obeys God rather than man, and, in the last resort, with Paul, "cares not a rap for the judgment of any human tribunal." [15]

The indwelling of Christ's Spirit means not only moral discernment, but moral power. Paul's count against the Law is that it was impotent through the flesh. Against this impotence Paul sets the ethical competence of the Spirit. "I can do anything in Him who makes me strong," he exclaims. For his friends in Asia he prays "that God may grant you, according to the wealth of His splendour, to be made strong with power through His Spirit in the inner man, that Christ may dwell in your hearts through your trust in Him." [16] This is the antithesis of the dismal picture presented in the seventh chapter of the Epistle to the Romans, and it comes, just as evidently as that, out of experience. Indeed, we may say that the thing above all which distinguished the early Christian community from its environment was the moral competence of its members. In order to maintain this we need not idealize unduly the early Christians. There were sins and scandals at Corinth and Ephesus, but it is impossible to miss the note of genuine power of renewal and recuperation—the power of the simple person progressively to approximate to his moral ideals in spite of failures. The very fact that the term "Spirit" is used points to a sense of something essentially "supernatural" in such ethical attainment. For the primitive Christians the Spirit was manifested in what they regarded as miraculous. Paul does not whittle away the miraculous sense when he transfers it to the moral sphere. He concentrates attention on the moral miracle as something more wonderful far than any "speaking with tongues." So fully convinced is he of the new and miraculous nature of this moral power that he can regard the Christian as a "new creation." This is not the old person at all: it is a "new man," "created in Christ Jesus for good deeds." [17]

The result of all this is that the Christian is a free man. It is here to be observed that the term "freedom" is ambiguous in common usage. It is sometimes used to imply that a man can do just as he likes, undetermined by any external force. To this the determinist replies that as a matter of fact this freedom is so limited by the laws which condition man's empirical existence as to be illusory. The rejoinder from the advocates of free will is that no external force can determine a man's moral conduct (and with mere automatism we are not concerned), unless it is presented in consciousness, and that in being so presented it becomes a desire, or a temptation, or a motive. In suffering himself to be determined by these the man is not submitting to external control, but to something which he has already made a part of himself for good or ill. When, however, we have said that, we are faced with a further problem. Not all that is desired is desirable, and in being moved by my immediate desire I may be balking myself of that ultimate satisfaction which is the real object of all effort. If that is so, then to "do as I like" may well be no freedom at all. There is a law of our being which forbids satisfaction to be found along that line, as it is written, "He gave them their desire, and sent leanness into their souls." He, then, whose action is governed by mere desire is not free to attain the satisfac-

tion which alone gives meaning to that desire. There
is no breaking through this law of our being. Every
attempt to do so proves itself in experience to be
futile. Hence we are in a more hopeless state of
bondage than that which materialistic determinism
holds; for the tyrant is established within our own
consciousness. One way, and one way only, out of
this bondage remains. If we can discover how to
make our own immediate desire, and the act of will
springing out of it, accord with the supreme law of
our being, then to "do as we like" will no longer be
to run our heads against the stone wall of necessity
which shuts us out from the heaven of satisfaction.
For we shall only "like" doing what we "ought." This
introduces a new sense of the word "freedom." It
does not now mean freedom from restraint to follow
our desires, but freedom from the tyranny of futile
desires to follow what is really good.

This is Paul's meaning. The state of slavery described in the seventh chapter of the Epistle to the
Romans is a slavery to wrong desires; not merely to
"flesh" in the abstract, as implying our material nature
and environment, but to the "mind of the flesh"—the
lower nature and environment made a part of one's
conscious self. The slavery is the more intense because there is the Reason or Conscience recognizing
the ideal of true satisfaction, and chafing more and
more at its impotence to resist. What the Law could
not do, God has done by the gift of the Spirit of
Christ: He has given the victory to the higher self.
"Where the Spirit of the Lord is, there is liberty."
"The Law of the Spirit—the law of a life in communion with Christ Jesus—has made me free from the law
of sin and death." Whereas life was a hopeless struggle, in which the higher self was handicapped against
a foe that had all the advantage, it now becomes a
struggle in which the handicap is removed, and victory already secured in principle, because God has

come into the life. The Law was external; it was a taskmaster set over against the troubled and fettered will of man. The Spirit is within, the mind of the Spirit is the mind of the man himself, and from within works out a growing perfection of life which satisfies the real longing of the soul. In the full sense freedom is still an object of hope; but the liberty already attained makes possible the building up of a Christian morality.

XI

THE DIVINE COMMONWEALTH DISCOVERED

From Paul's teaching about the Spirit of Christ flows naturally a thought in which we may find the consummation of his work. Where many individuals share an experience so intimate as the "partnership of the Son of God" there must be a very intimate unity among them. Moved and governed by the same Spirit, they are one at the deepest levels of life. The new life in Christ, while it rests upon a most intensely individual experience, is yet a life in which no man is a mere individual. He is a member of Christ's Body. We may recall that for Paul "body" meant a real organic identity such as that which makes a man a single self-identical individual through all the changes of the years. Wherever Christ's Spirit is at work, there is His body; and He has only one body. Thus the immense varieties of spiritual activity are only aspects of the one life, analogous to the functions of various organs in a living body—hand, eye, ear. Each is necessary to all, and each gets its significance only from its place in the whole. There is one Spirit. and therefore through the whole area of the

human race there can only be one body. Here the
evolution of monotheism reaches its necessary conclusion. "There are varieties of gifts, but the same Spirit;
and there are varieties of services, but the same Lord;
and there are varieties of activities, but the same
God, who is the source of all activity in us all." "There
is one body and one Spirit . . . one God and Father
of all, who is above all, and through all, and in all." [1]
This drawing of the last inference from the development of a great religious principle is a signal contribution of Paul to social philosophy. The Stoics had
already reached a doctrine of the unity of man. Here,
as in other points, Paul stands right in the midst of
wide streams of thought. But it may be observed that
the Stoic doctrine was worked out wholly within a system of naturalistic Pantheism, and suffered from the
limitations which such a philosophy involves. Paul's
Christian doctrine of the unity of man has its center
in a moral self-revelation of the one God, knitting
together all men who will accept a moral and personal relation to Him.

So much for the theory of the matter. But important as was Paul's theoretical contribution, it was not
a mere matter of theory. It represents the actual experience of the early days of Christianity. When a
number of individuals with varying and even clashing
interests have been caught by a revolutionary force
which has made some one new interest mean more
to each than any of his previous interests, then a new
unity is inevitably created. This is what actually
happened to the early Christians. The fact of Christ
and His dealing with them became more important
to each than any other fact of his experience. The
separate interests of master and slave, man and
woman, Jew and Gentile, man of culture and barbarian, faded into nothing before the absorbing fact
which made each of these a Christian. Christ lived
in each, and therefore the life of all was one. [2] One of

Paul's great words is that which is variously translated "communion" or "fellowship." The Greek word is *koinonia,* which was originally a commercial term implying co-partnership or common possession. Thus in the Gospels the sons of Zebedee and of John are said to have been *koinonoi,* or partners, in a kind of joint-stock company owning fishing-boats. This word seemed to the early Christians the most appropriate term to describe their relations one to another. They were co-partners in a great estate—the splendid spiritual "heritage" in which they were "joint-heirs with Christ." The ground of their corporate life was what they called "partnership of the Spirit"—a joint-ownership in all that was most real and vital to them all. Our liturgical phrase "the communion of the Holy Ghost" curiously obscures the vividness of the original words, as Paul passed them down to us.[3]

Here, then, as Paul saw with a sudden clearness of vision, was in actual being that holy commonwealth of God for which the ages waited. Here was a community created not by geographical accident or by natural heredity, not based on conquest, or wealth, or government, but coming into existence by the spontaneous outburst of a common life in a multitude of persons. The free, joyous experience of the sons of God had created a family of God, inseparably one in Him: "one person in Christ Jesus."

This is not to say that all distinctions between men are blurred in a dull uniformity. For the irrelevant distinctions of class, race, and nationality, which set men in hostility, are substituted those differentiations of function which bind men together in a co-operative commonwealth. Paul had much ado to induce his Greek converts, born individualists as they were, to give full play to this unity in difference. The Corinthians made even the varied endowments of the Christian life matters of competition and rivalry. They had no criterion of worth, but judged a man's gifts solely by their "rarity value." Paul bade them apply a new test; the up-building of the body. We have seen how Paul criticized the "revival" phenomena of the early period. This was the test by which he judged them. "Speaking with tongues" was of small value: it profited no one but the individual. "Prophecy" was of greater value: it benefited the community. The endowment of the Christian was an endowment for service; the variety of endowments pointed to an organism with a variety of functions. Since the endowments came from the Lord the Spirit, it was He alone who could give meaning and reality to the whole. It was as His Body that the whole community functioned.[4] Pursuing this line of thought, Paul was led to see that the gifts and endowments which are of vital importance are the moral virtues, and above all, love, which is "the perfect link." This divine love or charity is the subject of Paul's famous lyrical passage in the thirteenth chapter of his First Epistle to the Corinthians. It is the highest and most comprehensive gift of the Spirit. "The love of God is shed abroad in our hearts by the Holy Spirit given to us." [5]

Thus the highest category of Christian ethics is deduced by Paul directly from the experience of the indwelling Spirit of Christ, and we may find in the fact a confirmation of the reality of his claim to guidance by Christ's Spirit; for the central thing in the teaching of Jesus is His enthronement of love to God and man as the supreme and sufficient law of human conduct. Paul is moving in different regions of thought, yet emerges at the same point; and when he claims that in spite of the manifest differences of the route his guide to the goal has been Christ Himself, we must allow that his claim has reason. Love, then, is the sum-total of moral obligation: "Be under no obligation to anyone except the obligation of love. For love is the fulfilment of law." It is a creative principle of society, the actual force which builds and keeps in being the mystical body of emancipated humanity, the "Israel of God." It is the groundwork of the new "Law of Christ" or "Law of the Spirit." [6]

Here we find the necessary and sufficient correction to the individualism of Paul's ethic of the Spirit. The sense of a supernatural intuition of God and His will, independent of tradition or the mediation of any authority, is apt, if taken alone, to strengthen individual self-reliance to a morbid degree. It "puffs up," says Paul. But if the revealing spirit is the Spirit of Christ, then also it is the Spirit of love, and "while knowledge puffs up, love builds up"; builds up, not the character of the individual being—we do less than justice to Paul if we so interpret him—but builds up the commonwealth of God into an ordered and organic whole.[7]

As the initiation of the Christian life, that "immersion in one Spirit" in which the believer died and rose again with Christ, had its proper symbol in the rite of baptism, so also the fellowship of the Body of Christ had its symbol in the "Lord's Supper." From the beginning the Christian communities had their common meal, the "breaking of bread," and although we have not any explicit account of the meaning which before Paul's time was attached to the custom, yet the primitive record states that the Lord at His last meal with His disciples broke bread, saying "This is My body"; and His followers can hardly have continued to break the bread without some recollection of His words, or without attaching some special meaning to them. For Paul, at any rate, the breaking of the bread which Christ had called His body was "a sharing in the Body of Christ": "because there is one loaf, we, who are many, are one body, for we all share in the one loaf." [8] In order to understand what Paul meant to say by that, we must remember how absolutely seriously he took the thought that the life of the Christian is the life of Christ. As the "soul," or principle of life (*psyché*) animates the body of flesh, so the Spirit (of Christ) animates the community. When bread is eaten, the virtue of it passes into all the members of the body. So in receiving Christ, the Body, which is the community, nourishes all its several members and they are inseparably one in the sharing of the common life.

There is behind this a deep mystical thought resembling that of the higher mystery cults of the Greeks, in which the sacred food of the God was eaten, and the worshipper became one with Him. But Paul will not let the matter rest at that quasi-magical level at which the mere consumption of consecrated elements by itself sufficed to work some mystic change. The reality underlying the meal is Christ's impartation of Himself in His Spirit to His people. But that Spirit is love. If love be not an actual and effectual force in the gathering of believers, then the form is utterly empty and has no value. When at Corinth the Christians came together in a selfish and individualist spirit, they were not eating the Lord's Supper, but their own. There were quarrels and rivalries. The rich feasted in luxury; the poor looked on and hungered, and the rich despised them. Under these conditions, says Paul, it was quite impossible to eat a true "Supper of the Lord." It was useless to take the bread and say, "This is the Lord's Body," when you did not "discern the Body"—the unity which His Spirit creates among those who have the love of God shed abroad in their hearts. For the Supper was also a solemn memorial of the dying of Christ, and of all that the dying meant. It reminded the partakers that they were crucified with Christ—dead to the evil passions of the unsanctified heart, its selfishness and greed. The cup of wine was a participation in Christ's sacrifice—the blood of the new covenant. The Supper is therefore more than an ordinary community-meal, and more also than the consuming of sacred food which brings magical potency with it: it is the current renewal of a union with Christ both in His death and in His risen life, and so a repeated, "crucifixion of the flesh with the affections and lusts," and a repeated constitution of Christ's Body in the renewal of mutual love through His Spirit.

In this Body of Christ Paul sees "the *ecclesia* of God." *Ecclesia* is a Greek word with a splendid history. It was used in the old free commonwealths of Greece for the general assembly of all free citizens, by which their common life was governed. When political liberty went, the name still survived in the restricted municipal self-government which the Roman State allowed. It was taken over by the brotherhoods and guilds which in some measure superseded the old political associations. Among the Jews who spoke Greek this word seemed the appropriate one to describe the commonwealth of Israel as ruled by God—the historical Theocracy. Our translation of it is "Church." That word, however, has undergone such transformations of meaning that it is often doubtful in what sense it is being used. Perhaps for *ecclesia* we may use the word, simpler, more general, and certainly nearest to its original meaning—"Commonwealth." We have spoken throughout of the Divine Commonwealth. That phrase represents Paul's *"ecclesia* of God." [9] It is a community of loving persons, who bear one another's burdens, who seek to build up one another in love, who "have the same thoughts in relation to one another that they have in their communion with Christ." [10] It is all this because it is the living embodiment of Christ's own Spirit. This is a high and mystical doctrine, but a doctrine which has no meaning apart from loving fellowship in real life. A company of people who celebrate a solemn sacrament of Christ's Body and Blood, and all the time are moved by selfish passions—rivalry, competition, mutual contempt—is not for Paul a Church or Divine Commonwealth at all, no matter how lofty their faith or how deep their mystical experience; for all these things may "puff up"; love alone "builds up."

In the very act, therefore, of attaining its liberty to exist, the Divine Commonwealth has transcended the great divisions of men. In principle it has transcended them all, and by seriously living out that which its association means, it is on the way to comprehending the whole race. Short of that its development can never stop. This is the revealing of the sons of God for which the whole creation is waiting.

XII

THE LIFE OF THE DIVINE COMMONWEALTH

Paul, as a Pharisee, was supremely concerned with conduct, for in Judaism not orthodoxy but correctness of conduct was the test of a religious man. The standard of conduct was external and confused trivialities of ritual with the "weightier matters of the Law." But conduct was the all-important thing. When Paul became a Christian he did not lose his interest in practical religion. In his greatest theological epistle the high argument reaches a climax when with *"therefore, my brothers, I urge you . . ."* he turns to show how the sum and substance of the whole is moral holiness in practical life.[1]

In the ethical teaching he gives we must think of him as a missionary seeking to train a Christian community in the midst of a heathen society. He could not, and would not, do so by any attempt to impose a rigid code governing all behaviour. His aim was to see "Christ formed in them." He wished to see them enter into that self-determining life of fellowship with Christ which means emancipation of the spirit of man. That life of fellowship with Christ means

also membership of a body. From these two principles—the Spirit of Christ in the individual, the Spirit
of Christ creating the body—all morality must spring
by the pure and free submission of individuals to the
leading of that Spirit. All that Paul could do was to
set forth by way of example the kind of way in which
such leading tended for people situated as his correspondents were situated in the Roman world. In its
particulars his ethical teaching embodies a good deal
of the new morality which contemporary Stoicism
was proclaiming, as well as of the humaner Jewish
morals of the tradition of Jesus ben Sirach and the
"Wisdom" literature. The wise moral teacher will express the ideals he wishes to promulgate as far as possible in terms already appreciated by his hearers.
But the unity of the whole depends upon an inform-
ing spirit. It is the character of Christ which makes it
a whole. "I urge you by virtue of the meekness and
sweet-reasonableness of Christ"; "Bear one another's
burdens, and so fulfil the law of Christ"; "whatever
you do, in act or word, do everything in the name of
the Lord Jesus": when Paul uses such language it is
more than a form of words.[2] It represents a settled
and reasonable conviction, first that where there is
knowledge of good among men it is the work of
Christ the life-giving Spirit, and secondly that now
that Christ has lived the human life we have a clear
line of definition, a test for all our moral intuitions. In
the whole of Paul's moral teachings a single and self-
consistent ideal is implied, and that ideal is the character of Jesus Christ. If we take as the vital center of
Pauline ethics the poem of love in the thirteenth
chapter of the First Epistle to the Corinthians, we
shall not be wrong in recognizing in it a portrait for
which Christ Himself has sat. What Paul was trying to
do was to show how a man would live if Christ were
living in him, at Corinth, at Ephesus, at Rome, in the
reign of Nero.

There were certain things which he would avoid as a matter of course: they were forbidden by the best conscience of heathendom. Indeed, the catalogues of vices which Paul gives correspond fairly closely with those of contemporary moralists. He generally groups them broadly into two classes: sins of the flesh, of lust and appetite, and anti-social vices, especially the commercial vices, summed up as "greed" or "over-reaching" *pleonexia*.[3] I say "as a matter of course": and such it was for Paul, but not for his converts. We are startled to find gross unchastity at Corinth, theft at Ephesus, drunkenness at both. The fact is that Paul had addressed himself to an audacious enterprise in calling into the Church the very riff-raff of society. If we ask how this man—brought up in a narrowly pietistic Puritan sect—reached such faith in human nature, we remember that he was a follower of the Friend of publicans and sinners and find the answer there. But that these evil things must go he never doubted; and he assailed them in a steady confidence that Christ had given the victory.

Over against these vices Paul does not set any merely negative asceticism. He does not correct unchastity by demanding monkish celibacy, or avarice by insisting on Franciscan poverty, or drunkenness by erecting total abstinence into a law. In the Epistle to the Colossians he blazes out against the asceticism of certain circles as a denial of the supremacy of Christ over all creation and of the freedom of the Christian man. "All things are yours; and you are Christ's, and Christ is God's," is his broad principle.[4] His doctrine of "mortification" [5] is something far removed from that of subsequent Catholicism: it is not the ascetic discipline which is a kind of reversed self-pampering, but the complete dissociation of oneself from all selfish, self-regarding, self-protecting impulses, and the readiness to accept the consequences of that dissociation in loss, contumely, persecution or hardship to body or soul. In his First Epistle to the Corinthians there is a passage which affords an interesting study in the light of this.[6] Its conclusion is perhaps the most "ascetic" passage in Paul: and the context merits examination. The point at issue is Paul's refusal to take money for his services. It was the custom of wandering preachers of the Cynic, Stoic, and other sects to receive gifts from their hearers. Jesus Christ had sanctioned the expectation of hospitality on the part of His followers: and Peter at least seems to have interpreted this as including maintenance for his wife. "All quite right and proper," says Paul; "but I personally should find it a hindrance. I prefer to bear my own burden. Similarly I am prepared to yield even the liberty which I claim for every Christian; I am ready to put myself beside weakminded persons and accept restrictions which they consider necessary. I am prepared to give up anything which interferes with the success of my mission, as the athlete surrenders what would incapacitate him for running, and if 'brother ass, the body'[7] protests—so much the worse for brother ass! But I am bringing brother ass to heel: he shall not balk me in the end." If that is asceticism, then Paul is an ascetic. He has got work to do which must be done, and that work is his consuming passion. As the boxer trains hard and the racer runs light, so he will drop what hinders him from pressing towards the mark. That is different from the timid "touch not, taste not, handle not," of the Colossian ascetics, and from the later ecclesiastical prohibitions and restraints.

On one point, however, Paul seems untrue to himself. A little later, we learn there were ascetics at Ephesus who taught abstention from marriage, and probably claimed Paul's sanction.[8] If so, he had only himself to blame.[9] For himself he deemed the renunciation of family life necessary for his mission, though he had as much *right* to marry as Peter,

James, and the rest. So far, so good: but when he wished others, not engaged in mission work, to follow his example, and suggested that marriage was a *pis aller,* he was on less safe ground. There is much to be said for Sir William Ramsay's view that Paul was concerned in the first instance to maintain his right to be a bachelor if his work demanded it. To the normal Jew there was something eccentric, if not worse, about celibacy, and among the Greeks the man who did not marry was "asking for" scandal. Paul set out to claim that a full, pure, and honourable life could be lived, and by some must be lived, outside marriage. But he was carried away, as so many people are, into proving too much. We shall do best to hold him fast, in this matter and on the whole question of the relations of the sexes, to his more humane and truly Christian teaching that while in Christ there is neither male nor female, the pure love of man and wife is a sacrament of the divine love of Christ, and the marriage relation which it consecrates is indissoluble.[10]

The frontal attack on evil living is not by way of ascetic regulations, but by a steady appeal to the new life in Christ. Thus, he writes to the Christians of Salonica:[11]

God called us, not for an impure life, but into a life of holiness. And so any one who neglects (this calling) neglects not man but God who gives to us His Holy Spirit. About love for the brotherhood, again, there is no need for me to write to you, for you yourselves are taught by God to love one another; and indeed you act accordingly towards all the brothers in all Macedonia. But I beg you, my brothers, to do still better (in this direction), and to take pains to lead a quiet life, to mind your own business, and to work with your own hands, as I told you; so that your conduct may be respectable in the eyes of outsiders, and that there may be no destitution among you.

There is sound sense in these injunctions to an excitable and unsteady people. Here and everywhere Paul impresses us with his readiness to trust the Christian impulse and illumination in his very fallible converts. Again and again he echoes the appeal of Jesus, "Why do ye not even of yourselves judge that which is right?" [12] And from the same root grows as of necessity the whole new life. "The fruit of the Spirit is love, joy, peace, patience, kindness, goodness, loyalty, self-control." [13]

But further, the Spirit is a corporate possession and not a merely individual. There is a "partnership of the Spirit." That fact given full play creates from a new center the whole ethical life. In the twelfth chapter of the Epistle to the Romans we see the Christian ethic growing out of the thought of the claim of the body upon each of its members. The Epistle to the Ephesians supplies the fullest working out of this.[14] It is interesting to survey this broad sketch of Christian community-life and observe how at each stage there is an appeal to the central principles of life "in Christ." Speak the truth—for we are members one of another. Let the thief stop thieving, let him work hard—in order that he may have something to bring into the common store. Mutual regard must take the place of envy, hatred, malice, and all uncharitableness, "as Christ loved you and sacrificed Himself for you." Injuries must be blotted out by forgiveness "as God in Christ forgave you." "The Kingdom of Christ and God" rules out alike unchastity and avarice or the idolatry of Mammon. Mutual subjection is the rule. This begins in the family, where the relation of husband and wife is a "mystery" or sacrament of the relation of Christ and His Church. Parents and children have mutual duties and responsibilities "in the Lord." Slaves must give obedience "as Christ's slaves doing the will of God," and masters must "do just the same" to the slaves, because masters too are slaves of Christ.

What we need to observe here is the conception of mutual responsibility founded on an identical relation to Christ. Paul has taken over the framework of the household as known to Greek, Roman, and Jewish law: the housefather as supreme lord and disposer of his wife, his children and his slaves. But in doing so he has introduced a revolutionary principle which was bound to transform the whole conception. In regard to slavery Christianity brought reinforcements to Stoicism in the protest it was making against that deep-rooted institution. Its attack was made from a different side. Stoicism started in the main from the natural unity and equality of men, and showed that slavery as an institution was illogical. Christianity started from the slave himself as a son of God, and so a "brother for whom Christ died." It did not at the outset say that the institution was indefensible. It introduced a new attitude to the slave as a man. This new attitude is well illustrated from the letter which Paul wrote to his friend Philemon of Colossæ. He had lost a slave, Onesimus, who had run away with money belonging to his master. By some means Paul came in touch with the slave, and brought him to a better mind. He induced him to return to his master, with a letter from Paul. In this letter he wrote: "I beg you for my son Onesimus, born to me in my prison. A 'good-for-nothing' he was once, but now he is good for much, both to me and to you. I have sent him back to you as though I sent you my own heart. . . . It may be that he was separated from you for a time for this reason, that you might get him back no longer as a slave, but something better than a slave, a dear brother—dear certainly to me, and surely dearer far to you, both by natural relations and in (communion with) the Lord." There is here a transforming power which goes deeper even than the splendid humanism of the Stoics. We may recall that even Epictetus, one of the noblest of them, could dissuade a man from punishing a slave in the words "It is better for your slave to be bad than for you to make yourself unhappy." [15]

Passing beyond the household we have the growing community. In pre-Roman times the Greek city-state had formed a real community, where the individual was conscious of having his part in the "general will." The system had collapsed, and for all the elaborate organization of the Empire with its local and central government there was no real community wherein a man could find that whole-hearted fellowship with others in common concerns which is necessary to a full life. A similar problem faces us today, and provokes the various schemes of Syndicalism and the "Soviet" idea. The result in the Roman Empire was the formation of religious and semi-religious guilds, of which the central government was perpetually jealous, which it tried time and time again to cripple but never dared utterly to destroy. The Christian Church was the biggest attempt to create a real community within the amorphous society of the Roman world. In large measure it succeeded, because it based itself upon a real experience of fellowship founded upon a free and personal relation to a "Lord" whose character was definite and known—a personal relation which was one of "faith" or complete confidence. We see the conception of mutual responsibility working itself out in the community.[16]

We urge you, brothers, give good advice to the disorderly, console the timorous, hold the weak by the hand, and be patient with everybody.

Each member must have something worth bringing into the common store.[17]

For just as we have many organs in one body, and these organs have not all the same function, so we, many as we are, constitute one body in (communion with) Christ, while we are individually organs of one another. And so, since we have different gifts, corresponding to God's graciousness shown to us, if the gift be inspired preaching, let us preach up to the full measure of our conviction; if it be administration, (let us throw ourselves) into administration; if it be teaching, into teaching; if it be the encouragement of others, into encouragement; a man who gives should do it open-heartedly, one who takes the lead, with energy, one who does a kindness, with cheerfulness.

And this applies to material as well as spiritual things. The principle is enunciated by Paul quite incidentally. During the central portion of his career as a missionary he set on foot a great scheme by which he hoped to promote that unity between Jewish and Gentile Christians which was one of his dearest aims. The Christian community in Judæa was in great poverty, from various causes, including famine and probably persecution. Paul projected an extensive Relief Fund, to which all his communities of converts from paganism should contribute as a mark of brotherly love, and also as some acknowledgment of the real debt which they owed to the first promulgators of the Christian faith. The latter point Paul puts to the Romans in these terms:[18]

Macedonia and Achaia have decided to make a "sharing-out" (*koinonia*) for the poor among the Holy Community at Jerusalem. They decided—and indeed it was their bare duty; for if the pagans shared in (the verb is *koinonein*) their spiritual possessions, it is only fair that they should help the Jews with their material possessions.

It is almost impossible to reproduce in English the play upon the world *koinonia* which makes it clear that the "partnership" of Christians is a partnership in material goods as well as in spiritual. Here is a basis for a far-reaching Christian communism. Hence the motive Paul suggests for work, which is capable of a wider and more fruitful application. Paul, we may observe, brought into Greek society, with its affected contempt for the "vulgarity" of all handiwork, the healthier Jewish tradition of respect for the craftsman. But observe the motive: "A man should labour with his hands, that he may have something to give to him who has need." [19] In other words, Work not for gain, but to enrich the community. Mr. Bernard Shaw's dictum, "Do your work for love and let the other people lodge and feed and clothe you for love," is an equally good, if rough, expression for the teaching of Paul as it is for that of Jesus.[20]

The interaction of the two principles of individual autonomy and mutual responsibility is well illustrated by Paul's dealing with some questions of casuistry which arose out of the clash of different races and cultures in the Church. At Corinth a difficulty arose about the eating of food which had received a pagan consecration. The difficulty could not be avoided. If you belonged to any sort of social club or trade guild, you could not go to the members' dinner without having food over which a pagan "grace before meat" had been said. If you dined out with friends, the same thing might happen. And anyhow, you never knew but that the meat you bought at the butcher's had done duty in some sacrifice. In the Forum of Pompeii, indeed, the chapel of the Divine Emperor stands between the place of slaughter and the butcher's shop. The close connexion of sacrifice with the sale of meat is clear. Here was a strange dilemma for a person who believed that such a consecration brought demonic influence into the food. The Jew, then as now, would not touch such "unclean" meat. The conscience of the primitive Church was equally tender about it.[21] No wonder, then, that many at Corinth felt in the same way. But others, inspired by Paul's teaching, said: "No, an idol is nothing in the world; there is nothing in it." And they freely and openly ate the consecrated food, to the great scandal of the "weak-minded brother." "Everything is lawful" was their watchword. Had not Christ "made all meats clean"? Paul retorts: "Everything may be lawful; but not everything builds up (the community). It is not everyone who has this robust faith, and if a weaker-minded brother follows your lead and eats, in the ineradicable belief that he is incurring defilement, you have injured his conscience, and you are responsible for him." [22] A similar difficulty arose at Rome over Sabbath-keeping and vegetarianism, and Paul deals with it similarly: All days are alike; all foods are legitimate; but if your faith does not really rise to that height, then you must not go a step further than your conscience allows. "That which does not spring out of conviction is sin." And if there is a "brother" who has scruples you must not indulge your liking till you have won him to your way of thinking. "Do not ruin with your eating the brother for whom Christ died." [23]

What we have here to note is the immense value attached to the individual conscience. No community can be "built up," Paul says, except upon a tender and sincere regard for the conscience of its members, even though the conscience be mistaken or over-scrupulous. On the other hand, the robust conscience is bound to criticize with a candid eye the whole field of obligation and duty, unhampered by *tabus* or superstitious fears; moved only by the consciousness of a relation to Christ within the conscience which must never be desecrated, and by a perpetual sense of responsibility towards others; "for no one lives to himself and no one of us dies to himself."

Finally, the growing Christian community aims at comprehending all humanity. Meanwhile, its task unfinished, it has relations to "the outsiders." First, the Christian has a duty to the conscience of his pagan neighbours. He is bound to respect their moral standards to the utmost of his power. "Think out conduct which shall be honourable in the judgment of all men." [24] But further, the obligation to a general beneficence which love entails is not limited by the bounds of the Christian community: "as we have opportunity let us do good to *all,* especially to members of the family of faith." "Never return evil for evil, but always pursue what is good both towards one another and towards all." "I am debtor," Paul said, "to Greeks and barbarians." That debt he sums up in the same epistle as "to love one another." [25] That love will inspire the most scrupulous discharge of all social duties. The emperor and his government come within the scope of this general obligation, the more so because, however imperfectly, the empire does seek to embody something of that natural law of recompense which can only be transcended as men enter into the higher life of love and liberty in Christ.[26] But love will lead to something more positive than the mere discharge of duties. For all the measure of good that there is in paganism, there is also a power of evil, which is exerted by way of opposition to the Christian community. This is to be met always, not merely with non-resistance, but with an overplus of good. "If possible, keep the peace with all, so far as the decision lies with you. Do not seek revenge, dear friends, but let the Nemesis of sin have its course. . . . Do not be conquered by evil, but conquer evil with good." [27] This is surely an admirable summary and application of the teachings on non-resistance in the Sermon on the Mount. The outcome of it all is that the principle of reciprocity—"an eye for an eye, and a tooth for a tooth"—which in the old religion defined the nature of the divine dealing and therefore of moral obligation as between men, is superseded by the new positive and creative principle of love. Because love is the only principle upon which God deals with us, it is the only foundation of human morality.

In all this it is implied that society as constructed on a pagan basis must pass away. The future lies with the new community created by the Spirit of Christ. The future of mankind is entrusted to this community, and its history must be the growth and consolidation of this community. Its members are as "luminaries in the world, holding out the word of truth." [28] They are "elect" for a purpose—the purpose of bringing into God's way and into the fellowship of His Son the whole race of mankind without distinction. In looking forward, therefore, Paul can concentrate attention upon the fortunes of Christ's Body. In it he sees the promise of a true commonwealth of man. Already within the borders of the Christian Society the great distinctions of race, sex, culture, status, are transcended, and the autonomous company of believers at Ephesus or Rome is a real nucleus of the universal commonwealth. He sees this commonwealth growing up, built on the foundation of apostles and prophets —lives of men illuminated, inspired, and sanctified— with Christ for corner-stone; a temple inhabited by the Spirit of God. Or again, he sees it as a living organism—Christ the Head, every joint playing its part in consolidating the living structure, till it grows into perfect humanity. Then as his vision broadens he sees this "full-grown man" made the means of the redemption of the universe which waits in hope for the revelation of the sons of God. For God who "was in Christ reconciling the world to Himself" has purposed in the end "to sum up in Christ all things in heaven and earth." [29] That vision of a world made one and free was the inspiration of the apostle's life-work, and it is the word of hope he passes on to a distracted race.

APPENDIX

A LETTER FROM PAUL THE MISSIONARY TO THE SOCIETY OF CHRISTIANS IN ROME

The following abridged paraphrase of the Epistle to the Romans aims at presenting in a plain way the continuous sequence of the argument, while suggesting the free epistolary form of the original[1]:

My Dear Fellow-Christians of Rome,

Wherever I go I hear of your faith, and I thank God for it. It is a part of my daily prayers that I may be permitted to visit you. I believe such a visit would do you good, and I am sure it would do me good. In fact, I have tried again and again to get to Rome, but hitherto something has always turned up to prevent me. I shall not feel that my work as missionary to the Gentiles is complete until I have preached in Rome. My mission is a universal one, knowing no bounds of race or culture—naturally, since my message is a universal one. It is a message of God's righteousness, revealed to men on a basis of faith (i. 1-17).

Apart from this, there is nothing to be seen in the world of today but the Nemesis of sin. Take the pagan world: all men have a knowledge of God by natural religion; but the pagan world has deliberately turned its back upon this knowledge, and, for all its boasted philosophy, has degraded religion into idolatry. The natural consequence is a moral perversity horrible to contemplate (i. 18-32).

But you, my Jewish friend, need not dwell with complacency upon the sins of the pagan world. You are guilty yourself. Do not mistake God's patience with His people for indulgence. His judgments are impartial. Knowledge or ignorance of the Law of Moses makes no difference here. The pagans have God's law written in their conscience. If they obey it, well; if not, they stand condemned. And as for you— you call yourself a Jew and pride yourself on the Law. But have you kept all its precepts? You are circumcised and so forth: that goes for nothing; God looks at the inner life of motive and affection. An honest pagan is better than a bad Jew in His sight. I do not mean to say there is no advantage in being a Jew: [of this more presently;] but read your Bible and take to yourself the hard words of the prophets—spoken, remember, not to heathens, but to people who knew the Law, just as you do. No, Jew and pagan, we are in the same case. No one can stand right before God on the basis of what he has actually *done*. Law only serves to bring consciousness of guilt (ii. 1—iii. 20).

But now, Law apart, we have a revelation of God's righteousness [as I was saying (i. 17)]. It comes by faith, the faith of Jesus Christ; and it comes to *every one,* Jew or Gentile, who has faith. We have all sinned, and all of us can be made to stand right with God. That is a free gift to us, due to His graciousness. We are emancipated in Christ Jesus, who is

God's appointed means of dealing with sin—a means operating by the devotion of His life, and by faith on our part. It is thus that God, having passed over sins committed in the old days when He held His hand, demonstrates His righteousness in the world of to-day; i.e. it is thus that He both shows Himself righteous, and makes those stand right before Him who have faith in Jesus Christ. No room for boasting here! No distinction of Jew and Gentile here! (iii. 21-31).

But what about Abraham? you will say. Did not *he* win God's graciousness by what he *did*? Not at all. Read your Bible, and you will find that the promise was given to him *before* he was circumcised; and the Bible expressly says that "he had faith in God, and *that* counted for righteousness." The same principle applies to us all (chap. iv.).

[To return to the point, then.] We stand right with God on the ground of faith, and we are at peace with Him, come what may. God's love floods our whole being—a love shown in the fact that Christ died for us, not because we were good people for whom anyone might die, but actually while we were sinners. He died, not for His friends, but for His enemies. Very well then, if while we were enemies Christ died for us, surely He will save us now that we are friends! If He reconciled us to God by dying for us, surely He will save us by living for us, and in us. There is something to boast about! (v. 1-11).

[Christ died and lives for us all, I say. But, you ask, how can the life and death of one individual have consequences for so many?] You believe that we all suffer for Adam's sin; and if so, why should we not all profit by Christ's righteousness? Of course there is really no comparison between the power of evil to propagate itself and the power of good to win the victory, for *that* is a matter of God's graciousness. However, you see my point: one man sinned—a whole race suffers for it; one Man lived righteously—a whole

race wins life by it. [But what about Law? you say.]
Law only came in by the way, to intensify the consciousness of guilt (v. 12-21).

Now I come to a difficulty. I have heard people say,
"If human sin gives play to God's graciousness, let
us go on sinning to give Him a better chance. Why not
do evil that good may come?" (cf. iii. 8). What non-
sense! To be saved through Christ is to be a dead man
so far as sin is concerned. Think of the symbolism of
Baptism. You go down into the water: that is like
being buried with Christ. You come up out of the
water: that is like rising with Christ from the tomb.
It means, therefore, a new life, a life which comes by
union with the living Christ. You will admit that, once
a man is dead, there is no more claim against him
for any wrong he may have committed. He is like a
slave set free from all claims on the part of his late
master. Think, then, of yourselves as dead. When
you remember the death of Christ, think that you—i.e.
your old bad selves—were crucified with Him. And
when you remember His resurrection, think of yourselves as living with Him, a new life. And above all,
bear in mind that Christ, once risen, does not die
again: and so you, living the new life in Him, need
not die again. I mean, the sin that once dominated
you need not any longer control you; do not let it! You
are freed slaves; do not sell yourselves into slavery
again. Or, if you like to put it so, you are now slaves,
not of Sin, but of Righteousness (a very crude way of
putting it, but I want to help you out). Just as once
you were the property of Sin, and all your faculties
were instruments of wrong, so now you are the property of Righteousness, and every faculty you have
must be an instrument of right. Freed from sin, you
are slaves of God; that is what I mean. The wages
your old master paid was death. Your new Master
makes you a present of life (vi. 1-23).

Or take another illustration. You know that by law

a woman is bound to her husband while he lives; when he is dead she is free; she can marry again if she likes and the law has no claim against her. So you may think of yourselves as having been married to Sin, or to Law. Death has not released you from that marriage bond, [though here the illustration halts], for it is Christ's death that has freed you! Well, anyhow, you are free—free, shall I say, to marry Christ. You had a numerous progeny of evil deeds by your first marriage; you must now produce an offspring of good deeds to Christ. I mean, of course, you must serve God in Christ's spirit (vi. 1—vii. 6).

Now I admit that all this sounds as though I identified law with sin. That is not my meaning. But surely it is clear that the function of law is to bring consciousness of sin; e.g. I should never have known what covetousness was but that the law said "Thou shalt not covet." Such is the perversity of human nature under the dominion of sin that the very prohibition provokes me to covet. There was a time when I knew nothing of Law, and lived my own life. Then Law came, sin awakened in me, and life became death for me. Of course Law is good, but Sin took advantage of it, to my cost. I am only flesh and blood, and flesh and blood is prone to sin. I can see what is good, and desire it, but I cannot practise it; i.e. my reason recognizes the law, and yet I break it through moral perversity. If you like to put it so, there is one law for my reason, the Law of God, and another for my outward conduct, the law of sin and death. It is like a living man chained to a dead body. It is perfect misery. But, thank God, the chain is broken! The law of the Spirit of Life which is in Christ has set me free from the law of sin and death. Christ entered into this human nature of flesh and blood which is under the dominion of Sin. Sin put in its claim to be His master; but Christ won His case; Sin was non-suited, its claim disallowed, and human nature was free. The result is that all the Law stood for of righteousness, holiness, and goodness is fulfilled in those who live by Christ's Spirit. There are two possible forms of human life: there is the life of the lower nature of flesh and blood, of which I have spoken; and there is the life of the spirit. We have Christ's Spirit, and so we can live the life of the spirit. And in the end that Spirit will give new life to the whole human organism (vii. 7—viii. 11).

You see, then, that the flesh-and-blood nature has no claim upon us. We belong to the Spirit. Those who are actuated by that Spirit are sons of God. [I used a while back the expression, "slaves of God"]; but really we are not slaves but sons—sons of heirs of God, like Christ; and when we come into our inheritance, how glorious it will be! (viii. 12-18).

This, however, is still in the future. At the present time the whole universe is in misery, and in its misery it waits for the revelation of God's sons. *Now* all existence seems futile in its transience; and even we still share creation's pangs. But we have hope; and the ground of that hope is the possession of God's Spirit—in a first instalment only, but enough to reckon upon. The fact is that every prayer we utter—yes, even an inarticulate prayer—is the utterance of the Spirit within us. We know that all through God is working with us. His purpose is behind the whole process, and He is on our side. If He gave His Son we can trust Him to give us everything else. He loves us, and nothing in the world or out of it can separate us from His love (viii. 18-39).

[That concludes the present stage of my argument; but before I can proceed to final deductions, I must return to a difficulty already raised (cf. iii. 1-4).] If there is no difference between Jew and Gentile, does all the great past of Israel go for nothing? Do all the promises of Scripture go for nothing? First, let me say how bitterly I regret the exclusion of the Jewish nation as a body from the new life. I would surrender all my Christian privileges if I could find a way to bring them in. But we must recognize facts; and the first fact is that the nation as a whole never was able to claim the promises; from the beginning there was a process of selection. Of the sons of Abraham, Isaac alone was called; of the sons of Isaac, Jacob only. If we ask why, there is no answer save that God is bound by no natural or historical necessity, but intervenes according to His will. To question that will is as absurd as for the pot to arraign the potter. Then again, while some members of the Hebrew race have always fallen out, always God has declared His purpose ultimately to include others, not members of the Hebrew race—and that is just what is now happening. Now, as I said, I desire nothing more earnestly than that the whole nation should be saved. But the fact is that they have deliberately rejected the chance that was offered them. There is nothing remote or abstruse about the Christian message. It is a very simple thing: acknowledge Jesus as Lord, and believe that He is alive; that is all. And they cannot say that they have never heard the message, for Christ has His witnesses everywhere. It looks, then, as if God had rejected His people, as punishment for their obstinacy. I do not believe it. God's promises cannot go for nothing. In the first place, there has always been, and there still is, a faithful remnant of the Jewish people. And in the second place, as for the main body, their present rejection of the message is only a means in God's Providence for its extension to the Gentiles. The old olive-tree of Israel stands yet; many of its branches have been lopped off, and new branches of wild olive have been engrafted in their place. But God can engraft the lopped branches on again, if it be His will; and I believe it is His will, and that in the end the whole nation will return to Him and inherit the promises. And if the failure of Israel has meant such blessing to the world, how much greater blessing will its ultimate salvation bring! God's purpose, as I said at the beginning (cf. i. 16), is universal: He has permitted the whole of humanity, Jew and Gentile alike, to fall under sin, only in order that He may finally have mercy on the whole of humanity, Jew and Gentile alike. How profound and unsearchable are His plans! (chaps. ix.-xi.)

[So now I can take up again my main argument.] If *this* is the way of God's dealing with us, what ought to be our response? Can we do less than offer our entire selves to God as a sacrifice of thanksgiving? How will that work out? In a life lived as by members of one single body. Let each perform his part faithfully. Let love rule all your relations one to another, and to those outside, even to your enemies. Do not regard the Emperor as outside the scope of love, but obey his laws and pay his taxes. Yes, and pay all debts to every one. Love is, in fact, the one comprehensive debt of man to man. If you love your neighbour as yourself, you have fulfilled the whole moral law. But be in earnest about things, for the better day is already dawning (chaps. xii.-xiii.).

I hear you have differences among yourselves about Sabbath-keeping and vegetarianism. Take this matter, then, as an example of what I mean by the application of brotherly love to all conduct. Remember that the Sabbatarian and the anti-Sabbatarian, the vegetarian and the meat-eater, are alike servants of one Master. Give each other credit for the best motives. Do not think of yourself alone; think of your Christian brother, and try to put yourself in his place. If he seems to you a weak-minded, over-scrupulous individual, remember that in any case he is your brother, and that Christ died for him as well as for you, and reverence his conscience. If through your example he should do an act which is harmless in you but sin to him, you have injured his conscience. Is it worth while so to imperil a soul for the sake of your liberty in such external matters? If the other man is weak-minded, and you strong-minded, all the more reason why you should help to bear his burden. Remember, Christ did not please Himself. In a word, Sabbatarian and anti-Sabbatarian, Jew and Gentile, treat one another as Christ has treated you, and God be with you (xiv. 1 - xv. 13).

Well, friends, I hardly think you needed this long exhortation from me. You are intelligent Christians, and well able to give one another good advice. Still, I thought I might venture to remind you of a few points; for after all, I do feel a measure of responsibility for you, as missionary to the Gentiles. I have now accomplished my mission as far West as the Adriatic. Now I am going to Jerusalem to hand over the relief fund we have raised in Greece. After that I hope to start work in the West, and I propose to set out for Spain and take Rome on my way. Pray for me, that my errand to Jerusalem may be successful, so that I may be free to visit you (xv. 14-23).

I wish to introduce to you our friend Phœbe. She renders admirable service to our congregation at Cenchraeae. Do all you can for her; she deserves it.

Kind regards to Priscilla and Aquila, Epaenetus, Mary, and all friends in Rome.

(P.S.—Beware of folk who make mischief. Be wise; be gentle; and all good be with you.)

Timothy, Lucius, Jason, Sosipater, and all friends at Corinth send kind regards. (*So do I—Tertius, amanuensis!*)

Glory be to God!

With all good wishes,

Your brother,

PAUL,

Missionary of Jesus Christ

NOTES

FROM JESUS TO PAUL

[1] Forsyth, *Christian Ethic of War*, p. 87: "Did Christ not summon then, the legions it did not suit Him to ask for to avert the Cross?"

[2] Phil. iii. 5-14, Gal. ii. 19-20.

[3] On this matter see J. R. Coates, *The Christ of Revolution*.

A CITIZEN OF NO MEAN CITY

[1] Perhaps the earliest allusion to Jewish money-lenders occurs in a papyrus of the year 41 of our era. The papyrus is a letter to a man in money difficulties, and contains the salutary advice "Beware of the Jews!" See Milligan: *Greek Papyri*, No. 15.

[2] Ac. xxii. 25-28. The fact that Paul learned a trade, that of tent-making, does not necessarily conflict with what is here said of his family's social position.

[3] This assumes that 'Εβραῖος in Phil. iii. 5 has something of the same shade of meaning as in Ac. vi. 1. In any case Paul spoke Aramaic, Ac. xxii. 2, and Aramaic was the language of his inner life: cf. xxvi. 14.

[4] Ac. xxii. 3, Gal. i. 14.

[5] Ac. viii. 1-3, ix. 1-2, Gal. i. 13, I Cor. xv. 9.

[6] Ac. ix. 3-30, xxii. 3-21, xxvi. 4-23, Gal. i. 15-17.

[7] Ac. xv. 1-35, Gal. ii. 1-10.

[8] II Cor. xi. 23-28, I Cor. iv. 9-13, Gal. iv. 13, II Cor. xii. 7-9.

[9] This piece of information is given only in certain MSS. of Ac. xix. 9, but it probably embodies a good tradition.

[10] Ac. xviii. 2-3, 18-20, I Cor. xvi. 19.

[11] I Cor. i. 26, Rom. xvi. 23, Phil. v. 22, Phm. 8-16 (master and slave); the persons who are mentioned as entertaining the local congregation in their house must have been relatively well-to-do: see Rom. xvi. 5, 23, I Cor. xvi. 19, Col. iv. 15, Phm. 2.

[12] The personal traits of the man come out most vividly in the Second Epistle to the Corinthians and in those to the Galatians and Philippians. To read these letters rapidly through, either in the original or in a good modern translation, neglecting for the moment the details of the argument, is the best way to discover the Apostle as a real man.

[13] Ac. xxi.-xxviii. The epistles to the Ephesians, Philippians, Colossians, and Philemon probably belong to the Roman imprisonment.

[14] I cannot remember to whom I owe this allusion to San Paolo fuori le Mura. There seems no reason to reject the tradition that this noble building marks the actual burial-place of the Apostle.

THE HOPE OF THE WORLD

[1] What follows is mainly based on Rom. viii. 18-25.

[2] Quoted from the poem *To Everyman,* by Edith Anne Stewart published in the *Nation,* November 1918.

[3] This is a dominant idea, as I understand it, of Mr. Fearon Halliday's book, *Reconciliation and Reality.*

[4] Rom. i. 19, ii. 14-15.

[5] Rom. xiii. 1-6.

[6] II Thess. ii. 6-7.

[7] Rom. ii. 1-11.

[8] The στοιχεῖα of Gal. iv. 3, 9, Col. ii. 8, 20, are not the material "elements" of which the world is made, but the "phantom intelligences," as Mr. Thomas Hardy might call them, supposed to animate and control the visible universe. Cf. Eph. vi. 12.

[9] Rom. ix., xi. 1-12.

[10] Rom. i. 3-4, Gal. iii. 16-17, 19, iv. 4-5.

[11] Rom. viii. 28-39, Eph. i. 3-14, cf. Gal. i. 15.

[12] κατ' ἐκλογὴν πρόθεσις, Rom. ix. 11. A transposition of the terms would give us "purposive selection," as distinct from merely "natural selection."

[13] Gal. iii. 6-18, Rom. iv.

[14] Rom. ix. 6-29, xi. 4-7, Gal. iii. 7-9.

[15] I Cor. x. 1-10, cf. Rom. iii. 1-20. The word εὐδοκεῖν does not mean approval following upon conduct, but a free self-determination on the part of God; cf. Gal. i. 15, I Cor. i. 21, Col. i. 19, Eph. i. 5, 9, Phil. ii. 13.

[16] Rom. xi. 4, ix. 27-29.

[17] Gal. iii. 23-24, iv. 1-3: note that these statements are made not about any particular individuals, but about the People of God considered as a historical entity.

[18] This is the judgment also of the author of IV Ezra: see iii. 36, "Individual men of note indeed Thou mayst find to have kept Thy precepts; but nations Thou shalt not find" (c. A.D. 100).

[19] I Thess. v. 4-8, II Thess. i. 10, ii. 2, I Cor. i. 8, iii. 13, v. 5, II Cor. i. 14, vi. 2, Rom. xiii. 12-13, Phil. i. 6, 10, ii. 16.

[20] Rom. xvi. 25-26, Col. i. 25-29, and espec. Eph. iii. 1-12.

[21] I Thess. v. 5, I Cor. x. 11. Paul never says in so many words, as does his follower the author to the Hebrews, that Christians possess "the powers of the coming age" (Heb. vi. 5); but something of the kind is implied both in his constant antithesis of Christianity to "this age" (Rom. xii. 2, I Cor. ii. 6-8, II Cor. iv. 4, Gal. i. 4, Eph. ii. 2, etc.), and in his use of eschatological language in the present or perfect tense instead of the future (Rom. i. 17-18, ἀποκαλύπτεται, I Cor. i. 18, II Cor. ii. 15, σωζόμενοι, ἀπολλύμενοι, I Thess. ii. 16 ἔφθασεν ἡ ὀργή etc.).

[22] I Thess. iii. 3, Col. i. 24, Rom. v. 3-5, cf. II Cor. xii. 10, Phil. iii. 10.

[23] I Thess. iv. 13-v, 11, II Thess. ii. 1-10.

[24] Rom. xi. 11-33.

[25] I Cor. xv. 20-28.

[26] Col. i. 17-29, ii. 19, iii. 10-11, Eph. i. 3, ii. 23, cf. Phil. ii. 10-11.

THE QUEST OF THE DIVINE COMMONWEALTH

[1] For passages from Rabbinic tradition setting forth these ideas, see Weber, *System der altsynagogalen palästinischen Theologie* (1880), pp. 14-18. Much of this material is certainly late, but it doubtless represents earlier views. The earliest definite statement I can recall is the saying of R. Akiba, quoted p. 69.

[2] See especially IV Ezra (II Esdras) vi. 55-56: "Thou hast said that for our sakes thou hast created this world. But as for the other nations which are descended from Adam, thou hast said that they are nothing, and that they are like unto spittle, and thou hast likened the abundance of them to a drop on a bucket." This portion of IV Ezra is dated by internal evidence to A.D. 100. The proud self-consciousness of Israel in contrast to the idolatrous Gentiles is finely expressed in Wisdom xv. which offers an instructive comparison with Rom. i-ii.

[3] Mt. xxiii. 15.

[4] Ac. xvii. 26.

[5] Rom. iii. 9-23.

[6] I Cor. xii. 12-14, Eph. ii. 19-22, iv. 4-16; Gal. iii. 26-28, Col. iii. 9-11; Rom. iii. 21-30, Phil. iii. 3-9.

[7] Phil. iii. 20. Πολίτευμα is used specifically of a colony of settlers who in a strange land reproduce the institutions of their μητρόπολις.

[8] Ζωή αἰώνιος (Rom. v. 21, vi. 22-3, Gal. vi. 8, etc.) is properly the life of the αἰών of Messianic power and glory, begun here and now for those who are in "Christ."

[9] Gal. iv. 21-31.

[10] Romain Rolland, *Above the Battle* (Eng. transl. 1916), p. 54.

[11] Stephen was accused of speaking against the Temple and announcing the supersession of the Mosaic Law, Ac. vi. 13-14. It appears that Paul was present at his examination before the Sanhedrin (Ac. viii. 1, xxii. 20) and heard his defence, which, if it is at all faithfully represented by the rather tedious speech in Ac. vii, dwelt upon the temporary and relative character of both Temple and Law.

[12] I Thess. ii. 15-16.

[13] Ac. xv. 5, xxi. 20.
[14] Gal. ii. 1-10, Ac. xv. 7-11.
[15] Gal. ii. 11-14, cf. I Cor. i. 12.
[16] Ac. xxi. 20-30.
[17] Gal. i. 6-9, iii. 1-5, iv. 12-20, v. 1-12, vi. 12-16.
[18] II Cor. xi. 26.

THE ANCIENT WRONG

[1] Gal. v. 15.
[2] Rom. v. 10, Eph. ii. 14.
[3] The antithesis of the two orders of being runs through I Cor. xv. 40-50; cf. Rom. viii. 20-21, II Cor. iv. 16, v. 4.
[4] II. Cor. iv. 16, cf. Rom. vii. 22-23; Rom. ii. 14-15, Col. i. 21, ii. 18, Eph. iv. 18, Phil. iv. 7.
[5] I Cor. xv. 35-54, ii. 12, iii. 3, Gal. v. 17, Rom. viii. 12-13, 23, etc. I believe that the above is a fair description of Paul's "anthropology." But he is not a systematic theologian, and he sometimes uses terms loosely. Σῶμα, ψυχὴ, πνεῦμα, all appear at times in senses approximating more closely to their popular or vulgar meaning than to the strict Pauline usage.
[6] Rom. viii. 21.
[7] Eph. vi. 12, cf. Gal. iv. 3, 9, Col. ii. 8, 20; the "rulers of this age" who "crucified the Lord of glory" (I Cor. ii. 8) are discarnate intelligences working behind the actions of men. "Angels" are in Paul generally powers hostile to men's salvation, Rom. viii. 38, I Cor. vi. 3, xi. 10, II Cor. xii. 7, Gal. i. 8, Col. ii. 18.
[8] Rom. viii. 20.
[9] Rom. v. 12, 21, vi. 12, 14, 17-23, vii. 8-11, 20, viii. 3.
[10] Rom. v. 12-21, cf. IV Ezra. iii. 21-22, vii. 11-12.
[11] Rom. i. 18-23, 28; cf. passages cited in note 7 above.
[12] Rom. vii. 14, 18, viii. 5-8, Gal. v. 13, 19-21, vi. 8, Col. ii. 13, 18, Eph. ii. 3. It has to be added that in many passages Paul was σάρξ in an entirely non-moral sense as standing simply for the physical part of man, e.g. Rom. ix. 3, Gal. iv. 13, Col. i. 22, etc. How easily the one sense passed into the other is shown by a passage like II Cor. x. 2-4.
[13] (Ἡ)'οργὴ (τοῦ) θεοῦ Rom. i. 18, Col. iii. 6, Eph. v. 6;

ἡ ὀργή Rom. iii. 5, v. 9, ix. 22 (possibly with αὐτοῦ), xii. 19, xiii. 5, I Thess. i. 10, ii. 16; ὀργή Rom. ii. 5, 8, iv. 15, ix. 22 (σκεύη ὀργῆς), Eph. ii. 3, I Thess. v. 9.

[14] Rom. ix. 22-23.

[15] Rom. i. 18-32, xi. 8-10.

[16] Rom. ix. 22-24, ii. 4, xi. 32.

[17] Rom. iv. 5, v. 6, vi. 23.

[18] See N. Micklem, *The Open Light* (C.R.S.) ch. iii.

[19] See Mt. vi. 23=Lk. xi. 35, Mt. v. 13=Lk. xiv. 34, cf. Mk. ix. 50, Mk. iii. 29, cf. Mt. xii. 32=Lk. xii. 10, Mk. viii. 35, cf. Mt. x. 39=Lk. xvii. 33, Mt. xxiii. 34-36=Lk. xi. 49-51, Mt. xi. 21-24=Lk. x. 13-15, Lk. xiii. 1-9, etc. The principle running through all such sayings is that of the disastrous consequences of wrong choice in a moral universe: cf. Gal. vi. 7. On the other hand, the characteristic personal activity of God is illustrated in the patient love of the Shepherd and the Father of the Prodigal.

THE TYRANNY OF AN IDEA

[1] Rom. vii. 12, 14.

[2] Mk. ii. 18-20, Mt. vi. 16-18; *Teaching of the Twelve Apostles,* viii. 1.

[3] Deut. xiv. 3-21, xxii. 11-12, Lev. xix, 27, Mk. vii. 3-4.

[4] See especially the saying of Rabbi Akiba (died 135 A.D.) in *Pirke Aboth,* iii. 19: "Beloved are Israel, in that to them was given the precious instrument wherewith the world was created. Greater love was it that it was known to them that there was given to them the precious instrument wherewith the world was created, as it is said, 'For a good doctrine I have given you; forsake not my Torah (Law)'" (translation by Herford). Cf. Psalm cxlvii. 19-20, cxix. 89-96, lxxviii. 1-7, and Rabbinic passages cited by Weber, *op. cit.* pp. 18-25.

[5] "According to the Jewish mind, requital was deeply ingrained in the whole scheme of things. Exceptions there might be, but they were more apparent than real. The most solemn and the most true adage in the world was 'measure for measure.' 'All measures shall pass away, but measure for measure shall never pass away.' The Rabbinic uses of the word *Middah,* Measure, Attribute, Quality,

form a chapter in themselves."—C. G. Montefiore in *Beginnings of Christianity,* ed. Jackson & Lake.

[6] Rom. ii. 28-29.

[7] Gal. iii. 10-11. Several Rabbinic sayings to this effect are quoted in Wetstein's note on Ja. ii. 10, which is an early and unambiguous statement of the principle.

[8] J. A. Hadfield, in *The Spirit* (ed. B. H. Streeter), p. 87.

[9] Rom. viii. 1-2, Phil. iv. 13, Col. i. 24, Gal. ii. 19, vi. 14.

[10] II Cor. iv. 6.

[11] Gal. ii. 19-20.

[12] Rom. v. 6-8, viii. 35-39, II Cor. v. 14-15, 18-19, Col. i. 13-15, Eph. i. 4-7, ii. 4-10, iii. 18-19, v. 1-2.

[13] Gal. iii. 7-22, iv. 21-31, Rom. iv., ix. 7-13.

[14] Rom. ix. 22.

[15] IV Ezra (II Esdras) viii. 31-36, but contrast 37-62; cf. *id.* vii. 47-61, viii. 1-3, ix. 15, 21-22, x. 10; vii. 68, 133. The date is about A.D. 100; but surely it was out of some such position as this that Paul advanced into Christianity.

[16] Rom. ii. 4.

[17] Rom. iii. 25, cf. Ac. xvii. 30.

[18] Rom. x., iv. 3-8, Gal. iii. 11-12, I Cor. x. 4, cf. II Cor. ii. 4-18.

[19] See especially Is. xlv. 8-25, lv. 6-13, lvi. 1, lxi. 10-11, Jer. xxiii. 5-6, xxxiii. 15-16, cf. Dan. ix. 16. The idea is suggested, but scarcely adopted, in IV Ezra viii. 36.

[20] Rom. iii. 26, cf. i. 16-17, with 18 sqq., setting the problem which is solved in iii. 21 sqq.

[21] See Norman Robinson, *Christian Justice.*

[22] Mt. v. 45, xx. 1-16.

[23] Gal. iii. 15, iv. 7.

[24] Rom. v. 20, cf. Gal. iii. 19.

[25] Rom. v. 13-14.

[26] Rom. viii. 3, cf. IV Ezra iii. 20-22.

[27] Ἀκρασία : see *Nicomachean Ethics,* VII. 1-10.

THE SON OF GOD

[1] Rom. viii. 3.

[2] Gal. iv. 4-5.

[3] See especially *The Book of Enoch* (in Charles' *Apocrypha*

and Pseudepigrapha), and IV Ezra (= II Esdras in the English Apocrypha).

[4] I Cor. i. 24, 30. The "Wisdom" idea is best represented by the books of Wisdom and Ecclesiasticus in the English Apocrypha.

[5] Gal. i. 15-16, ii. 19-20, I Cor. ix. 1, xv. 4-8, cf. II Cor. iv. 6, xii. 1-9.

[6] *God the Invisible King,* p. 6, cf. pp. xiii-xiv.

[7] II Cor. iv. 4, Col. i. 13-19, cf. I Cor. viii. 6.

[8] I Cor. xv. 45-49, cf. II Cor. iii. 17.

[9] I Cor. x. 4.

[10] Gal. iv. 4, Rom. i. 3, viii. 3, II Cor. viii. 9, Phil. ii. 6-8.

[11] Eph. iv. 12-15.

[12] Col. i. 19, ii. 9.

[13] Phil. ii. 9-11, Col. i. 18-20, Eph. i. 20-23, I Cor. xv. 23-27, Rom. i. 4, viii. 34, xiv. 9.

[14] I Cor. x. 16-17, xii. 12-27, Rom. xii. 4-5 (cf. also I Cor. vi. 15), Col. i. 18, 24, ii. 19, iii. 15, Eph. i. 23, ii. 5-7, 15-22, iv. 4-16; Rom. viii. 9-11, 17, I Cor. iii. 11, 23, II Cor. iv. 10-11, Col. i. 27, iii. 9-11 (cf. Gal. iii. 28), Eph. iii. 14-19.

[15] I Thess. iv. 13, v. 10, I Cor. xv. 12-28, Eph. i. 10 *et passim.*

[16] II Cor. v. 16-17.

THE DECISIVE BATTLE

[1] Rom. v. 12-21, I Cor. xv. 21-22.

[2] II Cor. v. 21, Rom. viii. 3, vi. 10.

[3] II Cor. v. 14-15, Rom. vi. 5-8.

[4] Rom. xii. 1.

[5] Gen. ix. 4: so Rom. iii. 25, v. 9, I Cor. x. 16, xi. 25, 27, Eph. i. 7, ii. 13, Col. i. 20.

[6] Is. liii. 10-11.

[7] Col. i. 24, II Cor. i. 5-7.

[8] Rom. v. 17-19.

[9] Rom. iii. 23-26.

[10] From this sense of ἱλάσκεσθαι is derived the common usage in pagan inscriptions, ΘΕΟΙΣ ΙΛΑΣΤΗΡΙΟΝ, "a propitiatory offering to the gods"; but it is a mistake to argue directly from this to the Christian use of the noun.

[11] Unless ἱλάσθητί μοι, Lk. xviii. 13, is regarded as such a use; but though passive in form, the verb is virtually

intransitive in meaning—"be propitious," not "be pro-
pitiated."

[12] E.g. Ps. lxiv. 4 (LXX.=lxv. 3, E.T.) Dn. ix. 24 (LXX.).

[13] See Fearon Halliday, *Reconciliation and Reality*.

[14] Gal. iii. 13.

[15] Rom. v. 12, vi. 23, I Cor. xv. 21. This idea is part of Paul's
Jewish heritage. Cf. IV Ezra iii. 7, vii. 118. See also Fearon
Halliday, *op. cit.* pp. 141-146.

EMANCIPATION

[1] I Cor. xiii. 2, cf. Mk. xi. 22-23.

[2] I Thess. i. 8.

[3] Rom. iii. 22, 26, Gal. ii. 16, iii. 22, Eph. iii. 12, Phil. iii. 9
(the genitive is *not* subjective in any case); Col. ii. 5.
Πίστις ἐν Χριστῷ is probably not exactly what we mean
by "faith in Christ": it is rather faith towards God as con-
ditioned by communion with Christ, Col. i. 4, Eph. i. 15.
In Gal. iii. 26 it is doubtful if ἐν Χριστῷ Ἰησοῦ is to be
construed with πίστεως. Outside these three passages the
expression does not occur in Paul.

[4] I Cor. i. 9, x. 13, II Cor. i. 18, I Thess. v. 24.

[5] Eph. ii. 8, Rom. iii. 30, iv. 16, v. 1, ix. 32, Gal. ii. 16, iii. 24,
Eph. iii. 12, 17.

[6] Gal. ii. 19, iii. 1, vi. 14; cf. Ac. xxii. 8-10.

[7] Rom. ii. 15.

[8] Gal. vi. 7, Rom. vi. 23, interpreted by i. 18 sqq.

[9] *Breastplate of St. Patrick.*

[10] Rom. v. 18-19.

[11] *"Much good, some ill he did, so hope all's even,*
And that his soul through mercy's gone to heaven."
So runs the epitaph of Elihu Yale, the founder of Yale
University, on his tombstone in the churchyard of Wrex-
ham, North Wales.

[12] Phil. iii. 9, cf. Rom. vi. 1-11, xiii. 14, Gal. v. 24, Col. iii.
9-11. See also Fearon Halliday, *op. cit.* chs. x.-xii.

[13] Eph. ii. 9, Rom. iii. 27, I Cor. iii. 7 (cf. i. 18-31), iv. 7.

[14] Phil. ii. 13, cf. I Thess. ii. 13, II Cor. iii. 5, I Cor. xii. 6,
Col. i. 29, Eph. i. 19-20, iii. 20-21.

[15] J. A. Hadfield in *The Spirit*, pp. 106, 110.

[16] William James, *Varieties of Religious Experience*, pp. 209-

210. The passages here quoted are taken by James from Starbuck; but the whole of James' discussion of the type of conversion "by self-surrender," in Lecture ix. provides an illuminating comment on Paul.

[17] Rom. v. 1, 9, viii. 30, I Cor. vi. 11.

[18] Phil. iii. 12-14, cf. I Cor. ix. 23-27, Gal. v. 5.

[19] Phil. ii. 12-13. We may observe how this reproduces in new terms what Jesus had said about the Kingdom of God. "It is your Father's good pleasure to give you the Kingdom"; and yet "Seek ye first the Kingdom of God": "The Kingdom of God is like treasure hid in a field, which a man found, and . . . sold all he had and bought that field": "Strait is the gate and narrow the way that leadeth unto life."

[20] Rom. iv. 5.

[21] Ἀπολύτρωσις associated with δικαίωσις Rom. iii. 24, I Cor. i. 30, cf. Eph. i. 7, 14, Col. i. 14. See also Rom. vi. 6-7, 12-23, viii. 2, II Cor. iii. 17, Gal. iv. 1-7, 21-31, v. 1, 23.

[22] See Wordsworth, *Ode to Duty*.

[23] I Cor. vi. 11, i. 30, cf. Rom. vi. 19, I Thess. iv. 3-7, I Cor. iii. 16-17, vi. 19, Eph. ii. 21.

[24] Rom. vi. 1-11, Col. ii. 10-13.

[25] I Cor. i. 13-17.

[26] I Cor. x. 1-11.

[27] Rom. vi. 12-14.

[28] Gal. vi. 14, Phil. iii. 7-11.

[29] II Cor. iv. 7-11.

[30] Col. iii. 1-4.

[31] H. G. Wells, *The New Machiavelli*, pp. 291-292.

[32] Longfellow, *Saga of King Olaf*, xxii.

THE LORD THE SPIRIT

[1] Rom. v. 8-10.

[2] Gal. v. 22-23, vi. 8, Rom. viii. 23, II Cor. i. 22, v. 5, Eph. i. 14, Col. i. 27.

[3] The *locus classicus* for "pneumatic" phenomena is I Cor. xii.-xiv., which elucidates the references to similar phenomena in Acts.

[4] II Cor. iii. 17. Instead of multiplying references to show the identity of Christ's work with that of the Spirit, I

would suggest to the interested reader that he should take
a Concordance and discover for himself how often a statement made about Christ in one place can be confronted
with a closely similar statement made in another place
about the Spirit. He should have no difficulty in filling
a quarto sheet with such doublets.

[5] II Cor. xii. 1-9, Ac. xvi. 6-7, cf. I Cor. ii. 16, Gal. i. 12.
[6] Thomas Hardy, *The Dynasts*.
[7] Phil. i. 21, Gal. ii. 20, iv. 19, II Cor. iii. 12-18, Rom. xiii.
14, Eph. iii. 17. Cf. I Thess. i. 6, I Cor. xi. 1.
[8] I Cor. xii. 13, cf. Gal. iii. 27, Rom. vi. 3.
[9] Gal. iv. 6-7, Rom. viii. 14-17, I Cor. i. 9, Rom. viii. 26-27,
Eph. vi. 18.
[10] Rom. i. 19-21.
[11] I Cor. ii., xii. 8, II Cor. x. 3-6, I Thess. i. 5, Phil. i. 9-10,
Col. ii. 2-3, Eph. i. 17, I Cor. viii. 1-3, Gal. iv. 9, I Cor. xiii.
12.
[12] Rom. ix. 1, I Cor. viii. 12.
[13] I Cor. ii. 15, iv. 3-5.
[14] See especially Phil. iii. 15-16, which a false reading represented by the A.V. has changed into a plea for uniformity!
[15] Rom. xiii. 1, 4; I Cor. iv. 3.
[16] Phil. iv. 13, Eph. iii. 14-19, I Cor. i. 18, 24, iv. 20, Rom. i.
16, II Cor. xii. 9-10, xiii. 3-4.
[17] II Cor. v. 17 (cf. I Cor. iv. 15), Eph. ii. 10, iv. 24, Col. iii.
9-11, Rom. xii. 2.

THE DIVINE COMMONWEALTH DISCOVERED

[1] I Cor. xii., Rom. xii. 4-5, Eph. iv. 1-16, Col. i. 18-29.
[2] Gal. iii. 26-28, Col. iii. 11, I Cor. xii. 13.
[3] The following passages will illustrate the significance of
κοινωνία : II Cor. i. 7, cf. Phil. iii. 10 and Rom. viii. 17;
Phm. 6, cf. 17; I Cor. x. 16-21; I Cor. i. 9, II Cor. xiii. 13;
Phil. ii. 1.
[4] I Cor. xii. 4-11, 28-31, xiv. 1-5, Rom. xii. 6-8, Eph. iv. 7-16.
[5] Col. iii. 14-15, Rom. v. 5, Gal. v. 6.
[6] Rom. xiii. 8-10, Gal. v. 13-14, vi. 2.
[7] I Cor. viii. 1, cf. Eph. iv. 16.
[8] I Cor. x. 16-21, xi. 17-34.

[9] I Cor. i. 2, x. 32, xi. 22, xv. 9, II Cor. i. 1, Gal. i. 13; cf. Gal. vi. 16.

[10] Phil. ii. 5: that this, rather than the common translation, correctly renders the Greek original, I am convinced.

THE LIFE OF THE DIVINE COMMONWEALTH

[1] Rom. xi. 33, xii. 2.

[2] II Cor. x. 1, Gal. vi. 2, Col. iii. 17.

[3] Rom. i. 24-32, I Cor. v. 10-11, II Cor. xii. 20, Gal. v. 19-21, Col. iii. 5-8.

[4] Col. ii. 16-23, I Cor. iii. 21-23, x. 23-26.

[5] Col. iii. 5 sqq.

[6] I Cor. ix.

[7] I have ventured to make Paul speak the language of Francis: neither, I think, would object!

[8] I Tim. iv. 3.

[9] I Cor. vii.

[10] Gal. iii. 28, Eph. v. 21-33, I Cor. vii. 10-11.

[11] I Thess. iv. 7-12.

[12] Lk. xii. 57.

[13] Gal. v. 22-23.

[14] Eph. iv. 25, vi. 9, Col. iii. 5, iv. 6 goes over much the same ground.

[15] *Enchiridion*, xii. 1.

[16] I Thess. v. 14.

[17] Rom. xii. 4-8.

[18] Rom. xv. 26-27.

[19] Eph. iv. 28.

[20] Preface to *Androcles and the Lion*.

[21] Acts x. 11-14. The teaching of Jesus in Mk. vii. 14-15 had evidently not been assimilated. The following verses in Mk. may represent (by a device he adopts elsewhere), under the form of a private explanation, the process by which the early Christians came to understand the meaning of their Master's teaching upon this point.

[22] I Cor. viii. 1-13, x. 14-31. In the opening of the discussion, the words "We know that we all have knowledge," and "we know that an idol is nothing in the world," are probably to be taken as citations from the letter of the Corinthian church to Paul, expressing the view of the "strong-

minded" or ultra-Pauline party. Paul accepts both statements with qualifications.

[23] Rom. xiv. 1, xv. 6.
[24] Rom. xii. 17, I Cor. x. 32, I Thess. iv. 12, cf. Col. iv. 5.
[25] Gal. vi. 10, I Thess. v. 15, Rom. i. 14, cf. xiii. 8.
[26] Rom. xiii. 1-10.
[27] Rom. xii. 14-21.
[28] Phil. ii. 15-16.
[29] Eph. ii. 19-22, iv. 12-16, i. 10, cf. Col. i. 20; I Cor. xv. 25-28.

APPENDIX

[1] First published in *The Student Movement*, 1919.

INDEX OF REFERENCES TO THE PAULINE EPISTLES

185

Strategic Planning for
Corporate Success

Strategic Planning for Corporate Success

In the Context of
New Economic Policies

A Pathfinder for Indian Corporate Sector

V.S. Ramaswamy

S. Namakumari

First Published, 1994

MACMILLAN INDIA LIMITED
Delhi Madras Jaipur Patna Vapi
Bangalore Hyderabad Lucknow Trivandrum
Guwahati Coimbatore Cuttack Bhopal Madurai

Associated companies throughout the world

SBN 0333 92536 X

Published by S G Wasani for Macmillan India Limited,
2/10 Ansari Road, Daryaganj, New Delhi-110 002.

Lasertypeset by ADR Enterprises, G-51, Saket, New Delhi-110 017
Printed by Chaman Offset Printers, 1626 Sui Walan, New Delhi-110 002

Preface

Economic reforms are sweeping India. The country is, in fact, subjected to a totally new economic prescription. The policies launched since July 1991 have amounted to a radical route change for the nation. The experiment has just begun. But already, the nation has received enough indication of things to come. Industry and business are the entities most affected by this route change; they have to bear the brunt of this change. From the overdose of controls, industry and business are suddenly led into an environment free of fetters. While they have certainly gained entre-preneurial freedom, they are simultaneously exposed to a series of unexpected challenges. This book agitates this subject.

Indian industry and business are under trial. Their capabilities and mettle are under test. This is the first time they are made to experience the power of real competition that an open economy implies. In fact, if one were called upon to describe the impact of NEP in a nutshell, the answer would be—*competition, all round competition, no-holds-barred competition.* How do Indian industry and business propose to stand up to this competition created by deregulation, decontrol, delicensing? How do they propose to counter the new edge gained by the multinationals who will spearhead the new competition in this country? How do they propose to tackle this churning process and come out of it successful? This, precisely, is the theme of this book.

The era of licence-raj is over. Profits assured through the mechanism of licensing is also over. Corporate success is going to be the outcome of a conscious and long drawn out management process. Overnight, Indian industry and business are thrown into a situation of high vulnerability which can be tackled only through a process of strategic planning and strategic management, a process of building core competence and compe-titive advantage. Yesterday's strategies will not hold in today's vastly altered setting. Business firms of India have to redefine their very business and rework their mission and strategies. Resorting to core competence and competitive advantage as the real back up for corporate success has now become an inescapable requirement.

The book, in its first hundred odd pages gives an exhaustive exposition of the new economic policies. Starting with the July '91 announcement of the new industrial policy and flowing down to the budget of '93-94, all the steps initiated under NEP so far—the industrial and trade libera-lisation, the new fiscal reforms, the financial sector reforms, the structural adjustments—are presented in detail, giving an up-to-date and matter of fact account of NEP. The remaining part of the book deals with the consequences of NEP, its impact on industry and business, the business challenges of the emerging open regime, the management dilemmas and the possible management prescription. Drawing profusely from the cumulative wisdom of the management world, the book takes up the mission of explaining how Indian companies can stand up to the new challenges.

We hope the management men of India responsible for the growth of their organisations will be able to gather new insights from this book. With pleasure, we present this book to the decision makers in Indian industry and business.

V.S. Ramaswamy
S. Namakumari

Contents

1

The New Economic Policies—An Overview

The year 1991 stands out as a watershed in the economic history of India. Suddenly things changed. The country that had remained for many years unexposed to any significant economic change, was thrown open to revolutionary changes almost overnight. The series of new economic policies introduced during the year by the new government were stunning indeed, in their scope as well as in their significance. It was only natural that the year came to be reckoned as a landmark year for the country.

First came the decision on devaluation of the rupee. Closely following the announcement on devaluation came the New Trade Policies. Before the nation could digest the meaning of the New Trade Policies, the announcements on the New Industrial Policies started bombarding the people. The Budget that followed, a path breaking one by all counts, continued the sequence. More changes followed throughout 1991 and 1992, touching each and every aspect of the economy of the country. All these measures together constitute the New Economic Policies (NEP).

THE CONTEXTUAL SETTING

Before taking up a detailed discussion on the New Economic Policies, it would be a good idea to take a look at the contextual setting that forced the Government to unleash with such speed, the bunch of new policies, almost on a war footing.

It is recent history. By mid 1991, the economy of India had hit an all-time low. Government spokesmen as well as the Press were using expressions such as 'extremely difficult' and 'grim' to denote the economic situation faced by the country. It soon turned out that these expressions were gross understatements. These milder expressions soon gave way to the stronger phrase, 'unprecedented economic crisis'. In fact, it was precisely an unprecedented crisis which the country was facing in the days immediately preceding the introduction of the NEP. The Indian economy was facing a critical situation marked by a huge fiscal deficit, a serious balance of payments position, a double-digit inflation and stagnant industrial production.

Huge fiscal deficits

Over a period of time, the fiscal deficits of the Central Government had risen to a disturbing level. Rising interest repayment obligations, heavy outflow on subsidies, mounting budgetary support to PSUs and larger outflow towards assistance to States had pushed the budgetary as well as fiscal deficits up. The budgetary deficit for 1990-91 stood at the alarming figure of Rs 11,347 crore. Fiscal deficit had skyrocketed to Rs 44,650 crore. The budgetary deficit for the five year period 1985-86 to 1990-91, taken together, had exceeded Rs 48,000 crore.

An ever increasing internal debt had accentuated the effect of the fiscal deficit. The debt had risen to Rs 1,51,037 crore in 1990-91. In fact, if the other liabilities were to be taken into account, the total debt came to Rs 3,06,876 crore. Servicing of the borrowings by way of interest payment alone amounted to Rs 26,750 crore which formed more than one third of the total non-plan expenditure of the Central Government.

Alarming BoP situation

The foreign exchange reserves of the country were dwindling steadily and had nose dived to the rock bottom of Rs 2400 crore ($ 1.1 bn) by June 1991, which was barely enough to pay for two weeks imports. The situation was so serious that 67 tonnes of gold had to be shipped out of the country and mortgaged abroad to avoid default of international obligations. Trade deficits accumulated over the years was the main factor that led to the grave impoverishment of exchange reserves. In 1990-91 alone, the trade deficit was of the order of Rs 10,800 crore. While imports were burgeoning, exports failed to catch up. Besides trade deficits, the external debt was also mounting up year by year. The debt servicing obligations became a major contributor to the external deficits, the eventual BoP crisis and the steep decline in foreign exchange reserves. By 1990-91, foreign debts had zoomed to Rs 1,40,000 crore, excluding NRI deposits.

Economy reeling under high inflation

The economy was also reeling under high inflation and prices were continuously rising. Inflation rate had climbed to 13 per cent by June 1991.

Deficit financing and BoP crisis had together contributed greatly to inflation. Excess liquidity on account of fiscal deficits had increased price pressures and poor BoP position precluded imports of essential goods and containment of inflation through short term supply management.

Stagnant industrial production

The wheels of industry could not be kept moving. There were two main problems:

(i) shortage of bank credit, and

(ii) shortage of imported inputs due to the forex crisis.

The country was in the grip of draconian curbs on imports. Added to that, the banking system was on a tight leash. The Government had imposed severe restrictions on credit limits for industry. In respect of L/Cs for imports they had prescribed crippling cash margins. They had also brought in an erratic interest regime. These moves meant a double damage—curtailment of credit availability and enhancement of the cost of credit. As a result, industry became stagnant.

Crisis on all fronts

The other familiar ills of the economy also continued as in the past. The public sector did not generate the surplus it was supposed to generate. The Government had to continue providing budgetary support to many PSUs. Subsidies were also mounting and had an unsettling effect on Government's finances. Non plan expenditure of the Government on account of the overstaffed and underproductive Government establishments was also rising continuously. There was also a reduction in revenues, on account of slowing of industrial production.

The Eighth Five Year Plan of the country was a nonstarter in 1990-91, which should have been the first year of the plan. And even the allocations for the plan for 1991-92 had not been made.

Something drastic had to be done.

THE BOP CRISIS PULLED THE TRIGGER

While the country faced crises on all fronts and all of them were pushing the Government inexorably towards drastic economic reforms, it was the BoP crisis that actually triggered off the whole process and ushered in the new economic programme of the country.

An understanding of the background relating to the BoP position is essential for appreciating how the BoP crisis actually precipitated matters and became the immediate cause of action for the course correction of the economy. And at the outset, it must be appreciated that there were two crises on the foreign exchange front and they together gave rise to the BoP crisis:

(i) A crisis of falling exchange reserves.

(ii) A crisis of confidence on the part of the international community regarding India's ability to meet her foreign exchange obligations.

This needs elaboration.

Falling foreign exchange reserves

For the Indian economy, foreign exchange had always remained a scarce resource. The Government was all along exercising tight control over foreign exchange outflow. The industrial licensing system was used for exercising a curb on the foreign exchange requirements of industry. In addition, DGTD clearances and import tariffs were used as tools for further restricting imports. Similarly, foreign investment proposals were also subjected to close scrutiny from the forex angle. But despite all this control on the outflow of foreign exchange, India's exchange reserves were always low, since her exports never grew in any spectacular manner while her import requirements were always on the increase. As the economy grew, the exchange earned by the traditional exports was not at all sufficient to meet import requirements. The country began to borrow abroad in a big way, initially on concessional terms and in later years on commercial terms. The efforts at promoting exports especially of manufactured and value added items did not yield the intended results. Exporting proved difficult for an economy that had grown exclusively on the basis of a sheltered, non-competitive home market. So, the country borrowed still more. The difference was that in the later years, it was borrowing not only for importing capital goods but also for importing raw materials and for paying off the earlier debt and interest thereof.

Growing trade deficits and mounting foreign debts

An unfavourable balance of external trade became a persistent malady for India. The trade deficit grew steadily from Rs 99 crore in '70-71 to Rs 5831 crore in '80-81 and further to Rs 10,800 crore in '90-91. The Gulf war further worsened the position in this regard in 1990-91, compounding the problem in two ways:

> by making imports of petroleum products costlier, and
>
> by drying up remittances from expatriate Indians.

The Indian Government's efforts at curbing consumption of petroleum products by hiking their prices, produced only marginal results. The trade gaps continued to widen.

Moreover, as mentioned earlier, India had, over the years, also been incurring heavy foreign debts. The eighties especially was a decade of mounting external debt burden for India. The country's debt stock trebled during the decade. As stated earlier, by the end of the decade, the foreign debt excluding NRI deposits had sky rocketed to Rs 1,40,000 crore. With the debts mounting up the debt servicing obligations too mounted. The developments in this regard during '90-91 and the first quarter of '91-92 were particularly disturbing.

The continued borrowing through commercial loans and the utilisation of deposits in external accounts of NRIs for consumption purpose had brought about a situation in which repayments had to be effected on an unscheduled basis.

These developments resulted in a continuous depletion of the foreign exchange reserves of the country. Between March and June '91 alone there was an erosion of Rs 2,073 crore in the foreign exchange reserves which dwindled to Rs 2,383 crore.

International community loses confidence in India and de-rates India's creditworthiness

The crisis of confidence suffered by India among the international community worsened the matter further. India's precarious foreign exchange position combined with the political uncertainty then prevailing in the country and the inability of the administration to even present the annual budget for '91-92 were responsible for this erosion of confidence. The international community developed serious doubts about the ability of India to honour her payment commitments. Exporters started holding back their money abroad and NRIs had already repatriated $ 1 billion of their money. Foreign banks operating in India started refusing to endorse Indian L/Cs. All these served as signals for the international community to downgrade India's creditworthiness. There was an acceleration of outflow of foreign exchange on current account. The Government had to pledge the last of its gold. A severe compulsion came to be felt, for curtailing imports drastically. The RBI introduced draconian measures including severe curbs on opening of letters of credit.

On the verge of default

By June 1991, India was literally on the verge of default on her payment obligations. The disastrous implications of such a default were obvious.

Short term supplier's credit would have come to a grinding halt as the credit line would have dried up. Suppliers would not only have refused to extend any further credit, but would also have demanded immediate payment of all outstanding dues and also payments in advance for all future shipments. Simultaneously, at the other end, buyers of Indian goods abroad would have held back on their payments, anticipating the devaluation of the Indian rupee. India would have been deprived of export earnings just when she needed them most. And to make matters still worse, there would have been further flight of NRI deposits from the country. The result would have been a complete breakdown of imports— of even the most essential items like crude oil. The oil shortage would have created a transport crisis and a breakdown of the distribution system in the country.

Thus, by June 1991, India was on the verge of default and the grim consequences of such a default were haunting the nation.

The way out —The IMF loan

The disastrous consequences of an impending default compelled the country to look for a way out. In fact, the country had to find a quick and drastic solution. The Government felt that a hefty loan from the IMF alone could serve as the way out. In fact, the Government did not have any alternative. Even during the tenure of the previous Government, things had moved towards this end and negotiations had taken place with the IMF.

Appreciating the gravity of the situation, the new Government without losing a day, activated the IMF loan proposal.

IMF conditionalities

The IMF has consistently been maintaining that for achieving a respectable economic breakthrough, India must carry out radical economic reforms consisting of liberalisation, macro economic adjustments and structural reforms. Quite naturally, the IMF put forward a package of conditionalities to be fulfilled for India to become eligible for the large loan, as in its view such steps were essential for India to achieve the kind of breakthrough required. India's independent assessment too revealed that by and large the kind of reforms indicated by the IMF were actually required at this juncture.

The IMF conditionalities covered such areas as fiscal reforms, especially fiscal deficit reduction, tax reforms, liberalisation of industrial and trade policies, removal of the archaic barriers to the integration of the country's economy with the global economy, inflation control, prudent management of BoP, public sector restructure including disinvestment, removal of subsidies, ushering in market related price environment in place of administered price system, monetary reforms, financial sector reforms, capital market reforms and exit policy.

THE CONTEXT WAS READY

The IMF conditions were not at all light. In the normal course, a country like India would have found these conditions difficult to accept and implement, and hence would have wavered. But now, India's own judgement was that the predicament she was in called for such a remedy. There was a general recognition that things had gone too far, and it was time for the country to effect a major course correction. Under different circumstances, India would perhaps have opted for a softer alternative—a gradual process of course correction. But with the BoP position in such shambles and with inflation zooming as it did, there was no way the situation could be handled through a gradual process. The course correction had to be put through immediately. The IMF loan along with the conditionalities perhaps coincided with this general feeling getting formulated in the country. In short, the launching pad was set for India to embark on a massive programme of economic restructure.

Wide ranging economic compulsions was the real cause

A vital clarification is called for at this juncture. It should not be construed from the foregoing analysis that the BoP crisis and the consequent need for a hefty facility from the IMF was the real cause for the new economic policy. It constituted only the occasion. The real cause lay elsewhere.

It was the long felt need for a new economic path for the country that constituted the basic cause.

As far back as the mid 1980s, the country as a whole, was getting convinced that there was a huge gap between the performance and the potential of the Indian economy and that the economic policy followed in the previous three decades needed a thorough overhaul. In fact, the country was becoming aware that the policy had become outdated even by the '70s if not earlier and that the country was paying a heavy price in continuing to move on the old track.

The nation did make a number of rather feeble attempts at modifying the economic policy. But all these attempts centred around modifying existing regulations and controls, changing some of them, revamping some others and introducing some new ones. It never chose to altogether do away with the regulations and controls, though it had been known that what was required was precisely such a total goodbye to controls and regulations that had long outlived their relevance and utility. Situational factors as well as basic constraints were holding back the nation from a total change of the economic policy. But by June 1991, it had become an idea, whose time had come.

The Government places all its cards before the people

In a transparent and statesman like move, the new Government which assumed office in June '91, placed before the people a true picture of the gravity of the crisis facing the country. The Government also conveyed to the nation in unambiguous terms the tough reform programme it proposed to implement. The first indications on the programme came through the President's address to the joint session of the new Parliament. To quote from the address,

> Government recognises that the country is in the midst of an economic crisis of unprecedented magnitude. It has been living beyond its means and adopting soft options...

> Government is committed to the macro-economic stabilisation and structural reforms which will unleash the nation's latent energy to bring about accelerated development...

> We intend to take further concerted measures in the areas of trade policy reform to enhance the competitiveness of our exports...

Exports have a vital role in solving the balance of payment problems... . It is hoped that the export trade will get out of the circle of low growth, high cost and stifling controls and get on to a high trajectory of growth... .

Government is determined to work towards making India internationally competitive... . The opportunities provided by increasing internationalisation of industry and trade will be fully utilised... . Government will work for deregulation and reduction of bureaucratic intervention... . In order to raise the competitiveness and quality of Indian industry to global levels, technology will be liberalised and facilitated in areas where Indian technology does not measure up to international standards. Changes in procedures are being worked out so that the investment climate is made more conducive for participation by foreign companies, and non-resident Indians. Efficiency will be promoted in services required by industrial and other users of financial institutions and banks... .

Fiscal imbalance continues to be a major concern for the Government... . Government is committed to observing strict fiscal discipline.

The address gave an indication of things to come. It clearly signalled that there would be a severe tightening of the belt, that the nation could not continue to live beyond its means and that the people must be prepared to receive harsh measures. The address also explained that effective and urgent measures were being taken to rectify the BoP aberration and to reduce the deficits in the budgets. It also contained a specific mention about the proposals for removing the obstacles to liberal foreign investment and for carrying out a time bound programme for streamlining the industrial policies and programmes so as to achieve the goal of rapid economic growth.

AN OVERVIEW OF THE NEP

So far an attempt has been made to narrate the circumstances that led the country to the New Economic Policies. The remaining part of this chapter, presents a synopsis of the new policies.

The three components of the NEP

The policies and measures introduced under the new economic programme sought to serve three distinct purposes. Some of them were aimed at freeing industry and trade from the vice like grip of control, some others sought to reform the macro economy of the country and its economic institutions; and yet others had the objective of changing the structural infirmities which had accumulated over the years and were retarding the economic progress. In economic parlance, these are termed as liberalisation, economic reforms and structural adjustments, respectively.

Liberalisation includes changes in industrial and trade policies, aimed at freeing industry from the shackles of the licensing system and restrictions on imports and exports.

Economic reforms go beyond liberalisation. They include reforms of fiscal and monetary policies, besides liberalisation of trade and industrial policies. They also encompass reform of the economic institutions.

Structural adjustment is even larger in its sweep; it is an all encompassing process, containing elements of liberalisation, elements of economic reforms and other elements having a bearing on employment and income distribution. Structural adjustment amounts to a drastic course correction and therefore a more painful process for an economy to go through. The role of external agencies by means of conditionalities is also substantive in the case of structural adjustment. As an economy moves from liberalisation to structural adjustment, the scope, direction and rate of change in the policy parameters also alter drastically.

It should, however, be made clear that liberalisation, economic reforms and structural adjustment should not be viewed as watertight and mutually exclusive compartments of the NEP. To a large extent they are overlapping. This division has been made here only because these three elements do represent the three basic dimensions of the changes to which the Indian economy has been subjected since June 1991. Such a three fold division would facilitate a clearer understanding of the multifaceted shake up of the economy brought about by the package of policies and measures.

While the policies and measures launched in each of these groups are elaborately handled in chapters 2 to 5, a brief overview of all these measures is being provided here.

LIBERALISATION

One of the prime movers of the new economic policies was the sheer desire and compulsion of the Government to release industry and trade from the stifling Government controls. The effect was an all round liberalisation, changing the very character of the country's industry and foreign trade.

LIBERALISATION OF INDUSTRIAL POLICY

The liberalisation exercises began with the introduction of major changes in the industrial policy, which amounted to a radical transformation of the entire industrial environment of India. A whole range of industries were liberated from the clutches of licensing and control. Besides, substantive changes were also introduced in other aspects of industrial policy like foreign investment, import of foreign technology, MRTP, FERA and the role of public sector. Together, they have come to be known as the New Industrial Policy (NIP).

Delicensing of industries and removal of restrictions on foreign investment

All industries, except eighteen industries specified by the Government, were delicensed in a bid to eliminate the main obstacles to industrial growth. Another major measure has been the abolition of existing registration schemes. A new broad-banding facility was also announced, giving more flexibility of operations to industries. In a bid to attract direct foreign investment, automatic clearance for foreign equity up to 51 per cent has been allowed in 34 high priority industries. Automatic clearance will also be given for import of capital goods where foreign exchange availability is ensured through foreign equity. In order to obtain access to international markets, majority foreign equity holding up to 51 per cent will be allowed for trading companies as well. Another important move has been the creation of a specially empowered foreign investment board. An automatic permission scheme has been introduced for foreign technology agreements and for royalty payments in specified high priority industries. For industries other than those covered in the above scheme too, automatic permission will be given provided no foreign exchange is required for any payments.

The above mentioned liberalisations were only the starting point. In the next batch of moves, the Government further shortened the list of industries requiring licence, limiting it to a mere 14 items. As regards foreign investment too, the Government came up with a further dose of liberalisation. For example, it withdrew the restrictions on dividend repatriation by foreign investors. More importantly, the Government opened the power, hydrocarbon and electronics sectors for foreign investment in a big way.

Relaxation of FERA and MRTP

The new industrial policy brought about many changes in the Foreign Exchange Regulation Act (FERA) which had incorporated over the years a great deal of detailed administrative control over companies where the foreign equity exceeded 40 per cent. There were many other restrictions which prevented Indian companies and Indian residents from entering into various types of commercial relations with companies abroad. Initially, the Reserve Bank of India liberalised the procedure by granting general exemption from several of these controls. In a later move, the Government amended comprehensively the Foreign Exchange Regulation Act and removed many of the restrictions.

Sweeping changes were made in respect of MRTP regulations as well. The MRTP Act was amended to altogether do away with the threshold limit of assets which rendered a firm an MRTP company or a dominant undertaking. No MRTP clearance will now be required for investment applications. No approval is needed either for establishing new undertakings, for implementing expansions, mergers, amalgamations and takeovers. The existing restrictions on acquisition/transfer of shares also have been removed.

Curtailment of the role of the public sector

The new policy also restricted public sector's pre-eminent role. It now stands limited to eight core areas like arms and ammunition, atomic energy, railways, and mining and coal. Though reservation is retained for the public sector, there would be no bar against even these areas being opened up to the private sector. Another significant policy change is regarding disinvestment. According to the new policy, upto 49 per cent of Government's share holding in public sector units can be disinvested. Chronically sick PSUs are to be referred to the Board for Industrial and Financial Reconstruction (BIFR) for rehabilitation.

LIBERALISATION OF TRADE POLICY

The Government brought in radical changes in trade policy as well. At one stroke, most of the age old and unwarranted interventions in the export and import activities of the country were dismantled. The Government showed its determination to cast away the extreme caution that surrounded the trade policy and foreign investment policy all these years.

Liberalisation of imports, linking of imports to exports and lowering of tariffs

According to the new dispensation, foreign trade became totally free, with all controls removed, subject only to a small non-permitted list of items; and imports were completely taken out of licensing hassles. The Government also decanalised most of the foreign trade. The canalisation agencies would henceforth act as any other trading house.

Exports and imports would be governed by a self balancing system; imports will be made only with the forex earned and made available in the market by the exporters. Industrial units would enjoy all freedom to secure imports, step up exports, generate foreign exchange resources for imports and thus continue the cycle.

The Government also brought about a general lowering of import tariffs. Over the years, a sharp cut in import duties had been thought of by successive governments so as to expose Indian industry to global competition, to make Indian products cost competitive internationally and to boost India's exports. But the courage to act was lacking all these years.

It was as part of the new economic budget that for the first time, the Government actually carried out the experiment. Import of plant and machinery which will result in exports, was given special concession in import duty. In general, the new policy chose to rely on tariffs and exchange rates rather than quantitative controls for controlling trade flow.

Convertibility/New exchange rate systems

In the subsequent bouts of trade reforms, the Government came up with more innovative and daring changes. Introduction of Partial Convertibility of the rupee/dual exchange rate system and Full Convertibility/unified exchange rate system were the most striking in this series. The dual rate system, which was termed Liberalised Exchange Rate Management System (LERMS) replaced the system of Exim Scrips and allowed all foreign exchange remittances into the country, through export earnings as well as remittances by expatriates, to be converted into rupee under a dual pricing mechanism by which 40 per cent of the amount would be surrendered to the RBI at rates determined officially and the remaining 60 per cent would be converted at market determined rates. The Government also decided in principle that as soon as possible, exchange controls, except on capital transactions, should be removed and the rupee made fully convertible so far as current account transactions were concerned. And in the budget of '93-94,the Government implemented the decision and made the rupee fully convertible on trade account.

Encouragement to exports, encouragement to foreign investment and integration of the country's economy with the global economy

The chief aims of the reforms were to boost India's exports, to integrate India's economy with the global economy and to attract foreign investment. In particular, the Government wanted foreign direct investment to flow into India in ample measure, substituting India's borrowings from abroad—from institutions as well as NRIs.

Pegging down India's external debt and debt servicing obligations at a reasonable level was a major purpose of the new policies on the trade front. Since technology usually accompanies such investment, there was the powerful additional reason for wooing such funds. Measures specifically designed to bring in foreign investment formed a major part of the new policy. Appreciating that unless India carried out all round reforms, she would not attract foreign investments into the country, the Government employed a mix of trade reforms, industrial policy liberalisation and macro economic adjustments to attract foreign direct investment into the country.

The measures introduced through the '93-94 budget in particular constituted a major leap towards integrating India's economy with the global economy. Currency and trade barriers have been dismantled almost totally; import tariffs have been slashed drastically; liberation of even petro products from price/marketing control has been hinted at.

ECONOMIC REFORMS

Along with the liberalisation measures aimed at increased freedom of operation for industry and trade, the Government introduced a series of reforms with long term impact on the nation's economy and its economic institutions. The reform package included fiscal reforms, monetary reforms, financial sector reforms, measures to contain inflation, measures to curb accumulation of public debt, measures aimed at effective BoP management and measures towards long term macro economic stabilisation.

Fiscal and monetary reforms

The fiscal reforms centred around reduction of fiscal deficits, reforms of the tax system (direct and indirect tax system) and containment of public debt.

The Government brought down the fiscal deficit to 6.5 per cent of the GDP in '91-92 from 8.5 per cent in '90-91 and further down to 5 per cent and 4.5 per cent respectively in '92-93 and '93-94. In absolute terms the deficit was brought down to Rs 37,792 crore in '91-92 from the previous year's level of Rs 44,650 crore and further down to Rs 34,408 crore in '92-93. Though in '93-94, it slightly went up to reach Rs 36,959 crore, the policy of containment of fiscal deficit continued, as even in '93-94, the deficit as a percentage of GDP was only 4.5.

An overhauling of the tax system was also made, using the budgets for 1991-92, 1992-93 and 1993-94. The recommendations of the Chelliah committee on tax reform were partly implemented. Income tax rates were made moderate; maximum tax rate was limited to 40 per cent. The slabs also were rationalised. The income tax exemption limit was raised. Removal of some of the existing concessions and exemptions and a strengthening of tax compliance were the other features of the direct tax reforms. Modificaton in the treatment of capital gains tax and wealth tax, changes in the assessment of partnership firms, and introduction of presumptive tax also formed a part of the reforms relating to the direct tax system. In the case of the indirect tax system, the changes included reduction in import duties including that on capital goods.

The Government also took firm steps for containing public debt. The steps centred around establishing strict discipline in Government borrowings, reduction of interest liability through premature retirement of public debt and use of the proceeds from disinvestment in PSUs and sale of Government real estate for buying back public debt. The Government also took steps for creating a public debt redemption fund.

The reforms in monetary and credit policy aimed at slowing down monetary expansion and arresting inflation. With this end in view, the Government jacked up the Bank rate with corresponding upward adjustments in the deposit rates and lending rates. It also introduced a stringent credit squeeze. Industry was told that they were free to raise their working capital through various financial instruments at higher interest rates. Credit control measures were extended to the state governments as well. RBI issued orders denying the state Governments overdrafts beyond one week level.

Inflation control

The Government introduced a series of measures to contain the mounting inflation which had reached 17 per cent by August '91. Pursuit of tight money policy including credit curbs and high interest rates, reduction of fiscal deficits, reduction of Government expenditure, reduction of sub-sidies, reduction in budgetary support to public sector undertakings and reduction in transfers and assistance to states were the measures adopted for containing inflation.

Financial sector reforms

The Government realised that the financial institutions of India, especially the banks, have not been functioning as viable commercial institutions. It appointed an expert committee under the chairmanship of M. Narasimham, former Governor of the RBI, to suggest the line of reforms required in the banking sector. And the committee's report contained a whole gamut of suggestions for reforming the banking sector.

The committee pointed out that the profitability of the banks is adversely affected mainly due to 'directed investments' and 'directed credit'. To reduce directed investments, the committee recommended a substantial reduction of SLR, and opined that the SLR should be used only as a prudential requirement and not as a ready source of cheap finance to Government and the public sector. Regarding directed credit, the committee expressed the view that the pursuit of distributive justice should use the instrument of fiscal rather than the credit system and suggested that in any case there is no need for continuing to force the banks to lend at concessional rates to those who could stand on their own, whether in agriculture or in small industry. A specific recommendation of the Narasimham committee has been to gradually phase out the directed credit programme, which at present takes away as much as 40 per cent of the total income generating activities of the entire banking sector.

The committee also recommended new norms of capital adequacy, income recognition, and loan loss provisions. Noting that the expenditure side had also contributed sizeably to the erosion of profitability of the banks, the committee recommended a meaningful merger and amalgamation of the banks so as to eliminate the duplication and overlapping of operations.

As the first step towards the implementation of the committee's recommendations, the Government started a phased reduction of SLR and CRR and permitted a degree of flexibility to the banks in the matter of deposit interest rates. It also prescribed new norms of capital adequacy, income recognition, and loan loss provisions. In a more significant move, the Government allowed the public sector banks to go to the capital market and raise the required additional equity so as to strengthen their capital base and meet the new norms of capital adequacy. The Government also took the decision on partial disinvestment of the existing Government equity in the public sector banks. In fact, disinvestment upto 49 per cent of the total equity was permitted. And in a further move, the Government cleared the way for the setting up of new private sector banks in the country. How drastic this move is, could be easily understood if one noted the fact that for the past quarter century, ever since the bank nationalisation days, not a single private bank had been licensed in the country.

Clearly the Government was convinced that reform of the banking sector was absolutely necessary for not only facilitating the effective and productive deployment of the resources of individual banks but also to enable them to observe international norms and thereby meet international competition.

A series of innovative reforms were carried out in the capital markets. The private sector was allowed to set up mutual funds; the ceiling on the acquisition of shares/debentures of Indian companies by non-resident Indians and overseas corporate bodies was raised under the portfolio investment scheme from 5 to 24 per cent; the Securities and Exchange Board of India (SEBI) has been made a statutory body; a scheme for the registration of sub brokers has been introduced to ensure investor protection; all restrictions on interest rates on debentures and public sector bonds other than tax free bonds, have been removed; interest rates on such instruments would be governed by market forces; guidelines on large issues—Rs 500 crore and above—have been revised; and a new financial instrument, 'stock invest' has been introduced for payment of application money by investors. To cap it all, the office of Controller of Capital Issues (CCI) has been abolished, free pricing of shares has been allowed and bonus issues have been made more liberal. In fact, the capital markets of India have been allowed the liberalisation they have been clamouring for, all these years. Moreover, the package has been so designed as to attract the flow of public savings into the capital market and from there into industry.

The Government also opened up the capital markets of India to Foreign Institutional Investors (FIIs), by permitting FIIs such as pension funds, mutual funds, investment trusts, asset management companies, nominee companies and incorporated/institutional portfolio managers or their power of attorney holders to become players in the capital markets of India. A number of concessions were also extended to such investment. And by the beginning of 1993, investments by FIIs in Indian stock markets had become a reality, with a couple of FIIs actually putting in their money in some Indian scrips.

STRUCTURAL ADJUSTMENT

The liberalisation of industry and trade and the economic reforms were accompanied by programmes aimed at a structural adjustment of the economy. They were measures of course correction, and were supposed to demolish the very roots of some of the economic maladies faced by the country.

The structural adjustment measures consisted mainly of the elimination of subsidies and introduction of market driven price environment, pruning of Government establishment, restructure of the public sector undertakings, including disinvestment, and initiation of an exit policy for industry.

Axe on subsidies and introduction of a market driven price environment

Phasing out of subsidies and introduction of a market driven price environment for the products that were hitherto under the purview of administered prices, constituted the first package of structural adjustments. Subsidy on food, fertiliser and exports were the three major elements of subsidy by the Central Government. The adjustment process attacked all these subsidies. The CCS, which constituted the main element of export subsidy was completely abolished. Food subsidy could not be handled with the same ease. The Government tried to contain it within limits. At a point of time, the Government was even considering limiting the food subsidy to the really vulnerable sections of the population, taking the relatively better off sections out of the public distribution system/ subsidised food supply programme. A little later the Government withdrew the subsidy on sugar and increased the price of ration sugar by as much as 20 per cent. It also decided in principle that sugar would no longer receive any subsidy.

As regards fertiliser subsidy, the Government applied the axe very decisively and took a number of steps towards reducing the subsidy. As the first step, it increased the fertiliser prices by 30 per cent across the board in July '91. By this single decision, it brought down the fertiliser subsidy by Rs 3,000 crore per annum. And more drastic measures followed. In August 1992, the Government totally decontrolled phosphatic, potassic and complex fertilisers. As a result, the retention price system (RPS) and the subsidies which were in vogue in respect of these fertilisers for a decade and a half, were overnight dismantled. Only the nitrogenous fertilisers were left untouched; that too, as a matter of strategy. The withdrawal of the subsidies ushered in the era of market driven pricing in the fertiliser business, after a 15 year regime of administered pricing and subsidies.

Next came the turn of petro products. The Government increased the prices of petroleum products by 18 per cent so as to reduce the subsidies on them substantially. The Government even considered the complete decontrol of prices of all petro products barring kerosene meant for domestic consumption. Such a decontrol was also to be applied to aspects other than pricing, such as refining and marketing. The Government also decided to open up the petro product sector for private/foreign equity participation. It was even considering granting of freedom to private/ foreign companies to market petro products under their own brand names. These were moves towards making petro products eventually subsidy free and market driven. In fact, the entry of the private sector into kerosene and LPG, parallel marketing of the products at market determined prices and a dual price system had soon become a reality and the subsidies on these two products were brought down substantially.

Restructuring the public sector

Restructuring the public sector was the next major item on the adjustment agenda. Size reduction and efficiency improvement were the two main instruments employed by the Government for revamping the public sector. Size reduction was sought to be achieved through three different routes—partial disinvestment of the Government equity in a number of PSUs, cent percent privatisation of some units and closure of the unviable ones. Moreover, the very role of the public sector as a whole, was redefined and its scope considerably truncated. The Government also decided that budgetary support would no longer be made to facilitate the capital expansion of any PSU. The PSUs would instead go to the market for expansion of their capital. The intention obviously was that the Government's stake must be reduced through every possible route and thereby the size of the public sector component in the economy reduced.

By enacting the amended Sick Industrial Companies (special provisions) Act, the Government made it mandatory that all sick and potentially sick companies in the public sector be referred to the Board for Industrial and Financial Reconstruction (BIFR) for rehabilitation suggestions, including amalgamation, lease, outright sale and closure of the sick company. The most important feature of the new legislation is that the closure of a PSU is made possible by its provisions. Armed with the new legislation, the Government made it clear that it would close down patently unviable public sector units. The Government also announced its decision to totally phase out budgetary support to public sector units over a three-year period.

Disinvestment of Government equity in individual PSUs constituted the other major element of Government's scheme on public sector restructure. The Government believed that disinvestment would bring about size reduction and efficiency improvement of the PSUs and also release the locked up funds for deployment for better purposes. The Government in fact, went on record that it sought to disinvest the Public Sector units so as to use the proceeds for providing for social services like education, health, water supply, rural development and so on.

It was becoming clear that the new policy would act as a prelude to the eventual privatisation of a large part of the Indian Public Sector.

Exit policy

Recognition of the need to have an exit policy for industry, was another important outcome of the new exercises. Though the Government could not straight away spell out an exit policy for industry, it recognised that the new industrial policy has to be taken to its logical conclusion and that the removal of entry barriers to industry must be accompanied by removal of exit barriers as well. Obviously, the Government needed more time to act. It decided to deal with this issue sector by sector. Tripartite committees were formed for taking a close examination of selected categories of industries. In the meantime, in a strategic step, the Government created the National Renewal Fund (NRF) for providing support to workers affected by industrial restructuring. This in effect meant that without spelling out an exit policy, the Government took the sequence wise second step of providing a cushion for the adverse effects an exit policy would ultimately cause. The NRF signified an acceptance of a situation where an exit policy was becoming a reality even without a pronouncement from the Government to that effect. And, the country was slowly getting prepared to receive the final pronouncement of a formal exit policy.

INDIAN ECONOMY IN A NEW ORBIT

The sum and substance of the above moves was that the country's economy received a thorough shake up. And it happened with unbelievable speed. The country suddenly found itself in the grip of a new programme of economic reconstruction. It was changing track, the track it had got used to during the past forty years. Now it was on an altogether new orbit, backed by a new momentum and propulsion. And it was just the beginning.

2

The New Industrial Policy

The New Industrial Policy signified in the real sense the beginning of a new economic programme and amounted to a radical shift in the existing industrial policy. The new policy altered the industrial scene of the country overnight; liberated a whole gamut of industries from the clutches of licensing; and brought in a whole lot of other changes as well. It would be useful to make out a catalogue of these changes before proceeding with a detailed discussion on the New Industrial Policy (NIP), its meaning and importance, its impact on the industrial environment of the country and its distinctiveness over the entire bunch of industrial policy reforms undertaken hitherto .

LIBERALISATION BROUGHT ABOUT BY THE NIP

The NIP brought about significant liberalisation in practically all aspects of the industrial policy—industrial licensing, foreign investment, import of foreign technology, MRTP and the public sector. The details are presented below.

Liberalisation concerning industrial licensing

All industries, except the 18 specified in Annexure II of the 1956 Industrial Policy Resolution, stand delicensed, irrespective of the level of investment.

The 18 specified industries will continue to require licensing in view of considerations such as security and strategic importance, social importance, being hazardous in nature, environmental importance, and being items of elitist consumption.

Existing registration schemes (Delicenced Registration, Exempted Industries Registration, DGTD Registration) stand abolished. Entrepreneurs need only file an information memorandum with the Government, on the new projects and expansions.

A new broad-banding facility has been extended to existing units.

Convertibility clause for term loans from financial institutions is no longer applicable for new projects.

Liberalisations in respect of foreign investment and technology import

Encouragement of Foreign Direct Investment (FDI) would become the cornerstone of the New Industrial Policy.

Automatic clearance will be given for foreign equity up to 51 per cent in 34 high-priority industries if equity inflows are sufficient to finance the import of capital goods at the stage of investment and if dividends are balanced by export earnings over a period of time. (The condition regarding balancing of dividend outflow by export earnings, was withdrawn subsequently.)

Automatic clearance will be given for import of capital goods in cases where foreign exchange is available through foreign equity and where the foreign equity covers the cost of imports.

Automatic clearance will also be given for import of capital goods up to a maximum value of Rs 2 crore, if the CIF value of imported capital goods required is less than 25 per cent of total value (net of taxes) of plant and equipment.

In order to obtain better access to international markets, foreign equity holding up to 51 per cent will be allowed even for trading companies primarily engaged in export activities. Such trading houses shall be kept at par with domestic trading and export houses in accordance with the Import-Export Policy.

The capital market of India is opened up to Foreign Institutional Investors (FIIs) including pension funds. This is envisaged as a complementary move to the various other liberalisations aimed at attracting FDI.

Greater freedom will be available to the NRIs and the Overseas Corporate Bodies (OCBs) to play in the Indian capital markets; the ceiling on the acquisition of shares and debentures of Indian companies by NRIs and OCBs was raised from 5 per cent to 24 per cent under the portfolio investment scheme.

Facility of opening foreign currency accounts in India has been introduced.

A specially empowered foreign investment promotion board (FIPB) has been created for enlisting direct foreign investment in certain select areas. The board will negotiate with large international firms and approve foreign investment proposals.

An automatic permission scheme has been introduced for foreign technology agreements in specified high priority industries.

For industries other than specified above, automatic permission will be given subject to the same guidelines as above, if no foreign exchange is required for any payments.

No permission is needed for hiring of foreign technicians or foreign testing of indigenously developed technologies.

Technology transfer need not necessarily be accompanied by foreign equity participation.

Controls on dividend repatriation by foreign companies removed.

Terms relating to royalty payments also liberalised.

Sector after sector opened up for foreign direct investment; Power, Oil and Electronics included in the list.

In the power sector foreign investors invited to "build, operate and own power plants in India"; they can hold 100 per cent equity in power projects. Incentives like freedom to fix tariff ensuring 16 per cent ROI, liberal debt-equity ratio, long duration licence arrangements extending upto 50 years and freedom in repatriation of profits will also be available to foreign investors in this sector. Even freedom of marketing will be considered.

In the oil sector, foreign direct investment invited in production, refining and marketing of oil and gas.

In the electronics sector, a new scheme, the Electronic Hardware Technology Park Scheme (EHTP) introduced for attracting FDI; foreign equity upto 100 per cent allowed in such units and several other incentives also offered.

Substantial amendments to FERA carried out in order to remove the impediments to direct foreign investment.

Direct investment in the reverse—by Indians in other countries—also liberalised.

Liberalisation concerning MRTP

The Monopolies and Restrictive Trade Practices (MRTP) Act has been amended to altogether do away with the threshold limit (hitherto Rs 100 crore) for assets for MRTP companies and dominant undertakings; no MRTP clearance will therefore be required for investment applications.

No approval needed for establishment of new undertakings, expansion of undertakings, merger, amalgamation and takeover and for appointment of directors under certain circumstances.

Restrictions on acquisition/transfer of shares removed.

A newly empowered MRTP Commission will initiate investigations *suo moto* or on complaints received from individual consumers in regard to monopolistic, restrictive and unfair trade practices.

Changes concerning public sector

Public sector's pre-eminent role will be restricted to eight core areas like arms and ammunition, atomic energy, railways, and mining and coal.

Private sector can enter practically all areas; though reservation of some areas for the public sector is being retained, there would be no bar for even these areas to be opened up to the private sector selectively.

The public sector too can enter all areas; it need not confine itself to a few areas as in the past.

Professional management and greater autonomy will be encouraged in the public sector.

Up to 49 per cent of the Government's shareholding in public sector units will be sold to financial institutions, mutual funds, employees and the general public.

Chronically sick PSUs will be referred to the Board for Industrial and Financial Reconstruction (BIFR). A National Renewal Fund (NRF) is to be created to help rehabilitate the workers affected by industrial restructure.

THE SIGNIFICANCE OF THE VARIOUS LIBERALISATIONS

Let us try to understand the meaning and significance of all these liberalisation measures.

Significance of licensing liberalisation

Licensing liberalisation is one of the most significant aspects of the NIP. As per the new policy, all but 18 industries have been taken out of licensing requirements. While the original reasons for introducing licensing might have been convincing, over the years, the licensing requirements tended to delay decision-making, reduce competition, shelter inefficiency, discourage initiative, and stifle the growth process. A change became necessary and inevitable.

The new policy aims at freeing the Indian industry from the many needless and irksome controls. It accords the pivotal role to market mechanism in determining the allocation of resources. It seeks to ensure the elimination of costly delays, inefficiencies and wastages. It has consciously opted for the development of an industrial structure based on technological dynamism and international competitiveness. And finally, it has the mission of making India a truly formidable industrial power.

In the earlier era, entrepreneurs and industrialists were required to wage a battle, sometimes extending to a few years, for getting industrial licences of their choice. Since the powers for approving and refusing applications for licence, were concentrated in the capital of the country, those seeking licences had to make repeated visits to New Delhi, establish liaison offices in the capital and organise follow up of the application at different levels of the bureaucracy and at the political level. They also had to attend a plethora of meetings called by the different departments and agencies in the Government and answer their never-ending queries. And finally, in many cases such laborious and time consuming efforts may turn out to be a totally infructuous exercise as the expected licence may not be granted at all. The loss of time resulting from the licensing hassles were costing the nation enormously. Project costs went up and in many cases the projects became unviable as the parameters changed drastically in the long intervening period. With the licensing liberalisation, entrepreneurs can concentrate on setting up the industries of their choice instead of spending their time and energy on the procurement of the licences.

The abolition of the registration requirements also amounted to a welcome relief to the industrialists. In the revised scheme, after just filing an intimation with the Government regarding their proposals, they can go ahead with the implementation of the project.

The licensing liberalisation was extended subsequently to more industries such as 'white goods' (refrigerator, washing machines, microwave ovens and air conditioners). The Government in addition indicated that it was examining delicensing of certain other industries such as passenger cars, electronics, drugs and pharmaceuticals, petroleum and sugar.

Significance of liberalisation of foreign investment and technology import

While global outflow of foreign direct investment (FDI) has been rising since early 1980s, at the rate of 30 per cent per annum, India did not benefit from this substantial growth in the FDI during all these years. The highly regulated economic regime of India had created a negative image about India in the minds of the foreign investors. In the absence of FDI, India was resorting to commercial borrowings from abroad and deposits from NRIs. In the new era, the Government however planned to sharply reduce its reliance on external commercial borrowings. The country wanted access to capital, technology and markets, all of which direct foreign investment would provide. In addition it would expose the Indian industrial sector to competition from abroad in a phased manner. Cost efficiency and quality would begin to receive the attention they deserve.

The prime significance of the liberalisations in respect of foreign investment is that most of the obstacles in this matter have been removed by the new provisions. In as many as 34 industries, direct foreign investment upto 51 per cent of equity ownership has been allowed by the new policy. Subsequently the Government enlarged the list. Hotels and tourism related industry, industrial synthetic diamonds, glass shells for television tubes, printing machinery, optic fibre, energy efficient lamps, jelly filled communication cables were included in the revised list. Later, the Government included the software industry also in the list. In addition the new drug policy under consideration proposes to declare drugs as a priority sector where 51 per cent foreign equity projects will get automatic approval. Even existing companies will get automatic approval to raise foreign equity up to 51 per cent as part of expansion programmes. The company need not be engaged in industries listed in Annex III; only the proposed expansion need be in the high-priority   industries. Subsequently, the Government liberalised the provision still further, by which existing companies can raise foreign equity up to 51 per cent even without an expansion programme. The only condition was that the increase in equity level must result from expansion of the equity base of the existing company, and the foreign equity must come through remittance of foreign exchange. With this provision, several companies with a foreign equity of 40 per cent or below at present can automatically increase it to 51 per cent.

The Government also removed all controls on dividend repatriation by foreign companies including the condition that foreign investors have to balance their dividend outflow by export earnings. The foreign investors had protested earlier that this condition was forcing them to export in order to balance their dividend payments and that foreign shareholders would be deprived of their dividends till the company was in a position to export and this was inhibiting the flow of foreign investment into India. As per the new provision, the condition will be applicable only to the consumer goods industry. In fact, it has been stated that removal of even this restriction would be considered later.

In a further move, the Government declared that India would liberally consider allowing cent per cent foreign equity in certain industrial projects depending on the economic benefits of the projects. To make things more attractive to foreign investors, provisions relating to royalty payments have also been relaxed. Now it is possible to pay royalty payment of Rupees One crore lumpsum, five per cent on domestic sales and eight per cent on exports, subject to total payments of eight per cent on sales, over a ten year period from the date of agreement, or a seven year period from the date of commencement of production. These payments will be net of taxes and calculated according to standard procedures.

Sector after sector opened up to foreign direct investment

In tune with the new thinking, the country opened up several areas of industrial activity to foreign investment. The size of investments envisaged too, is expected to be pretty substantial. The conditions governing investment have also been liberalised in an equally big way. Quantitative and discretionary controls have also been removed. And industries which were hitherto the exclusive domain of the public sector have been opened up for foreign investment. Power, Oil and Electronics are the industries thrown open initially.

The power sector

In the earlier days, infrastructure like power, was the exclusive domain of the Government sector—the Central Power Corporations and the State Electricity Boards. Even the Indian private sector had nothing to do with it, let alone the foreign private sector. Now, at one stroke, Indian as well as foreign private investments are allowed in power generation and power distribution. The logic in seeking foreign investment in a massive way in the power sector was simple. The Government of India just did not have the massive resources needed for establishing on its own, the required capacities in this crucial infrastructure sector. Indian private sector investments would not have sufficed either. Foreign investment thus became a must. Moreover, it was recognised that even from the technology and efficiency angle, foreign participation in the sector was necessary and desirable.

Accordingly, the Government decided to let the private sector, Indian and foreign, into the power sector. The Government in fact, made the offer that they can 'build, operate and own power plants' in the country.

Obviously, appropriate incentives were called for if the foreign companies, NRIs and the Indian private sector were to bring in the expected massive investments into the business of power. Appreciating the reality, the Government improved the attractiveness of the offer as under:

Foreign investors will be allowed to hold 100 per cent equity in the power sector.

In the price structure, 16 per cent return on investment can be built in.

Repatriation of profits by foreign investors in the power sector can be made without the requirement to balance dividend payments with export earnings.

The power sector to be liberalised from the administrative, legal and financial angles. The enactment has been changed to the effect that any company (in the private sector) registered under the Companies Act can carry on the business of power generation.

The licenses will be issued for a period extending up to 50 years.

The debt equity ratio would be raised to 4:1.

A five year tax holiday from corporate taxation is allowed to private enterprises entering the power sector from the date they begin generating power. (This incentive was given in the 1993-94 budget.)

On the administrative side, it would be a single window clearance.

The Government may even consider granting freedom to the new entrants in the matter of marketing.

The oil sector

The oil sector too was opened up to foreign investors by allowing foreign equity investment to the tune of 26 per cent in refineries and development of discovered oilfields. Simultaneously, the Government also decided to offer oil blocks for exploration on round the year basis. Even small discovered oil and gas fields, were opened to the private/foreign investments on 'production sharing basis'. Initially, 28 such fields would be offered for collaboration. The moves would hasten exploration and increase crude availability during the Eighth Plan period, besides attracting foreign investment.

In respect of collaborations relating to refineries, the Government liberalised the position with the stipulation that the public sector oil companies will have 26 per cent equity, the foreign investor will have 26 per cent equity and the balance 48 per cent will be offered to the Indian public. The objective of the policy was to mobilise foreign private capital into oil refining which until now remained the monopoly of the Indian public sector. The Government stated that it would also welcome proposals for domestic and foreign private investment in the production, refining and marketing of oil and gas. With a view to making the offer more attractive to investors in the oil sector, Government was also prepared to allow them to deal in speciality products.

The fact that the oil sector too has been opened up to foreign investors, even in the matter of marketing, is of special significance. Refinery alone is not a very profitable investment and if people have to be attracted to this highly capital intensive investment, there has to be some supplementary activity that is attractive from the profitability angle. Marketing being one such activity, the Government decided to include it in the package. Marketing of specialised items within the petro products range has been specifically thought of in this regard. The idea is that the foreign companies can enter into some sort of an arrangement with Indian companies and market the petro products, including the specialised items.

The electronics sector

The Government liberalised the foreign investment policy for the electronics sector as well. From now on, multinationals setting up manufacturing facilities in computer hardware and peripherals under 100 per cent export-oriented scheme will be allowed to sell up to 30 per cent of their production in the domestic tariff area. Similarly, component manufacturers will be allowed to sell up to 35 per cent of their production in the domestic market. These companies will also be allowed to have 100 per cent foreign equity.

Electronic hardware technology park (EHTP)

The liberalisations in the electronics sector were largely brought about through the Electronic Hardware Technology Park (EHTP) scheme. The scheme had been specifically designed to help build a strong electronics industry in India, with the focus on enhancing India's export potential.

An EHTP is basically a duty-free and bonded area. An EHTP unit can import free of duty all types of goods, including capital goods required by it for production, provided they are not items on the negative list under the import policy. Second-hand capital goods can also be imported in accordance with the policy. Foreign equity up to 100 per cent is allowed in the case of such units. Such a park can be set up by the Central Government, State Governments and public or private sector organisations. An EHTP can be an individual unit or a part of a cluster of such units located in an area designated as EHTP. The unit will be exempted from payment of income tax for a period of five years in the first eight years of its operation. All tax benefits as well as other benefits available to the 100 per cent EOU and EPZ units will be extended to the EHTPs as well.

The EHTP scheme is expected to enable a number of multinationals in the electronics field to invest in India in a big way and to make a contribution towards strengthening the electronic component industry of India. The scheme will be administered by the Department of Electronics.

The mining sector

As per National Mineral Policy, 1993, the Government has thrown open even the mining industry to the private sector, except for uranium, coal and mineral oil. The move is to attract foreign investment and boost exploration and exploitation of the mineral potential in the country. Thirteen minerals are now open for investment by private sector: iron ore, manganese, chrome, sulphur, gold, diamond, copper, lead, zinc, molybdenum, tungsten, nickel and platinum. The revised policy raises the ceiling on foreign equity in the mining industry by providing for foreign equity participation up to 50 per cent.

A large number of foreign investments approved

Following the launching of the new industrial policy, there has been a spurt in the number of foreign investment proposals approved by the Government. According to RBI figures, between August '91 and October '92, foreign collaboration approvals were granted in 1876 cases. Of these, 808 were approved by the RBI and the remaining by the SIA and the FIPB. The CCFI cleared 10 major proposals in power and oil sectors. Of the total 1876 proposals approved, 740 involved foreign equity participation amounting to $ 1.2 billion. Of these, 38 proposals related to existing companies enhancing foreign equity to 51 per cent.

FERA Amendments and removal of hurdles to foreign investment

FERA was acting as a hindrance in attracting foreign investment and foreign technology. Many foreign companies have been staying away from India because under FERA laws, they were not in a position to hold majority equity control in their Indian ventures. And they were not eager to bring into India their Hi-Tech know-how without a controlling interest in the venture.

The Government decided to bring about comprehensive amendments to the existing Foreign Exchange Regulations Act to remove the wide ranging impediments to foreign investment and to facilitate efficient business activity by Indian companies and foreign investors. While initially it brought the amendments through notifications, it later felt that appropriate changes should be effected in the statutes. Foreign investors, Japanese in particular, were keen that the Government provide a sustainable legal framework for the various FERA changes already announced during '91-92.

FERA Amendment Ordinance

In January '93, the Government promulgated an ordinance to amend the FERA. The amendment incorporated all the changes to FERA which had been issued in '91-92 as notifications of the RBI or the Government.

The Ordinance substantially liberalised the regulatory provisions of the FERA and brought it in line with the already liberalised industrial, trade and exchange rate policies. It removed a large number of existing restrictions on companies with more than 40 per cent non-resident equity. Simultaneously, it also removed FERA controls on Indian firms setting up joint ventures abroad.

The main changes in FERA brought about through the Ordinance are as follows:

FERA companies will be allowed to acquire whole or part of any undertaking in India, carrying on trade, commerce and industry, excepting those in agriculture and plantation activities.

FERA companies exempted from the prohibition imposed under Section 29 on establishment of a branch office or a liaison office even when the non-resident interest in such company exceeds 40 per cent.

Restrictions regarding assets held in India by non-residents have been removed.

Deletion of the FERA provision under Section 12, which provided that the Government could direct certain payments to be made by FERA companies in a special account.

Import and export in gold and silver has been exempted from FERA.

Section 17 conferring on the Government the power to regulate uses of imported gold and silver has been deleted.

Section 15, which confers on the Government the power to direct FERA companies to make payment in foreign currency in certain cases, has also been deleted.

Restrictions on transfer of any security from a register in India to a register outside India have been removed, as these were intended to take care of erstwhile sterling companies, which had dual registers.

Restrictions on transfer of shares by a non-resident to another non-resident have been removed.

A new section has been introduced which permits taking out of goods on rental, lease, hire or on any other arrangement, which does not amount to the disposal of such goods. This will greatly benefit exporters.

Investment abroad by Indians also liberalised

After the removal of hurdles to foreign direct investment into India, there was no logic in continuing with the hurdles faced by Indian firms in investment abroad. The Government liberalised the policy as under:

Automatic permission for Indian direct investment upto $ 2 million in joint ventures and wholly-owned subsidiaries abroad; investment proposals involving more than $ 2 million to be routed through an inter-ministerial committee, which will take a decision within 90 days of the receipt of the application.

Permission to joint ventures in which Indian companies are minority shareholders or majority shareholders to diversify their activities, participate in the equity of another company, promote a subsidiary, or alter its share capital — without the prior approval of the Indian Government.

Indians allowed to hold immovable property abroad, subject to certain conditions to be stipulated by the Reserve Bank of India.

The FERA ordinance is expected to build up the confidence of the foreign investors to invest in a wide range of industries in the country. It has given a legal shape to various notifications issued by the Government in the past liberalising the FERA provisions. It would also reassure the foreign investors about the permanency of the liberalisation of FERA provisions.

The ordinance would likewise facilitate setting up of Indian joint ventures abroad as the order removes many restrictions which inhibited setting up of such ventures in the past. It may also help Indian exporters to make their presence felt in the international markets and generate additional exports.

Significance of MRTP liberalisation

MRTP liberalisation is the second major hallmark of the NIP. In fact, licensing and MRTP liberalisations have been complementary to each other. It is to make the licensing liberalisation genuinely effective, that the MRTP impediments have also been removed. Henceforth, the emphasis of MRTP will be on controlling restrictive and unfair trade practices. The threshold limits of assets in respect of MRTP companies and dominant undertakings shall cease to operate; consequently, the pre-entry scrutiny of investment decisions by so-called MRTP companies will no longer be required and therefore, in the case of expansion, establishment of new undertakings, merger, amalgamation and takeover, there will be no need for these companies to obtain prior approval of the Central Government. Even the most optimistic were only hoping that the MRTP threshold limit would be increased by the Government from Rs 100 crore to Rs 500 or Rs 1000 crore at the most. It was a pleasant surprise to them to learn that the Government totally abolished the threshold limit.

Curtailment of the role of the public sector

Curtailment of the role of the public sector is another significant feature of the NIP. A commanding role for the public sector had all along formed the cornerstone of India's industrial policy. The policy all through was aimed at expanding endlessly the role of the public sector in the nation's economy. The New Industrial Policy presents a striking contrast to all these earlier prescriptions by voting for a substantive reduction in the role of the public sector in the industrial development of the country. Only eight industries are now exclusively reserved as the core industry for the public sector, and having regard to their weightages, it would be evident that the role of the public sector has been reduced by almost 50 per cent of what it used to be all these years. As a corollary, as much as three-fourths of the total industrial activity of the country is now being made available for the private sector and only one fourth for the public sector.

Another significant reform relating to the public sector in the NIP is the extension of BIFR's purview to the public sector. The Government amended the Sick Industrial Companies Act (SICA) and armed itself with powers to tackle the sick PSUs. According to the provisions of the amended SICA, sick PSUs would get referred to BIFR for rehabilitation suggestions. Through this route, even closure of PSUs became possible.

THE UNIQUENESS OF THE NEW INDUSTRIAL POLICY

A comparison of India's past industrial policy and the present policy formulations under the new economic programme, would readily highlight the total route change now adopted by the country in the matter of industrial policy. It is precisely for highlighting this contrast that we present below a gist of the policy formulations of yester years. We shall then see how the reforms now attempted constitute a total break with the earlier policy.

Evolution of India's industrial policy over the years

Following the country's independence in 1947, the nation adopted a clearly spelt out Industrial Policy in 1948 through the well known Industrial Policy Resolution (IPR) of 1948. The adoption of a mixed economy was the cornerstone of the Industrial Policy of the young nation. The subsequent important steps in the evolution of the policy have been the enactment of the Industries (Development and Regulation)Act, 1951, the Industrial Policy Resolution, 1956, the MRTP Act 1969, the Licensing Policy Statement of 1970, the Industrial Policy Statement of 1973, the Industrial Policy Statement of 1977 and the Industrial Policy Statement of 1980.

The IPR of 1956 accorded a pivotal role for the public sector in the industrial development of the country. Strident growth of a few business houses in the private sector, led to the formulation of the Monopolies and Restrictive Trade Practices (MRTP) Act 1969 and the Industrial Licensing Policy Statement 1970. The latter had classified industries into core sector, non-core sector, heavy industries sector, middle sector, joint sector, unlicensed sector and the small-scale sector. It was also indicated that investment by large houses would be encouraged in certain areas needing heavy investment while the core sector would be reserved for the state.

The Industrial Policy Statement of 1973, identified certain high priority industries where investment from large industrial houses and foreign companies would be permitted. A secretariat of industrial approvals (SIA) was set up to speed up the issue of licences and to deal with all aspects such as letter of intent, foreign collaboration, capital goods clearance, etc.

The Industrial Policy Statement of 1977, emphasised the need for greater decentralisation, and a much bigger role for the small scale and cottage industries so as to create more employment opportunities. It raised the exemption limit for licensing and introduced the concept of tiny sector within the small-scale sector.

The Industrial Policy Statement of 1980 laid stress on the optimum utilisation of installed capacity, technological upgradation and modernisation, selective regularisation of excess capacities, improving the efficiency of public sector enterprises and the promotion of export-oriented units. It was also decided to promote 100 per cent export oriented units.

In practical terms, industrial policy followed by India since independence, was the offshoot of a controlled economy where both private and public sectors shared the responsibility of industrial activity, under the strict supervision of the Government. Industry as a whole, was subjected to various administrative and legal controls. The objective was to deliberately channelise resources according to the social and economic priorities of the nation. The Government invested directly in industrial activity, mostly in the core sector by setting up public enterprises while consumer products were by and large left in the hands of the private sector.

There was a specific background to the adoption of such a policy. At the time of independence India was primarily an agricultural economy. To come out of the shackles of a backward economy, the country had to adopt an industrial policy that encouraged establishment of basic industries and infrastructure. Control and regulation formed an integral part of the policy.

The New Industrial Policy marks a clean break with the past

It would be clear from the foregoing presentation of the historical evolution of India's industrial policy, that the NIP is not just another amendment to the hitherto followed industrial policy. On the contrary, it meant a wholesale revision of the entire policy framework relating to the country's industry. The new package was full of drastic and fundamental policy departures, compared with all the previous attempts at policy modification in this sphere. In fact, it represents the opposite of the IPR, 1956 which had become the bible of industrial policy for the country and remained so till 1991. And that is why, the new policy has been widely described as a new chapter in India's economic history.

What has to be grasped essentially from an analysis of the evolution of India's industrial policy is the fact that the original policy as well as every reform or amendment thereof till 1980 increased the role of the state in regulating and controlling the industrial activity in a variety of ways. It was only during the 1980s that changes that could be termed as policy departures or reforms in the true sense of the term were getting incorporated, and that too in bits and pieces. And when it came to the NIP, it simply outweighed all the reforms of the '80s.

Another important difference between the policy initiatives of the earlier era, especially the pre 1980s and the NIP, is that throughout the earlier period, the basic strategy was one of import substitution, while the NIP gave emphasis to exports. In the earlier regime, the domestic industry was protected throughout from external competition either by the imposition of a total ban on imports or by a high tariff wall. It was no doubt necessary to protect the domestic industry during the early stage of economic growth. But it is being realised, in retrospect, that the protection given was not only excessive but was also continued for too long. The result was that the infant refused to grow; the industry was saddled with outdated and obsolete technology, productivity declined, and the country's share in World market declined steadily.

Yet another difference is that while in all previous policy formulations, the Government was always trying to improve existing regulations, in the NIP, it chose to bid goodbye to regulations altogether. Delicensing, deregulation, decontrol and debureaucratisation became the pillars of the new industrial policy. In the earlier era, the economy of India not only got itself entangled in a maze of regulations, it also got highly complicated, with a multiplicity of sectors, which in turn meant more of regulations. Moreover, several products came under price control; some under floor prices, some under ceiling prices and yet others under a dual pricing system. Private trade and public distribution system charged different prices for a variety of products. Subsidies and state trading added to the confusion of the system. Naturally, the economy came under total bureaucratic control. Under the NIP, not only were these controls sought to be dismantled, but the complications created over the years with the multiplicity of sectors, were also sought to be eliminated.

To put it in a nutshell, the NIP represented a clear departure from the earlier ideological fixations which were totally out of tune with contemporary realities. The new policy relies greatly on the market mechanism and globalisation impulses. It envisages a more open, efficient and quality-conscious industrial sector equipped to face global competition. In sweep and tenor, it is novel, compared to the earlier policies. While the earlier policies encouraged industry to remain wrapped up smugly in the cocoon of an excessively protected economy, the New Industrial Policy compelled industry to acquire competitive strength and pursue business excellence.

3

The New Trade Policy

Like industrial policy, trade policy too has been an area of significant reform under the new economic programme. In fact, the reform in trade policy has been absolutely radical. The Government dismantled at one stroke, most of the restrictions that were acting as stumbling blocks in the export and import activities of the country. It also brought in, for the first time, a clear and specific link between the country's exports and imports. The reform meant that Exim activities will henceforth have to operate on the premise that "you cannot import if you don't export".

While the reform measures contained in the trade policy notification of July 4, 1991, constituted the core of the New Trade Policy (NTP), the NTP actually encompassed several other measures announced subsequently. The '92-93 budget, presented on February 29, 1992, introduced the partial convertibility of the rupee; on April 1, 1992, the Government announced yet another instalment of changes; and full convertibility followed during the course of the next year. All these moves together constitute the New Trade Policy.

SALIENT FEATURES OF THE NEW TRADE POLICY

The salient features of the New Trade Policy are listed below:

Foreign trade would be freed totally from all controls; a small list of non-permitted items will be the only restriction that would remain.

Industrial units will have all freedom to secure imports, step up exports, generate the forex required for imports and continue the cycle.

Imports of the country would be linked to exports of the country. Imports and exports will be governed by a self balancing system; imports will be made only with the forex earned and made available in the market by the exporters. 'You cannot import, if you do not export' would be the new maxim.

Trade gap will be limited to the difference between the forex portion surrendered to the Government by the exporters and the value of Government imports of essential items. (With full convertibility, this position has been modified further.)

There would be a general liberalisation of imports; import of capital goods would become particularly easy; these goods would no longer be in the negative list of imports; second hand capital goods will also be allowed, in some sectors without licence, and in others with licence.

All items listed in the permissible list, OGL items imported by PMP units, all capital goods, and machinery and spares, can now be imported through the REP route. Unlisted OGL category is abolished. All imports in this category would also now come through the REP route.

All supplementary licences stand abolished except for the small scale sector and life saving drugs and equipment. All additional licences granted to export houses also stand abolished. Advance licensing will stay, REP rate for advance licence exports is increased from 10 per cent to 20 per cent of net foreign exchange.

Baggage rules liberalised and the customs duty slashed on a number of items brought in as baggage by returning Indians.

A new scheme permitting liberal import of gold and silver by Indians returning from abroad brought in. As per this scheme, they can legally bring in 5 kg of gold every time they visit home. The import will attract only a nominal duty.

Import of all items except the essentials will be decanalised; and the canalisation agencies will function as any other trading house without any special advantage or control over imports.

Import licences would vanish from the scene completely in the near future.

Exports would be encouraged with a number of incentives.

On all export earnings, REP licences would be available at the uniform rate of 30 per cent of the earnings.

Exim scrips would replace REP licences; the scrips would become the principal instrument of imports; they would be freely tradeable and financial institutions will be allowed to trade in them. (Subsequently, partial and full convertibility of the rupee followed)

Concessions will be provided in import duties on import of plant and machinery which results in exports; industrial units can avail of this advantage, for boosting their exports.

Special incentives introduced for export oriented units (EOU); EOU scheme and EPZ scheme liberalised; the schemes extended to agriculture, horticulture, aquaculture, poultry and animal husbandry.

Inter-unit transfers allowed in the schemes. Permission granted to instal machinery on lease. EOU/EPZ units may export through Export Houses, Trading Houses and Star Trading Houses.

A special Export Promotion Capital Goods Scheme (EPCGS) providing for import of capital goods at 15 per cent concessional duty, with an export obligation of 400 per cent introduced.

Deemed exporters, manufacturers with ISO 9000 and IS 14000 certification and Export Houses, Trading Houses and Star Trading Houses made eligible for special import licences.

Definition of Deemed Exports streamlined. Supplies to EOU/EPZ units, supplies against EPCG licences and supplies against Advance Licences, recognised as deemed exports.

Cash Compensatory Support (CCS) which formed the lion's share of export subsidies abolished completely.

All procedures for imports and exports simplified to a great extent.

The Rupee made a partially convertible currency on trade account by the 1992-93 budget and a fully convertible currency by the 1993-94 budget.

SIGNIFICANCE OF THE NEW TRADE POLICY

The new trade policy is marked by radicalism as well as pragmatism. It represents a radical departure from the past, conceptually as well as in details. At the same time, there is nothing utopian about it; it is out and out pragmatic. The significance of the new policy is elaborated below.

Freer trade and open exim regime

To begin with, the new trade policy has liberated the Exim trade from the shackles of controls. The Government realised that India has to gain a real competitive edge in the international markets. It also realised that it was not possible to achieve this edge in a system of licensing and controls. And this realisation has permeated the new trade policy. In other words, 'freer trade and a more open Exim regime' is the most significant and the most distinctive feature of the NTP.

Linking imports with exports

Linking imports to exports and developing a system of self balance between them is the second major feature of the new trade policy. In the new scheme of things, imports cannot endlessly bulge, without any reference whatsoever to the export level. Industry as a whole, has to necessarily match its imports with its exports. Foreign exchange just will not be available beyond the free market portion of forex earned by exports.

In fact, the Exim scrip scheme and the subsequent partial convertibility scheme are essentially intended to ensure that the import growth does not go out of line with exports. Events soon demonstrated that the

Government was steadfast in the implementation of the self balancing linkage of imports with exports. The Government decided not to make any additional allocation of forex at the offical rate for the import of additional crude and other petroleum products during '92-93. The IOC, the canalising agency, was advised to purchase the forex from the market at the market rate. The official forex would be limited to the originally approved level of $ 5.1 billion. Had the Government compromised on this issue, the concept of self balancing linkage between imports and exports would have gone haywire. The subsequent full convertibility scheme pushed the process another big step forward, as under that scheme, even essential imports by Government will have to depend on the market and pay at the market rate. These moves in fact, have linked Indian economy with the global economy, besides linking India's imports with her exports.

Relying more on exchange rates and tariffs than on quantitative restrictions, for controlling trade flow

The new policy was formulated on the clear recognition that in regulating India's external trade, dependence on quantitative controls ought to be dispensed with and exchange rates and tariffs should become the principal instruments for controlling the trade flow. The policy also appreciated the fact that the tariffs in India are among the highest in the world and that they should be brought down in a gradual manner, if India has to avoid becoming an extreme example of a high cost economy. At the same time, the policy had to use tariffs wherever necessary, for controlling trade flow including possible dumping. This was obviously necessary since reliance on quantitative restrictions for controlling trade flow was being given up.

Steep reduction in tariffs

Since high tariffs have been pushing up the investment costs as well as the production costs in the country, the Government decided that tariffs on import of capital goods as well as inputs should be slashed. In accordance with the above recognition, the '92-93 budget brought about modest reductions in the import tariffs on a number of items. And the '93-94 budget slashed the tariffs in the most uninhibited manner.

Reduction in tariffs have been particularly hefty in respect of project imports and import of capital goods. While the 1992-93 budget brought about modest reductions in this regard, the 1993-94 budget made very significant cuts. In 1992-93, the duty on projects and general machinery imports was brought down from 80 per cent to 55 per cent. In 1993-94, it was brought down to 35 per cent. In respect of the power sector, the rate was lowered to 20 per cent. In absolute terms, the give away in tariff in respect of projects and machinery import was more than Rs 835 crore in 1993-94. The 1992-93 budget brought customs duty rates down from an average of 150 per cent to 110 per cent. In the 1993-94 budget, the maximum has been brought down to 85 per cent, from 110 per cent. The budget actually gave a relief of Rs 3,273 crore in import duties. More details of the tariff cuts are presented in chapters 4 and 6.

The Chelliah Committee on tax reforms has recommended that by 1997-98, import tariffs should be slashed to a maximum of 30 per cent, except in respect of non essential consumer goods where the duty could be 50 per cent. The Government is in agreement with the trend of the recommendation and it is just a matter of time for the tariffs in India to register further steep falls.

Partial convertibility of Rupee/Dual Exchange Rate System

The Government had appointed a high level committee on BoP with a view to getting recommendations on a new exchange rate system for the country. The committee looked at the issue of exchange rate in the light of the country's experience with the Exim scrip scheme. The Exim scrip scheme had helped to put in place a generalised incentive structure for all exports with a wider commodity coverage, a higher average entitlement and a smaller dispersion in rates, as compared with the REP system. It also reduced the need for budgetary subsidies for exports. The scheme had also been well received by the exporters. There were demands for expanding the coverage of Exim scrip scheme beyond areas of goods trade and professional services, to include other foreign exchange inflows. The committee identified its task as one of modifying the Exim scrip scheme, correcting inadequacies and drawbacks in the operation of the mechanism and expanding the coverage of the mechanism. And the recommendation in favour of a dual exchange rate system was the outcome.

The Government felt that the dual rate system recommended by the committee did contain a number of advantages. Specifically, it could help contain the current account deficit, impart some flexibility to the exchange rate system, ensure that the cost of essential imports does not rise abruptly, keep capital outflows under close control, and replace unnecessary, burdensome, case-by-case, regulatory mechanisms of exchange control with a simpler, more efficient and transparent system and thereby enhance the productivity, efficiency and ease of the operations. The Government realised that there were certain risks too in the scheme but felt that the balance of advantages favoured the scheme. Accordingly, the Government brought in the dual rate system which was called the Liberalised Exchange Rate Management System (LERMS). The new system which came into effect on 1 April, 1992, replaced the Exim scrip scheme.

Under LERMS, 40 per cent of the foreign exchange remitted will be converted at the official exchange rate while the remaining 60 per cent will be converted at market determined rate. The foreign exchange surrendered at official exchange rate will be available to the Government to meet the exchange requirements of essential imports such as petroleum products, fertilisers and defence requirements. All imports required by industry will be made, using the foreign exchange obtained from the market at the market determined rate. The Government felt that with LERMS, it had hit upon a self balancing system to manage a large part of the balance of payments — a mechanism which can achieve what the Exim scrip was designed to achieve but failed to, namely, to ensure that the country's requirements of forex for meeting its import requirements will be met by the earnings from exports and that there is no shortfall which will have to be funded by the Reserve Bank.

The new system did have certain merits. In the first place, there will be no need in the new system to issue Exim scrips for each export transaction as the new system will operate through the banks. Industry can have free access to foreign exchange at market rate for its imports. Instead of the premium on Exim scrips, exporters will now have the premium on their earnings of foreign exchange. Secondly, earlier, release of foreign exchange for imports was at the discretion of the Government, depending on the purpose for which the exchange was sought; but the exchange rate applied was official. Now, the exchange has to be obtained at the market rate, but the procedure for obtaining the exchange is quite simple; moreover, the list of prohibited items is made very small.

From the exporters point of view, the new system meant that the entitlement ratio at market rate will be up from 30 per cent to 60 per cent of exchange earnings. Workers remitting money from abroad would also gain, since they would also be eligible for market rates to the tune of 60 per cent of the remittances. The other welcome effect was that the new system inflicted a severe blow to the illegal foreign exchange market or *Hawala* market. The legal market rate and the *Hawala* rate came close to each other.

In opting for partial convertibility instead of total convertibility, right at the beginning, the Government has taken a cautious approach. The disquieting experience of some other similarly placed countries which had opted for total convertibility at one go, had weighed with India when she took her decision. By retaining the provision that 40 per cent of all the exchange earned would remain with the RBI for meeting the essential imports at official rate of exchange, the Government was trying to protect the economy from possible hyper-inflation and the shooting up of prices of essential imports. By limiting the convertibility, the Government achieved a sort of insurance in respect of imports of essentials.

Partial convertibility a partial success

Even though the Government had high hopes about the partial convertibility scheme, when the scheme was actually put into operation, it proved to be just a partial success. The intended spurt in exports did not materialise. Exporters complained that the system imposed a tax on them; they could convert only 60 per cent of their foreign exchange earnings at the market exchange rate; the remainder had to be converted at the officially set rate; and partial convertibility meant subsidising the Government's essential imports through industry's exports.

The experience worldwide has been that dual exchange rates are inefficient in terms of allocation of resources and cumbersome to operate.

Full convertibility/Unified Exchange Rate System

Subsequently, through the '93-94 budget moves, the Government made the rupee fully convertible on trade account and brought in a unified exchange rate system in place of the earlier dual exchange rate system. The unified system means that exchange rates of rupee will be fixed on the basis of the prevailing market rate, which in turn will be determined on the basis of demand and supply of the foreign exchange. The system is christened as Unified Market-determined Exchange rate system and is termed for convenience, as modified LERMS.

Under the full convertibility, all receipts, out of export earnings or remittances, whether on Current account, or on Capital account of the Balance of Payments, will be converted entirely at market rate of exchange. Likewise, in the case of payments too, the market-based rate of exchange will apply uniformly to all foreign exchange payments whether on Government or private account.

The Government veered round to the view that full convertibility of the rupee on trade account was essential for boosting exports and for promoting foreign direct investment. It was recognised that partial convertibility in effect acted as an 8 per cent tax on exporters and to that extent made exports less competitive and less profitable. It was felt that exports could be promoted through full convertibility as full convertibility would remove the existing disincentives of exporters under LERMS. Similarly, partial convertibility was acting as a disincentive to foreign direct investment (FDI). The Government felt that full convertibility would provide confidence, more than anything else, to foreign direct investors and therefore is likely to give a fillip to FDI.

Full convertibility and unified exchange rate system is expected to give a boost to exports as in the new system, exporters would benefit from higher rupee realisations at market rate for the entire value of their exports. The expectation is that the profits of exporters will go up by 10 per cent at the minimum. In other words, full convertibility confers a new competitive edge to India's exports. Full convertibility is expected to bring more foreign exchange into India in yet another way. It is common knowledge that millions of dollars are stashed abroad by Indians. Full convertibility provides the required climate for them to bring back these amounts into India.

It was feared that full convertibility might push up inflation, especially by pushing up the prices of petro products which will now have to bear the market rates of exchange for all imports. The fears however were allayed by the Government's assurance that (a) the move coincided with a declining trend in international oil prices and (b) the oil coordination committee had enough surplus to take care of moderate fluctuations in the international prices of oil or in the exchange rate of the rupee.

INTEGRATING INDIA'S ECONOMY WITH THE GLOBAL ECONOMY

The crucial fact that emerges from the series of trade policy liberalisation is that globalisation of India's economy is no longer a glib phrase; it is becoming a reality. Liberalisation of imports and hefty cuts in import tariffs combined with convertibility of the rupee have already given a major push to the process. The exchange rate mechanism has emerged as the main instrument in regulating the trade flow of the country. The full floating of the rupee is a clear signal to international investors about the Government's determination to integrate India closely with the world economy. It is also a signal to Indian companies that they should become globally competitive if they want to survive and prosper. Tariff restructure too has given a big push to the process. The viability and competitiveness of the products manufactured in India have all along been under great strain, because of the high import tariffs on raw materials, capital goods and project imports. Not only have the tariffs been generally high, but the tariff structure has also been totally topsy-turvy, without any rational backing. For example, in several industries, duties on inputs and components have been out of tune with duties on finished products.The new trade policy has altered the scene completely. The liberalisations in other areas such as industrial licensing and foreign direct investments and the permission to Indian companies to raise equity abroad, have reinforced the process of integration.

From REP to Exim scrip to partial convertibility to full convertibility—A step by step process of integration

The journey, the trade policy and the exchange rate system have made, from REP to full convertibility is in essence a multi step transition from Government regulated allocation to market driven allocation of foreign exchange. It has been a steady progress to a stage wherein imports of the country are free from all controls, being regulated only by the relative scarcity of foreign exchange and the actual price of the import. The exchange rate adjustment through the 20 per cent devaluation of the rupee in July 1991 was the first step. With every successive step, the Government allowed the rupee to float more and more freely. With the introduction of Exim scrips in August 1991, 30 per cent of the foreign exchange earnings could be converted at the market rate. Then, in March 1992, under the system of partial convertibility, the 30 per cent entitlement at market rate was increased to 60 per cent. And now there was no need for the exporters to go to the Government to get their entitlements certified; the banks could directly encash 60 per cent of the export proceeds at the market rates. With full convertibility brought about by the 1993-94 budget, 100 per cent of the export proceeds could be encashed at the market rates. Along with all these adjustments in the float of the rupee, there have been parallel changes on the side of imports, permitting unfettered import of capital goods, raw materials and components. The Government chose such a step-by-step process of integration in order to keep under check the possible hardships.

Encouragement to exports

Encouragement to exports was the other dimension of the process of integration of India's economy with the global economy. The new trade policy sought to provide encouragement to exports in a number of ways. It not only contained a number of incentives but also a number of procedural simplifications designed to promote exports. The policy totally hinged on the thesis that export growth has to be accelerated, if India has to survive economically and if India's BoP position has to be rescued out of the perpetual crisis into which it has got entangled.

To help Indian exporters compete better in the international markets, Government announced higher duty drawback in respect of 161 items, effective June 1, 1992. Duty drawback being the provision to compensate exporters against the high import and other duties on raw materials used in the manufacture of export commodities, higher quantum of drawback facilitates the Indian exporters to compete effectively in the international market. Subsequently, effective June 1, 1993, the Government announced revised duty draw back rates for 331 more items.

The Export Promotion Capital Goods Scheme (EPCGS) of the new Exim Policy was another measure to encourage exports. The special merit of the scheme is the encouragement it provides to the new manufacturer-exporter with viable project ideas; the scheme affords consideration of their proposals on merits.

Subsequently, the Government also enlarged the scope of the Exim Policy by widening the definition of 'manufacture' and 'capital goods' to boost exports of agricultural and marine products.

Incentives are but one part of the strategy of the NTP. The other part consisted of creating an element of compulsion. The new trade policy compelled industries to look towards exports. In the new regime they cannot survive without export.

The globalisation budget

The 1993-94 budget has been aptly called the real globalisation budget for India. The budget gave the clear message about India's globalisation endeavour. Currency and trade barriers have been dismantled almost totally; trade has become almost totally free. The '93-94 budget gave special encouragement for boosting exports—a unified exchange rate, abolition of export duties, cheaper export credit and cuts in import duty which meant lower costs of production and improved competitiveness. The exporters have been granted a reduction of one per cent in lending rates and banks have been exempted from the interest tax on transactions with exporters. This would ensure a greater flow of resources to the export sector.The budget also sought to harness agriculture for exports. The expectation is that the encouragement provided by the budget will help the country achieve a 16 per cent growth in exports in dollar terms in 1993-94.

Simplification of procedures and transparency in trade policy administration

Simplification of procedures is another hallmark of the new trade policy. In the past, trade policy used to be spelt out in two bulky volumes running to more than 400 pages. Now, the policy book is drastically reduced in size and is brought out in a single sleak volume of less than 100 pages. And that in itself is an indication of the extent of simplification that has gone into the matter. As per the new policy only one application is required for exports and imports, as also for legal undertakings and bank guarantees as against several sets of application forms prescribed in the earlier policy. The umpteen annexures that used to form an integral part of the earlier policy books have been eliminated in the new version. There is just one annexure now against 17 in the earlier one. The new Export Promotion Capital Goods Scheme (EPCGS) of the new Exim policy in particular, stands out as a model of simplification in bureaucratic policy formulations. While it is very vast in scope, it is very brief and simple in pronouncement. Likewise, flexibility of approach is yet another welcome feature of the new policy.

The multiplicity of controlling agencies has also been considerably reduced as per the new policy.

The Duty Exemption Scheme (DES) for import of various goods for production for export, is another noteworthy measure in the new policy. The new regulations offer considerable freedom to exporters to operate in accordance with their own priorities. The advance licences can be either value based or quantity based. Flexible value addition is made possible by giving advance licences for a class or classes of export products in the same sector, though this is selective for the time being. The new self-declared pass book scheme for the three categories of recognised trading houses is another example of flexibility. It provides for self-regulation on the part of the export houses. Furthermore, in the new policy, the import entitlement of one licensing year can be carried forward either in full or in part to the two succeeding licensing years. Designs and drawings may be imported without any restriction and Indian goods already exported can be imported back without a licence, for repairs and re-export. The very move to replace the REP licences by Exim scrips was a major exercise in simplification of procedures. REP licences were cumbersome in operation and their replacement by Exim scrips did make the operations smoother.

Along with simplification, the new trade policy is also marked by transparency. The Government has stated that unlike in the past, no ad hoc modifications of the policy would be introduced every now and then. Instead, there would be a methodical approach to policy changes and the changes would be announced at the beginning of each quarter. The policy promises that the political and bureaucratic hand would be restrained and a systematic approach to changes would be the new order.

The self certification procedure introduced in the new policy, testifies to the new intentions of the Government. The Government has placed trust in the exporters of the country by offering them the self certification procedure. The new policy in addition, provides greater powers and role to the regional licensing authorities.

THE NEW TRADE POLICY, A MAJOR INSTRUMENT OF LIBERALISATION

It can be seen from the foregoing analysis that the Government has used the trade policy as a powerful instrument in its liberalisation endeavour. The Government's expectation is that the new trade policy on the whole would help boost exports, provide a self balancing mechanism for balancing exports and imports, encourage efficient import substitution, liberalise trade in general, reduce bureaucratic controls and eliminate the incentive for illegal transactions in foreign exchange.

4

Economic Reforms

The Government was aware that in addition to liberalisation of industry and trade, macro economic adjustments and reforms were also necessary for restoring the health of the country's economy. It accordingly prepared a package of economic reforms for implementation over the medium term which touched practically every aspect of macro economy. Fiscal reforms with a major thrust towards fiscal deficit reduction, monetary reforms, capital market reforms and banking sector reforms were the items that were high on the agenda on economic reforms. BoP management and inflation control formed integral parts of the scheme of things. Prudent management of the macro economy was the basic aim. The Government recognised that fundamentally the reforms should be able to eliminate waste and inefficiency in the macro economy and improve its productivity. Simultaneously they should inject a new element of dynamism into the growth processes of the economy so that the economy becomes vibrant and internationally competitive. The reforms should also help curb the exponentially growing internal and external debt and the resultant debt servicing burden.

FISCAL REFORMS

The fiscal reforms centred around reduction of fiscal deficits, reform of the tax system (direct and indirect tax systems) and containment of public debt.

The path breaking budgets

The fiscal reforms including taxation reforms were implemented largely through the budgets for '91-92 and '92-93. It is therefore essential to make a reference to these budgets before proceeding with a discussion on fiscal and taxation reforms. Fiscal '91-92 witnessed the unique phenomenon of the presentation of two budgets—one presented in July for the fiscal year 1991-92 and the other presented in February for the year 1992-93. And the significance of these budgets did not stop with the novelty that both of them were presented in the same year. They indisputably were path-breaking budgets. They represented a clean break from the past in their economic and fiscal content.

The twin budgets epitomised the Government's determination to bring about drastic economic reforms. Normally, an annual budget is a short term document and no one expects a Government to spell out or implement all its long term economic policies through an annual budget. But, the twin budgets presented in 1991-92 were specifically used to implement a number of far reaching policies with long term impact on the nation's economy. They also signified a whole-hearted vote in favour of fiscal discipline and deficit reduction, an uncommon feature again, as far as budget exercises in recent times are concerned.

Reduction of fiscal deficit

The Government chose fiscal deficit reduction as the topmost item of priority in its agenda on fiscal reforms. Fiscal deficits and budgetary deficits have been a familiar weakness of India's Public Finance for several years now. In more recent years, the problem got very much compounded. The crisis faced by the country on the fiscal front by '91-92, was indeed serious. The fiscal deficit had mounted to more than eight per cent of the GDP in 1990-91, as compared with six per cent at the beginning of the 1980s and four per cent in the mid 1970s. This deficit had to be basically met by borrowing. As a result, internal public debt of the Government had accumulated to about 55 per cent of the GDP by '90-91; and the burden of servicing the debt had become quite onerous. Interest payments alone formed four per cent of GDP and 20 per cent of the total expenditure of the central government. No wonder, deficit reduction figured as the prime item in the reform package.

Deficit reduction became important for yet another reason. Inflation control, the other priority item in the reform package, also depended heavily on deficit reduction. In other words, deficit reduction was to be the instrument for facilitating inflation control as well as for achieving the various macro economic adjustments that were required for putting the economy back on rail.

The new thrust at deficit reduction was characterised by two unique features : (i) a radical change in the very approach of the Government to deficit financing and (ii) target bound fiscal deficit control.

Over the years, India had embraced deficit financing as a strategy of public finance. Though aware of the pitfalls of this strategy, successive governments persisted with it, in view of the advantages it offered. However, as years rolled by, the limitations came to be felt more. The new Government thought it appropriate to reverse the very approach to deficit financing.

The Government brought down the fiscal deficit to 6.5 per cent of the GDP in '91-92 from 8.5 per cent of the GDP in the previous year and further down to 5 per cent in the '92-93 budget. In absolute terms, the fiscal deficit was brought down to Rs 37,792 crore in '91-92 from the previous year's level of Rs 44,650 crore and further down to Rs 34,408 crore in '92-93; the budget deficit was brought down from Rs 11,347 crore in '90-91 to Rs 7032 crore in '91-92 and further down to Rs 5,389 crore in '92-93; and the revenue deficit was brought down from Rs 18,562 crore in'90-91 to Rs 17,081 crore in '91-92 and further down to Rs 13,882 crore in '92-93.

The 1993-94 budget was one better in this regard, compared with the 1992-93 and 1991-92 budgets. Revenue deficit, budget deficit and fiscal deficit were contained at Rs 17,630 crore, Rs 4,314 crore and Rs 36,959 crore respectively in the 1993-94 budget. Even though in absolute terms, the fiscal deficit in 1993-94 was slightly higher than that of 1992-93, expressed as a percentage of GDP, it amounted to only 4.5 per cent, while the corresponding position in 1992-93 was 5 per cent. Budgetary deficit was pegged down at the very modest level of Rs 4,314 crore in 1993-94 budget. Actually, this meant that the budgetary deficit had been slashed down to just Rs 333 crore on the basis of existing taxation. It was only due to the hefty cuts in indirect taxes extended in the year, that budgetary deficit could not be kept at the low level of Rs 333 crore. The Government rightly contended that it could have kept the fiscal deficit between 3.5 and 4 per cent in 1993-94 but for its keenness to stimulate economic growth by tax cuts, shedding Government's existing revenues.

Moreover, in order to ensure that fiscal discipline is maintained all through the year, the Government set quarterly and monthly targets for deficit reduction and started a tight system of monitoring.

In controlling fiscal deficit, the Government chose to reduce the expenditure rather than mobilise additional income through fresh taxes. This strategy was adopted in order to keep inflation under check. And the expenditure reduction was sought to be achieved by cutting the capital/plan expenditure, rather than the revenue expenditure of the Government.

Fiscal deficit reduction acquired such a great importance in the reform regime that a line of thinking emerged at the policy making level that there is need for a law restricting the extent to which the Government can run a deficit and the extent to which the Government can borrow overall with a sub-ceiling on borrowing from the Reserve Bank.

Reduction of Government expenditure

The Government took the unpalatable decision to effect a sizeable reduction in its expenditure during '91-92 and '92-93. As already mentioned, the cut was effected on the capital/plan account rather than on revenue account. The reason for adopting this route was quite simple; the Government just could not effect a cut on its revenue expenditure. The Government was however quite serious about curtailing its total expenditure. In fact, it limited its expenditure growth in 1992-93 to less than 5 per cent over the previous year. The significance of this can be appreciated from the fact that the growth in Government expenditure in 1991-92 over the previous year had been as high as 14.2 per cent. The importance accorded for inflation control in the '91-92 and '92-93 budgets also strengthened the expenditure reduction move. As a consequence, the Government's role as a buyer was shrinking. In a country like India, if the Government as the single largest buyer trims down its purchase, it will set off a chain reaction throughout the economy. Fully aware of such a reaction, especially of the ill effects it will have on industrial production, Government effected a cut in its expenditure. It seemed that a long term trend had been initiated, by which the level of Government spending in India and the role of Government as a buyer would shrink continuously.

The Government also explored the possibilities of reducing its unproductive revenue expenditure. It constituted an austerity committee to give recommendations on pruning the unproductive expenditure of the Government and simultaneously initiated certain other steps to restructure the bureaucracy and trim the Government machinery. It decided not to fill up vacancies that arose in non priority areas.

In addition to the above steps the Government also tried to reduce its expenditure by effecting cuts in its grants and transfers to states and PSUs.

Phasing out subsidies and budgetary support to PSUs

Phasing out subsidies of various kinds and budgetary support to PSUs formed another important part of the fiscal reforms. This is being dealt with in detail in the chapter on Structural Adjustment (Chapter 5).

Savings policy

As part of the fiscal reform package, the Government also introduced new measures for encouraging savings and channelising it into risk taking types of investments. In the earlier era, the Government used taxation as the means for capital formation. In the new era, the capital markets have come of age and the people have understood the importance of savings. More importantly, they have understood the merit of channelising the savings into the capital markets. In other words, people's capitalism has already taken roots in the country. The Government no longer needs to rely on taxation for capital formation. Nor does it need to provide artificial props for channelising people's savings into the capital markets. This is being dealt with in greater detail in the sections on tax reforms and capital market reforms that follow.

Tax reforms

Reform of the tax system was an integral part of the fiscal reforms of the new regime. And the reforms were carried out through the budgets of '91-92 and '92-93.

As regards direct tax system, the reforms were as follows:

Income tax rates made moderate; maximum tax rate limited to 40 per cent; narrower spread between the entry point and maximum slab; avoiding too many slabs in between; raising of IT exemption limit; minimising concessions and exemptions; strengthening of tax compliance; clubbing of minor children's income; introduction of presumptive tax; modification in the treatment of capital gains tax and wealth tax; exempting shares and financial assets from wealth tax; and simplification of the tax system.

The reforms were designed to provide the direct tax structure, a reasonable measure of stability. The recommendations of the Chelliah Committee on tax structure reform were partly implemented through these measures. Expansion of the tax base, reduction of the tax shelters, lowering of tax rates, simplification of the tax structure and modernisation of the tax administration were the main general recommendations of the Committee.

An indication was also given by the Government that in the next couple of years corporate taxes would be brought down. The Chelliah Committee had recommended a phased reduction of corporate tax rate from 51.75 per cent to 45 per cent by '93-94 and to 40 per cent by '94-95. It had also recommended bringing farm income under the tax net.

The 1993-94 budget however, did not bring down the direct taxes—corporate or personal. Fiscal compulsions obviously did not permit the Government to reduce them during the year. It persisted with the previous year's levels in this regard, except for some very minor concessions. The Government clarified that it was committed to reducing the corporate tax in the years to come.

The tax reforms were also designed to promote savings. The logic was that India's capital markets have become reasonably mature and no artificial props or concessions are required from now on for savings. If there is money in the hands of people, they know how best to save; and lowering of tax rates will leave more money in their hands. Savings will flow automatically into risk taking type of investments.

The above logic too was in tune with the Chelliah Committee's thinking. According to the Committee, concessions artificially divert savings to particular channels and reduce the tax liability of some individuals as against others. The concessions also force taxpayers to take uneconomic decisions and change the flow of resources. It would be a wiser move to reduce overall tax rates, withdrawing the concessions.

As regards the indirect tax system, the 1991-92 and 1992-93 budgets concentrated on reduction in import duties including duty on import of capital goods. And it was through the '93-94 budget that the Government carried out in a big way, the indirect tax reforms, covering both customs and excise duties. This budget not only restructured the indirect taxes, but also brought about a substantial general reduction in the tax levels. A total amount of Rs 4,522 crore was sacrificed by the Government in the form of customs and exise tax cuts; Rs 3,273 crore was shed out of customs duties and Rs 1,249 crore out of excise duties. The duty cuts have also been well spread out over a large variety of products, so that the effect will be felt across the board. Consumer durables such as entertainment electronics, white goods, automobiles including passenger cars, LCVs, HCVs, and two wheelers and a large number of items in consumer softs including soaps and detergents, toiletries, tea and textiles have all been covered by the restructure of the indirect tax system.

It was clear that progressive reduction in customs and excise duties will be part of the future trend. As regards customs tariffs, an indication was given by the Government to the effect that in three or four years time, the tariff rates would be brought in line with international levels. To quote the finance minister, "The Indian industry has been given adequate notice of the tariff reduction, it has come of age and I believe, it can face international competition. Indian industry could not remain an island cut off from the rest of the world." As regards excise duties, the Chelliah Committee had recommended that the maximum excise duty should not exceed 50 per cent with few exceptions like cigarettes. Indications are that the Government may implement the recommendation over a period of time. The Government also prepared the ground for moving towards full-fledged Value Added Tax (VAT) and suggested a three-slab MODVAT system. It also proposed to broaden the base of indirect taxes by bringing in services under the tax net and reducing the scope for exemptions. Commodity and user specific exemptions and a review of the current tax sharing arrangements would also be undertaken. The Government however needed time for implementing these recommendations.

Containment of public debt

The Government realised that containing public debt was of utmost importance. The bulk of the fiscal struggle waged by the Government, year after year, had been caused by the mounting interest burden on public debt. Table 4.1 provides the details of the steep growth in the interest burden on public debt.

Table 4.1

Growth in interest burden on public debt — '84-85 to '92-93

Year	Interest burden(Rs Crore)
1984-85	5974
1985-86	7512
1986-87	9246
1987-88	11251
1988-89	14278
1989-90	17757
1990-91	21471
1991-92	27250
1992-93	32000

It can be seen from this table that the burden has risen by five and a half times in nine years, from Rs 5,974 crore in 1984-85 to Rs 32,000 crore in 1992-93.

To quote Dr. Raja Chelliah, "Traditional measures of cutting expenditure through economy measures are geared to gaining a temporary reprieve. As the underlying long term tendencies are not addressed, the crisis surfaces repeatedly." One of the major long term tendencies that Dr. Chelliah refers to is the rising interest payments.

The interest burden on Government debt could have been eased, had the Government got better return while investing the borrowed funds. But it was not possible, given the low net profitability of the public sector and concessional loans to state governments. Evidently, certain measures had to be adopted to reduce the stock of public debt. The RBI in its annual report for '91-92, cautioned that the upsurge in the Central Government's borrowing in the 1980s, the steady rise in coupon rates on Government securities and the compression of maturities of the loans have led to bunching of repayments and unlike in the past, repayments could by far outstrip fresh loan flotations in the foreseeable future. It suggested the reintroduction of a Consolidated Sinking Fund to redeem the public debt. It felt that the salutary system of redeeming the Government debt should not have been dispensed with. An early reintroduction of this system would in its view, go a long way towards establishing long term viability of Government borrowings.

More stringent proposals for containing public debt

The Government was now bent on taking decisive steps. Retirement of public debt became a subject of active consideration. Withdrawal of budgetary support to the public sector undertakings, and withdrawal of concessional loans and advances to state Governments were also actively pursued. These were aimed at enhancing the return on Government funds. The Government was also prepared to use the funds mobilised through public sector disinvestment for purchasing back its public debt. Though in '91-92 the proceeds of public sector disinvestment were used for financing Government expenditure and for reducing the fiscal deficits, the idea is now getting accepted by the Government that the proceeds from the sale of Government assets should be matched by a correspon-ding reduction in Government liability. The Government was even prepared to consider the sale of real estate owned by it for retiring a part of the public debt.

The Government was considering the possibility of bringing down the stock of public debt by Rs 25,000 crore over three years. That would result in a saving in interest of Rs 2,875 crore per year. In fact, the various measures of the Government that will be discussed in this chapter, had the ultimate purpose of putting an end to the profligacy of the central and state Governments and introducing financial discipline so that finally the Government's liabilities, especially the dependence on borrowings, is reduced. The stark reality has dawned on the Government that without liquidation of a substantial part of the existing stock of internal debt it would not be possible to eliminate the revenue deficit even within the next five years.

Containment of RBI credit to Government

As a part and parcel of the new thinking on fiscal reforms, a proposal also came up for introducing some kind of a ceiling on the net RBI credit made available to the Government. The Reserve Bank of India also suggested, in its Annual Report for 1991-92, that there ought to be a ceiling on the amount of net RBI credit made available to the Government of India.

The RBI had already taken steps denying overdrafts beyond one week to state Governments, as part of the measures to impart financial discipline at state level. It was in this context that proposals for introducing similar measures with respect to the credit made available to the centre, were coming up. The encouraging thinking on the subject in the circles of economists, as well as the RBI was that the RBI credit should take the form of only ways and means advances to the central Government upto an agreed level which is to be cleared at the end of each year. The Government was also accepting the fact that massive reliance of the centre on RBI credit was contributing to considerable monetary instability. The Government had already started exercising control on utilising RBI credit by fiscal adjustments as well as through activation of internal debt management instruments. In fact, its decision introducing a phased reduction of the statutory reserve ratios was an acceptance of the position to rely less and less on captive bank funds. And, the reduction in SLR and CRR announced by the Government had resulted in increased bank credit to industry, indirectly cutting the net RBI credit available to the central Government.

MONETARY REFORMS

During '91-92 and a major part of '92-93 the Government faced the unenviable task of meeting two diametrically opposite objectives through its monetary policy. On the one hand, it had to contain the overall liquidity in the economy and on the other it had to provide resources for reviving economic activity. The Government decided to stay with the priority of containing liquidity, unmindful of the adverse effect of such a policy on the other important objective of reviving the economy. The RBI categorically stated that its ultimate mission in the prevailing context, was to use the monetary policy at any cost, for controling inflation.

Monetary and credit policy was somewhat modified in '92-93. While formulating the monetary and credit policies for 1992-93, the Government still kept in mind the primacy of the objective of inflation control, but introduced measures to revive industrial and agricultural production. In particular, it brought down the minimum lending rate, from the high level of 20 per cent which was prescribed in October 1991, to 18 per cent in two stages. Early next year, it brought it down to 17 per cent and in July 1993 to 16 per cent.

Inflation control

The Government introduced a series of measures to contain the mounting inflation which had reached 17 per cent by August '91. Besides pursuit of tight money policy, reduction of fiscal deficits, reduction of Government expenditure, reduction of subsidies, reduction in budgetary support to public sector undertakings and reduction of transfers and assistance to states were the major routes employed for containing inflation. Since deficit financing and excess liquidity arising on account of it push up price pressures enormously, an attack on fiscal deficits was indirectly an attack on inflation. Coupled with this were the tight money policy, credit squeeze and high interest rates which served as a frontal attack on the galloping inflation.

The Government set specific and time bound targets in respect of inflation control. Inflation was targeted to be brought down to 9 per cent during '91-92. Though the Government could not achieve the target, (the actual for the year was 13 per cent) the new approach did result in a focused endeavour and the fact that a reduction of 4 percentage points was achieved compared to the peak of 17 per cent in August '91 was significant. The Government set a target of 8 per cent for '92-93 and effectively used the budgets of '91-92 and '92-93, which were truly path breaking endeavours, for controlling inflation. In fact, the Government was determined to carry on with its crusade over inflation over the longer term and set itself the objective of bringing it down to 3 per cent over a three year time frame.

Relentless pursuit of tight money policy ... stringent credit squeeze ... high interest rates...

A severe tight money policy was the result of the above perception. Besides inflation control, BoP management too necessitated the pursuit of such a policy. Not only was credit squeezed to the utmost, cost of credit was also hiked to the maximum. The bank rate was jacked up to 11 per cent and then to 12 per cent with upward modifications in deposit rates and lending rates. Industry was subjected to the combined travails of credit compression and interest rate hike. While interest rate hike affected the cost of credit directly, credit compression produced an indirect adverse effect on it. And industry was told that it was free to arrange its working capital requirements through different financial instruments, at higher interest rates.

Earlier, by May '91, the credit limits of industrial units had been pinned down to their actual peak borrowing in the previous three year period and penal interest was being charged by the banks when the units exceeded the limit. Cash margins for L/Cs were also made very stringent. While the regular interest, even for the most worthy borrowers, was 20.5 per cent, the penal interest ranged between 25 and 30 per cent.

Containment of broad money

The Government consciously chose to direct its monetary reforms at containment of broad money (M3) within reasonable limits. Though it could not achieve the goal to the desired measure, it prevented a run away expansion of M3. The growth rate of M3 has generally been in excess of 18 per cent during recent years, with 1990-91 as the only exception. During '91-92 the Government took a number of measures to cut down the excess liquidity and to prune demand. However, in spite of these measures, the stock of broad money grew by 18.5 per cent during that year. The Government continued its efforts at containing broad money during '92-93 as well.

India had agreed with the IMF that broad money growth would be kept below 10.5 per cent during '92-93. The IMF was not happy over the actual achievement in this regard in the previous year. During that year as stated already, broad money supply grew by 18.5 per cent. The agreed target was 13 per cent. The IMF wanted to fix the target at 6 per cent for '92-93 so as to compensate for the slippage of '91-92. Finally, 10.5 per cent was agreed to by India and the IMF. The actual growth as at end of September 1992 was however as high as 18.9 per cent, way above the target of 10.5 per cent for the full fiscal year 1992-93.

Gradual easing of credit squeeze and modification of SLR and CRR

Monetary policy finally started moving, albeit at a very slow pace, in the direction desired by the Government when inflation came under reasonable check by the middle of '92-93. The Government started slowly relaxing the tight money policy. Resources were freed up to an extent and increased flow of credit to different sectors of the economy was made possible. Though in industry's view, it was a case of too little coming too late, it served as an indication of Government's thinking. The Government loosened the screws on the credit squeeze further and also made a token cut in interest rate. It also decided to reduce SLR and CRR in a phased manner. This is being dealt with in detail in the section on banking sector reforms.

The Government was certainly hamstrung in its pursuit of monetary reforms in the immediate aftermath of the introduction of the new economic programme, in view of its overriding priority for inflation control. It had to bide its time for introducing many of the monetary measures which it desired to implement. And throughout '91-92 and for the most part of '92-93 tight money policy, credit squeeze and high interest rate formed an important part of the monetary policy of the Government.

BoP management

In the matter of BoP management, the new policies sought, as the immediate step, to provide the much needed first aid. The aim was to see off the crisis in the shortest possible time. It was to be followed by more substantive measures designed to stabilise the position in the medium term and put it on a strong footing in the long term. In other words, the policy consisted of a fire fighting component, a stabilisation component and a restructuring component.

The fire fighting component aimed at restoring India's credibility in the eyes of the world. Emergency measures such as pledging of gold held by the RBI for mobilising temporary liquidity abroad, were resorted to for achieving this aim. It helped the country to avert a default in international payments. The Government then took two major decisions (i) to devalue the rupee and (ii) to avail of a hefty loan from the IMF. These two decisions helped in improving instantly, India's credit rating in the international markets. In a way, the two decisions were interlinked.

The devaluation was intended to tackle the BoP problem by boosting India's exports by making Indian products more competitive in the world market, and by compressing India's imports by making them costlier in terms of domestic currency. The devaluation decision and the decision to go for the IMF loan together led to a quick salvaging of the situation; enough exchange flowed into the kitty; the capital flight was reversed ; and the confidence of the international community and the NRIs was fully restored. In addition, the country mobilised 2.5 billion dollars from the sale of special bonds denominated in foreign currencies and from an Amnesty scheme to encourage the repatriation of assets held abroad. As a result, the country could achieve a quick rebuilding of net foreign exchange reserves. The reserves rose in a short time, by over $3 billion, the equivalent of three months imports. The reversal of capital flight, in fact, was the result as well as the cause of the restoration of confidence in India.

Measures designed at medium and long term benefits included industrial and trade policy liberalisation, and macro economic adjustments and reforms, specifically aimed at bolstering the BoP position and reducing the exchange deficits. Of the various moves in this regard, inflation control deserves a special mention. Appreciating the close linkage of BoP position to internal inflation level, inflation control was accorded top priority in the new policy. Inflation control, in its turn, involved several other measures.

The Government had also by then, negotiated a $2.2 billion standby loan from the IMF, $900 million from the World Bank, and $1.25 billion from the Asian Development Bank. It also made it clear that it would take another medium-term structural adjustment loan from the IMF, after the economy had weathered the immediate crisis.

India's foreign exchange reserves rose to $6.4 billion by September 1992, though its own funds out of this amount was only $1.1 billion and the rest was made up of borrowing from different sources. India also brought down the current account deficit to $3 billion in 1991-92 as against $9 billion in 1990-91. Though the increase in exchange reserves was more due to import compression, inflow of loans and control of exchange deficit on current account than due to export earnings, it was a great relief to India. Though a lasting solution for the BoP problem had not been found, a good respite had been obtained by the Government in this regard. BoP no longer posed a crisis to the nation.

The restoration of further confidence, following up-front structural reforms and fiscal action in the next budget, which included politically difficult decisions like cuts in fertiliser subsidies and transfers to states, boosted up the BoP position further. By the beginning of 1992-93, the focus was shifting from short run adjustments and averting of external default to lowering of inflation and revival of the economy.

BANKING SECTOR REFORMS

In respect of the banking sector too, the Government wanted to implement a number of far reaching reforms. During the 25 years since nationalisation, the banking sector of India has turned out to be a particularly enfeebled component of the ailing economy of the country. The banks have not been able to function as commercial financial institutions, as they were subjected to excessive regulation and political interference. The capital structure of the banking system too has been woefully weak. The profitability has been weaker still. The quality of loan assets has also been poor. It was only natural that the Government wanted to carry out a thorough reform of the banking sector. It however needed expert advice for formulating the reform package. It therefore appointed an expert committee under the Chairmanship of M. Narasimham, former Governor of the RBI, to suggest the required line of reforms in the banking sector.

Narasimham Committee Report

The Narasimham Committee Report provided a wide range of recommendations for reforming the banking sector. It pinpointed in detail the maladies afflicting the banking sector and offered a number of suggestions for rectifying them. It would be interesting to see the exact thinking of the committee on the subject.

Maladies afflicting the banking sector

To quote from the report of the Narasimham committee,

> Despite the massive expansion of the banking services in the country, particularly after the nationalisation in 1969, there has been a noticeable trend of declining productivity and efficiency in the banking system, along with the continuing problem of low profitability.

> Directed investment, directed credit programmes, unnecessary duplication of infrastructure and overstaffing are some of the basic ills of the banking industry.

> In the case of directed investment and directed credit programmes, the interest income available to the banks was less than the market related rates or what they could have secured from alternate deployment of funds.

> The erosion of profitability of banks has also emanated from the side of expenditure, as a result of fast and massive expansion of branches many of which are unremunerative, especially in the rural areas, a considerable degree of overmanning, especially in the urban and metropolitan areas and inadequate progress in updating work technology. Both management weaknesses and trade union pressures have contributed to this. There have also been weaknesses in the internal organisational structure of banks such as insufficient delegation of authority, inadequate internal controls and deterioration in what is termed as 'housekeeping' — balancing of books and reconciliation of inter-branch and inter-bank entries.

Reforms suggested by Narasimham Committee and Government's programme of action

The Narasimham Committee recommended a number of reforms, which in its view would serve as remedies for these ills afflicting the banking sector. The major recommendations of the Committee are briefly analysed below.

Recasting the very objectives of the banking sector

The first major recommendation of the Committee related to the recasting of the very objectives of the banking sector. For more than two decades, 'social objectives' constituted the crux of the corporate mission of the banks, which in effect meant the extension of credit to borrowers in the priority sectors on a preferential and cheaper basis. The banks have also been required to cross subsidise this forced discharge of 'social responsibilities', setting off the losses they incurred on such lending against profits earned on more lucrative business. And their performance was being rated against these objectives.

The Committee felt that it should not be the business of the banks to fulfil such social objectives. The Committee instead felt that a commercially viable lending policy should become the objective of the banking sector. Credit should be made available only in respect of bankable schemes. It was the Committee's view that the pursuit of distributive justice should make use of the instrumentality of the fiscal rather than the credit system. Drawing particular attention to the cross subsidisation of priority sector lending and charging of higher interest rates to the other sectors, the Committee recommended elimination of such cross subsidisation from the objectives of the banking sector.

Phasing out priority sector lending/directed credit

As regards directed credit/priority sector lending, the Committee specifically recommended the phasing out of such lending. It noted that in any case there was no justification for continuing to force the banks to lend to the relatively better off borrowers on this basis. Priority sector lending/directed credit gobbles up as much as 40 per cent of the income generating activities of the banks.

Appreciating the practical difficulties involved in such a move and the fact that the phasing out would in any case take some time, the Committee suggested that in the meanwhile, the priority sector lending could be restricted to the really poor sections. Priority sector could be redefined to mean only the small and marginal farmers, the tiny industrial sector, small transport operators, village and cottage industries, rural artisans and other similar weaker sections of society. Additionally, and importantly, the Committee said that the quantum of funds earmarked for the purpose should be slashed to 10 per cent of the aggregate credit.

De-regulation of deposit interest rates

While many of the reforms planned in the banking sector remained on paper for a considerable length of time, a few ideas went through the implementation stage quickly. One move in this category was the loosening up on the deposit interest rates offered by the banks. For the past several years, under the regimented structure, all banks in India offered the same interest rates for deposits. The system had been in vogue for so many years that both the banks and the depositors had almost forgotten that it was possible for the acceptors of deposits to show some distinctiveness in rates of interest paid for the deposits.

In the new regime, the RBI thought it fit to permit the banks to make distinctive offers on deposits within defined parameters and limits. The stipulations were: the maximum interest rate should not exceed 13 per cent; there should be a minimum differential of quarter per cent interest between one block of maturity and the other and as a policy, there must be a minimum of three blocks of maturities for fixed deposits. That the banks did not stretch themselves to the full in experimenting with the new-found flexibility is a different matter. The relevant point is that a new flexibility was offered by the RBI to the banking system. Evidently, a pro-active banking role was getting initiated.

The RBI also took steps to improve the spreads available to the banks, albeit in a small way to start with. Since profitability of banks very much depends on the spread that they enjoy between lending and deposit rates, improving the spread will amount to a significant and crucial reform in the banking sector. The RBI not only deregulated the interest rates but also reduced the multiplicity of interest rates.

Lowering of SLR and containment of Government's dependence on Bank funds

The excessive dependence of the Government on bank funds and the requirement relating to the Statutory Liquidity Ratio (SLR) has been another major factor that contributed to the present state of the banking sector. The SLR was as high as 38.5 per cent. This meant that a massive part of the bank resources was being utilised to finance the Government/ Public sector at extremely low rates of interest. In other words, the SLR prescription was one major factor that eroded the profitability of the banks. The Narasimham Committee recommended that SLR could be brought down to a level of 25 per cent. The Committee also recommended that SLR should be used only as a prudential requirement and not as a source of low-cost, available-on-tap finance for the Government/Public sector.

The Government accepted the recommendation and as a first step in implementing it, reduced the SLR on incremental domestic liabilities of the commercial banks from 38.5 per cent to 30 per cent with effect from 1992-93. Besides, in the credit policy for the 1992-93 busy season, the Government reduced the SLR from 38.5 per cent to 37.5 per cent. It also decided that the SLR will be gradually reduced to 25 per cent.

The above decisions were in line with the objective of reduction of fiscal deficit. Obviously, Government's need to borrow from the commercial banks will get reduced with a reduction in fiscal deficit. And for the banks, it will release funds to expand credit to agriculture and industry.

The Government also initiated steps to develop an active market for Government securities which would make it less dependent on statutory borrowing from the banks in future.

Adherence to healthy norms on capital adequacy, income recognition and provision for bad debts

The Narasimham Committee also recommended that proper norms must be formulated on capital adequacy, income recognition and provision for bad debts and that the banks must invariably adhere to the norms. This was especially so for banks engaged in international operations, as they had to conform to international practices. The Committee highlighted the fact that the banking sector of India cannot hope to achieve international credibility without achieving international norms. Even in the case of banks which may not be engaged in international business, the stipulations under the proposed reforms would necessitate the adoption of new norms. For example, with the shift to more transparent accounting, there would be no escape from an expansion in the capital of the banks.

Accepting the recommendation, the RBI prescribed new norms relating to capital adequacy, income recognition and provision for bad debts. The banks however felt that the new norms were quite stringent. In their view, strict implementation of the norms could push many of them into the red. Clearly, the changeover was going to be a painful process for the Indian banking sector, used as they were in the past, to an entirely different culture.

The apprehension that was uppermost in the minds of the banks related to the high degree of capital requirement implied in such a reform and the ways and means of raising such capital.

*With the new norms, massive inflow of fresh
capital became inescapable*

Evidently, the new norms meant a massive inflow of fresh capital into the banks. According to finance ministry estimates, resources to the tune of Rs 14,000 crore would be needed over the next few years to help the banks follow the new norms. Though theoretically, there were two options before the Government for raising the resources—to go to the capital market and raise the amount by issue of fresh equity or to finance it from its budgetary resources—in practice, it had only Hobson's choice: it could only direct the banks to go to the capital market with the attendant implication of partial privatisation of the banks. Resources of such magnitude were simply not available with the Government. The chief executives of public sector banks appreciated the reality and favoured mobilising funds from the market. They also suggested that part of the equity could be offered to the employees, which would not only support the effort at mobilisation of capital but also instil a greater sense of participation in the employees.

Way cleared for partial privatisation of public sector banks

By mid '92, the Government started seriously considering the idea of disinvesting a portion of its equity in public sector banks to raise resources for the banking sector. The Government also considered issue of fresh equity so as to enlarge the equity capital base of the banks. Both these moves would have the effect of partially privatising the banks. The

Government however felt that in case of disinvestment of equity, as well as enlargement of the equity base through issue of fresh equity, the control over the banks should still remain with the Government. This would mean that Government intended to limit the private share to a maximum of 49 per cent of the total equity of the banks. The significant point is that a proposal for a major change was on the anvil.

By February '93, the thinking crystallised and the decision was announced. The Government allowed the nationalised banks to go to the capital market and disinvest Government equity in them. Besides disinvesting existing Government equity, the banks were also permitted to raise the capital required by them by floating fresh equity or through other instruments. And the private equity can go up to 49 per cent of the total paid up equity. It is clear that the move is a step in the direction of denationalisation of the banks. The Banks will not be the same any longer.

Way cleared for new private sector banks

By the beginning of '93, the stage for starting new Private Sector Banks in the country was also set, with the RBI releasing its guidelines on the matter. As mentioned already, the importance of this move can be correctly understood if one noted that for the past quarter century, since the bank nationalisation days, not a single licence has been issued for a private player to start a bank in the country.

The RBI guidelines stipulated the following:

The banks to be started must have an equity base (paid up equity) of Rs 100 crore at the minimum.

They will have to adhere to the prescribed capital adequacy norm from the very beginning—eight per cent of risk weighted assets.

They will have to follow the RBI rules on all aspects of credit management including priority sector advances. There can be a relaxation relating to credit to priority sectors in the initial stages, in order to ensure a reasonable level of profitability.

They will have to lay down their loan policy within the overall policy guidelines of RBI.

They should be registered as a public limited company under the Companies Act, 1956, and be governed by the provisions of the Reserve Bank of India Act, 1934, the Banking Regulation Act, 1949, and other relevant statutes with regard to their management set-up, liquidity requirements and the scope of their activities.

To prevent domination of particular interest groups, no shareholder would be allowed to have more than one per cent of the voting rights.

Limits would be set for "cross advances" to related companies and associates. Exposure limits would also be set for any single loan account.

Evidently, the new policy to license private sector players to set up banks will exercise a significant impact on the competitive character of the banking industry. In fact, the RBI note on the subject speaks of the 'increasing recognition of the need to introduce greater competition which can lead to higher productivity' as the context for allowing the setting up of new banks in the private sector.

ICICI, UTI and HDFC permitted to set up new banks

By July '93, the RBI gave final approval to ICICI, UTI and HDFC for setting up fresh banks. The ICICI bank will have an initial paid up capital of Rs 100 crore which will be fully contributed by ICICI. It will go for public issue shortly after its operations stabilised. Its headquarters will be Baroda. The bank being set up by the UTI will also initially have a paid up capital of Rs 100 crore. It will, after a year, go in for a public issue of Rs 150 crore. It will reduce its holding over a period of three years. The bank's objectives are to create a 'financial market' catering to diverse needs of the clientele. The proposed bank by HDFC will have an initial paid up capital of Rs 300 crore. The share will be widely held among HDFC, and the public. It will provide the full range of banking service and will be fully computerised from the beginning.

The new banks will set up branches in rural, semi-urban and urban areas, fulfil the requirements of priority sector credit and meet the capital adequacy norm of eight per cent of the risk weighted assets from the beginning. UTI is scouting for reputed foreign partners to start divisions in foreign exchange, money markets, equities, merchant banking, custodial services and investment banking. ICICI has already set up an investment bank along with J.P. Morgan of the United States. The new banks will be listed on the stock exchanges and would have a widely spread out shareholding. This will make them accountable to the shareholders. Till end May 1993, the RBI has received 123 requests from public limited companies, trusts, associations, firms and individuals for permission to start new banks. The new generation of private banks is expected to usher in an era of automated and financially strong banks which could offer world class financial services. The new banks can be set up without any of the problems that existing banks face, like overstaffing, frequent demands for wage hikes and resistance to computerisation. The new banks will open in a new liberal regime where profit is no longer a dirty word.

World Bank loan to part finance the banking reforms

The Government also felt that the World Bank could be approached for a structural adjustment loan (SAL) to help implement the banking reforms.

It completed the preliminary work in this regard by mid 1992 and started formal negotiations with the Bank. On its part, the World Bank had promptly sounded the possible donor countries for contributions to the SAL.

Transparent accounting and fair disclosures

The Narasimham Committee had also felt that greater transparency in the operations should be an objective of the banks. At present, the accounting system does not provide a clear picture of how funds have been lent, what is the extent of non-performing assets and whether adequate provision had been made against bad, doubtful and sticky advances. It is estimated that the bad and doubtful debts of Indian banks average 15 per cent of all advances, four times the international norm, adding up to Rs 22,000 crore today.

Over the years, the banking sector of India had kept its entire operations shrouded in secrecy. Improper accounting practices and absence of proper disclosures were the order of the day. In the view of the Narasimham Committee, publication of balance sheets in a transparent manner, stoppage of the practice of concealing losses and observance of disclosure norms should be strictly enforced under the reform package. The Committee also underscored the need for effective supervision and vigilance. It proposed the setting up of an independent agency for this purpose, under the aegis of the Reserve Bank of India. The Committee also stressed the importance of updating of work technology and computerisation of operations.

Tackling the sizeable non performing assets

Over the years, there has also been an unchecked rise in the non-performing assets of the banks. As per RBI report on the trends and progress in the banking sector, the aggregate domestic non-performing assets of all public sector banks accounted for 14.46 per cent of their total domestic advances during 1991-92. Over Rs 10,000 crore got locked up in advances to sick units; and the repayment rate of loans in respect of agriculture and small industries was below 60 per cent. The loans and advances thus became non performing assets. The recovery of loans and advances to different classes of borrowers had not been attempted assiduously and consequently, profitability of the banks was getting seriously affected. The Narasimham Committee suggested that bad and doubtful debts be segregated and special efforts be made for examining how these locked up funds can be recovered.

Restructure of organisation, operations and systems

The Narasimham Committee also proposed to strengthen the structure of the banking system by cordoning off from each other, its four main spheres of activity, namely, international banking, national banking, local banking and rural banking. This may help check open-ended cross-subsidisation and usher in a system in which no one sphere need feed the other in order to survive. Merger and amalgamation of banks was the other major proposal of the Committee in the mattter of restructure. In the Committee's view, the expenditure side had contributed sizeably to the erosion of profitability of the banks, largely on account of unremunerative and haphazard expansion of branches, especially in the rural areas, and any restructure of the banks should take into account this reality. There was also considerable degree of over-manning, especially in the urban and metropolitan centres. Inadequate progress in updating the work technology aggravated the situation. Both, management weakness and trade union pressures, have contributed to this situation. In the Committee's view, a meaningful merger and amalgamation of the banks would reduce the total number of such institutions and more importantly, do away with the duplication and overlapping of rural operations which do not yield much revenue. The Committee recommended a slowdown in the pace of branch expansion, particularly in respect of the forced opening of branches at centres of doubtful promise. Expenditure could be contained through such a restructure.

Creation of an Assets Reconstruction Fund

The Narasimham Committee also recommended that banks be directed to more adequately make provision for sub-standard, bad and doubtful loans and that high-value, bad and doubtful accounts be taken over from banks, at an independently estimated discount, by an Assets Reconstruction Fund (ARF). The refreshing aspect about the ARF proposal is the suggestion that the discounts on transferred accounts be 'independently evaluated'. If this suggestion is implemented, at least the ignorance about the magnitude of bad and doubtful debts would be exposed.

The banks will have to be provided a subordinated loan by the Government to finance the write off represented by the extent of the discount at which the ARF takes over the bad debts. Securitisation of debts by the ARF will shift the load from banks. The Government will then have to reclaim the debts by providing funds for the ARF. The financially well off banks may not need the ARF to clear bad debts; the others may have to take recourse to it.

Banking reforms are bound to take place, though the pace may be slow

The Government is likely to implement most of the recommendations of the Narasimham Committee. Now, only a beginning has been made. As mentioned earlier, the Government is considering disinvestment of a portion of its equity in public sector banks to raise the resources required for the banking sector. Resource mobilisation has become inescapable to enable the banks to comply with the new norms on capital adequacy and bad loan provisions. Banks having an inadequate capital base and a bad loan portfolio might not have much scope for operation in the future. Thus, the bank managements are compelled to streamline their funct-ioning. In short, the Government is all geared up to see that this crucial sector of the economy is overhauled and strengthened to function as typically commercial institutions. The dependence of the central and state governments on the banking system for their requirements of funds will also get reduced and the banks would mainly function as bankers to industry and commerce of the country rather than bankers to the Government.

The Government's intention is very clear; it wants to create a competitive, efficient and modern banking system which could effectively serve the needs of the economy.

CAPITAL MARKET REFORMS

As a part of the economic reforms, the Government introduced several measures towards liberalising the capital market of India. In addition, it also gave a big boost to the market through its savings and investment policy and taxation policy. Encouraging the flow of savings into the stock markets and therefrom to industry was one main aim of the new policy of the Government. Industry in search of capital and investors in search of investment avenues were put face to face. The Government gave up its role of mobilising capital and protecting investors and left the investors to decide for themselves.

And the new initiatives did produce quick and welcome result—an increased flow of money to industry from the investing public via the capital market. The Government felt that the stock markets had attained reasonable maturity and it was time to give it the kind of freedom it was clamouring for, for the past few years.

Liberalisation of capital markets

The Government liberalised the capital market of India through a series of new measures. The measures in fact changed the very character of the market. The important ones among them are listed below.

Making the Securities and Exchange Board of India (SEBI) a statutory body. The Board is now vested with powers to protect the interests of   investors and to promote the development of the capital market and to regulate the working of stock exchanges.

Abolition of the institution of the Controller of Capital Issues (CCI), free pricing of equity shares for public as well as rights issues, liberalisation of bonus issues and freedom to raise equity capital from abroad.

Permission to private and joint sectors to operate mutual funds.

Raising of the ceiling on the acquisition of shares/debentures of Indian companies by non-resident Indians (NRIs) and overseas corporate bodies (OCBs) from 5 to 24 per cent under the portfolio investment scheme.

Directive to the stock exchanges to ensure greater transparency in transactions for the benefit of the investing public and stricter regulation of trading in specified shares, timely settlement of transactions and broad-basing the governing bodies of stock exchanges.

Introduction of a scheme of registration of sub-brokers, as a measure of investor protection.

Amendment of clause 41 of the listing agreement to provide for greater disclosure of financial information on a half-yearly basis by the listed companies.

Direction to the major stock exchanges to work out a scheme of market makers in the exchanges to improve the liquidity of listed shares.

New guidelines on Employees' Stock Option Scheme in order to restrict the maximum number of shares that can be allotted to an employee at 500 shares of Rs 10 each or 50 shares of Rs 100 each.

Removal of all restrictions on interest rates on debentures and public sector bonds other than tax-free bonds. Interest rates on such instruments will from now on be governed by the market forces.

Revision of the format of the prospectus in respect of public issues. (Among the disclosures, the companies are now required to highlight the risk factors of the projects in the prospectus)

New guidelines on large issues (Rs 500 crore or above). Proceeds of such issues, till deployment, can be invested in fixed deposits with cooperative/nationalised banks, UTI, financial institutions and public sector undertakings, other than in public sector bonds

Revised guidelines on good and bad delivery of securities in stock exchanges so as to improve and simplify the operation of stock exchanges.

Introduction of a new financial instrument, Stockinvest, to be used by the investors as application money for new capital issues.

Permitting foreign investors to play in the Indian stock markets.

Boosting capital market by channelising savings into productive and risk taking investments

While formulating its '92-93 budget the Government heavily relied on the premise that old mechanisms of promoting savings through tax concessions have outlived their utility in the current Indian economic scenario and a new approach for channelising savings into more productive and more risk taking type of investments was called for. Keeping this requirement in view, the Government abolished concessions like 80 L, 80 CCA and 80 CCB. It recognised that the Indian economy had reached a stage where reasonable tax rates would be the one single influence on the way people would use their income. The '92-93 budget lowered the rates of tax so that people could decide what to do with their income. It went by the assumption that the people of India no longer needed any artificial props for savings. The Government recalled that way back in the sixties, when the Unit Trust of India (UTI) was set up, the concept of savings through units was new and it was necessary to induce people to save through units. By '92-93 the situation was quite different; there were 11 public sector mutual funds in the country including the UTI. And with its new policy, the Government had also cleared the way for competition from the private sector mutual funds. This was bound to have a major and positive impact on the stock markets of the country and in channelising the savings of people into the stock markets via the mutual funds. With the lowering of tax rates, a greater part of the incomes of people was becoming available for saving in a manner of their choice. Combined with this situation, if instruments which would encourage risk taking were devised, the objective of channelising savings into these productive and risk taking types of investments could be achieved easily. This in fact was the main logic of the '92-93 budget. By reducing tax rates, by liberalising the provisions relating to capital gains tax, and by exempting investments in productive instruments from wealth tax, the Government sought to create the climate that was necessary for savings to flow into risk accepting investments. The Finance Minister in fact argued strongly in his budget speech that the time had come for India to reward the entrepreneurial spirit of Indians.

In stimulating the capital market the Government had one more aim. It wanted to wean industry away from artificial props so far provided by the Government. In fact the '92-93 budget refrained from offering any artificial props for industrial production. Instead, it chose to revitalise the capital market. Moves such as freeing the capital market from the controller of capital issues, and granting of freedom of pricing of shares to the firms were designed to make industry depend more and more on the capital market for its resources.

Opening up of Indian capital markets to Foreign Institutional Investors (FIIs)

Opening up of the Indian capital markets to the Foreign Institutional Investors (FIIs) was another bold and important move in capital market reforms. The 18-point scheme in this regard formulated by September '92 not only permitted Foreign Institutional Investors (FIIs), including pension and mutual funds, to make investments in Indian capital market, but also provided them a package of incentives, including tax concessions. The salient features of the scheme are listed below:

> FIIs such as pension funds, mutual funds, investment trusts, asset management companies, nominee companies and incorporated/

institutional portfolio managers or their power of attorney holders are the ones permitted to invest in India under the scheme.

The FIIs will be allowed to invest in all the securities traded on the primary and secondary market.

No restriction on the volume of investment—minimum or maximum—for the purpose of entry of FIIs in the primary/secondary market.

No lock-in period prescribed for such investments.

The FIIs will be allowed to collectively hold a maximum of 24 per cent of the issued share capital in any one company. The maximum holding of any single FII in any company shall be five per cent of the total issued capital. The RBI will monitor the limits.

Portfolio investments in primary or secondary markets would be subject to the ceiling of 24 per cent of issued share capital for the total holdings of all registered FIIs in any one company.

A concessional tax regime of a flat tax rate of 20 per cent on dividend and interest income earned from such investment.

The tax rate on long-term capital gains (one year or more) will be 10 per cent.

RBI's general permission under FERA would enable the registered FII to buy, sell and realise capital gains on investments made through initial corpus remitted to India, subscribe or renounce rights offerings of shares, invest on all recognised stock exchanges through a designated bank branch, and to appoint a domestic custodian for custody of investments held.

Open foreign currency accounts in different foreign currencies, if it is so required by FII for its operational purposes.

Open a special non-resident rupee account to which could be credited all receipts from the capital inflows, sale proceeds of shares, dividends and interests.

Transfer sums from the foreign currency accounts to the rupee account and vice-versa, at the market rates of exchange.

Make investments in the securities in India out of the balances in the rupee account.

Transfer repatriable (after tax) proceeds from the rupee account to the foreign currency accounts.

The FIIs will have to get registered with the Securities and Exchange Board of India (SEBI) and the Reserve Bank of India.

The liberalisation and reform programme entered a significant phase with the announcement of guidelines for foreign investment in Indian stock markets. This is likely to be reinforced in the near future with permission to foreign brokers to operate in the Indian market.

By the beginning of 1993, investments by FIIs in Indian stock markets had become a reality. At least a couple of FIIs had put in their money in some Indian scrips by then. Of course, these were in the nature of forays or trials. The FIIs were trying to understand the settlement procedures, custodial services, regulation, brokers services, stock exchange rules and systems. By July 1993, the number of FIIs registered with SEBI and RBI had swelled to 55.

Private mutual funds

The removal of entry barriers to private mutual funds and PMS is an equally important reform in the financial sector. Following the issue of guidelines by the Union Finance Ministry, many non-banking finance companies and banks in the private sector had submitted their applications for approval by SEBI to promote asset management companies and mutual funds. By the beginning of '93 SEBI gave 'in principle' clearance to six private mutual funds including 20th Century Finance Corporation, ICICI, Tata Sons, Creditcapital Finance Corporation, Ceat Financial Services and Apple Industries. Many more players may soon join the fray and operate mutual funds in the private sector in the coming years. 20th Century has already announced that it would be launching two funds of Rs 50 crore each out of which, one fund would be open-ended and the other close-ended. Creditcapital Asset Management Limited would have a technical and training tie-up with Lazard Investors which manages funds to the tune of $30 billion worldwide.

Temporary setback to capital market reforms
on account of the stock scam

When the Government was half way through with the capital market reforms, the stock market of the country got messed up with the scam of '92. Had it been a simple fraud relating to the stock and securities market, a reference to it in a treatise like this would not at all have been necessary. Since the scam has produced deep adverse impact on the functioning of stock markets and has put the clock back on the entire process of reform, it is essential to make a reference to it in this work.

The scam arose basically on account of the gross disregard of rules, regulations and guidelines by the banks, Indian as well as foreign. Banks got involved in unconventional means of improving their profitability which, in the absence of effective control mechanism led to diversion of bank funds into the stock market and to further manipulation and misappropriation.

The scam did affect, albeit in the short term, the credibility of India's stock markets. Morgan Stanley, one of the world's biggest investment bankers, and the fund manager of the India Magnum Fund said in one of its memorandum, "...the scandal has generated investor anxiety about India. Interest in India has ground to a halt as investors are questioning the stability of Indian stock markets and the integrity of the participants in it. The overall uncertainty of the future of the Indian stock markets is reflected by the fact that the India Growth Fund has plummeted by 40 per cent since its pre-scandal peak on April 1, 1992."

By causing a severe setback to the capital market, the scam also made it difficult for the Central and State Governments, public sector units and Indian entrepreneurs to mobilise the resources required for executing their schemes. There is no doubt however that the reform package in respect of the financial sector, especially the banking sector and the stock market sector was held up because of the scam. Having invited the people to take a constructive attitude to the mobilisation of capital by investing funds in the share market and designing incentives for it as part of the economic reforms, the process necessarily had to be carried further. The Government however realised, after the first package of reforms of the capital markets, that the markets were really not mature enough for a sudden surge of total independence and that some regulations were still necessary towards investor protection. In a document issued around this time on the Asian Investment Strategy, the well-known financial consultant Merrill Lynch had commented on the Indian capital markets, as follows:

"The longer-term story about India and its economic reforms remains intact for the time being. However, it almost goes without saying that the Government has its work cut out to strengthen the regulatory framework of the equity market as well as other securities markets. This should be especially important if India hopes to attract any foreign capital to its market ... Much will depend on how quickly and effectively the Government acts to strengthen the regulatory framework. Any hint that the reforms are inadequate could see foreign investors giving India a miss for some time to come."

Not surprisingly many of the subsequent moves of the Government concerning the capital market, had as a cardinal element investor protection and fair market transactions. The Government was determined to ensure that the confidence of investors, Indian and foreign, in India's financial institutions is restored. And it kept an ambitious agenda for banking and stock market reforms. The Government reiterated that its objective is the creation of a vibrant and internationally competitive financial system.

5

Structural Adjustment

Presenting a synopsis of the new economic policy in the opening chapter of this book, we had mentioned that structural adjustments stood as a class apart, from all other reform measures. For, compared to the liberalisation and reform measures, structural adjustment is invariably a far more difficult game. It was also a novel game for India. It amounted to a drastic reversal of past policies and a radical route change for the economy. It was with full awareness of this fact that the Government decided to implement the structural adjustment programme (SAP). The Government in fact had no choice but to implement the programme, for, structural adjustment constituted the core of the new economic policies and without it the whole exercise would have been futile.

The structural adjustment initiated by the Government consisted of a wide range of measures. We shall discuss them under the following heads:

(i) Phasing out of subsidies and introduction of market driven price environment.

(ii) Pruning of Government establishment and reduction of expenditure on staff.

(iii) Restructure of Public Sector including disinvestment of Government equity in the PSUs.

(iv) Exit policy for industry.

We shall narrate the various moves taken by the Government in each of these spheres and explain the economic and other implications of each of these moves.

PHASING OUT OF SUBSIDIES AND INTRODUCTION OF MARKET DRIVEN PRICE ENVIRONMENT

Reduction of subsidies and progressive introduction of a market driven price environment for the products that were hitherto under the purview of administered pricing was the first programme of adjustments launched by the Government in the wake of the NEP. It was also perhaps the most difficult of all the adjustment exercises attempted by the Government.

The Government came round to the view that prices that are kept down by subsidies favour the present at the expense of the future. Everyone including the poor suffers on account of it in the long run. Subsidies are a drain on the public exchequer and lead to undesirable fiscal deficits. They also result in diversion of money that could be utilised for creating new projects.

Over the years, subsidies had become a Frankenstein in the Indian economy. Traditionally, food subsidy, fertiliser subsidy and export subsidy have constituted the main chunk of Central Government's subsidies. These three put together constituted 87 per cent of the total Central Government subsidy. In absolute terms, it amounted to Rs 14,000 crore, in '90-91, food accounting for Rs 5,000 crore, fertiliser Rs 6,000 crore, and export Rs 3,000 crore. In recent years, petro products have also been accounting for an appreciable share of the total subsidy.

Under the terms of its '91-92 agreement with the IMF by which it secured a $2.2 billion loan to help the country implement its economic reform programme, the Government had promised to slash its subsidies as a part of SAP. The specific understanding was that through a package of measures, overall subsidy would be brought down to a level of 1.1 per cent of GDP in '92-93 from 1.6 per cent in '91-92.

Export subsidy eliminated at one stroke

With its commitment to the SAP, the Government made a frontal attack on the various subsidies that were being doled out by it to the different sectors/sections. Right at the beginning, in a single stroke, the Government eliminated the export subsidy, by abolishing the CCS. The devaluation decision came handy to implement the move.

Containment of food subsidy

The Government found that containing food subsidy which was threatening to cross Rs 3,000 crore during '91-92 was a different cup of tea. With the subsequent all round increase in the procurement prices, especially as a chain reaction of the increase in fertiliser prices, containment of food subsidy actually became an all the more difficult proposition. In other words Government's dilemma with regard to food subsidy continued in the post NEP era as well. But the significant difference was that the Government now used every possible opportunity for containing the subsidy. It defined its task as one of limiting the subsidy to below Rs 2,500 crore in 1992-93. It increased the issue prices to the extent possible. It also thought of many new ways of bringing down the subsidy, chief among which was the limiting of the subsidy to the really vulnerable sections, taking the relatively better off sections out of the benefits of the Public Distribution System and subsidised food supply.

Subsidy on sugar abolished

In a further move following the compulsion to allow a higher statutory minimum price for sugarcane, the Government increased the price of ration sugar by 20 per cent. Concurrently, it allowed the price of free market sugar to go up based on cost and market factors. While adjustments in prices of commodities is not a matter of great importance, the point to be noted is that whereas in the previous era, such increases in minimum prices of farm products, would have been absorbed partly or fully by subsidy, this time, the increase was fully passed on to the consumers including those depending on the public distribution system. Sugar sector was obviously entering the subsidy-less era. In fact, the Government made a policy statement to that effect subsequently. It also increased the free sale quota as a further step towards market driven price environment.

Axe on fertiliser subsidy and decontrol of phosphatic, potassic and complex fertilisers

The Government applied the axe most forcefully on fertiliser subsidy. In July '91, it increased fertiliser prices by 30 per cent across the board. In fact, it increased the prices by 40 per cent and then brought it down by 10 per cent as a concession, in view of the vehement protests by farmers. This steep increase in fertiliser prices was a bold move by all counts. For, during the past ten years fertiliser prices were not touched by successive Governments, despite the mounting increase in the cost of fertilisers, both imported as well as indigenously manufactured varieties and the consequent sky rocketing of fertiliser subsidies. In July '91, by a stroke of the pen, the fertiliser subsidy was brought down by Rs 3,000 crore. In fact, subsidy on account of fertilisers was threatening to cross the Rs 10,000 crore mark during '91-92 and the Government's bold move effectively curbed the threat.

That the Government had in its scheme, reforms which were far more radical and which went far beyond the above described 30 per cent price hike , became evident by the next financial year. In August '92, in a bolder move, the Government completely decontrolled phosphatic, potassic and complex fertilisers and brought in market related pricing for fertilisers after a 14 year regime of control and subsidies. The retention price system (RPS) and the subsidies which were in vogue in respect of these fertilisers for the past 14 years were completely withdrawn. Henceforth, the subsidised RPS was to be available only in respect of nitrogenous fertilisers. Left to itself, the Government would have done away with the RPS and the accompanying subsidies in respect of the nitrogenous fertilisers too. It was because of fear of the political fall-out of the unpalatable decision and also to arrest a possible sudden fall in agricultural production, that the Government kept the nitrogenous fertilisers outside the decontrol move.

The move was expected to bring about a saving of Rs 3500 crore per annum in fertiliser subsidy. If we reckon that the above cut was over and above the cut of Rs 3,000 crore in the previous year, its formidable impact could be correctly gauged. The Government reduced the outlay on fertiliser subsidy to Rs 3,500 crore in '93-94 from Rs 5,800 crore in '92-93. It was hoping that the subsidy on fertiliser account could be contained further in the coming years.

Petro product subsidy drastically reduced

After the initial round of price rises across fertiliser, fuel and food in 1991, there was some slowdown in the pace of subsidy reduction. And this fact had drawn some criticism from the IMF as in its view, the slowdown in the handling of subsidies affected the progress of reforms. By Aug-Sept '92, the Government acted again and drastically cut the subsidies on fertilisers as explained in the foregoing paragraph. The Government also increased petro product prices, which could fetch perhaps as much as Rs 3,000 crore in the remaining six and a half months of the financial year. The average increase worked out to 18 per cent. The increase could not really be postponed any longer because the oil pool account was running a deficit of Rs 5,400 crore at the end of fiscal '91-92. Since the Government had committed to the IMF that it would bring the pool back into surplus there was no alternative to raising petro-products prices. The stiff hikes in the prices of petro products was also influenced by the need to mop up rupee resources which would be required for financing petroleum imports at market exchange rate beyond the level of 5.1 billion dollars for which foreign exchange at the official rate had been provided. And through the bold move on petro products, the Government conveyed the message that the reforms and structural adjustment were back on track.

Move towards total decontrol of petro products

The Government did not stop with subsidy cuts and price increases. As a follow up measure to the steep 18 per cent hike in the prices of petro products, the Government started considering total decontrol of prices of all petro products barring kerosene for domestic consumption. The Government was in fact convinced that in respect of petro products too, the market mechanism should replace the control mechanism and market determined prices should replace Government determined prices. The decontrol was also to be applied gradually to other aspects besides pricing, such as import of petro products including crude, refining and marketing.

As a step towards this goal, the Government announced that all new refineries coming up in the private sector would be free to import crude directly from the international market. With three new refineries in the private sector and three more in the joint sector expected to come up shortly, Government's decision to allow them to directly import crude for refining meant a substantial policy change.

Partial decontrol, dual pricing, and parallel marketing by private sector in kerosene and LPG

Subsequently, the Government allowed parallel marketing by the private sector in kerosene and LPG with a view to cutting down the heavy subsidies on these products. By then despite the price hike, the Government was still subsidising LPG and kerosene to the tune of about Rs 4,000 crore. In addition to allowing parallel marketing the Government also decanalised the import of these products. With these moves, the private sector, Indian and foreign, can enter into this business; they can import and market the two products in an unfettered manner. And the public sector which has all along handled the business on an exclusive basis is pushed into the era of competition. The Government also allowed actual users of LSHS to import the product for their captive consumption.

The Government/Public sector agencies would continue feeding kerosene to the public distribution system (PDS) at subsidised rates fixed from time to time. Likewise, the public sector oil companies would also continue to supply LPG and LSHS under the administered pricing system.

The decision thus means introduction of parallel marketing and dual pricing for these three products which were hitherto reserved for marketing by the public sector oil companies exclusively and were sold at prices fixed by the Government. Now, the private sector can establish their own marketing network and sell at their own prices. The move would pave the way for major international oil companies to enter the petro product sector in the country. This may also turn out as the precursor to complete decontrol of petroleum products. To facilitate import of the products and to make the operations cost effective, the Government also allowed the private suppliers of these products, international/Indian, to set up the required inland tankage facilities or onshore or offshore floating storages.

Decanalisation of naphtha imports

Continuing the efforts towards pushing petro products into a free price and free market environment, the Government also decanalised the imports of naphtha and allowed actual users to import naphtha directly from suppliers abroad. With this move, domestic prices of naphtha are expected to come in line with the prices ruling in the world markets. Prior to the above decision, prices of naphtha based end products in India were far higher compared to international prices, since price of naphtha in India was substantially higher in relation to international price. These products started facing severe price competition from the imported supplies. After all, with the trade liberalisation, the products could be imported into India freely. The Government had to bring in anti-dumping duties on some of the naphtha-based end-products. And finally, the Government decanalised import of naphtha enabling Indian producers of petro products to get naphtha at international prices and compete on level ground with imported supplies. It was a case of restructure leading to more restructure. And in many cases such restructure measures had an adverse impact on the public sector corporations of the country which were till then enjoying the advantage of a monopoly producer/canaliser of imports of the concerned product. In this case, the Indian Oil Corporation (IOC) had all along been the canalising agent for the import of naphtha. Now, not only has it lost this position, but has also to face the reality of the price of its naphtha going down by at least Rs 1,000 per tonne. Domestic producers of naphtha like CRL and HPCL also were the sufferers.

Steel decontrol

Between July 1991 and January 1992, the Government took a series of measures relating to the steel industry, which collectively had the effect of total decontrol of the steel industry. The new industrial policy announced in July 1991 opened up the iron and steel industry to private entrepreneurs by removing it from the list of industries reserved for the public sector. With a view to encouraging fresh investment in this sector, it was also included in the list of industries of high priority for foreign investment. The controls on prices and distribution of iron and steel, which were in operation since the Second World War, were removed in January 1992. The producers are now free to determine their prices without any Government control whatsoever. The freight equalisation scheme was also abolished with effect from January 10, 1992, giving consumers located near the integrated steel plants, the advantage of lower freight.

Axe on subsidies to SSI sector

Around the same time, there were also indications that the subsidies provided to the small scale sector (SSI) would be withdrawn gradually. In the view of the Government, the era of concessional lending was fast coming to an end. The banking system was under great strain and concessional lending was becoming unsustainable. While concessions and protection had a role in fostering the SSI sector, the very same concessions and protection acted in many cases as an inhibitor. They tempted the units to go by the perverse logic that if only they remained stagnant and stunted, they would be eligible for the concessions and protection.

PRUNING GOVERNMENT ESTABLISHMENT AND REDUCING GOVERNMENT EXPENDITURE ON STAFF

The Government also devoted some attention to reduction in the expenditure on Government staff. The Government was no doubt too sensitive to touch the wages of Government employees. The National Development Council (NDC) was asked to take up the matter and the latter appointed a subcommittee known as the austerity committee, to suggest ways and means of cutting down Government expenditure on all possible accounts. The subcommittee recommended among other things, a one year freeze on dearness allowance to Government employees, Central and State. The basic idea was that there should be a DA freeze in respect of the Central Government employees, since any payment by the Central Government to its employees led to a chain reaction among State Governments as well. This had undermined the financial position of the States to a large extent, since they were unable to raise additional resources to meet this demand. The subcommittee felt that while DA was intended to neutralise the inflationary impact, it nevertheless pushed up prices and set in motion a chain reaction leading to further rise in inflation and DA. A freeze on DA to Government employees was also a part of the policy prescriptions suggested by the International Monetary Fund (IMF) and the World Bank as a means to curb fiscal deficit of the Central Government.

The other recommendations of the NDC subcommittee included a ban on fresh Government employment in non-essential sections and removal of leave travel allowance for Government employees. The subcommittee also felt that no bonus should be paid to Government servants and that there should be no encashment of surrendered earned leave, except at the time of superannuation.

The committee felt that it was necessary to break the vicious circle in order to contain inflation. The organised sector, which could bear some impact of inflation without undue burden, should be asked to make some sacrifice for a limited period of time.

RESTRUCTURE OF THE PUBLIC SECTOR

Public sector restructure was the next major aspect of the structural adjustments. With each passing year, the nation and the Government were becoming increasingly aware of the need for restructuring the Public Sector undertakings (PSUs) of the country. Many of them had become a drain on the economy. In the four decades between 1950 and 1990, the public sector had expanded enormously in physical as well as financial terms. And such a large sector remaining unproductive for years together did have severe adverse effect on the nation's economy.

The two basic strategies usually applied in public sector restructure

Public sector reforms usually involve a two pronged approach:

(i) Reduction of the size of the sector.
(ii) Performance improvement.

And size reduction is usually attempted through

(i) privatisation,
(ii) partial disinvestment, and
(iii) closure.

India is also trying to follow this basic approach. It seeks to achieve size reduction as well as performance improvement. And it seeks to achieve size reduction through closure of certain units, privatisation of certain others and partial disinvestment of a large number of units. In fact, India chose partial disinvestment as the main route, closure as a supplementary route and privatisation as the exceptional route.

Government takes certain fundamental policy decisions

Before the Government set itself to the task of restructuring the public sector including disinvestment of its equity in the individual PSUs, it took certain fundamental policy decisions. First, it decided against setting up any new public sector enterprises. Secondly, it decided that there will be no further expansion of existing public sector units. There may be some exceptions, but the broad policy thrust will be such that it enables the Government reduce the size of its public sector operations. Thirdly, the Government decided not to provide any fresh budgetary support for new investments to be made by PSEs. If a public sector unit wants to expand its operations, it would have to raise the capital from the market.

The Government also decided to totally phase out budgetary support to public sector units over a three-year period. It had already made reductions in the budgetary support for loss making units and given them the message that they must undertake a process of restructuring, and become selfsufficient. Government would help units which could be restructured. But patently unviable units will have to face closure; they could not expect continued budgetary support from the Government.

The Government also abolished the prevalent system of a 10 per cent price preference to PSUs in purchase tenders floated by the Government. Instead of the price preference, the PSUs will now be given "purchase preference". This means that the PSUs will be given a chance to revise their bids to match the lowest bidder to bag the order. The step was taken to induce competitiveness among the PSUs vis-a-vis the private sector. The new purchase preference in lieu of the earlier 10 per cent price preference is a part of the overall Government strategy to phase out the discretionary support system so far provided to the PSUs. The introduction of the purchase preference will pave the way for the PSUs to become more competitive and cost effective. In effect however, the Government has withdrawn another implicit subsidy to PSUs through the above step.

Poor performance of the PSUs compel drastic reforms

As on March 31, 1990 there were 244 public sector units owned by the Central Government, employing 22.2 lakh persons with a total investment of about Rs 1,00,000 crores. Returns evidently have not been in proportion to the massive investment.

Though, compared to 1985-86, the performance of the PSUs somewhat showed an improvement by 1989-90, it still left much to be desired. As many as hundred Central PSUs were incurring losses year after year. The story of the state PSUs had been infinitely worse still. The state PSUs are excluded in the analysis provided here.

The combined performance of the 244 Central public sector enterprises in 1989-90 constituted a slight improvement over the levels of 1985-86 in the sense that during the period, the percentage of their net-profit to capital employed increased from 2.73 to 4.48 per cent. In absolute terms, the profits of all the 244 enterprises taken together, increased from Rs 1,172 crore in 1985-86 to Rs 3,782 crore in 1989-90. While the oil group of enterprises increased their net profits from Rs 1,651 crore in 1985-86 to Rs 2,900 crore in 1989-90, the non-oil group enterprises moved up from a net loss of Rs 479 crore in 1985-86 to a net profit of Rs 822 crore in 1989-90. A disaggregated analysis however indicates that during 1989-90, out of the 244 PSUs, 131 enterprises earned an overall net-profit of Rs 5,741 crore while 98 incurred a net-loss of Rs 1,959 crore. A substantial amount of the profit has thus been eaten up by the loss-making concerns. The latter accounted for 15 per cent of the total capital employed in the public sector.

The poor overall performance of the public enterprises could in fact be traced to the 98 loss making PSUs. As per an official document, these 98 enterprises were inefficient in more than one sense; all these units showed 'negative profits' in 1989-90; they also had an accumulated loss of Rs 10,000 crore, which amounted to 78 per cent of the total accumulated losses of all public enterprises. Of these 98 units, 15 PSUs were monopolies and 83 were operating in competitive markets. The 15 monopoly public enterprises were functioning in core sectors like steel, coal, mines, shipyards, transportation services and essential trading services. The 83 PSUs operating in competitive markets contributed 79.3 per cent of the accumulated losses. The annual loss per employee of chronically sick enterprises was Rs 38,714 in 1989-90, the capital employed per employee in these enterprises was Rs 13,093 and the accumulated loss per employee as on March 31, 1990 was Rs 2.09 lakhs.

Government initiates concrete steps towards PSU restructure

The Government drew up concrete restructure schemes for the PSUs which included, referring sick PSUs to BIFR, turn-around strategies for individual PSUs, retrenchment of surplus workforce with the help of voluntary retirement schemes, disinvestment of Government equity in PSUs and provision of greater autonomy to them.

It can be easily seen that these schemes went far beyond the normal support measures adopted by the Government from time to time. These were programmes with long term impact on the Public Sector as a whole. It included some very substantial schemes which could be implemented only with appropriate new legal enactments.

Sick PSUs to be referred to BIFR

According to an exercise carried out by the Bureau of Public Enterprises, it would require a massive capital infusion of Rs 24,000 crore if a revival package for the 98 loss making PSUs were to be put through. Even if a revival package for the 58 chronically sick units were to be implemented, it would require Rs 15,000 crore. After analysis, the Government concluded that it would mean poor economics to pump in such massive investment just to keep these sick units going. The Government also did not have such vast resources for ready deployment. Even from the angle of preserving the employment in these units, the Government felt that pumping in fresh investment of this order would not be worthwhile. For, it found that by making a far lesser investment in fresh projects, a much larger volume of fresh employment could be generated. The Government's considered view was that fresh Government investment should flow into core and socially important sectors and not for revamping and rehabilitating sick PSUs. The problem of sick PSUs has to be tackled differently. It is in view of this fact that the government decided to refer sick PSUs to the BIFR. Since the existing legal frame work did not permit referring PSUs to BIFR, the Goverment amended the law.

By February 1992, the amended Sick Industrial Companies (Special Provisions) Act became law and it became mandatory that all sick and potentially sick industrial companies in the public sector be referred to the Board for Industrial and Financial Reconstruction. The Act would apply to all industries which fall under the First Schedule to the IDR Act 1951 with the exception of the scheduled industry relating to ships and other vessels drawn by power. The Central Government in consultation with RBI could extend the coverage of the Act to these latter industries as well, by a notification. In case a public sector unit is declared sick through an order, the Government could appoint an operating agency which will have to prepare a scheme within 90 days for the sick company providing various options such as amalgamation of the sick company with any other industrial company, lease of a part or whole of the sick company, or outright sale of the sick company. The Government notified four Central financial institutions and eight nationalised banks as operating agencies for this purpose.

If the report of the operating agency revealed that it was not possible to revive a sick industrial company even by measures like amalgamation, reconstruction, sale of the whole or part of the company, the Bench of BIFR may form the prima facie opinion that the company be wound up. Show cause notice for winding up may be issued following the prescribed procedures including, if necessary, a reference to the High Court.

After the passing of the amendments to the Sick Industrial Companies Act (SICA), the Government decided to refer 58 PSUs to the Board for Industrial and Financial Reconstruction for preparing detailed programmes of restructuring or closure. Of the 58 units, 33 had been actually referred to the BIFR by August '92. Twelve more were about to be referred, making the total 45. By the end of '92-93, the total had swelled to 54. The Government also requested the BIFR to constitute a special bench to hear these cases.

The Government was trying to work out a methodology of reviving these units that was acceptable to both the managements and the workers of these units. It was clarified that sick units had been referred to the BIFR as a procedural formality; it did not mean that all units that are referred to the BIFR would be closed.

The Government however decided that it would not finance any rehabilitation of the sick public sector undertakings which have been referred to the Board for Industrial and Financial Reconstruction. Instead, it will explore the possibility of private sector participation; alternatively, it would help workers run the units.

Patently unviable PSUs may be closed down

The BIFR would evidently go about its task much the same way in respect of public and private units referred to it and there will not be any special treatment to the PSUs. It will prepare a scheme for rehabilitation if it is feasible to do so or recommend closure if it is impossible to rehabilitate the unit.

The Government made it clear that it would close down patently unviable public sector enterprises. In what appeared to be a statement of policy in the case of the perpetually loss-making units, Government declared: "Efforts made in the past to improve their performance have not produced the desired results so far. It does not, therefore, stand to logic to perpetuate such losses in the future as well."

Individual PSUs get ready for restructure

With Government's thinking on the subject becoming clear, many PSUs started developing restructure plans, appropriate to their respective conditions.

The restructure did not mean mere retrenchment of workers. While surplus workforce had to be retrenched as a part of the restructuring process, the process incorporated several other elements aimed at improving the competitive position of the concerned unit. Identification of areas of business in which the units should remain and areas they should vacate, elimination of loss making activities, improvement of efficiency, compensation packages for redundant employees and retraining of workers formed integral elements of the restructure plan. Some of the PSUs even hired management consultants for this purpose, including in some cases, foreign consultants funded by the World Bank.

The NTC restructure plan

A brief reference to the restructure plan brought out by the National Textile Corporation (NTC) would be of help in getting a correct idea of the kind of PSU restructure that was being considered.

The NTC had incurred an accumulated loss of over Rs 2,300 crores by '91-92. In August 92, the Government gave its approval to a comprehensive restructure of the textile mills owned by the National Textile Corporation (NTC)

The restructure strategy involved several elements such as selective modernisation of units, amalgamation of some units, closure of unviable units and technology upgradation for the revamped units. Financial restructuring and rationalisation of workforce through a Voluntary Retirement Scheme (VRS) also formed integral components of the restructure strategy. The outlay involved Rs 1,250 crore, of which, Rs 700 crore was meant for the Voluntary Retirement Scheme and Rs 550 crore for modernisation. The funds for modernisation were to come from the financial institutions and that for the VRS from the National Renewal Fund. The scheme spread over three years, would cover a workforce of over 73,000.

The NTC while opting for modernisation had to necessarily consider workforce reduction as well. Modern looms need only one-fifth the labour that obsolete ones do. If the company cannot shed labour, modernisation will saddle it with both high capital costs and high labour costs. The NTC therefore developed three special schemes for the rehabilitation of the workers likely to be rendered surplus by the restructuring measures.

Under the first scheme, a worker would be given two mini or four maxi powerlooms by the corporation at a nominal cost of Rs 500 to Rs 1000 a loom, for starting his own unit. The worker would require Rs 44,000 of capital investment and some working capital for making the unit functional. The worker has to contribute one-third of the finance required and the balance would be arranged through bank loan. He would function on "job work basis" and those running their units successfully for at least six months would get a production incentive from the corporation, which could be almost equivalent to their contribution to the scheme. Under the second scheme, the worker will purchase two or four new looms from the open market. Purchase of looms in the open market would need an investment of around Rs 2 lakhs per loom. While one fourth of this amount would be the worker's contribution, the balance was to be obtained by way of bank loan. Under the third scheme, the worker will start a reeling unit. Since such a unit required an investment of Rs 188 lakhs, it was proposed that the unit could be run by groups of 24 workers on a cooperative basis. The financing pattern envisaged would be 25 per cent contribution by members and the remainder coming through bank loans.

Public sector disinvestment

Disinvestment of Government equity in the Public Sector was the next major element of Public Sector restructure. While some commentators have referred to this as 'privatisation', we have consciously preferred the phrase disinvestment as we feel that 'privatisation' may not be the appropriate phrase to denote Government's offloading of a limited part of its equity in PSUs. It is possible that such a disinvestment turns out as the forerunner of eventual privatisation of the PSUs. But, as far as the current moves are concerned, 'disinvestment' or 'partial disinvestment' may be the more appropriate phrase than 'privatisation'.

The thinking behind the disinvestment

At the beginning of this section, we had clarified that PSU reform the world over, has two objectives—size reduction and efficiency improvement. Disinvestment is one main route leading to size reduction and efficiency improvement in the individual PSUs and the sector as a whole. India also had in mind these objectives when it embarked upon PSU disinvestment.

Another objective, however, took precedence in India's scheme of things. The Government wanted to divert its locked up resources in PSUs to the social service sectors for which the Government could not provide adequate resources otherwise. In fact, the Government had gone on record that it sought to disinvest the public sector units so as to use the proceeds for providing for social services like education, health, water supply, rural development and so on. The feeling had grown increasingly stronger that enough resources were not available with the Government for providing for these social services largely because resources were locked up in the PSUs without getting returns. The Government came to the conclusion that the resources had to be taken out of the PSUs without any more delay and ploughed into the social service sectors.

Besides these objectives, India had yet another objective in mind, when it went for PSU disinvestment. During '91-92 and '92-93 it badly needed funds for a multiplicity of purposes. First and foremost it needed

funds for bridging its fiscal deficit. It had given a commitment to bring
down the fiscal deficit to 6.5 per cent of the GDP in '91-92 and to 5 per
cent of the GDP in '92-93. And PSU disinvestment provided an easy and
tempting route for raising the funds. It also meant a non-inflationary route
of raising resources. In fact, the Government had gone on record that it
was going in for PSU disinvestment as it preferred to mop up resources
without fuelling inflation.

The Government was ready to disinvest its equity in the profit
making PSUs, the loss making PSUs and the sick PSUs. It was projecting a
distinct rationale for each of these moves. In its view, disinvestment in
profitable PSUs would in effect mean that the money needed for their
own modernisation and growth could be raised from the market. As
regards the loss making PSUs, benefits of disinvestment would be far
greater. It would mean minimisation of the drain caused by these units on
the public exchequer and also help raising of resources for the
Government. As regards the sick PSUs, as much as Rs 15,000 crore was
required for revamping the 58 sick PSUs. And, as it was not possible for
the Government to pump in such funds, it started considering private
equity participation "on a joint venture basis". And in all the three cases,
the Government would be mopping up revenues which could be put to
many different uses. In '92-93 alone, the Government planned to mop up
about Rs 3,500 crore. It could use this amount for bridging its budgetary
deficit or for building the National Renewal Fund or for carrying out the
Jawahar Rozgar Yojna.

Thus from every angle the idea of public sector disinvestment found
acceptance with the Government. Eventually, it did release substantial
blocked up funds; and these funds were coming without causing further
inflation. Government's stake in the PSUs was getting reduced and
private ownership was getting slowly injected into them. As a by product,
the efficiency improvement too was on the cards.

Disinvestment in '91-92

During '91-92, the Government disinvested varying proportions of its
equity in 31 select, profit making PSUs and gathered Rs 3,038 crore. The
disinvestment was limited to a maximum of 20 per cent of the total equity
in any given PSU.

Selection of PSUs for disinvestment

The first criterion in the selection of PSUs for disinvestment in '91-92 was
that the undertaking should have a positive net worth. That brought
down the list of probables to 136 out of a total of 244 public sector
undertakings. Then, undertakings in defence and those with small capital
base were excluded. Air India and Indian Airlines were dropped as they
were not organisations incorporated under the Companies Act. Finally,

the Government had just 31 PSUs for consideration. All of them were currently profitable.

Procedure followed

The disinvestment was actually carried out in two rounds. The offer was limited to public sector mutual funds, banks and financial institutions. Disinvestment in individual PSUs ranged from two to 20 per cent of the total equity of the respective units. While a maximum of 20 per cent was fixed for each unit for disinvestment, the actual offer was just eight per cent of the total equity of these enterprises put together which incidentally constituted 1.5 per cent of the total equity base of the entire central public sector. The offers were in assortments/bundles of different units' equity in different proportions.

Extent of disinvestment

The disinvestment in '91-92 totalled up to Rs 3,038 crore. While in respect of 14 enterprises, the disinvestment was to the maximum of the specified extent, i.e., 20 per cent, in other cases, the percentage ranged from 0.7 to 18. In other words, the Government realised 3.4 times the aggregate paid up value of the shares involved.

Disinvestment in '92-93

The Government planned to raise Rs 3,500 crore through PSU disinvestment in 1992-93 and Rs 7,500 crore over the three year period, '92-93 to '94-95. As the Government mopped up Rs 3,038 crore by divesting just 8.2 per cent in 31 units in '91-92 another 20 per cent divestment in just these 31 units would be enough to collect the targetted Rs 7,500 crore.

Selection of PSUs

The Government decided that the disinvestment will cover 20 select PSUs as under:

Steel Authority of India, Hindustan Zinc, Bharat Petroleum, Hindustan Petroleum, Rashtriya Chemicals, BHEL, Shipping Corporation of India, Indian Telephone Industries, Mahanagar Telephone Nigam, Videsh Sanchar Nigam, National Fertilisers, FACT, HMT, Nalco, Neyveli Lignite Corporation, Bongaigaon Refineries, Hindustan Organics, Bharat Aluminium Corporation, Hindustan Copper Limited and National Minerals Development Corporation. This meant that of the 31 PSUs taken up for disinvestment in '91-92, 14 were not considered for further disinvestment during '92-93. The three additions proposed for '92-93 were Bharat Aluminium Corporation , Hindustan Copper Limited and National Minerals Development Corporation. In the first phase only eight PSUs out of the list of 20 mentioned above were to be covered. They were: Steel Authority of India, Bharat Petroleum, Hindustan Petroleum, Hindustan Zinc, Rashtriya Chemicals, Neyveli Lignite Corporation, HMT and NALCO. These PSUs were selected as their shares were already being traded in the premium market and their values had begun to be quoted in stock markets.

Procedure followed

After the experimental disinvestment in '91-92 the process however got into some trouble. The Government was somewhat confused regarding the procedure to be followed. It considered two ideas: (i) selling the shares directly to public at a fixed price and (ii) selling it through a number of financial institutions and mutual funds, with an appropriate widening of the network of bidders as compared to the '91-92 disinvestment. The Government also felt it would be better to include foreign banks, select stock brokers, select NRIs and select private mutual funds, in addition to the public sector financial institutions and mutual funds. The Government was also of the view that it would be better to fix a separate price for the shares of each PSU unlike in '91-92 when shares of different PSUs were packaged into different assortments and sold on the basis of offers for the bundles as such. The Government also considered a proposal for allotment of the PSU shares to workers of the PSUs, at the rate of 200 shares per worker at face value.

The following are the highlights of the procedure finally chosen for the '92-93 disinvestment:

The shares would be sold through an 'open auction' method in which anybody "permitted to deal in equity or debenture in the Indian stock market" would be allowed to participate. The Government would notify the auction through advertisements in newspapers. A minimum subscription amount of Rs 2.5 crore would be prescribed, and offers below that would not be accepted. The Government would set a "reserve price" for the shares of each PSU after consultations with merchant bankers and based on parameters such as trading price of the shares concerned, the intrinsic worth of the enterprise and its earning potential.

The disinvestment was to be carried out in phases. A phased approach was presumably adopted with a view to determining how maximum profits could be realised through minimum sales. Response from the first phase would guide the second phase of disinvestment.

In the first phase, the Government decided to offer five per cent shares each, of the eight PSUs mentioned earlier. The subscribers could offer one rate for a certain number of shares and another for additional shares of the same unit but each of the offers should be for a minimum of Rs 2.5 crore. The offers would be accepted in the descending order of the bid. There would be no restrictions on the maximum number of shares an individual could apply for.

The Securities and Exchange Board of India (SEBI) was asked to identify about 100 clients who could participate in the auction.

Extent of disinvestment

The disinvestment in 1992-93 totalled up to Rs 1,912 crore. The first round of disinvestment which was in October 1992, moppped up Rs 802 crore through sale of 12.7 million shares of eight companies. In the second round which took place in December 1992 Rs 1,110 crore was mobilised; the Government was to pick up the balance in the third round in March 1993 so that the overall mobilisation met the targetted figure of Rs 3,500 crore. But all through 1992-93 the market response to PSU disinvestment weakened stage by stage and the prices offered by the buyers (mostly public sector mutual funds) dropped steeply. Since the prices quoted by the bidders were less than the referral price fixed by the Government, the latter had no alternative but to accept a shortfall of more than Rs 1,500 crore.

Possible direction PSU disinvestment may take in the future

It is likely that after an interval of time, PSU disinvestment will go far beyond the limits set by the Government in its opening gambits. The possibilities are seen to be as follows:

(i) The Government may go beyond the list of 34 PSUs covered in '91-92 and '92-93 together and include for disinvestment practically all the profit making PSUs (around 150 in all). It may even consider all the PSUs for that matter, without making any distinction between profit making and loss making units (around 244 in all).

(ii) The Government may go beyond the 20 per cent limit and disinvest higher percentages of Government's equity in the PSUs. (As a matter of fact, approval in principle has since been given by the Government for going up to 49 per cent).

(iii) The Government may go beyond even the 49 per cent limit, at a later date and in a selective manner. This means foregoing Government's majority equity control in the PSU concerned (An example has already been set in respect of Maruti Udyog Ltd).

(iv) The Government may sell cent per cent of its equity in some of the loss making units and thus privatise them cent per cent.

(v) The Government may go to the public directly and sell the shares to them, instead of limiting the sale to institutions and prescribing minimum investment.

(vi) The Government may even sell the shares in the international market, gaining foreign direct investment in the process.

Government decides to sell HPC

The probability that the Government might attempt outright sale of some of the PSUs became an actuality quite soon. The Government decided to put up for outright sale the Hindustan Paper Corporation (HPC). Employing around 8,800 persons on its pay rolls, including those in the two units of the corporation and its three subsidiaries, HPC was the first public sector undertaking to be handed over to private sector. The sale was to be administered by a high-powered committee to be set up for the purpose.

Disinvestment in state PSUs

Following the initiatives taken by the centre, the states too took some steps regarding disinvestment of their equity in the state PSUs. While disinvestment in the central PSUs was to be without Government losing management control, in the state PSUs, the disinvestment generally meant Government giving up its managerial control, as it involved outright sale of the units. However, where the units had substantial accumulated losses, the problem was not merely one of handing over Government equity and management control. It became necessary to make the sale of the unit attractive enough to the private bidder by giving some incentives. In fact, the states found that there were no takers for some of their PSUs, without such incentives. At the same time, there was also the impression that the states were handling the task in a rather haphazard manner. It was generally felt that the states could have made the units more attractive to the prospective bidders before offering them for sale. For example, it was felt that the states could offer their PSUs for sale after carrying out some restructure including implementation of a golden handshake to surplus workers, so that they could fetch greatly improved sale value.

Though unpalatable and unpopular, public sector reforms are inescapable and will gain momentum

In any country, public sector reforms are politically unpalatable and experience the world over shows that a Government takes to PSU reform only when it faces a major economic crisis. This is also true of India.

Any structural adjustment invariably produces an impact at the micro level, which will be felt by producers, consumers, and workers. And of the various measures of structural adjustment, public sector reforms are the most painful ones at the micro level. Because, its adverse repercussions are immediate and they affect a sizeable segment; they often imply withdrawal of facilities and concessions hitherto enjoyed by the segment, facilities that had become a taken for granted part of their benefits. Withdrawing them all of a sudden does hurt.

Besides being politically unpalatable, public sector reforms are also generally characterised by a great amount of complexity. This is perhaps all the more true in the case of India. The sheer size of the sector, the plethora of administrative problems associated with the reforms, the bargaining power of the organised groups likely to be hurt in the process, the time consuming nature of the reform operations are all factors that add to the complexity of public sector reforms.

That is why the Government is cautious with public sector reforms. It is however firm in its resolve. As such, despite its unpopularity, public sector reforms will be pushed through step by step. In fact the reform is likely to gain momentum with each passsing day. When action is initiated on the several aspects relating to this matter, it will have its own logic and momentum and will take the sector through a substantive and irreversible change. In fact, what has been done so far in the sphere of public sector reform, marks only the beginning of the reform process. Much had been indicated on this front on which action remains to be taken. For instance, Government had indicated that efficiency improvement in PSUs is one of its aims. But, precious little has been done in this direction. Even in the case of size reduction of PSUs, nothing significant has been done. In spite of all these limitations, the measures already initiated do symbolise a substantial breakaway in the role assigned to the public sector so far. They constitute a literal redefinition of the role of the public sector. The concept that had been prevalent so far—the concept that once a PSU is constituted, it should go on forever, even if it keeps eroding the precious resources of the nation—has been demolished by the PSU reforms. The widely shared mental conditioning of the nation that public sector units should be run like philanthropic institutions has also been exploded. This misconception had from time to time, been strengthened by certain pronouncements by successive Governments to the effect that profit making is not the main objective of the public sector. Now the story is different.

The philosophy and role of the public sector bound to change

The public sector of India will obviously acquire a new look in the coming years. Its very role would be redefined and restructured. Public sector investment would be stepped up in the social services such as health and education. It might also flow in a greater measure into the infrastructure sectors, while it would be curtailed in the manufacturing sector. Public sector might gradually withdraw from areas where no public purpose is served by its presence.

EXIT POLICY

An exit policy for industry is an inescapable requirement of an industrialised economy. And an economy that has set itself on a course of restructure of its industry, has to necessarily offer an exit policy to industry.

In the wake of the NEP, the entry barriers to industry were being removed through delicensing and other liberalisations. The recognition naturally became stronger that the exit barriers too will have to be dismantled if industrial resurgence has to become a reality. It was also felt that removal of exit barriers was particularly essential for attracting foreign investment. The Government understood that the demand for a viable exit from unviable industrial units is basically unexceptionable in the context of economic reforms and structural adjustments.

The Government however, approached the subject with great caution, as it could not afford to overlook the social and political risks involved in implementing an exit policy that does not enjoy broad public support. The Government was also keen to ensure that the socio economic fabric of the nation does not crack up because of the restructure measures. It was also keen to ensure that industrial peace was preserved to the extent possible. The Government preferred to deal with this issue sector by sector. Tripartite committees were formed for taking a close look at different sectors. The Government made all attempts to convince the workers that protection of existing jobs in non-viable units might not serve the larger interests of employment. It was also publicising the idea that the process of restructuring sick units will be accompanied by a credible social safety net to redeploy and retrain the affected workers and to provide suitable compensation where redeployment was not possible and retrenchment became unavoidable.

It was becoming clear that the Government wanted to take its time to evolve and announce an exit policy.

There has also been a view that India already has an exit policy through the provisions of the ID Act and the Sick Industrial Companies Act and all that is now required is to bring about the required modifications in the provisions of these Acts. While there may be some merit in this view, the point is that industrial entrepreneurs are not satisfied with the existing law. What industrial entrepreneurs want is a system that helps them quickly and painlessly close down industries if they feel the market conditions and economics of operations do not justify the continued existence of the units. Entrepreneurs would like some of the existing provisions of the law deleted and certain others amended. For example, there is a provision in the Industrial Disputes Act which says that a company will have to get the permission of the State Government before closing or shifting an industrial unit. The provision is used quite often to stonewall the exit of a sick industrial unit, even when it is clear that there is no alternative to closure. The entrepreneurs may like a more rational approach in this regard; they may like the veto power of the state Government nullified, for otherwise, the concept of exit freedom might remain a myth.

Voluntary Retirement Scheme becomes almost a substitute for exit policy

In the post NEP era, the term exit policy has come to signify some kind of a Voluntary Retirement Scheme (VRS) that would help the restructuring process. The Government was clearly in an uncomfortable position in the matter of exit policy. On the one hand, it was under compulsion to announce a policy of exit as the logical conclusion of its structural adjustment and on the other hand, it was scared of the consequences on the labour front of a cut and dry exit policy. It found the VRS or the golden hand shake scheme, as the convenient instrument to get over the problem. In fact, the VRS was projected as the painless substitute for exit policy. And, the Government brought in heavily budgeted VRS schemes for the PSUs. And when the Government came out with tax relief for Voluntary Retirement Scheme of even the private sector, the 'golden handshake' schemes became attractive for the private sector as well.

National Renewal Fund (NRF)

Even though the Government was taking its time to come out with an exit policy, it was never in doubt regarding the need to create provisions for absorbing the effects of structural adjustments on the labour force. In the Budget for 1991-92 the Government announced its intention to establish a National Renewal Fund with the objective of providing a social safety net to ensure that the cost of technological change and modernisation did not fall too heavily on the workers. The rationale behind the NRF and the Government's guidelines regarding its functioning are explained below.

The Government announced that the National Renewal Fund is set up to provide assistance to cover the costs of retraining and development of employees arising as a result of modernisation, technology upgradation and industrial restructuring. The NRF will also provide funds, for compensation of employees affected by restructuring or closure of industrial units, both in the public and private sectors. In addition, it will provide funds for employment generation schemes and for creating and operating a social safety net for labour, in the specific context of industrial restructuring.

The fund is of a non-statutory nature and will be constituted in two parts—National Renewal Grant Fund (NRGF) and Employment Generation Fund (EGF).

National Renewal Grant Fund (NRGF)

The National Renewal Grant Fund (NRGF) will deal with the immediate requirements of labour in sick units. The funds will be disbursed in the form of grants for compensation payments to employees affected by rationalisation schemes. It will also be used for paying compensation to workers when industrial undertakings or parts thereof are to be closed as a consequence of sickness as recommended by the Board for Industrial and Financial Reconstruction (BIFR). These payments may include the payment of legal dues and dues under Voluntary Retirement Schemes to the employees. The payment of legal dues, if made from the NRF, would form a claim on the assets of the closed units as and when they are disposed off. In addition, it may be used for providing resources for interest subsidies to enable financial institutions to provide soft loans for funding labour rationalisation schemes.

Employment Generation Fund (EGF)

The Employment Generation Fund (EGF) will provide resources for approved employment generation schemes in sectors affected by industrial restructuring. The funds will be disbursed in the form of grants.

The NRGF and EGF will be in operation for a limited period of time up to a maximum period of ten years from the date of their inception. An industrial unit requiring modernisation, technology upgradation or rationalisation, will raise funds in the normal way from the capital market/term loans from the financial institutions at the available rates of interest. The funds from NRF will serve exclusively the requirements of labour resulting from such schemes.

Funding of the NRF

The NRF may receive funds from budgetary allocations by the Government of India/state Governments, contributions from financial institutions, insurance companies and industrial undertakings. Proceeds from disinvestment of public sector equity and multilateral or bilateral aid will also be used to build the fund. There will be no open ended Government liability for the NRF which would be in operation only for a limited period of time.

The administration of the NRF

The NRF will be administered by a high level Empowered Authority in the Department of Industrial Development, Ministry of Industry. The Authority shall consist of the Secretary (Industrial Development) as Chairman, and Secretaries of the departments of Expenditure, Public Enterprises, Company Affairs, Labour, Education and Economic Adviser, Ministry of Industry, a labour representative to be nominated by the Ministry of Labour, Employers' representative to be nominated by the Department of Industrial Development, and two experts in management/ industrial relations as members. Additional Secretary, Department of Industrial Development, will be the Executive Director.

The Empowered Authority can approve proposals for disbursement of funds up to a limit of Rs 100 crore. Other proposals would require approval of the Minister for Industry. The Empowered Authority will be free to make funds available in different forms. In order to ensure a proper scrutiny, the Authority will consider only schemes prepared or underwritten by an accountable agency like the Board for Industrial and Financial Reconstruction, State Governments or the administrative ministry concerned.

It was decided that the fund would for the present have a corpus of Rs 2,200 crore. Rs 200 crore has already come in as the contribution of the Government, Rs 1,000 crore is envisaged to flow from the proceeds of the partial disinvestment of Government equity in the PSUs, and the balance Rs 1,000 crore is envisaged to flow in the form of a structural adjustment loan (SAL) from the IDA/World Bank. The fund is to be deposited with the General Insurance Corporation, which would devise a special insurance scheme determining the premia to be paid.

The Government had only modest aims in this regard for the fiscal year 1992-93. The limited amount already available was proposed to be used in two ways: Rs 175 crore for supplementing funds required for voluntary retirement schemes and the rest for PSUs which are to be partially or totally closed.

Social Safety Net

The Government has also been thinking in terms of a Social Safety Net. The NRF is not a substitute for a social safety net. Their purposes are different. While the NRF has the specific role of rehabilitation of affected workers, the aim of social safety net is to provide benefits and welfare amenities to all citizens including labour. The very presence of a social safety net will reduce the fear associated with structural adjustments. In fact, industrial restructure in European countries and the UK, could succeed only because these developed countries had built up since the thirties a social safety net in the form of housing, education and health benefits and doles and pensions. This is missing in India. And the Government is keen to introduce a social safety net so that the structural adjustments can take place with minimum strain.

STRUCTURAL ADJUSTMENT WITH A HUMAN FACE

There is no denying that in the short run, structural adjustments may deal a severe blow to the poor and also put a large number of people out of work. Structural adjustments involve price decontrol and drastic cut in subsidies. These moves push up prices. And the poor are the worst sufferers. Again, structural adjustment necessarily makes the market more competitive, and liberalises the entry and exit of firms and technologies. Greater competition means that inefficient units get driven out, and their employees lose their jobs.

In fact, there is little dispute about the adverse consequences of structural adjustments. The difficulties inherent in the adjustment process have been highlighted even by World Bank evaluations dealing with the Bank's own structural adjustment lending programmes. That is one reason why the Bank has consistently advocated that the Structural Adjustment Programmes (SAPs) should be supplemented by investment that is specifically aimed at cushioning the SAP impact on the poor. Anticipatory positive action can reduce the hardships arising out of adjustment for workers as well as for society at large. The longer a country waits without anticipatory action, the more painful is the adjustment process.

The Government has been insisting that the structural adjustments will be implemented without losing sight of the human element. Heartlessly and unwisely implemented, the adjustments can hurt several sections of the society, especially the weaker ones. It is mainly on account of this fact that the Government is proceeding rather cautiously with the structural adjustment programmes. It prefers to evolve the policies carefully and implement them gradually. In other words, it votes for "structural adjustment with a human face".

6

The Aftermath

What exactly has been the outcome of the new economic policies, the liberalisation, the reforms and the structural adjustments? What happened in the period that immediately followed the launching of the new policies? And what is going to be the long term effect of these policies on the economy of the country?

THE ECONOMY SUFFERS A SETBACK

Immediately after the launching of the new economic policies, the economy of India suffered a setback. A number of negative developments stared at the nation. The main problem was the slump in economic growth. A steep rise in inflation was the other major setback. On other fronts too, things were bad, indeed. Let us take a look at the indicators.

State of the economy by February '92

The economic survey for 1991-92 presented by the Government in Parliament at the end of February '92 depicted the economy of the country as under:

GDP growth rate expected to fall to 2.5 per cent in '91-92, compared to 5.8 per cent in '90-91 and 8.5 per cent in '89-90. (The actual was much worse than the estimate. It was just 1.2 per cent, the lowest in living memory)

Zero growth in agriculture.

Negative growth in industry, after a consistent growth in the previous three years.

Nothing to write home about on export performance.

Inflation continued to reign around 12 to 13 per cent, after touching the peak of 17 per cent in August '91.

Growth in Real National Income comes down to three per cent in 1991-92 because of stagnant agriculture and low industrial growth. In 1990-91, the real income growth was five per cent.

Slump in economic growth

Economic growth indeed went down drastically in the first year of the reform era. The growth in GDP in fact hit the lowest mark at 1.2 per cent, as against 5.8 per cent in the previous year i.e., '90-91 which in itself was a year of relatively poor growth on account of the Gulf war. The extent of the slump could be appreciated still better, if it is noted that during '89-90 the growth rate was as high as 8.9 per cent. In fact, throughout the Seventh Plan period the growth rate was 8.5 per cent.

Slump in industrial production

There was a big slump in industrial production in '90-91. In fact, it was the industrial slump that largely contributed to the fall in economic growth.

Import compression, credit squeeze and interest hike cause the industrial slump

Industrial production suffered largely on account of import compression and credit squeeze. Import compression though essential from the BoP angle, certainly came in the way of industrial performance; credit squeeze compounded the problem. The Bank Rate was jacked up to 11 per cent and then to 12 per cent with upward adjustments in deposit rates and lending rates of banks. In fact, the Reserve Bank tightened the monetary screw by hiking interest rates to levels which could have been rightly termed usurious in character. The import squeeze, the tight money measures and the condition regarding heavy cash margins for letters of credit for imports, were intended to check the BoP slide and to reduce the inflationary pressures. They subjected industry to the compounded travails of credit compression and interest rate hike. While interest rate hike affected the cost of credit directly, credit compression produced an indirect adverse effect on it.

Reduction of fiscal deficits and pruning of Government spending, adds to the slow down

The deficit reduction exercise and the curtailment of Government expenditure, particularly on capital account, were the other major causes of the slump in industrial growth. Through the '91-92 budget, the Government reduced the fiscal deficit from 8.5 per cent of GDP to 6.5 per cent. Had this been achieved through an expenditure reduction on revenue account to a significant measure, it would have been a more welcome correction. Given the realities concerning Government's limitations in curtailing its revenue expenditure and the compulsion to effect the agreed lowering of fiscal deficit, the Government chose the course of compressing its capital expenditure. This obviously rendered the budget growth-deflationary. In fact, the exercise at deficit reduction continued during '92-93; and industry's travails too continued.

Reduction in plan investment

There was also a marked slowing down in plan investment consequent to the fiscal deficit reduction and expenditure cut imposed by the Government, which, as mentioned already was mostly on the capital/plan account. The two successive years, 1991-92 and 1992-93, witnessed a big shortfall in plan investment, especially in the public sector. The plan assumption of raising Rs 6,058 crore through securities and debentures had also run into difficulties. This shortfall naturally affected the industrial growth. Budgetary support to the PSUs was also withdrawn making matters worse for industrial production. The net result was that industry witnessed a recession in '91-92. While overall GDP registered a low growth of 1.2 per cent and agriculture registered a marginal growth of 0.5 per cent, industry witnessed zero growth.

Steep rise in inflation

On the inflation front too, the developments were quite disturbing in the months that followed the launching of the new policies and measures. The annual rate of inflation, as measured by the wholesale price index on a point to point basis reached the peak of 17 per cent by August '91. The Government had a strong apprehension that the reform package might flounder on the rock of inflation and therefore concentrated its attention on inflation control throughout '91-92 and '92-93. It, however, could not achieve much success in the matter during '91-92. Though the improvement in the foreign exchange reserves and the relentless pursuit of tight money policy were giving hopes that inflation would be contained, no significant fall in inflation took place in '91-92. The year ended with an inflation rate of 13 per cent.

The economy was thus simultaneously badgered by recession as well as inflation, a phenomenon which Samuelson had described as Stagflation.

BoP continued as a problem area

The BoP position too continued to pose worry to the country in the aftermath of the NEP. While it did not pose a crisis any longer, it remained a problem as exports did not catch up as expected. The earlier optimistic expectations about exports were based on the new trade policies and other relevant reform measures under implementation. While these were useful to an extent, export resurgence depended equally upon the revival of industrial activity, which had been noticeably depressed throughout '91-92.

The fact that the BoP position required continued vigilance was appreciated by the Government very well. In fact, the Government was aware that only a respite had been obtained with regard to BoP and not a solution to the problem. The solution required a relentless pursuit of a coherent policy over a fairly long period of time.

The economic downtrend was no surprise to the Government

The economic downtrend was no surprise to the Government. In fact, the Government as well as the economists in the country were predicting that a deterioration in the economic conditions would take place in the short run. They explained that the J curve effect of economic growth, inherent in any such massive programme of economic reform, was taking place in the country. The downtrend was a transition phase and the growth curve had to look up finally. It was a case of the nation consciously sacrificing growth rates in the short term for the sake of long term economic benefits. In any reform process, stabilisation must precede growth, and the time lag in stabilising the economy inevitably affects growth. The Government was predicting that the growth rate would fall to 4 per cent in '91-92. The actual was much lower, at 1.2 per cent. The sluggishness continued in '92-93.

SIGNS OF RESURGENCE AND REVIVAL

That the setback to the economy was only transitional, was becoming clear by the middle of fiscal '92-93. Signs of resurgence and revival of the economy emerged. Economic growth and growth in industrial production in particular, picked up; inflation came under firm control; BoP position too had become manageable; there was some welcome turn on the export front too.

Industrial activity looks up

There were clear signals suggesting industrial revival. A number of sectors were getting out of the production slump caused by the severe import compression that plagued the industry in 1990-91 and 1991-92.

Buoyant corporate investment

There was a big step-up in fresh investment in industry. The capital market was witnessing a rush of public and rights issues. During 1991-92, the capital market (primary market) raised an amount of Rs 13,193 crore registering a 41 per cent increase over the previous year. In fact, the primary capital market has been characterised by significant buoyancy, both in terms of number and amounts of new capital issues by non-Government public limited companies. During the first eight months of the financial year '92-93, the number of new issues more than doubled, compared to the previous year, increasing from 259 to 596. The average amount per issue also increased substantially. The year also witnessed the largest ever public issue, Mangalore Refinery and Petrochemicals, for Rs 1,142.66 crore. The primary market continued to remain buoyant despite the secondary market crash that followed the scam.

Corporate investment forecast, based on projects for which assistance had been sanctioned by term-financing institutions, also suggested a sizeable increase in capital expenditure by industry during 1992-93 as against a decline in 1991-92.

Taking advantage of the liberalised procedures for implementing modernisation and expansion of existing units and setting up of new units, almost all major industrial establishments embarked on a number of schemes involving heavy capital outlay. A number of altogether new enterprises also were coming up, venturing out in various spheres. There were also indications of a good inflow of foreign investments, especially in hi-tech areas.

Since investment trend in the corporate sector is a reliable index of the mood of the country regarding industrial prospects, the above developments clearly pointed to industrial revival.

Monetary and credit policy modified

It has already been explained that tight policies on the monetary and credit front greatly contributed to the industrial slump in 1991-92. In formulating the monetary and credit policies for 1992-93, while the primacy of the objective of inflation control was kept in mind, measures were introduced to revive industrial production. In particular, interest rates were brought down from the high level of 20 per cent which was prescribed as the minimum lending rate in October 1991, to 17 per cent in three stages. The lowering of the minimum lending rate of commercial banks by three percentage points including one announced in the budget for 1993-94, coupled with the reduction in the lending rates of the term lending institutions by two percentage points over the same period, brought in substantial gains to the corporate sector. For the top 500 companies in the private corporate sector, the estimated gain worked out to a massive Rs 376 crore for the year 1993-94 and was a big relief to industry reeling under the impact of demand recession and poor profitability. Subsequently, bank lending rate to industry was brought further down by one percentage point in July '93.

Unwinding of credit squeeze

The Government also relaxed the credit squeeze considerably. The volume of bank credit to industry and business is a key indicator of the state of industrial operations. Bank credit for purposes other than food procurement, increased by over Rs 10,355 crore between March and August 1992, against a decline of nearly Rs 800 crore in the same period of the previous year. Subsequently, in January '93 a special allocation of Rs 1,000 crore credit was made available to industry and agriculture. The RBI came up with the massive credit support, routing it through IDBI and NABARD. The RBI would provide accommodation to the IDBI to the tune of Rs 400 crore by way of re-finance limits. Another Rs 200 crore would be available out of IDBI's own resources. The remaining Rs 400 crore would also come from the RBI and go to agriculture via NABARD, whose general line of credit would go up from Rs 2,700 crore to Rs 3,100 crore. The RBI also relaxed norms for calculating maximum permissible bank finance and enhanced the threshold limit for providing term loans by banks for projects. As a further move towards credit liberalisation banks were advised to treat only two-thirds of the term loan instalments falling due for repayment during the next 12 months as current liabilities and to keep the remaining one-third outside the current liabilities for the purpose of calculating maximum permissible bank finance. This move will enhance the borrowers' eligibility for maximum permissible bank finance. As regards term lending by banks, the RBI enhanced the threshold limit for extending term loans for projects by banks from Rs 3 crore to Rs 10 crore.

The objective was to stimulate output of capital goods and intermediate goods industries in particular. Machinery manufacturers, manufacturers of commercial vehicles, road transport corporations and hire-purchase and leasing companies were to benefit from these moves.

The massive cut in customs and excise duties in the '93-94 budget, bound to stimulate industrial production further

It was with the presentation of the 1993-94 budget in February '93 that the optimism about industrial revival and resurgence acquired full credibility. Industrial production now enjoyed all the facilitating factors—easier imports, easier credit, buoyant corporate investment, substantial cuts in customs and excise duties and cuts in interest rates. Excise and customs duty cut was no doubt the crowning factor. Described as a 'Give away' budget, the '93-94 budget offered excise duty cuts in a host of items. The cuts in customs and excise duties together amounted to Rs 4,532 crore.

Import duty on projects and general machinery has been reduced to 35 per cent from 55 per cent in the budget. Infrastructure sector areas like power, coal mining and petroleum refining currently attracted a duty rate of 30 per cent. This has been reduced to 25 per cent for coal mining and petroleum refining. The duty on power projects has been reduced to 20 per cent. In the case of electronics industry, the duty on project imports on specified capital goods for electronics has been reduced to a uniform 25 per cent. Besides the import duty on raw materials, piece parts and components has also been scaled down. As for the telecom sector, the import duty on optical fibre has been cut sharply to 20 per cent from 90 per cent. To improve export capability in the select thrust areas like textiles, leather, marine products, gems and jewellery, the import duty on specific capital goods has been reduced to 25 per cent.

With the slashing of the duty on capital goods imports, Indian industry can now set up new and technically superior plants. This coupled with the reduced duties on raw materials and components should enable Indian industry to cut costs and increase output and sales. It should also spur investment, both by Indians and foreigners; many investors have in fact been waiting for these duty cuts for ordering new plants.

Coming to exise duty, on a large number of capital goods and instruments, it has been brought down to 10 per cent from a peak of 23 per cent. The auto industry minus two-wheelers has been given special sops so as to pull it out of recession. The excise duty on motor cars has been brought down to 40 per cent from 55 per cent. Excise duty on tractors, colour television, air conditioners and refrigerators has been reduced substantially. Some of the other concessions include total exemption for coffee, tea and instant tea, reduction from Rs 1,900 to Rs 1,500 per tonne for vanaspati; from 17.5 to 10 per cent on electric fans, from 23 to 15 per cent on specified domestic electrical appliances, from 34.5 to 25 per cent on dry cell batteries, from 23 to 10 per cent on radio sets, from 69 to 30 per cent on mattresses and bedding articles and total exemption for footwear up to a value of Rs 125 per pair. And duty rates on basic feedstocks like ethylene, propylene, butadine, benzene, styrene and ethylene dichloride which were ranging between 25 per cent and 80 per cent, have been drastically reduced to a uniform level of 15 per cent.

Increased plan investment

Earlier, the curtailment of plan investment had affected industrial production. This inhibiting factor also was reversed by the 1993-94 budget which provided for a 32 per cent increase in central plan outlay.

BoP position improves considerably

By the second year of the reform regime, BoP position too improved considerably. Foreign exchange reserves of the country touched the level of $6.4 billion by July '92. Though it dipped subsequently to $4.8 billion by November '92, it rose to $5.3 billion by end of calendar year '92. It again touched $6.4 billion on March 31, 1993. And in the next fortnight it crossed the $7 billion mark. Around the same time two years ago, when the country was compelled to launch its New Economic Programme, the reserves were as meagre as $1.1 billion. Though much of the reserves is attributable to the IMF loan, the fact that India could enjoy a comfortable forex reserve of over $7 billion after providing for a trade deficit of $3.75 billion in 1992-93, is quite significant indeed. Subsequently, the balance of trade position too improved significantly. The first quarter of fiscal 1993-94 witnessed an export growth of 28 per cent in dollar terms over the corresponding period of the previous year. Even by August 1993, the exchange reserves stood well above the $7 billion mark. The strengthening of India's foreign exchange reserves exceeded the most optimistic expectations.

Inflation also comes under control

Inflation also came under reasonable control during the second year of the reform regime, i.e., '92-93. By end July/early August '92, for the first time since October 1990, the annual rate of inflation, as measured by the wholesale price index on a point to point basis, dropped to a single digit, 9.28 per cent. In the weeks that followed, it declined further to 8.3 per cent, 7.7 per cent and 7.4 per cent. Thereafter, it however showed an upward swing, reaching close to a double digit figure once again by the week ending October 3, 1992. This was mostly on account of the steep hike in the prices of petroleum products effected during the previous month. The inflation rate however promptly reverted back and stabilised at 8 to 9 per cent after the steep rise following the petroleum product price hike. Thus, a consistent and large decline in inflation had occurred during fiscal '92-93. The RBI projected the 1992-93 rate of inflation for the year as a whole, on a point to point basis in terms of the wholesale price index, around 8 per cent. According to National Council of Applied Economic Research (NCAER), it was likely to be between 9 and 10 per cent.

Subsequently, by the week ending June 5, 1993, the inflation rate fell to 5.8 per cent on a point-to-point comparison with the corresponding week in the previous year. This was the record low inflation rate over the past six years. The rate of inflation at the end of the year 1992-93, on a point-to-point basis, stood at 6.75 per cent.

The fact that inflation could be contained to this extent, despite the compulsions and constraints, is a significant achievement and is indicative of the economy's resilience and the inherent strength of the reform measures. The Government's expectation is that inflation would fall below 3 per cent within 3 years. A low level of inflation is a necessary condition for sustainable growth. In fact, a low level of inflation is as much an initiator of a virtuous cycle of growth, as spiralling inflation is an initiator of a vicious cycle.

The economy bounces back

In short, the economy of the country was slowly bouncing back. It was certainly getting out of the mood of doom that dominated the scene between mid '90 and mid '92. The Government faced with confidence the immediate adverse effects of its new programme of economic restructure.

The country showed that it has the resilience to withstand the new treatment. According to advance estimates released by the Central Statistical Organisation (CSO), the economy was poised for a growth rate of 4.2 per cent in the financial year 1992-93. And economists became confident enough to predict a growth rate of 5.5 per cent for 1993-94, mainly on account of the expected resurgence on the industrial front, where they placed the projected growth rate upwards of 7 per cent. And the Government was going ahead with renewed confidence and conviction with a continuing agenda of reforms.

The NCAER has forecast a real GDP growth of 5 per cent for 1993-94 as compared to 1.2 per cent in 1991-92 and 4.2 per cent in 1992-93. According to the council, the GDP growth scenario for 1993-94 appears better than it was in the last two years, with a growth oriented budget, a substantial increase in public sector expenditure, adequate levels of foreign exchange reserves and foodgrain stock, a positive environment for exports, lower excise duties/customs tariff, increased commercial credit supply potential, lower interest rates, and normal monsoon prospects. The Council's 'business expectations' survey of May 1993 has shown industry judging the economic scenario of 1993-94 as better than last year.

THE CONTINUING AGENDA

Economic jolts like the stock market scam, social upheavals like the Ayodhya episode and tragedies like the Bombay blasts did affect the momentum of the reform process. For a while, the Government became preoccupied with the socio-political issues. But as soon as the nation and society calmed down, it was back on the stage with its priority item—economic reforms. To doubting Thomases, the Government gave the reply that it was bent on going ahead with the reform programme and that there was no going back on the subject. It explained further that many of the processes it had started are irreversible; they can only gain further momentum and surge ahead. In fact, the subsequent announcements and activities of the Government were proving that it had a long agenda on hand. The mission of economic restructure was here to stay.

As part of its continuing agenda of liberalisation, the Government delicensed the manufacture of motor cars, white goods (refrigerators, washing machines, airconditioners etc), raw hides and skins, leather and patent leather, including chamois leather. In the past, the delicensing of items like cars and white goods would have been unthinkable. The concept of luxury has undergone a change with the rise of a large middle class which exceeds 100 million. Refrigerators and washing machines are now viewed as middle class staples rather than luxuries for millionaires. Moreover, the earlier logic for retaining some of these industries under licensing are fast getting eroded in the compulsions to become really competitive and global. In addition, following the unification of the exchange rate and new export import policy, licensing requirements have really become redundant. The combination of the market rate of exchange and the Exim policy would direct allocation of investments in industries. In fact, the industry ministry had suggested that except for electronic, aerospace and defence equipment, furskins, industrial explosives and hazardous chemicals, all other industries may be delicensed. The Government has been planning to delicense most of the service industries in the immediate future. Retaining just a select few services like banking and telecommunications under licensing, other service industries like hotels, tourism, leasing, advertising, software and medical services may be delicensed and liberalised. The very fact that 51 per cent foreign direct investment is allowed in some of the industries will pave the way for further liberalisation in licensing requirements in respect of those industries.

The Government has unveiled its comprehensive economic reforms agenda for the next three years, in its discussion paper entitled *Economic Reforms—Two years after and the task ahead*. The agenda envisages major changes in Government policies in the areas of fiscal management, taxation structure, employment and poverty alleviation, financial sector, external sector, industry, agriculture and infrastructure.

On the fiscal front, the agenda envisages a sharp cut in central fiscal deficit from 5.6 per cent of GDP in 1992-93 to 3 per cent of GDP in 1996-97. The Government's commitment to switch over to a new tax system with a wide base and moderate rates, promoting economic efficiency, growth and equity was becoming evident. The Government has also indicated its desire to reduce subsidies and implement a new approach to administered prices with further cut in budgetary allocations to PSUs. In the fertiliser sector, already all fertilisers other than straight nitrogenous ones have been decontrolled and taken out of subsidy. Soon, this is likely to be applied to the straight nitrogenous fertilisers as well. Similarly, in petro products too, total decontrol and free pricing may emerge.

On the trade policy front, the commitment is to further phase out the remaining import restrictions and replace them with appropriate tariffs. Imports of some 300 intermediate and capital goods still remain on the negative list; the Government proposes to review the position and eliminate most of the restrictions. Only on considerations of security, ethical and environmental factors, would any restrictions be retained. The agenda also suggests that the current account deficit in the balance of payments be brought down from about 2.2 per cent of GDP in 1992-93 to below one per cent in 1996-97.

In the case of tax reforms, thus far just a beginning has been made. Many reforms are sure to follow. The bulk of Chelliah Committee recommendations will be taken up for implementation. The very shape of the tax structure would be rendered different. Indirect tax reforms would ensure a gradual reduction in the average customs tariff to 25 per cent.

The continuing agenda will especially involve radical reforms in respect of the infrastructure sector including power and transport. The monopolistic nature of these sectors will change. This will involve inclusion of private service providers and decentralisation of function and autonomy within existing public sector entities. In the absence of budget support, public entities will have to operate on commercial principles. These entities may have to sell equity to the public to broaden their ownership base and accountability. Pricing and distribution strategies will be wholly revamped consistent with commercial and economic principles. Foreign investment will involve build-operate-transfer (BOT) approaches.

Reforms of financial sector are also likely to be pursued with greater vigour in the continuing agenda. As regards the banking sector, the reforms are likely to result in a complete ban on generalised loan waivers, institution of speedy and effective loan recovery processes and phased reduction in the statutory liquidity ratio to 25 per cent and in the cash reserve ratio to 10 per cent. These measures will increase the banks' lending potential to the commercial sector. Phasing out of ceiling and floor rates respectively on bank deposits and lendings, and careful targeting of concessional lending to the really needy would be the other major reforms in the banking sector. In fact, in respect of banking sector reforms, the Government is only biding its time for going full swing with the implementation of the Narasimham Committee recommendations. A number of new private banks will soon emerge, changing the competitive character of the banking industry.

Exit policy is another subject that may receive the attention of the Government. Being a highly sensitive issue, politically and socially, Government has chosen a cautious approach. But the encouragement given to the voluntary retirement schemes and the constitution of the National Renewal Fund are sure indications that the Government will not, for long, shy away from the formulation of an exit policy for industry. In fact, with the Government's desire to attract private investment, especially foreign investment, removal of exit barriers will have to follow.

In this chapter, we have just seen the economic situation in the immediate aftermath of the new policies. It is just a period of transition. What would be the long term effect when the Government moves ahead with greater speed in its liberalisation and restructuring policies? What would it mean to the economy and to the participants in it?

A discussion on this subject is the theme of the remaining part of this book.

7

Business Challenges of
the Open Regime

We have now come to the mission of this treatise. The mission unfolds in this chapter.

The first part of this book has been devoted to a portrayal of the new economic prescription administered on the Indian industry and business and the new milieu in which it has to operate. An exposition of the actual challenges that emanate from the new environment and the possible means and methods by which industry and business can meet the challenges, is the burden of the second part of this book. This chapter is the curtain raiser. It introduces the challenges posed by the open regime and the new demands on management in such a regime.

The most striking and self evident feature of the open regime is that it can release the blocked up growth impulses and entrepreneurial talents of the country. In the first place, the open regime offers absolute freedom to business houses and entrepreneurs in arriving at their investment decisions. The dismantling of the multitude of regulations and controls, the abolition of industrial licensing in respect of most industries, the scrapping of the threshold assets limit for MRTP companies, the relaxations in the Foreign Exchange Regulation Act, the toning down of the all pervasive role of the public sector and the opportunity of entry to the private sector into a number of areas till now reserved for the public sector, are all factors facilitating the full display of entrepreneurial talent.

The time old grouse that several vital sectors of the economy were out of bounds for private enterprise is now broken. The entry barriers have been thrown off and more than four-fifths of the country's industry has been opened up for private enterprise. In fact, the bid to open up the economy for private enterprise has been carried very much further by the whole hearted welcome extended to foreign investment into the country and the removal of rules and procedures that were blocking the entry of such investment. In other words, the open regime has not only released the competitive forces internally, it has also paved the way for foreign investment and along with it, technology transfers, all forming a package of mutually reinforcing factors in favour of private enterprise's place in the economy of the country.

Does this all mean that Indian business and industry will from now on go through a very cushy time?

Far from it. While the new environment certainly unfolds many attractive opportunities to them, it also poses simultaneously a variety of business challenges—challenges of a kind which they have never faced before. And this is precisely why Indian industry is now in a state of anxiety.

Let us take a close look at the challenges posed by the open regime and the implications they hold for industry and business.

EMERGENCE OF INTENSE AND VIBRANT COMPETITION

Fuelling of competition is the foremost of the many challenges posed by the open regime. With the opening up of the economy, Indian industry and business will face infinitely tougher competition, competition of a kind unknown till now. Competition among the companies already operating in India will hot up immensely, and competition from the multinationals that may enter India afresh will add a new dimension.

Competition among firms already in operation in the country is bound to hot up further as every one of them will now be eager to consolidate their position in the market. Some will gain, while others will lose out. And a foretaste of this phenomenon is what we have seen in the case of HLL and Tomco recently. Though both HLL and Tomco have been giants in the Indian soaps and detergents market, HLL, through its competitive strengths, especially marketing clout, has overshadowed Tomco. Having lost out in the competitive battle, Tomco did the next best thing under the circumstances—it allowed HLL to take over Tomco on mutually advantageous terms. The coming years will see many such instances of competition intensifying among the companies already operating in India, some winning and the others losing out.

As regards competition from the newly entering MNCs, it will be a different phenomenon altogether. While the MNCs need the Indian market to saturate their immense capacity to expand and grow and the Indian companies need the management knowhow, the investment and the technology of the MNCs, the result is going to be an uneven battle. The advantage which the Indian companies enjoyed all along, will now vanish, as they face the multinationals who are light years ahead of them. A powerful competition is now knocking at their doors. Indian companies will thus have to play on two grounds simultaneously—with their rivals at home and with the newcomers from abroad.

ENTRY AND CONSOLIDATION OF MULTINATIONALS

The powerful thrust emanating from the aggressive entry and consolidation of the MNCs, is by all counts, the most significant of the many dimensions of the new competition. The MNCs already operating in the country are enthusiastically consolidating their position; and many are entering anew and entering with the strategic intent of having a strong presence in the Indian market.

A large number of MNCs acquire majority equity stake in their Indian enterprises

With the liberalisation of foreign direct investment, removal of FERA restrictions and the new freedom to raise their equity stake to 51 per cent, that too at prices of their choice, a large number of MNCs operating in India have hiked their equity stake to 51 per cent and acquired majority control in their Indian enterprises. Unilever has been one of the first to consolidate their position in this manner in their Indian companies. A detailed reference to this has been made elsewhere. Besides Unilever, more than two dozen MNCs have already taken to this route. To name a few: Ashok Leyland, Cadbury, Glaxo, Hoechst, Merck, ABB, Alfa Lavel, P&G, Madura Coats, Singer, Indian Oxygen, Philips, PSI Data Systems, Bata India and Indian Shaving Products have already consolidated their position with 51 per cent equity stake. Indications are that out of the nearly 300 MNCs operating in the country, almost a third are emerging as companies with 51 per cent equity control by the foreign parent firms. More may join the list.

While the MNCs already in operation are acquiring majority equity control through consolidation and capital restructure, the new entrants are securing majority control at the entry itself. For example, the French multinational, Alcatel, which has promoted three ventures in the country has secured majority stake in all the three ventures right at the entry stage.

Majority stake by the parent MNCs means additional competitive edge to their Indian enterprises

For the MNCs, going in for 51 per cent equity is not just a matter of securing increased control over the show. The new position provides them with several strategic advantages. With majority stake, the MNCs will bring in their latest technologies and state-of-the-art products. More importantly, they will bring the original brands of the parent company. They will also bring in their full marketing and management might. Support of more advanced management knowhow and resources will naturally be available. And an opening for exports through the parent company's expertise will also be available in many cases.

More than anything else, acquisition of majority control is an expression of the parent company's commitment to the growth of their business in India. P&G for example, will now give a new importance to the Indian market in its scheme of things, especially in respect of cleaning products, the market for which is growing at 30 per cent per year in India compared to the one per cent growth in the US market. P&G now plans to flood the Indian market with P&G brands like Head & Shoulders Shampoo and aims at a five fold growth in turnover. Similarly, Cadbury's parent company, Cadbury Schweppes hiked its stake in Cadbury India to 51 per cent from 40 per cent and along with it launched its new range of confectionery products in India. For ABB, India certainly tops the list in its non-European markets. ABB will bring in Rs 700 crore in various projects and the Indian company will exploit the strength of the parent company in robotics, transportation and environmental control systems. Glaxo will help its Indian company secure the required foreign exchange resources for implementing new schemes and upgrading technology. Indian Shaving Products will use the Gillette brand name for its blades and also for new products like swivel-head razors, in addition to gaining the corporate name Gillette India. It will also diversify into deodorants and writing products, the parent company's line of products. As for the Indian Sewing Machine company, it becomes Singer India. Singer Corporation of USA will lend new help to boost up exports. Singer India will produce the latest series 900 range of sewing machines for exports, using Singer's new technology. The company also plans to diversify into washing machines, audio and video systems, dish washers, toasters and food processors. PSI Data Systems will become Bull India and using the parent, Groupe Bull of France, it will introduce the full range of hardware, including large and medium range IBM hardware, which can be had through using the strategic alliance of Groupe Bull with IBM. For Bata India, expansion and modernisation are on the anvil. It also plans to launch new Adidas products in line with its new ambitions of growth.

List of MNCs entering in partnership with Indian firms is also growing

While a number of MNCs already in operation in India are thus consolidating their position, many more MNCs are entering Indian market afresh in alliance with a chosen Indian partner. Ford has a venture in alliance with Maruti Udyog for the manufacture of aluminium radiators. GM has tied up with Hindustan Motors for a car project. Itochu, the leading Japanese industrial group has struck a major financial tie-up with Reliance Industries for two projects, a refinery and a methanol based petrochemical unit. Hewlett-Packard, the US computer multinational, is in India in partnership with HCL, a growing Indian computer firm. In the financial sector business, the Japanese investment firm Orix International has tied up with Infrastructural Leasing and Financial Services (IL&FS) and J.P. Morgan with ICICI.

General Electric enters with Godrej as partner

General Electric has promoted a venture in alliance with Godrej for the manufacture of compressors, refrigerators and other white goods and home appliances. The joint venture involves a technology tie up and strategic alliance. The new company will manufacture the entire range of GE's home appliances, beginning with refrigerators and washing machines. Later, it will take up production of dish washers, microwave ovens and cooking ranges. The transfer of Godrej's refrigeration business to the joint venture and the placement of GE's equity in the new venture would help the business. In fact, GE's equity in this venture would be one of the biggest foreign equity investments in India among joint ventures in recent years.

Bayer enters into partnership with Herdillia

Bayer AG, the German multinational, has entered into an alliance with Herdillia Chemicals, the Bombay-based flagship company of the GP Goenka group. Under the arrangement, Bayer AG has licensed its closely-held knowhow and trade mark for the manufacture of heat transfer media to Herdillia Chemicals. Heat transfer media are high-value chemicals (landed price in India is Rs 1,60,000 per tonne) used in the manufacture of synthetic fibres, polymers, chemicals and drugs. At present, Bayer group manufactures heat transfer media only at Leverkusen, Germany. The heat transfer media will be manufactured by Herdillia at its Thane site and will be marketed by Bayer (India) in India and by Bayer AG in the far eastern markets. Bayer AG proposes to use its proposed Indian facility as a manufacturing-cum-export base and is planning to export at least 1000 tonnes from India.

GE Capital sets up consumer finance company in alliance with Godrej

GE Capital, a part of the General Electric group of the US and one of the largest financial services companies in the world, is setting up a consumer finance company in collaboration with Godrej. GE Capital is expected to have majority stake in the proposed venture and the initial capital of the company is expected to be around $3 to 5 million. The company would finance all types of consumer durables.

The joint financial venture is a logical extension of the GE-Godrej partnership and the new finance company will exploit the potential of the new range of consumer durables turned out by the GE-Godrej combine. It can also profitably serve the financing needs of the vast dealer network of Godrej.

It was becoming clear that GE was developing its presence in India through strategic alliances. GE had in fact, worked out eight alliances in India, three with partners in the public sector and the rest with the private sector. Each alliance is planned to become a leader in its sector, drawing on and contributing to the GE network in India.

Re-entry of IBM and Coca Cola

The re-entry into the Indian market by American multinationals, IBM and Coca Cola sums up the story. Pushed out of India in the '70s, their re-entry in the '90s typically signifies that with the new economic programme, the wheel has turned a full circle. For IBM, it is a re-entry in alliance with the Tatas. Coke has staged its re-entry directly. Coca Cola South Asia has been allowed to set up a 100 per cent owned venture in India to manufacture beverage essence and beverage base. A new wholly owned subsidiary would be set up with a capital of Rs 60 crore for implementation of the project. Initially, Coke is projecting an annual sale of 25 million cases of its soft drinks in India, against estimated current annual sales of 15 million cases by Pepsi and 60 million by Parle.

Entry of McDonalds food chain

The American fast food chain, McDonalds Corporation is also entering India and setting up a wholly owned subsidiary. The chain's restaurants in India will be developed and operated primarily through a joint venture between the McDonalds subsidiary and Indian partners. The proposal envisages McDonald's participation in the equity capital of the venture to the tune of $100,000 to start with, which will be increased to $20 million over a period of seven years. The significance of the entry of McDonalds chain of eating joints and big hamburgers lies in the likely spread of a life style and tastes of the American kind.

MNCs may enter the oil sector too

In the near future, we may see the entry of MNCs into the oil business as well. As per the new industrial policy, a number of fresh concessions have been extended to foreign direct investment into the oil sector. The multinational oil companies who were active in India decades ago and who had left the country in the wake of the oil policy of the late '50s and early '60s, are now returning to the country. And some others are entering anew. Mobil has returned in alliance with IOC and is putting up a lubricant plant. Caltex has returned to put up blending plants in partnership with IBP. It will market a wide range of lubricants and petroleum products. Caltex/IBP are also planning to set up 3 million tonne oil refinery in Assam. Shell too is striking a partnership with BPCL for setting up a refinery in Madhya Pradesh. Castrol which is already present in India is implementing an expansion. Another giant likely to enter India is the French Societe Nationale Elf Acquitaini through its subsidiary Elf Lube.

The MNC Traders

There is yet another dimension to the new MNC competition, besides what has been referred above. The country is going to witness competition from MNC traders. For example, Mitsui & Co. are going to bring special types of papers for the Indian market—heat sensitive paper, computer paper etc. They have 150 offices round the world, eight of them in India. Mitsui was already supplying India major items like phosphoric acid, sulphur and ammonia. The other Japanese giant, Mitsubishi is aiming at the steel business of India. Their plans are to import electrical steel from Nippon Steel, Kawasaki Steel and Sumitomo Metal. Samsung, Korea's largest trading company, is planning to bring into India newsprint, non-ferrous metals, phosphoric acid, ammonia, sulphur, rubber and steel.

A strong presence in service businesses too

In addition to operating industrial enterprises/joint ventures and trading activities, the MNCs may have a strong presence in India in services too. At one go, eleven foreign companies have been allowed to set up branches in India for carrying on various service businesses. The centres chosen for the present are New Delhi, Bombay, Bangalore, Madras and Calcutta. The areas of activity relate to export of goods, promotion of exports, promotion of technical collaborations, promotion of joint ventures, rendering technical support for high technology systems, development of new products and promotion of research.

MNC Consultancy firms like McKinsey and Anderson become active

World's top ranking management consultancy firms like McKinsey and Arthur Anderson have already established their outfits in India. The open regime makes India a particularly fertile ground for these consultancy firms. Though they may not totally take over the consultancy business in India, the MNC consultants are bound to make a mark in this sphere. They have high reputation, strength of specialisation and business clout. They also have to their credit, rich global experience in management consultancy, especially in the major market economies of the world. They have also become status symbols; and in any reference group, they will be the first names to be recommended and considered. When P&G world wide and GE engage them, P&G India and GE-Godrej would also naturally engage them. Their entry and consolidation in India has already made every Indian consultancy firm, from Ferguson to Tata consultancy to sit up.

Increased MNC presence will also enlarge the challenge in marketing communications

Advertising and promotion battle in particular, will intensify with the large scale entry/consolidation of multinationals. Marketing communication will become more aggressive and the Indian consumer will be pulled towards several new products. The multinational companies will naturally be followed by their ad agencies. While it may be argued that even today, many Indian ad agencies have tie ups with foreign expertise, the participation of foreign agencies till now has not been substantial. But now, when their principals wage a direct war in the Indian market, the agencies will come in a big way to their support. For example, though OBM is already in India and is doing a good job for many Indian companies, it may be a different story when one David Ogilvy directly handles his accounts in India. Similarly, while HTA is already serving a number of clients, JWT may produce a different effect altogether. The challenges on the marketing communications front will dramatically increase. In the matter of media availability too, there will be new developments, especially arising from the aerial satellites.

A major shift in the offing in the power equation between Indian firms and the MNC partners

The fallout of MNC consolidation is not limited to its impact on competition in the country. There is another aspect, a totally different one for that matter—the imminent shift in the power-equation between Indian companies and their MNC partners. The shift, obviously, is going to be in favour of the MNCs. It is on the cards that in the new environment, the MNC will ask for greater control and a more active role in their ventures in the country. There are scores of companies in India, promoted by Indian entrepreneurs, with MNC collaborations, where the Indian partners have all along exercised control. Now, the Indian partners in these companies may have to settle for a change in the power equation between them and the MNC partners. The response of the Indian firms to this new demand may not be uniform; it may vary depending upon the specific realities of the units concerned and the perceptions of the Indian partners in each case. If the MNC partner insists on greater control, it may be difficult for the Indian partner to resist the demand, especially if the price to be paid is the loss of the alliance with the MNC. It seems that many Indian enterprises are going through this process. Companies like Kinetic Honda and LML Piaggio have allowed their foreign partners to hike their equity and control in the joint ventures. Many others too seem to have recognised the inevitability of the new situation. In many cases, if the Indian businesses do not let their foreign collaborators increase their equity stake, the former may be the losers. Because, some important advantages are obviously derived by them from the association with the

MNCs. For example, Kinetic Honda decided to allow Honda Motor Company to have majority stake so as to retain the advantage of the global reach of the Japanese giant. The company felt that it was better to become a part of Honda's global network rather than merely remain an Indian company. For most companies, such logic may hold good and they may go along with their MNC partners even at the cost of losing control. There will also be companies who would not like to forego their majority stake.

In the case of NOCIL of the Mafatlal group for example, the new situation resulted in the termination of the Shell-Mafatlal relationship which had worked smoothly for thirty years. In fact, Shell was about to participate in the Rs 6,000 crore naphtha cracker project of NOCIL by providing the latest technology as well as an investment of Rs 1,000 crore. However, in the new context, Shell wanted to enhance its equity from the present 33 per cent to 51 per cent. Mafatlal did not want to lose control of the company. It was finally decided that Shell will disinvest its 33 per cent equity in NOCIL to the Mafatlal group at a mutually agreed price.

It is obvious that either way, Indian firms with MNC partners, have to face the issue of readjustment of their relations with their MNC partners.

Formidable challenge for Indian companies

Thus, it is not a matter of simple entry by a few MNCs. It is a strong entry with the clout that goes with majority control in the ventures concerned. It is bound to have its impact on the business environment of India and the competitive position of the companies in India.

In the existing scheme of things, Indian companies may enjoy some competitive advantage compared to their multinational counterparts—the very advantage of operating at home, for instance. The Indian firms are already here, with well entrenched products and channels of marketing and distribution. They have already built up some brand patronage. Culturally too, the Indian companies are close to the Indian consumer. But like any other advantage, this advantage of the domestic enterprises is not invincible. The MNCs are invariably strong enough to nullify such competitive advantage enjoyed by a particular player. Resources and perseverance are the only requisites. And that is precisely why successful companies continuously build on substantive competitive advantages, by consolidating and extending them and by developing some new forte. The point is that the limited inherent advantages enjoyed by the Indian companies can put them on a strong footing, only if they can develop these advantages further and work on them and gain tangible competitive edges in their respective businesses. Otherwise, these apparent advantages can be easily countered by the stronger contestants. After all, many of the MNCs have already got long built connections in India and are familiar with the Indian market and the ways of Indian business. And for the MNCs who are really newcomers, they also have the experience gained by operating already in a variety of countries and cultures. MNCs the world over, operate on the principle that no culture is really alien to them. Their very success in many lands is proof to them that any customer in any part of the world will respond favourably to a good product. In other words their clout is essentially a product clout. And that is what most of the Indian companies unfortunately lack today. And that is precisely why one has apprehensions about the Indian companies losing out their fragile natural advantages in the new setting.

IMPORT LIBERALISATION ADDS A FURTHER DIMENSION TO THE INTENSIFICATION OF COMPETITION

Increased competition on account of the increase in the number of players and the entry and consolidation of MNCs is just one dimension of the new competitive scenario. There is another equally significant dimension—the competition emanating from imports.

In chapter 3 on the New Trade Policy, the new efforts at integrating India's economy with the global economy has been discussed elaborately. The main measures in this direction came in the form of liberalisation of imports and steep reduction in import tariffs. Except for a small negative list, imports have been opened up completely; and tariffs have been reduced drastically. One major offshoot of this liberalisation has been the intensification of competition through imported goods.

For example, in the wake of the import liberalisation, several naphtha based petro chemical products faced stiff competition from imported products. The price of naphtha in India being substantially higher than the international prices, the naphtha based products made in India were costlier, compared to the imported products. In the earlier era, the domestic users of these products could not get the benefit of the lower international prices due to two reasons: (a) prevailing restrictions on imports and (b) the high tariff walls. The domestic users had no other alternative but to patronise the indigenous products. With the change in the rules of the game, the domestic users started patronising the imported products. The domestic manufacturers were caught in the heat of competition from imported products and had to woo customers with price cuts and discounts. They even sought Government intervention.

Liberalisation of imports will add to competition in another manner as well. Improved availability of imported raw materials, that too at a reduced landed cost, would help increase the production in several industries. The net impact would be that the supply of products in several sectors will becomes liberal, adding to the competition. And, as the negative list of imports becomes progressively leaner and the tariffs lesser, as the process of liberalisation gains further momentum, the competition from imported goods will become more intensive.

Competition from the technology angle too

In the past, Indian industry did not have free and easy access to the best technologies of the world. While in every sphere of industry and business, the rest of the world was leaping ahead with newer and newer technology, Indian companies unfortunately lagged far behind in technology, products and processes. The consequences of staying with older generation technology were severe on the cost front and quality front. Indian products could not compete with state-of-the-art products of the world. With older technologies, the scale economies of the Indian companies also remained non-competitive. The access to modern technology all these years was blocked because of the country's preoccupation to protect domestic industry from outside competition. The restrictions on the size of royalty payments and time allowed for making royalty payments to suppliers of technology encouraged the suppliers to favour lumpsum transfers. By discouraging long term relationships between suppliers and buyers of technology, this practice often made suppliers less responsible for ensuring successful technology transfers. Now things are different, with the liberalisations of direct foreign investment, import of technology and conditions on royalty payments. More than these relaxations, what will facilitate most, the easy access to modern technology is the freedom given to MNCs for operating in India and for repatriation of profits. They will be bringing their proven products and technologies to India to reap the benefits offered by the vast market of the country.

This means that there will be a new dimension to the competition—older technologies vs new technologies.

From shortages to surplus

One ubiquitous feature that has pervaded the Indian economy all these years is shortages. The people of the country were the victims of all round shortages, shortage practically in every sector, consumer goods, industrial goods and services. Many companies were going on with old plants and out-dated processes; many others could not expand on account of the controls and restrictions. Naturally, output was affected leading to shortages. To make things worse, a number of industrial units with their vested interest in shortages, managed to perpetuate the shortage situation. In some cases, even artificial scarcities were created. Demand and supply both were the outcome of Government imagination; and within the given framework, industry played the role that suited them.

Price controls by Government acted as another major cause of shortages in a number of industries. Quite often, the price controls served as a disincentive for production and as an incentive for production cutbacks. In the words of T. Thomas, former chairman of HLL, "...As the rigours of price control continue, honest manufacturers will find it unviable to continue the manufacture of products. They will even try to minimise their losses by reducing their production. This happened in the soap and vanaspati industries in the '70s, which created widespread shortages and rampant black marketing. Whereas the trade was able to sell the products at unofficial premia of 100 per cent, the manufacturers were forced to sell at highly unremunerative prices. They had to discontinue production in order to curtail cash losses which they incurred on every tonne of product. Black-marketers among the manufacturers thrived on the shortages and amassed unaccounted tax-free money which they shared happily with those who could be of use to them."

The country, the markets, and the people suffered the shortages. This situation is going to change now. The Government has taken away the controls on capacity, as well as on expansions and diversification of industries. Now that decisions on investments will be left to the entrepreneurs concerned, industry will function based on market mechanism, not by Government dictates. Investments will take place in areas of demand; and production will rise to meet demand. And the country will very soon witness a true transition from rationing of shortages to marketing of surpluses.

The challenge of graduating from shoddy products to products of excellence

It is a very peculiar phenomenon: while India is reckoned as one of the largest of markets in the world, Indian products sadly, are rated among the shoddiest of products in the world! Here lies the biggest threat and hence the severest of challenges for the Indian companies. To transnational companies, India is a wonderful market with unlimited potential for many products. Most naturally they will rush in when the doors are open to them. The Indian companies never bothered to cultivate this gold mine. Production mastery and product excellence were never their concern. And over a period of years, most of them have simply acquired the image of the shoddy producer. When commerce round the world was operating on the singular principle that innovation and marketing are the only key functions of business, companies in India were excelling in producing low quality products and dumping them on the hapless Indian consumer.

In several product categories, the Indian consumer was paying the highest price for the shoddiest product. From garments to motor cars this position has been almost always true. Every product carried an invisible tag for the consumer—'take it or leave it'. While a low level of quality was a common phenomenon among almost all sectors of industry, quality of products in sectors under price control deteriorated to lowest common standards. Because, under the price control regime the inevitable reaction of the manufacturers is to survive by adopting the lowest possible standards of quality and service that they can get away with.

The rules of the game now stand changed. The Indian consumer is now face to face with the best producers of the world, or perhaps to put it better, he is face to face with the best products of the world. He is no longer required to subsidise the antiquated production processes and products, the inefficiencies and the myopia of Indian companies. He can now readily switch over to a well made product. Though all along, he had the money to spend, and the willingness to spend, he could not get a well engineered product. Now, there is someone round the corner ready to give him the promised product, a product that will perform. And therefore, for the companies of India it becomes a question of their survival—they have to graduate from shoddy products to products of excellence.

This problem relating to quality will acquire a particularly difficult dimension in the context of the new focus on exports and globalisation. Indian companies will feel the pinch as they have never done before. For example, BHEL found that it could not achieve its planned exports without paying attention to quality and obtaining international certifications. As a part of its new strategy to boost exports, BHEL set a target date to obtain ISO-9000 certification for its products. Such a move was taken by the company following loss of orders worth several hundred crores on the ground that it did not have ISO-9000 certification. The company faced disqualification in several cases. A supplier without the certification was also required to pay higher insurance rates. The company realised that in international markets, third party quality assessment and registration is a must for doing business. It organised a crash programme for obtaining ISO certification for its plants and products. Philips India too had to face a similar challenge on the quality front when it wanted to export its audio systems. It later secured the ISO certification.

THE EXACTING DEMANDS OF A BUYER'S MARKET

The Indian business scene has already started feeling the exacting demands of a buyer's market. This is true of all sectors—consumer products, industrial products and services. In fact, even before the effect of industrial liberalisation could be seen in the form of expansion of installed capacities and actual production in various industries, the liberalisation of imports and the reduction in imports tariffs in respect of several products have expedited the changeover to a buyer's market situation. It has already exposed the vulnerability of several companies who were practically in a monopoly situation, with customers always at their mercy in all matters, from pricing to quality to availability.

In the past, the artificial barriers to entry and limits on growth of firms, had led to an increase in monopolies. The shackles served the interests of the producers, rather than the interests of the buyers. There was inadequate emphasis on reduction of costs, upgradation of technology and improvement of quality standards. And the buyer suffered.

If the suffering of the buyer in the consumer goods sector was bad enough the industrial buyer's dilemma had been worse still. He has always been at the mercy of a couple of manufacturers, and in certain cases, he had only one supplier to bank on. Because of the Government policy of restricting imports, the industrial buyers of the country were literally tied to one or two Indian suppliers. The Government tied them up! That was the extreme situation of a total seller's market making the life of a buyer more than miserable.

Cost escalations can no longer be passed on automatically to buyers

The emerging buyers market will alter the situation drastically. And one area where the difference would clearly manifest itself will be pricing. With the emerging buyers market, it will no longer be easy for firms to pass on cost escalations automatically to buyers. In the petrochemicals market, for example, the earlier practice was that the producers were passing on all their costs to the ultimate buyer, unconcerned about the buyer's viability. How things changed overnight for such sellers, at the dawn of the open regime can be best appreciated through IPCL's distress sale of 10,000 MT of paraxylene, to Bombay Dyeing. For paraxylene, IPCL was the only producer in India and Bombay Dyeing the only customer. All along, IPCL could dictate the price and sell because for Bombay Dyeing the alternative source was imports which was obviously costlier because of the 85 per cent import duty on the product. When there were indications that Government might reduce the duty from 85 per cent to 25 per cent, IPCL had to think it over. It had 15,000 MT of paraxylene stocks, with an additional 1000 MT coming every month. Bombay Dyeing, in the new situation, was unwilling to buy at the sticker price of Rs 22,000 per MT though the cost of importing paraxylene was higher. IPCL went in for a distress sale, well below the declared price, just recovering the variable cost for the corporation. Obviously things were turning to a situation where the seller and the buyer had to come together and sort out pricing problems which is the normal pattern in an industrial product marketing situation.

And when the Government turned its magic wand once again, IPCL was the beneficiary—in naphtha. When the Government decanalised the import of naphtha, IPCL as a major buyer, was the biggest beneficiary; the monopoly sellers, the public sector refineries and the IOC were the losers. The prevailing global price of naphtha was cheaper by Rs 1,000 per tonne compared to the price of the domestic product.

Change in business style already discernible

The new environment has already started working. A change in business style on the part of the earlier day monopoly sellers is already discernible. After the massive increase of the prices of petro products in September

1992, there were expectations that prices of petrochemicals would go up. But many petrochemical companies ruled out immediate hike in their product prices following the increase in feed stock prices announced by the Government. Their explanation was that the market will not accept the increase. Such a response was a new phenomenon for India.

Marketing men in India in varied businesses, who all along had it easy, will start feeling the pressure of the new demands thrown up by the changing market conditions. And companies who never felt the compulsion to devote due attention to the marketing function will suddenly find that they are getting stuck with stocks, which all along used to 'move out' without their having to toil. They did not anticipate a situation where their customers can by-pass their products and instantly turn to another brand or a substitute product, superior in quality and perhaps even cheaper. The new market with its crucial feature being choice and free availability, will now force the companies to behave differently—to offer the products the way the consumer wants.

The consumer gaining new importance

In the new business environment, the consumer is going to be the enviable beneficiary. The companies who could all along afford to disregard the consumer are today in the unenviable position of having to compete—compete to win the favour of the consumer. Rules of business which were unilaterally in favour of the producer are now being rewritten in favour of the consumer. Companies and managements will now witness the situation where the consumer calls the tune. Rules which would have automatically changed long back but for the overdose of protection showered on the Indian manufacturer now stand repealed.

In the new context, the Indian consumer is going to be a highly demanding creature. Industrial units are going to see a new consumer whose expectations keep soaring. Indian businessmen have been too pre-occupied with their product to find any time for the consumer for whom the product was intended. To their surprise, they will now find that the consumer is gaining the dominant place in their business schemes without their being even aware of it.

INDUSTRY STRUCTURE WILL ALTER

The new policies will also lead to change in the structure of several industries. The dismantling of industrial licences and controls and the relaxations in policies relating to foreign investment, foreign technology import and MRTP, will all result in a thorough rehashing of the number of players, capacity and relative shares in the industry concerned. There may be expansions in capacities by the existing units in the industry; there may be new entrants. In the licence era, industrial production was governed by the licensing system. In the new de-licensed regime, production patterns would be market driven, conforming to demand patterns and income distribution patterns. The change will have its impact on industry structure in several industries. The opening up of a number of industries hitherto reserved for the public sector to the private sector and the reversal of roles between the public and private sectors will also contribute to the change in industry structure.

The new diversification spree also will contribute to changes in industry structure. Liberalisation and deregulation have the natural potential of driving companies into unrelated diversification. When entry barriers are absent, many companies may like to have a piece of the action in many unrelated businesses which may seem to them as attractive. A combination of the desire to have a piece of the action in the unrelated fields and the herd psychology may act in concert and lead to over-crowding in some industries. Naturally, the industry structure will alter in such industries. The new regime also permits and facilitates mergers. Industry structure will naturally alter on account of the mergers too.

Industry structure may also alter on account of the entry of a number of new and substitute products. It is natural to expect that in the open regime, with the easy access to technologies and investments from different corners of the world, many new and substitute products may enter on a scale hitherto unknown. And the process may have a powerful impact on the existing products and the units producing them. The market shares of the various operators in the industries concerned may change, leading to the alteration of the industry structure.

Notions on scale economies will alter

In the new scheme of things, it seems that small is no longer beautiful. With liberalisation and deregulation, ideas associated with scale economies have drastically changed. In the past, operating on a smaller scale enjoined some benefits on the enterprises. And in many cases, the enterprises had to be content with smaller scale units out of compulsion, since licences were just not available for larger capacities. With the opening up of the economy, and entry of MNCs backed by substantial investment and state-of-the-art technology, 'Going big' is going to be the order of the day. When substantial cost advantages accrue out of large sized operations, even the big companies of India will have to redefine their optimum scale structure and cost-volume-price equations.

In fact, the rush seen in the wake of the NEP in the matter of corporate mergers sprang from the need and desire for scale upgradation. For example, HLL, already the unquestioned market leader in soaps and detergents, found it necessary to still go bigger and went in for acquisition of Tomco, the second largest player in the industry. Overnight HLL which already had a high capacity at 2,05,186 MT of soaps and detergents, increased it to 2,82,084 MT by the acquisition of 76,898 MT of Tomco's capacity. In the bargain, HLL enhanced its market share to a formidable

70 per cent. Many other companies also took to the merger route. Mergers of EEC and GEC, David Brown Greaves and Greaves Cotton, Renusagar Power and Hindal Industries, Quest International India and Pond's, and NOCIL and PIL were mooted.

The proposal for the setting up of an international size radial tyre unit is another example. Radial tyre units set up so far in India have been of much smaller size compared to world standards. Now, Modis, JKs and Apollo Tyres who are competitors in the tyre industry are turning out as collaborators and are going to put up a joint venture for the manufacture of (bus and truck) radial tyres. Naturally, size upgradation and superior technology come hand in hand in the proposed venture, which is expected to cost Rs 1,000 crore and will be using the technology of Continental of Germany, a tyre giant and a major technology supplier in the radial tyre business.

The attempts towards integration of India's economy with the global economy will also contribute greatly to the alteration of Indian concept of scale economies. In the new context, economic size need no longer be linked to the size of the Indian market. It can assume a truly global connotation. The passenger car industry in India is an example. Though India constitutes a vast market for many other products, for a product like passenger car, the Indian market is minuscule by international standards. Annual sale of passenger cars in India is of the order of 90,000, whereas in the US, annual sale is in the order of 9 million or around 100 times that of India with about a fourth of India's population. A car unit enjoying economy of scale in the country has been out of question all these years. And with the fragmentation of the small size demand over four or five car manufacturers, there was no possibility for any one of them to do well. In the years to come, the story may be different. Car units of international size may be established in India, catering partly to the Indian market and largely to the global market. It is because of this new potential following the liberalisations that international giants in the auto industry have turned their eyes towards India. As soon as indications came from the Government that the Indian car industry too would be delicensed soon, the foreign auto giants started their scouting. The big companies of India in the auto industry have also started gearing up to seize the opportunity. While they are examining initially the possibility of putting a new Indian car on the Indian roads, they are also looking at the possibility of setting up a global size car unit in India which will serve mostly as the manufacturing base to serve a world wide market. Obviously, if the idea clicks, the ideas associated with minimum economic size will undergo revolutionary change. And the scenario may apply to any other product, not merely passenger car. Now that the law and the environment permit such operations, concepts relating to scale economy, economic capacity and minimum investment will all change in course of time in several industries.

INVESTOR PRESSURE WILL MOUNT ON CORPORATE SECTOR

There is another challenge that is equally certain to materialise in the post-liberalisation era. Investors' pressure on enterprises and managements would mount like never before, requiring a strategic response from them. It may perhaps take some time for the pressure to become perceptible and forceful. But once the momentum is gained, it would become a big force and the entire corporate sector would come under the pressure. The large community of middle class investors who constitute today the investor force in the corporate sector, would vociferously demand efficient and profitable performance from the industry. Since a large part of the investment by this group comes via the mutual funds (public sector mutual funds till recently, private funds too now) the pressure would mainly come via the mutual funds. There are already 12 mutual funds in operation in the country, 11 in the public sector including the UTI and those of LIC and GIC and one in the private sector. The Unit Trust is by far the largest and its investible funds surpass Rs 35,000 crore. The remaining ten mutual funds also have been making impressive progress, of late. Today, the number of subscribers to mutual funds exceeds a million. For private mutual funds, approval has already been given by SEBI to six parties and more are on the way. In a couple of years time, the private mutual funds will become a big force in the investment scenario. Public or private, mutual funds in the new scenario will be subjected to the same type of pressure—the real investors behind the funds will assert themselves and exercise pressure on the funds, on investment decisions. Investment will be made with the sole aim of earning good returns including capital appreciation. Financial institutions and mutual funds may keep aloof from scrips that are not backed up by performance. The capital market will be made to mirror the earning capability of the enterprises. And enterprises which cannot provide attractive dividends and capital appreciation, whether in public or private sector, would lose investor support. As it invariably happens in all market economies, in India too, the investors would now call the tune.

As Government sheds its role as the biggest buyer, industry will face new challenges in marketing

In India, the Government has all along been the biggest purchaser. This was so because Government was the biggest investor in the industry of the country, holding the reins of production in the country. Government was the biggest purchaser of stores, machinery, projects and services. While the significance of the change in the Government's role as producer seems to be well understood, what is not so readily appreciated is the fact that Government's role as the largest buyer is also vanishing, with severe implications to the sellers of goods. Several companies of India, big and small, in a variety of businesses, existed and thrived mainly by selling to the Government. They could pursue just one customer and make their sale and profits. And the rules of selling to the Government, an institutional buyer, an impersonal buyer, have been vastly different from selling to individual buyers. Even among institutional buyers, selling to discriminating private business firms is a far more difficult job. Selling to the impersonal machinery, the Government, was infinitely easier. Government as a buyer operated on different norms. It was overconcerned with cost/price. Quality and performance were subsidiary considerations. Now, when Government buying is replaced by hundreds of companies, selling will be possible only on the planks of quality and performance. Those who want to sell will have to deliver the promised product, the guaranteed product, the performing product, and not "the lowest quoted product".

The example of the cement industry will illustrate the point well. Following the emphasis on deficit reduction and expenditure cuts, the Government slowed down its purchase of cement among many other products. The Director General of Supplies & Disposals (DGSD) virtually did not buy any cement during April-September 1991. One can well imagine the impact of this on an industry which supplies 35-40 per cent of its output to the Government. Cement business suffered a substantial setback.

CHALLENGES EMANATING FROM THE CHANGES IN INTERNATIONAL ENVIRONMENT

The challenges emanating from the new environment of India presents just one part of the picture. There is the international environment posing another set of challenges. It is not as if only companies going global need an understanding of the global environment; even firms that are confined to the domestic market will be affected by the process of globalisation of the Indian economy and the changes taking place in the global environment. The activities of the Indian firms aspiring to go global as well as the manoeuvres of international firms who would contribute to the de-insulation of India, would compel all firms operating in India to be alive to the global scenario.

It is of particular significance that India's liberalisation of industry and business coincide with a time when substantial changes are taking place in the global business scene. New business/market alliances, new market blocs and new geopolitical entities are emerging. The resurgence of Germany, the reshaping of the former USSR into the new Russian market, the demise of Comecon, China that is fast turning into a market economy, the EC, emerging anew as a powerful business bloc, the emergence of Japan as the new monitor of world business and of course the US becoming more powerful as the new arbiter in world affairs in the new unipolar world and trying to regain its supremacy in world business, are all shaping an altogether new situation. It is into this juggernaut of global business environment that India is entering backed by her newly designed globalisation process.

Besides the changes in global geopolitical equations and international economic relations, another unique phenomenon is taking place right now in the mega environs. More and more nations are today turning to the market economy concept as the viable route for their well being. Economics, business and marketing dominate the world today. Politics, military and security concerns have taken the backseat. And the world is emerging as one big market, one great bazaar. It is into this great shopping centre that Indian businessmen are poised to enter, and they will now be compelled to get attuned to the new global dynamics.

Exporting becomes everyone's priority

In the new regime, exporting has become a must for every enterprise. The new trade policy has made every entrepreneur and industrial organisation sit up and reorient their strategies. The new policy actually has brought a compulsion on them for earning the foreign exchange required by them for the import of whatever raw materials or components they needed for keeping their production lines going.

In the earlier era, procuring an import licence was a problem, but once an import licence was obtained, foreign exchange was available from the RBI at the offical exchange rate. In the new era, while licence is no longer a problem, the import has to be financed by the forex bought from the market at the ruling market rate. And with the full float of the rupee, the exchange was becoming costlier for the importer. In addition to the cost aspect, the risk associated with depending on the market for the entire exchange requirements of the enterprise was also coming to the fore. The only long term and viable solution lay in setting up one's own export base.

Earlier only a handful of companies like Tata Exports and ITC had taken to exports seriously and systematically. Now, many companies are turning to the overseas market. In fact, it seems that practically every company in India has started feeling the compulsion to take to export. Reliance Europe, Essar World Trade, Ceat, Fairgrowth Exim are all newcomers. Eicher, Videocon, Salora and SRF had entered a little earlier and are now trying to consolidate the small foothold they had gained. Essar World Trade has a Rs 500 crore target. Reliance Europe, too, has high targets. They have tied up with Itochu. Companies like Videocon who were solely relying on the USSR market are now shifting their focus to other countries.

Tata Steel has made exports a thrust area. It realised the importance of exports in the new context and decided to market a good part of its steel internationally. During '91-92, the export of the company came to Rs 450 crore. Bharat Forge Ltd., (BFL) is another company that has made exports a thrust area. Earlier, BFL's main export customers were USSR and Poland. Now, it has shifted the focus to Japan, the US and Europe. It is actually negotiating major export contracts with Mitsubishi Motors,

Toyota and Mazda of Japan, Daimler-Benz of Germany, and Cummins Engine National Forge of the U.S. The company recently invested Rs 100 crore in a highly automated plant to produce forgings of international quality.

Mafatlals also has turned to exports. The company invested Rs 90 crore on modernisation exclusively aimed at export. Fresh investments had to be made not only in the factory, but even in office and communication systems. Mafatlals export grey cloth to some of the best companies in the world in the retail garment business. London's Mark and Spencer regularly sources its materials from Mafatlal. The next aim of the company, is to export fabric and then garments under its own brand name.

Thapar group is also taking to exports. It has set up Thapar International which will handle exports of the group's firms — Ballarpur Industries, Crompton Greaves, JCT, Toscana Shoes etc. Leather and glass will be one of the thrust areas. Modelled after ITC's international business division, Thapar International would re-group exports under one company to acquire a star trading house status. Companies like Sundaram Fasteners and Parle Agro have also turned to exports. Sundaram Fasteners has set up an exclusive export division. It is aiming at a Rs 100 crore turnover by '95. Parle Agro has started exporting its Frooti mango drink to the middle east. The company now plans to export the product to Europe and the US.

While exports become everybody's business in the new context, it is certainly not going to be an easy business for everybody. In fact, the compulsion to expand export and the difficulty in accomplishing it, together constitute one major business challenge of the open regime. India's position is definitely peculiar in the matter of exports. The concept of exportable surplus which many other countries in the world recognise and practise does not apply to India. The 880 million strong market or demand base does not really allow anything to become exportable surplus. Most products that are made in India can really get consumed within the country on account of the huge population and the growing purchasing power of a vast section of that population. Companies in India have to necessarily enlarge output of various products and also earmark a good portion of it for exports; they can not embrace the concept of "exporting the exportable surplus". And there is no shortcut to boosting exports. Indian companies have to produce quality goods and services that will serve the needs of global customers, stand global competition in terms of price and technological excellence and follow the best marketing practices. Through improved scales of production and technological upgradation, the companies have to become cost competitive, too.

R&D and innovation become inescapable

R&D and innovation now become crucial to business success. Indian companies have been by and large neglecting R&D and product innovation for a variety of reasons. Government controls of various types, especially the control on prices of products have been one main reason. It is natural that when an industry is kept under price control, the firms in that industry will neither have the resources nor the motivation to invest in modernisation or R&D. But Government controls and paucity of resources cannot be cited as the only reason behind this position. Even some of the big companies who could afford the cost of research and development chose to by-pass this route, as in their scheme of things it was an activity that could be dispensed with, a cost that could be spared. For example, in the pharmaceutical industry investment in R&D is just 2 per cent of sales, whereas in the developed countries it is 12 per cent. Hardly any new product has materialised out of Indian firms' R&D efforts. What we have seen on the consumer product front as well as the industrial product front, were some me-too products. But now when the real thing, the original brands are going to be here with the full and direct support of the concerned foreign companies, competing with them with me-too products will obviously become a losing game. The pointer is clear. Companies of India have to necessarily spend on R&D and develop new products suitable to the Indian market in their respective businesses. Only through original product ideas that will specifically suit India, can Indian firms hope to meet the new competition. R&D and innovation is the only route to such new ideas. Since many companies have not developed even the infrastructure required for such an activity, and since this cannot be done overnight, having a shelf of new product ideas will take time. And this is the threat they face.

VULNERABILITY, ANOTHER MAJOR CHALLENGE

It is not a sudden development. It is the exposure that is sudden. Many of the Indian corporations have all along been vulnerable on a variety of counts. With liberalisation, vulnerability has come to the fore.

In many industries, vulnerability arose primarily out of a one-product-syndrome, one-technology-syndrome and a captive-market-syndrome. A textile company is stuck with one product, sari, a shoe company thinks of only shoes for its product portfolio, a soap company can have just soap and perhaps shampoo too. The vulnerability would have been offset if the companies concerned had built up some entry barrier in their businesses. They did not accomplish this either. The only barrier to entry was the Government licence and control and it stands removed today. Every business is now entry free and every company is vulnerable. All these years, the companies have not built up any edge in respect of suppliers or raw materials or trade channels. Nor have they acquired any other advantage that would reduce their vulnerability. They do not have a special knowhow or technology to compensate. The vulnerability of several industrial enterprises of India is bound to get exposed in the new environment. And since there are many facets to the vulnerability of the enterprises, the exposure would also be on several fronts.

Vulnerability from one product syndrome — SCICI example

In the case of, SCICI the vulnerability has emerged essentially from its one product syndrome, its sole dependence on shipping finance business. The free market of today is forcing the SCICI to change track completely. The five year old shipping financier is going in for a wider portfolio of businesses. The company feels that remaining with just one business, namely shipping, is risky, making the company highly vulnerable. In its scheme of diversification, the company is looking for businesses far removed from its current product line of shipping finance. It is considering businesses like food processing, power generation, communication networks and even tourism. As per its restructure plan, five years from now shipping will account for only 50 per cent of its business portfolio. To quote the company "we would not like our entire fortunes to be tied down to one industry". And the new environment expedited the restructure process.

Vulnerability consequent to the disappearance of monopoly

The changes effected in the roles of the public and private sectors, the decanalisation of imports and the removal of privileged positions enjoyed hitherto by public sector organisations, have exposed the vulnerability of several public sector units.

MMTC, STC and MSTC

With decanalisation of imports of major items and the ending of monopoly state trading, the giant corporations, MMTC, STC and MSTC suddenly stand exposed. It is a case of a huge business segment being suddenly snatched away from them due to the opening up of the economy. Several commodities have been decanalised in the wake of the NEP, and the volume of annual business snatched away from MMTC, STC and MSTC has been to the tune of Rs 1,500 crore phosphoric acid and ammonia, Rs 500 crore steel, Rs 1,400 crore in sulphur, rock phosphate and non-ferrous metals, Rs 1,600 crore in metal scrap and Rs 400 crore in newsprint.

As far as MMTC is concerned, the decanalisation of a number of items including non-ferrous metals, steel and fertiliser raw materials, has caused great havoc to the fortunes of the company. It has pruned its metal imports division and wound up the export trade group; and slashed its turnover targets for '93-94 by 30 per cent. It has lined up restructure plans to revive its fortunes; the plans include engineering and textile joint ventures. While MMTC is trying for restructure, hundreds of key people have left STC availing of the VRS. MSTC who had only one business, metal scrap, is in deeper trouble.

The large private business houses of India, Reliance Europe, Essar World Trade, Salora International, Birla International, Raunaq International, ITC, TISCO and Hindujas have already entered the scene to secure the new business that is opening up with the abolition of the monopoly of the public sector trading corporations.

IL&FS

Infrastructure Leasing and Financial Service (IL&FS) is another example of vulnerability coming to the fore, the moment the advantage of monopoly disappeared. IL&FS was set up by the UTI, Central Bank and the HDFC to finance and pioneer infrastructure projects. With the Government's new policies on throwing open the infrastructure sector to private participation, IL&FS has decided to diversify to new areas of business including communication, broking and data services.

IOC, HPCL and CRL

With liberalisation, petro products are no longer the exclusive preserve of the public sector petroleum companies. In kerosene and LPG business, companies like HPCL, the domestic producer of kerosene and IOC, the erstwhile sole importer of kerosene have suddenly lost out. It was a business over which they have enjoyed monopoly for many years. A good part of the business has now been snatched away from them, with the entry of the private trade into the business.

In the benzene business, petroleum refineries like CRL and HPCL have been for years the main domestic producers and suppliers. And IOC has been the sole importer. All users of benzene in the chemical, petrochemical, pesticides, pharmaceuticals and dye business were totally dependent on these companies. With the decanalisation of benzene import and the liberalisation of import procedures, several actual users of benzene in the country have turned to international suppliers bypassing the domestic suppliers. The users are no longer obliged to buy their requirements from the domestic sources; and the foreign suppliers offer the product at cheaper rates. The first casualties in the new scenario have been CRL and HPCL. They are now required for the first time, to face competition and market the product in a non-monopoly and non-administered price environment. IOC is the next casualty, losing an attractive monopoly business—the canalised import of the product.

THE CHALLENGES ON THE FINANCE MANAGEMENT FRONT

The open regime has thrown up special challenges on the finance management front, too. The financial climate in the country has vastly changed.

The interesting variety of financial services now available in the country is a pointer to the changes taking place in the corporate finance scene of India. While prudent corporations all along knew the importance of strategic management of their finance, now, the requirements have become more complex and pressing. In fact, a number of new finance functions/tasks have emerged due to the changes in the economic scenario of the country and the new globalisation endeavour.

The new need for gaining expertise in forex management

The new trade policy with its reliance on balancing of exports and imports and full convertibility of the rupee, has made forex management an important job. In addition, it has also brought in a number of relatively new tasks in forex management such as:

Exchange risk management—Finance men now have to watch exchange rate movements and tackle their exchange risks through swaps, options and futures. Such instruments/modalities and their management have become important.

Asset management—Export proceeds are tangible foreign exchange assets and deploying them efficiently is a crucial task, today.

Liability management—Imports and borrowings of foreign funds also need expert handling. Finance men will have to use swaps and options and manage their liability in an innovative manner.

Keeping track of credit rating—They have to track interest rates and credit rating of countries, measure the movement of relative exchange rates and assess the risk involved.

Raising equity abroad

As Indian companies undertake world scale projects, funds cannot be sourced from the domestic markets alone. Global issues are now likely to be resorted to more frequently. In fact, taking advantage of the new provisions for raising equity abroad, more than 30 Indian companies have planned to raise equity abroad to fund their projects.

The job obviously becomes one of developing an altogether new financial expertise. It means acclimatisation with international finance, which is undergoing fast changes. To aid corporations in these matters, financial service firms have cropped up. But even to avail of the service of such firms, the corporate finance people ought to have a comprehensive knowledge of the new context, the new instruments and the new services. Globalisation compulsions anticipate not only marketing skills, but financial skills and expertise in line with the international standards.

Many new developments on domestic finance front, too

On the domestic business front too, a number of new dimensions to the finance job have emerged; new business trends and hence new compulsions to money management have emerged. While some of them have been short term trends answering short term problems, others are settling into more stable patterns.

Greater resort to equity and a sea change in debt-equity ratio

In the earlier days, companies went to the market and raised equity capital mainly for implementing projects—new projects or expansions. Recent trends show that the corporate sector uses the equity route for a variety of new purposes like repaying borrowings, augmenting long term working capital, meeting periodical requirement of capital expenditure and meeting cost overruns of projects. And with the free pricing of capital issues and abolition of CCI, more and more companies are entering the capital market and the equity route. The frequency of equity issue has been particularly high in 1991-92 and 1992-93. Charging of high premium is the other equally pronounced development. Industrial enterprises are keen on securing the maximum premium for their issues of equity shares and fully and partly convertible bonds. Free pricing regime is freely being used for achieving diverse financial purposes—purposes for which equity issues were never resorted to in the earlier era.

In the recent past, the cost of short-term money has been going up, with minimum rate pegged as high as 20 per cent. Long term funds which were available at 14 or 15 per cent in the late '80s have moved up to 18 or 19 per cent. In fact, companies pay out nearly one-fifth of their total costs to banks and institutions as interest. With interest costs becoming more and more of a burden, companies are trying to replace debt with equity with a view to slashing interest liability. And many of them are choosing to rely on equity for working capital requirements as well. Though servicing equity is going to be costly and difficult, many companies go in for expansion of their equity.

A sea change has taken place in the share of debt finance in project cost. In the past, a 4 : 1 debt : equity ratio was the common pattern in most manufacturing concerns. And in trading projects, the ratio was higher at 5 : 1 or 6 : 1. In the first place, debt finance was available in good measure. Secondly, there was no ban on going for a high debt component. Thirdly, the debt finance was not expensive; in fact, some incentives were available under certain conditions, to those who took debt finance.

This trend has, now, vastly changed. Debt : equity ratio now hovers around 2 : 1. Because of the anxiety to minimise dependence on borrowing from term lending institutions and to prevent an undue increase in interest burden, the accent has now been on equity issues and fully and partly convertible debentures. As donors, financial institutions are also not happy now to finance projects with a higher debt component. Constraint of funds and increasing risks have made the financial institutions and banks prefer a low component of debt. Simultaneously, the boom in the stock market has promoted the increase in the equity portion. Moreover, debt is becoming costlier day by day, whereas equity comes with a good premium. Cutting interest costs and paying off debt assume top priority now. The new possibility for realising hefty premium means more funds flowing into the reserves and an opportunity for the company to reduce its debt burden. No wonder, industry has been showing distinct preference for equity over debt.

Turning to the market instead of the banks, even for debt capital

Companies now find that their working capital requirements will be constantly on the increase and it is going to be a long term phenomenon. Logically, then, they had to raise funds on a long term basis rather than on a short-term basis. They do not mind paying a premium interest for such long term facilities as the short term facilities are just not available with the required degree of reliability. And, the business stakes of fund-shortage are quite high. As such, with the short term bank finance becoming costly and scarce, companies naturally looked to other avenues—from using call money markets to raising equity to meet their working capital requirements. Videocon for example, quickly went to the capital market and raised the required funds through five year bonds at 20 per cent, as its requirement of finance far exceeded what the banks could provide.

Taking to equity route even for working capital

Similarly, companies do not now mind expanding the equity base to meet the growing working capital requirement. As the short term money became very volatile besides becoming very costly, they have started shoring up their equity capital, using it to meet their working capital requirement.

P&G is one example: By raising equity at a premium, P&G mobilised Rs 37 crore and used it to reduce its interest burden. The company utilised Rs 15 crore out of the newly generated funds towards working capital and brought down its borrowings on working capital account from Rs 30 crore to Rs 15 crore. The remaining Rs 22 crore was utilised for repaying loans to banks, carrying an interest rate of 16 per cent. These borrowings were actually in the nature of a bridge loan to fund advertisement expenses, till the equity came in. Ballarpur Industries is another example. The company is poised to raise Rs 125 crore through its issue at a premium of Rs 165 per share of Rs 10 face value. A substantial part of the resources thus raised will be used for liquidating working capital loans.

Pressure on margins & profits

For many companies, the days of assured sales and profits are over. They have to be extra vigilant about costs. Only through effective cost control coupled with a high level of productivity and quality assurance, can companies now ensure their bottomline targets. Financing costs have been going up considerably besides material costs and labour costs. Similarly, distribution and marketing costs have also been escalating. In the new era of hi-competition, all these higher costs cannot be automatically passed on to the consumers, as done in the earlier era. For many products, there will be no takers on those terms. The rise in costs coupled with the inability to pass it on to the consumer will erode the profits of companies.

Evidently, liberalisation will not automatically bring in profits to industries. In fact, the converse is true. Liberalisation will put corporate profits under severe pressure. It was the licence-control regime of yesteryears that used to guarantee profits to corporations even when they turned out shoddy products at high cost.

To make matters more difficult, domestic supplies of many products would increase, with de-regulation, putting pressure on sales volumes and market shares of many firms. Furthermore, the progressive cutting down of tariff and non-tariff barriers should mean a bigger supply of imported goods. The net effect of an increased supply of goods in the market, a widespread hike in costs and a drop in sales would be a pruning of profit margins.

The need to understand and utilise the new crop of financial services

The range of financial services has widened enormously. They include: lease and hire purchase finance, broking, consumer finance, corporate finance, corporate funds management, mutual funds, merchant banking, money market operations, equity trading, venture capital finance, corporate advisory services, international finance, fixed deposits and portfolio management.

The entry of foreign institutional investors, private sector mutual funds and tie-ups with international broking firms are widening the scope for financial services. The more agile companies are not only using the available new financial services, they are also launching new companies of their own, in the financial services business. They are developing financial expertise in key areas—providing financial advisory services to transnational companies operating in India, providing advisory services to Indian companies raising capital abroad and providing research and development support to FII's coming to India. Ceat Financial Services Limited, to cite one example, is gearing up to the challenge of globalisation by developing expertise in forex advisory services, and lease financing.

THE TRAUMA OF TRANSITION

It would be evident even to a casual observer that Indian business is in a stage of transition. There is hectic activity all round. Well known companies of the world with their tempting brands, are ready to initiate the Indian consumers, especially the urban middle class consumers, into a hi-consumption life style. A new production-consumption chain will be set in motion. Not only will new companies and new businesses emerge; even new ways of doing business will emerge: Mergers, amalgamations, takeovers, technology tie-ups, strategic alliances, investment partnerships, marketing collaborations, and franchise arrangements to name but a few.

The Government is going ahead with the economic reforms. The 1993-94 budget, the third since the commencement of the new economic programme, is also out announcing more measures towards strengthening the course of reform. Full convertibility of the rupee on trade account has been brought about, to the surprise of every one, especially the economic commentators who were calculating that the country would take another two years to introduce it. The entire corporate sector of India will feel the impact of this reform process. Many companies may not right now know how exactly their companies and their businesses are going to be affected. The economic environment is in a state of flux; existing rules and existing patterns are undergoing a major change, but new patterns are taking their own time to take shape.

The companies of India are obviously experiencing the trauma of transition. An element of confusion and chaos is inherent in this state of transition. As Charles Dickens said,

> *"It was the best of times*
> *It was the worst of times*
> *The epoch of belief*
> *The epoch of incredulity"*

Whether and to what extent the companies of India will withstand this trauma of transition and pull out of it successfully, will depend upon their management strength.

THE TIME FOR STRATEGIC MANAGEMENT HAS ARRIVED

The foregoing discussions would clearly indicate that the task ahead for Indian industry and business is an uphill one; their existing systems and styles will have to be honed the way they have never before been done. They will have to change their styles, systems and structures; they will have to bring in fresh investments to reap the benefits of scale economies; they will have to even change the way they used to think about their businesses. The very mindset of Indian businessmen will be required to change. The way the new economic policies are pushing India on the path of change, is sure to transform Indian industry and business beyond recognition. It is almost like the sea taking a sudden deviation. But it is happening. It is a turn which people thought India would never take. And when it really happens the participants in the drama of change are bewildered.

Does this all mean that Indian industry and business will wither away? Where does Indian industry and business stand in the chess board of this new commercial battle? Do they have any defence?

Strategic management is the obvious answer. In the regulated and centrally planned regime, the need as well as scope for strategic management of enterprises has been rather limited. While in a market economy, corporate growth is always achieved as the result of strategic management, in a regulated economy it is achieved as the concomitant of the overall developmental planning of the economy. For countering competition too, strategic management is the obvious route in a market economy. In India, the intensity of competition has all along been limited. Naturally, there was no compulsion to apply the concept of strategic management on a wide basis in the industrial and business activities of the country. Active Government intervention in industrial and business operations, in the public as well as the private sector, was another inhibiting factor. Throughout the past regime, the Government had unfortunately promoted a myopic view of what management is all about. The country developed a wrong perception of the very aims of industry and business. There was an excessive concern with vaguely specified social objectives in the running of industry and business. The ground was not at all fertile for the application of strategic planning and strategic management. The excessively protected industrial environment acted as a cover for the serious weaknesses in the running of industrial enterprises and they were able to carry on.

Now, things will change. As big private investment is flowing in into many industries, supported in several cases by foreign direct investment, a powerful idea of real ownership will now be at work in industry and business, as a contrast to the notional ownership implied in the public sector concept that dominated the scene in the earlier regime. Another feature of the open regime is investor pressure about which mention has already been made in an earlier section. Investor pressure of a new kind contrasted to the era of big Government investment, will mean totally new demands on the way industry and business are going to be run in the country. Companies will now suddenly search for management techniques, techniques that can take them through their new-found problems. They will find that what they need is strategy evolved through a painstaking strategic planning process. They will also find that there is no shortcut to corporate success except through the long drawn out process of strategic planning. Techniques have to emanate from strategy and from long term strategic intent. Companies will be forced to understand that their most important task is to ensure profits and growth for the enterprise; their major job is marketing and innovation; and their major concern is creating and retaining customers and finding and developing markets. And the route for all this is strategic planning. Obviously the time for strategic management has arrived in India.

This chapter is an exposition of the travails, the challenges, the open threats, and the hidden dangers, the Indian industry will be subjected to in the open regime. What we are providing are only pointers or indicators of what could be in store for industry and business, in the private as well as the new-look public sector, for entrepreneurs, big and small, and for professional managers. This is just an alert or alarm call to Indian business so that the concerned can get up in time and prepare for the travel.

8

Strategic Planning for Corporate Success in the Open Regime

When we look at the world scene, we find that companies like GE, Siemens, Honda, Coca Cola, P&G and Johnson and Johnson which have become universally known cases of business success, have something in common: all of them have been strong on the strategy front, working with a clear cut and long term strategic intent. In India, however, a good majority of the companies, even big companies, have been playing a hit or miss game. Only a few companies have opted for a formal strategic planning frame and a systematic planning process. Even this small group of firms have confined themselves to short term plans. As for the large majority of Indian firms, they have not even tried out strategic planning in its rudimentary form, let alone work the future in their favour, which strategic planning is ultimately supposed to do.

END OF CONTROL–LICENCE ERA AND BEGINNING OF STRATEGIC PLANNING ERA FOR INDIAN FIRMS

The industrial and business units of India cannot be faulted for the above unsatisfactory situation. All these years, Indian industry and business were under a Control-Licence Raj. Governmental rules, regulations and controls imposed severe constraints in their attempts on a meaningful planning exercise. As J.R.D.Tata put it, "... even the bureaucrats of India themselves confess their inability to understand the total maze and multiplicity of rules, regulations, schedules, quotas, licences and reservations which seek to control any venture." In such a fettered environment where competition was at a very low ebb and demand-supply was artificially controlled, companies could attempt only some short term planning. They were mainly adjusting to the ever-changing rules of the government. Besides, the need for strategic planning was also very limited. All that companies had to do was to woo the government, obtain licences and manipulate the markets. Companies were neither compelled nor attracted to exploit the process of strategic planning. This was a function they could dispense with.

In the new regime of freedom of operation to industry and business, not only will the environment become conducive to the play and application of strategic planning frameworks, the environment will actually compel the companies to turn to scientific ways of managing business. When multifarious challenges raise against the companies, they will naturally find that the old ways no longer work; they will automatically turn to strategy, as they will find it the rewarding and cost-effective way of conducting their business. They will realise that strategic planning is their hedge against risk and uncertainty, the hedge against costly mistakes and overnight vulnerability. Strategic planning will thus become crucial to all companies of India, big and small, market leaders and followers, the mature players and the new entrants, the global operators and the niche planners.

The search for strategies

For the companies of India, the search for strategies will really begin now. In their anxiety to somehow tide over the new complex situation, they will in fact, resort to a mad rush for strategies. They may try to push their products offering some special incentives to the distribution channels, they may resort to price cuts, they may advertise more, they may go in for a new ad agency, they may try a change of their brand name, some of them may even try their hands at new businesses like imports and exports. While such a search is understandable under the circumstances, one cannot be sure about the value, the utility and the relevance of these strategies to the particular situation faced by the corporation.

How does one ensure he is forging the appropriate strategy for his business at this juncture? What is the strategy requirement in the long run? Strategy is not something that can be taken out of one's hat and pushed into the market all of a sudden. To forge the appropriate strategies, a company has to work backwards, do a lot of planning and home work, bring to the fore the corporation's ambitions, understand where its core competencies are, identify the competitive advantage it enjoys, pinpoint the gap in these areas, decide the broad businesses where it should stay and have a strong presence and only then can it decide on the kind of strategies it can employ. Strategic planning means performing these activities for the corporation. It is a process where an entire corporation commits itself to an important self-surgery. It involves knowing the organisation, its businesses and its environments so that the very excercise throws up the strategic alternatives in front of the firm. The aim and purpose of strategic planning is to ensure that the market front strategies of the firm have the back up of certain core competencies and competitive advantages lying with the corporation. Locating these core competencies and competitive advantages and developing and orchestrating the strategies in this direction is the main task in strategic planning.

This book is not intended to be a basic text on strategic planning. Still we are dwelling at some length on the essentials of this subject so as to provide the perspective needed for understanding and handling the strategic planning challenges of the open regime, which is the central theme of this book.

THE STRATEGIC PLANNING PROCESS

Strategic planning is a stream of decisions and actions leading the firm to the development of effective strategies which would in turn help the firm achieve its objectives. Strategic planning helps the firm to anticipate new trends and thereby enjoy the benefit of the lead time for all its crucial decisions and actions. As the saying goes, chance favours the prepared man. Strategic planning does this preparation. Through the strategic planning process, a corporation takes long term decisions concerning the mission of the organisation, the businesses it will pursue and the markets it will serve; lays down all its objectives and policies; and formulates strategies. Strategic planning also ensures that there is the required structure to support the strategy and its implementation.

Decisions of highest significance and serious consequence to a company are taken through the strategic planning process. In fact, the focus of the company gets decided through this route. Starting from the formulation of the corporation's broad philosophy of functioning and its core faiths and beliefs, to specifying its businesses and formulating its strategies at various levels—corporate level, business unit level and product level—all vital aspects come under the purview of the strategic planning task. Strategic planning originates right at the point a corporation conceives of its corporate mission. It starts by clarifying the very relevance of the business.

In other words, the task of strategic planning is to provide a route map for the corporation. A strategic organisation does not travel in a haphazard manner; it does not go here and there undirected, knocking at wrong doors, covering long distances on the wrong track; instead it travels with the support of a route map which will show up in advance, alternative routes, by-passes, short-cuts, dangerous terrains etc. Strategic planning endows a corporation with hedges against totally unexpected developments on its business horizon. In other words, instead of totally banking on the gut feelings of the Chief Executive or a few individuals, strategic planning lends a framework, a flexible and scientific framework, where decisions are taken not in a haphazard way, but systematically and in a guided and guarded manner, so that every move of the firm is purposeful and rewarding.

Strategic planning has the ultimate burden of rendering a corporation with certain competitive advantages in its fight for survival and growth. It is competition that makes strategy and strategic conduct essential in a business. The more intense the competition, more critical is the need for competitive advantage and competitive strategies, both of which emanate through an enduring strategic planning process. In a successful corporation, strategic planning works as the pathfinder to the various business opportunities; simultaneously, it also serves as a corporate defence mechanism.

Strategic planning combines in its fold both intuition and logic, and one supplements the other. While the intuitive part draws from the experience, knowledge and vision of the crucial people in the organisation, the logic part draws from information, systems and quantitative techniques. As could be expected, in the new context, the earlier excessive reliance on intuitive thinking is yielding place to a meaningful blend of intuition and logic. Because of the complex demands affecting business today, corporations are now leaning more on a methodical frame, information and systems for their strategic planning task. Business has become so complex that the chief executive or a few individuals, cannot successfully handle the strategic planning task of the business through their gut feeling. As a result strategic planning based on a good blend of logic and intuition is fast becoming widely accepted.

Strategic planning is not just a matter of projecting the future—what the future holds in terms of threats or possibilities. On the other hand, it is an attempt to prepare the corporation to face the future and even shape the future in the corporation's favour. In fact, it amounts to inventing the future of the company. Its ultimate burden is influencing the mega environs in the corporation's favour, working into the environs and shaping it, instead of getting carried away by it.

Business history has an abundance of instances of failures directly traceable to lack of strategic planning. This is quite natural since it is strategic planning which provides the framework for right business decisions—decisions on markets, products, manufacturing facilities, investments and so on. When the strategic planning framework is faulty or inadequate, the vital decisions on these areas go wrong. To quote George Steiner, "Strategy is the central and unique core of strategic management. Strategy refers to the formulation of basic organisational missions, purposes and objectives; policies and programmes to achieve them; and the methods needed to assure that strategies are implemented to achieve organisational ends... one framework for formulating and implementing strategies is the formal strategic planning process...".

Quite naturally, considerable thought, expertise and effort have to go into the process of strategic planning. The success of the efforts and activities of the enterprise depends heavily on the quality of strategic planning, i.e., the vision, insight, perception, sense of realism and clarity of ideas and the perfection of methods and measures that go into the strategic planning job. Through strategic planning the corporation generates several scenarios for the future. Contingency strategies are prepared for each of these likely future scenarios.

To present it in a nutshell, the major tasks undertaken through the strategic planning process are:

> spotting the opportunities and threats thrown up by the environment,

> defining the business mission on the basis of environmental and internal scanning,

> deciding on the individual businesses of the corporation and their relative priorities,

> setting the broad objectives of each of the businesses as per the priorities set,

> identifying and developing core competencies and competitive advantages, and

> forging the strategies required for the attainment of the objectives.

THE NEW COMPULSIONS FOR TAKING TO ENVIRONMENTAL SCANNING

All along, in India, companies could manage their business with just a cursory look at the macro and micro environments. Because of the highly regulated industrial environment, enterprises did not feel the need for a very careful and systematic assessment of the environment. As there was very little competition, the risk involved in skipping the essential function was never so grave. The converse is true in the open regime. Today, every firm has to closely observe its business environment and spot correctly the business opportunities and threats it faces. The main purpose of the exercise is to identify the favourable as well as unfavourable factors emerging in the environment.

For a business enterprise, its environment is comprised of diverse factors like the socio-economic conditions, the technology related matters, the supplier factors, the competitive environment and finally the government. In analysing these environmental factors, the enterprise is trying to monitor the current changes in the environment and also forecast the likely changes that may take place in the future. If the environmental factors change significantly, what should be the corporation's response on the strategy front? Can the organisation get going with the same objective-strategy framework, or should it come up with alternative programmes and strategies to meet the changed scenario?

In its attempt at environmental scanning, basically, a firm tries to understand how its business environment is behaving currently, and how it is poised to behave in the near as well as distant future. The firm gathers all available information relating to its environment, studies them, filters them and analyses them. It studies the changes in the socio-economic scene, and the impact of the changing government policies on its business; it studies the emerging trends in the business; it studies the programme of competitors; it also plots the likely fortune pattern of the business. In addition, it evaluates the alternative technologies and scope for substitute products available in the business and their relative cost-effectiveness. The purpose of this comprehensive X-ray of the environment is to locate the emerging opportunities as well as the problem areas. The firm also studies the structure of the market and the nature of competition. It locates the leaders in the business, builds up a profile of each of them and studies their programmes and practices and strengths and weaknesses. It evaluates their success stories and plots their failures. And after this elaborate environmental scanning, it may prepare scenario predictions, like the most probable scenario, favourable scenario and unfavourable scenario.

The new business environment of India

Right now, in the Indian business scene, all companies of India, in almost all businesses find that their business environment has drastically changed. In fact, the entire discussion in the chapter on 'Business Challenges of the Open Regime' has dealt with the changes that have taken place in the business environment of India. Normally, at any given time, environmental changes take place in one or two of the factors, say, social environment or technology environment or competition environment. And such changes affect only a select few businesses and industries. For others the changes may not make any perceptible impact on their business. But now, in the peculiar situation obtaining in India today, industry and business of the country in its entirety is affected by the environmental changes. Because, here is a situation where the entire country is taking a substantive route change. No wonder, all the participants are affected by this change. And quite naturally, the task of environmental analysis assumes special significance. The existing protected environment is yielding place to a vastly altered scene where business opportunities, challenges and threats of a wide variety await the Indian companies. The days of entrepreneurs and corporate planners struggling hard with the interpretation of the finer prints of the Industries Development and Regulation Act or the Monopolies and Restrictive Trade Practices Act to pinpoint industrial opportunities are over. The battle for economic survival and prosperity of the corporate sector will no longer be decided in the corridors of Udyog Bhavan in New Delhi; it would instead be determined in the market. For decades, the Indian corporate sector yearned for this sort of business environment and was clamouring for a liberal industrial policy. Sizing up the new developments, evaluating their impact on one's business, and responding to them with the right programmes and strategies is the task facing them now. Creating new opportunities and options is what the new reforms are all about, and companies have to examine closely the opportunities thrown up by the reforms and exercise their options wisely. For example, policy decisions such as convertibility of rupee, reduction in import tariffs and liberalisation of the trade policy have thrown open significant business opportunities for several industries. Understanding such substantive alterations in the business environment, studying them, evaluating them, weighing their pros and cons to one's own industry is the burden of environmental scanning.

Environmental scanning helps formulate strategy in line with fresh opportunities in the environment

Environmental scanning does not stop with providing some clues to the firm on the opportunities and threats present in the environment. It actively helps formulation of strategies. This is especially true of times of significant changes in environment. With the radical changes in the economic and industrial environment of India following the new economic programme, many firms have been keeping track of the environmental changes with extraordinary alertness and are putting the knowledge to good use in formulating potentially rewarding strategies.

Several companies take to mergers

For instance, many Indian companies in the wake of the NEP are taking to mergers. The new environment has enabled them to recognise that in the new scenario, the altered economic environment rendered mergers ever more attractive while the altered policy/legal environment rendered them absolutely feasible. The new policy/legal environment has removed the barriers to mergers. Actually three specific policy changes spurred the companies to think of merger: radical modifications in MRTP, relaxations in FERA, and delicensing. In the past, the policy/legal environment had frustrated the companies in their attempts at mergers. Whenever the companies tried a merger, they collided either with MRTP restrictions or the FERA barriers. And they were forced to set up separate companies in the same business because of the restrictive licensing policy. The rewards of operating on a mega scale in a particular business could never be realised by them. Some of the mergers now being debated would have taken place long back but for the restrictions. Now that the obstacles have been removed and the companies concerned have understood the changed environment, they could embark upon mergers and acquisitions.

Companies now saw several attractions in mergers. To some of them, product/business synergy was the chief attraction; the synergy driven mergers would reap the benefits of stronger distribution and marketing network, inter brand support, and larger market. To others, scale economies and financial advantages were the main attractions. In a dog-eat-dog market, survival depends on economies of scale. Capacities cannot be overnight enhanced to critical volume levels. By mergers and acquisitions, such quick expansion in capacity can be easily achieved. MNCs, in particular, found it attractive to merge some of their enterprises into larger entities.

No wonder then, within a short while from the announcement of the liberalisations, a great deal of news about company mergers/amalgamations started coming in. Mergers of EEC and GEC, David Brown Greaves and Greaves Cotton, Renusagar Power and Hindal Industries, Quest International India and Pond's India, NOCIL and PIL, Tea Estates/Doom Dooma and Brooke Bond and even a merger of Brooke Bond and Lipton, the two large beverage and food products companies in Unilever group were talked about. The other merger moves were: VST Industries with ITC, Wardhaman Auto Electric with Kirloskar Electric, GEC-English Electric with GEC-Alsthom, Gujarat Heavy Chemical with Dalmia Industries, Mafatlal Apparels with Standard Industries, Amar Dyechem with United Phosphorous, Sakthi Soya with Sakthi Sugar, Tetra Pak with Alpha Laval, and Orissa Synthetics with Straw Products. And most of these mergers have already materialised, subsequently. To cap them all, Reliance Petro merged with Reliance Industries. It has been the largest merger in the Indian corporate history. In addition to all these mergers, acquisition of Sewa Paper by BILT, Andhra Cement by India Cement, UB Petro by Manali Petro, Western Foods by Nikumbh Dairy Products, ACC Babcock by ABB, Consolidated Coffee by Tata Tea, Tribeni Tissues by ITC, Shriram Industrial Enterprises by Shriram Refrigeration Industries, Sathavahana Chains by Tube Investments and Amrit Protein Foods by Amrit Banaspati also took place.

In the earlier era, incentive to grow was almost non-existent and in fact some companies preferred to "demerge" by splitting one company into two or more so as to escape from the harsh provisions of the MRTP Act. But now, as soon as the new environment started unfolding, companies started taking a right about turn.

Several companies seize the new opportunity
in the import business

Just as a number of companies went in for mergers, several others have cashed in on the opportunities opening up in the import line, consequent to the altered environment.

When the Government ended the import monopoly of the public sector in several spheres, it led to a total freecarting of trade—any company can do trade from anywhere to anywhere. It meant that a huge business segment has suddenly become available for the Indian private sector to seize. The major commodities decanalised in the wake of the NEP, and the volume of business involved have been as follows:

Commodity	Annual imports (in Rs crore)
Phosphoric acid and ammonia	1,500
Steel	500
Sulphur, rock phosphate and non-ferrous metals	1,400
Metal scrap	1,600
Newsprint	400

Large business houses of India have been quick to sense the fortune involved in the change in environment—Reliance Europe, Essar World Trade, Salora International, Birla International, Raunaq International, ITC, Tatas and Hindujas are already there to grab the new import business from the public sector giants like MMTC and STC who till now enjoyed a monopoly in these import businesses. For example, ITC, TISCO, Reliance and Essar were already scouting to get into the Rs 1,600 crore steel scrap import business. ITC is in fact planning imports of fertilisers, seeds, pulses, newsprint and edible oil besides steel scrap. For Tatas, the import thrust will be on metals and minerals. Essar plans to import iron ore pellets. Reliance intends to import petroleum products, chemicals and yarn, products which they are already familiar with.

With the decanalisation of most of the commodities, import as a business has become an attractive activity. The idea of being a trading house is catching up among big companies. Since there is a large number of small and medium sized companies who would like to get such a service, import trading will work out to be a promising new area.

BPL seizes the opportunity in hi-tech communication and forges a joint venture with Alcatel

Similarly, watching closely the changes in the technological environment and the new possibilities for joint ventures in the liberalised regime, BPL decided to enter into a joint venture with Alcatel Business Systems of France. Through this alliance BPL is trying to capitalise on the expertise of Alcatel in areas like EPABX, key telephone systems, push button telephones, answering machines, videotex terminals, payphones and net works. BPL also hopes to get a share of the European market where Alcatel is a leading supplier.

Passenger car units size up the environment and reformulate strategies

While the New Industrial Policy of June 1991, delicensed a large number of industries, the passenger car industry continued to remain under licensing. But alert firms knew that the car industry would soon be delicensed. Existing players kept track of the Government moves as well as the plans of the aspiring new entrants. The latter, on their part, started formulating their moves taking delicensing of the industry for granted.

TELCO was quick to revive its earlier plans to enter the car industry. After locating a niche for its new indigenously developed diesel vehicles, Tata Sierra and Tata Estate, TELCO now became busy giving final shape to its project of producing passenger cars in partnership with Honda of Japan.

The existing players, Maruti Udyog, Premier Automobiles and Hindustan Motors understood the emerging competition from TELCO. They also gathered that other commercial vehicle leaders like Mahindra and Mahindra, DCM Toyota and Eicher Motors can become their competitors in addition to TELCO. Hindustan Motors promptly tied up with General Motors. GM's model 'Opel Kadett' is likely to be the new entrant, constituting the central piece of HM's survival strategies in the changed environment. Premier Auto too, started its search for strategic alliances, with Peugeot of France, Nissan of Japan and Fiat of Italy.

As regards the new entrants, DCM-Toyota was planning to enter with the same Toyota support. Mahindras, who already had the Peugeot tie up for its jeeps, preferred the Peugeot alliance for passenger cars as well. Eicher Motors who have a tie-up with Mitsubishi for commercial vehicles evinced interest in bringing out Mitsubishi's Mira or the Pachermo in India.

All these firms were taking all these moves when the passenger car industry continued to remain in the list of industries requiring a licence. Environmental scanning had given them the clue and when the delicensing actually came in April 1993, it was no surprise to them. Not only had they clearly anticipated it, but had also drawn up the possible scenario in the industry, consequent to delicensing.

The ability to carry out proper environmental scanning and the skill to precisely assess the opportunities are very important for strategic planning. Because, the success of subsequent tasks depend on the quality of environmental analysis. A missed opportunity or a wrongly sized up opportunity misplaces the focus of strategies. Till now, Indian companies brought up in an era of licence raj had been taught that the first rule is to grab a licence wherever possible. Grabbing a licence was equivalent to grabbing the best of business opportunities. It is no longer so; in fact, there is no licence to be grabbed. On the other hand, business opportunities available in the environment have to be sensed and grabbed through strategic planning and environmental scanning. The companies can no more seek shelter under Government policy and neglect their responsibility for strategic planning as they have done in yesteryears.

The multi-dimensional changes
warrant a close scan

In the chapter on Business Challenges of the Open Regime, in a 30 page discussion, the many-sided challenges and threats emanating from the new Indian environment were portrayed in detail. All these identifications are environment related findings. At micro level, the exercise will in fact reveal an even more comprehensive and certainly much deeper picture of what the concerned firm can expect of the environment.

This is the main concern of environmental analysis. But to make sense out of the multifarious features of the changing environment, to understand what is a possible benefit and what could be a hidden threat, or to identify what are the major shifts that might affect the fortunes of one's industry, a corporation must first understand what exactly are its own ambitions, aspirations, where exactly it would like to reach, what it would like itself to be in the future. In other words, to exploit the environment, a company should have done its homework on these fundamental subjects relating to its business and existence. Only when these ideas are clearly laid out for the benefit of the company and its planners, can one derive good advantage from the exercise of environmental scanning. This implies that even before the first exercises on environmental scanning are undertaken as part of the overall strategic planning process, the corporation has to clarify the fundamentals of its very existence and being. This takes us to the other major task of internal scanning, which any corporation taking to the strategic planning route has to carry out.

INTERNAL SCANNING—ASSESSING STRENGTH AND WEAKNESS, IDENTIFYING COMPETITIVE ADVANTAGE

While environmental scanning may help identify the various possible opportunities in areas of interest to the firm, the firm obviously cannot tap all the identified opportunities. It has to apply the principle of selectivity and decide on the opportunities it has to tap and the businesses it has to pursue. It also has to build defences against impending problems. To facilitate this work, the firm attempts an internal scanning taking a close look at its aspirations, capabilities, weaknesses and competitive advantages.

Companies in India have, by and large, been working with closed assumptions regarding their strength and weaknesses. There is no systematic scanning regarding this aspect. While a small enterprise can straightaway list out its strong and weak areas, for multi-business, multi-division corporations, such a route may not lead to a correct picture of its competitive profile. Especially when one's strength or weakness has to be rubbed against that of competition and the changes taking place in the environment, the assessment needs expertise and a professional approach. Moreover, understanding and pinpointing the company's strength and weaknesses in relation to competition is also important from the point of view of identifying the competitive advantage the company enjoys. As we shall see later, gaining a competitive advantage is a core task for corporate success. For carrying out that process too, the beginning is systematic internal scanning.

As an illustration, let us see how TISL, a newly launched venture of the Tatas, approached its internal scanning task.

TISL: Internal Scanning

Strength

> Excellent workstations and placed in the price-inelastic segment of the market
>
> The brand dominance of the collaborator, IBM
>
> IBM's reputation and the consequent pull of the best talents in the industry to work for TISL

Weaknesses

> Late entry
>
> Limited marketing reach, as per current plans
>
> Reliance on PS/2 which is a virtually unknown PC in India
>
> The omission of IBM name in the company name

Opportunities

> The large scope for expansion of the market. The Indian market is potentially one of the largest in the world for the chosen product mix
>
> Opportunity to pioneer vendor-cum-consultant role, perfected by IBM abroad
>
> The position of IBM as one of the world's largest buyers of software

Threats

> Present market leaders in India, HCL-HP, Wipro Infotech and PCL are all well entrenched
>
> Other transnational players have also already got a headstart here
>
> Lower priced vendors dominate an increasingly price conscious market

Obviously, to undertake such an internal scanning, a corporation like the TISL would be having the required clarity about the true nature of the new business into which it is entering, its ambitions in the venture and its stakes. The corporation, in other words, would have undertaken the more basic exercise relating to its business mission.

Clarifying one's business mission, what business are we really in?

Years ago, the well known management experts, Peter F. Drucker and Theodore Levitt emphasised that any firm desirous of tapping the emerging business opportunities and successfully staying in the business must find answers to certain basic questions concerning their business, like:

What business are we in?

Do we define and understand our business correctly and in its broadest connotation?

What are our basic strengths and distinctive capabilities to pursue this business?

In what business would we like to be in, tomorrow?

At the time these management thinkers addressed these questions to industrial and business managers, especially of the US, no one understood the full import and relevance of such a thinking to the successful management of coporations. Because, those were days when management was a relatively less complex task even in countries like the US. Only in subsequent years, captains of industry and business understood the wisdom and prophecy that lay behind these words of Drucker and Levitt.

Defining one's business accurately is the real starting point of strategy formulation. It is the prime requisite for selecting the right opportunities and for steering the corporation in the right direction. Many firms fumble in this task, because they lack a correct perception of the business they are engaged in.

Mission statement—The Ford Motor Company

To get an idea of how a global corporation perceives its mission, the mission statement of the Ford Motor Company is cited below. The company laid down the "mission statement" as part of its rejuvenation exercise.

> Ford Motor Company is a worldwide leader in automotive and auto-related products and services as well as in newer industries as aerospace, communications and financial services. Our mission is to improve continually our products and services to meet our customers' needs, allowing us to prosper as a business and to provide a reasonable return for our stockholders, the owners of the business.

Mission lends direction for planning

A mission justifies the organisation. It provides a statement to insiders and outsiders on what the corporation stands for. Mission statements cannot be vague. When they are vague, they are of no use to the corporation. The specificity and breadth of the mission statement are important considerations for the strategy formulation job. The mission should carry the grand design of the firm and convey what it wants to be. Not many companies in India have attempted to define accurately their business mission.

Proper definition of the business and its basic mission do bring several benefits to the firm. It reveals to the firm many relevant facts about its functioning which it may not be aware of otherwise. It brings to the fore the weaknesses if any in the very conceptualisation of the business of the firm and errors in judgement already taken place on these aspects. Most important, the exercise invariably brings the purpose and objectives of the business into clearer focus.

As business boundaries keep changing, mission development has become a difficult task

Clarifying one's business mission is not going to be easy in the new business scene of India. When product-market-boundaries get extended and different product categories of yesteryears blend and merge and when new products keep invading the market, when substitute products also keep entering in diverse fields, especially with the support of the MNCs and their new technologies, changing the existing business boundaries, understanding the nature and composition of one's own business becomes difficult. Definition of one's business becomes a highly shifting and difficult task.

Business boundaries are indeed becoming highly volatile. Unless one is careful, one may err in identifying the nature and boundaries of one's business. The narrower a corporation defines and perceives its business, the larger are the probabilities of its loss. When the definition of the business is narrow, quite naturally, the assessment about the competition will be narrow; and the vision of the likely changes that will invade the business and of new opportunities that will spring up in the business will also be narrow. Evidently, the corporation has to define its business as broadly as possible; it has to go beyond its immediate product, beyond its immediate competitors, beyond its immediate market boundaries; it must relate it to the functions performed by the product or the benefits provided by the product and the basic needs which the product seeks to satisfy and must even encompass as many related functions as possible. The definition must also be wide enough to embrace new opportunities and provide a vision of latent sources of competition.

Spotting the strong points and weak spots

The basic purpose of internal scanning is not only to clarify and define the purpose and mission of the business which the corporation is in, but also to pinpoint its strength and weaknesses in the various areas of performance. A corporation will not be strong in all areas of functioning. But its weaknesses will not normally come to the fore unless it makes a conscious search to spot them. In internal scanning, the idea is precisely to spot the strength and weaknesses. Through this exercise the organisation prepares itself for the matching of its ambitions and competence, bridging it as required. The exercise is also the starting point for locating and developing the core competencies and competitive advantages required by the firm in its fight for survival and growth.

SETTING OBJECTIVES BECOMES CRUCIAL
IN THE NEW CONTEXT

In a highly competitive environment, setting one's objectives with the highest degree of clarity becomes crucial to success. Carefully laid down objectives serve two important purposes for the corporation—they facilitate the progress towards the mission; they ensure that with minimum errors, least wastage of resources and minimum diffusion of effort, the corporation implements a clearly identified plan of activity.

While for a single product corporation, the task of setting the objectives may be a comparatively easier exercise, for a multi-business corporation, objective setting is a far more difficult, time consuming and risky job. It demands a lot of experience, knowledge and skill at analysing and weighing different trade offs. In fact, the first responsibility of such corporations is to decide the future of each of its businesses. Setting time bound goals comes only next. Goal setting should start with the more basic decision on what should be done on each of the distinct businesses of the enterprise.

The firm has to decide which are the businesses that should be cultivated through fresh investment and care, which ones should be given a mere maintenance without committing much of further investments, which are the businesses that call for a closer observation before committing further resources and which are the businesses that could be phased out. In other words, to go by the Boston Consulting Group terminology the enterprise decides what is to be done in respect of its Stars, Cash cows, Question marks, and Dogs. It may decide to expand the market of the Stars by committing heavy resources; it may decide to totally milk one of its Cash cows and preserve the resources; it may choose one of its Question marks for special observation and treatment, with an all-out mission to see whether it can turn out to be a Star; and it may decide to straightaway dispose of some of its Dogs. Only after such corporate level decisions are taken, can the business units' objectives be framed. Because, the objectives in respect of a Star poised to enter new territories will be vastly different from those in respect of a Cash cow. Similarly, the objectives to be set for the Question marks selected for a special growth push will be distinct from those of the Dogs or Cash cows.

Setting priorities for individual businesses
—The example of Tatas

It is interesting to see how the Tatas recently divested of Tomco, which was thus far considered as one of its prominent businesses. Though the soap business of India was constantly growing, Tomco had of late been faring badly. Tatas concluded after an in-depth analysis that it was a business not worth pursuing. Competition was becoming rampant and bigger competition was coming in. HLL was already acquiring further strength; and the new Godrej-P&G combine was posing more trouble. The company's own consultancy wing and outside consultants studied the matter and finally the Tatas decided to divest its soaps business. Tatas allowed HLL to acquire Tomco.

While Tatas decided to divest and get out of the soap business, they decided to give a new thrust to their tea business. They are seeking a substantive international presence in the tea business by penetrating the Russian and European markets and are targeting to enhance tea exports from Rs 85 crore to Rs 200 crore in just two years. They have reckoned tea as a Star for them. The corporation has gone to the extent of enlisting the support of its former international rival, Tetley of the US. The new Tata-Tetley combine will jointly promote global marketing of Tata Tea. The tea business obviously, is getting top attention of the Tata management.

The Tatas are also providing new support and fresh investment to their cement business which is now in trouble. Till a couple of years back it was a prospering business for the group. Some of the new economic policies adversely affected its cement business. The corporation decided to give a new growth push to the cement business by providing a new investment of Rs 700 crore, adding marketing skills and offering more group support of the corporation.

In its relatively new business of watches also, Tatas are committing additional resources and planning expansions with the objective of nurturing and cultivating the business. The core business of steel and the business of chemicals are receiving the existing level of priority. And for further growth through diversification the corporation is adding new businesses to its portfolio—car, computers, petrochemicals, minerals and metals.

The example of ITC

ITC too, is taking a close look at its different businesses and their relative priority to the corporation. The business of cigarettes, which all along remained the mainstay of ITC is being played down. Though it is the Cash cow of ITC, ITC has taken the policy decision to reduce its dependence on cigarettes. It has already reduced its dependence on cigarettes from 100 per cent a few years back to 65 per cent of total turnover now and has decided to bring it further down to 50 per cent by 1995.

ITC has all along been watching with concern the international trends in this matter. Cigarette continues to be under attack from an increasingly health conscious world. Accordingly, ITC is anxious to reduce its over dependence on the cigarette business, so that its vulnerability on that count is reduced. One business that is going to receive high priority is the agri-business. It is a Star for ITC. Hotels and exports too are receiving relatively high planning support. In its future plans for growth, the company is considering the new business of imports in diverse products like fertilisers, seeds, pulses, steel scrap, newsprint and edible oils.

Redefining of objectives —The example of Indal

Now let us see how a single business company is looking at its objectives. Indal (Indian Aluminium Company) is in the midst of a major rethinking in its business objectives. Confronted with problems on all fronts, high cost of power, power shortage, glut in international markets, falling domestic demand, threat from substitute products and lower profits, Indal is taking a fresh look at its business. From $550 per tonne in 1989, world alumina prices fell to $350 in 1990 and further crashed to $140 in 1991. And Indal's profit from exports of alumina which was Rs 42 crore in 1989-90 fell to Rs 18 crore in 1990-91 and further down to Rs 1 crore in 1991-92.

The company's new objective is summed up in the pithy statement, "From the position of a metal producing company with some interest in semi-fabs, today we are a semi-fab company, with some metal of our own." This reshaping of objectives has already been given effect to. In the early eighties, the product pattern was: 70,000 tonnes of primary metal and 36,500 tonnes of semi-fabs. In 1991-92 the pattern was 63,000 tonnes of primary metal and 69,000 tonnes of semi-fabs. From a business of primary metal, the company is fast shifting into aluminium products business. It is giving substantial thrust in downstream products, customisation and branding. And its requirements of primary metal in the future is planned to be met through outsourcing and product exchanges.

The increasing relevance of the SBU concept in business planning and setting objectives

Historically, companies in India have been conceiving and implementing business plans with a divisional orientation. The divisional structure mostly came from the geographic or manufacturing dictates. This often led to related products getting included in different divisions and getting different planning treatment and priorities. And sometimes it also led to unrelated products getting included in the same division and getting identical planning priority and treatment which they did not warrant. Evidently, such mix-up led to sub-optimal results. The concept of Strategic Business Units (SBUs) helps avoid this pitfall.

As per the SBU concept, a multi-business corporation groups its portfolios into a few distinct business units. All related products from the standpoint of 'function', will fall under one SBU. Every SBU will have its own set of competitors; and it will have its own distinct strategies. In all basic matters, mission, competition and strategy, one SBU will be different and distinct from another.

Several of the big Indian companies are already multi-business corporations, active in diverse products. And many others are right now taking advantage of the new environment and are developing diversification plans. They would be soon entering a variety of new businesses. These corporations can ideally benefit from an understanding of the SBU concept of business planning, which many leading corporations of the developed world have applied successfully, in their business planning job.

Many Indian firms are trying out the SBU concept

Many Indian firms are now taking to the SBU idea in their strategic planning efforts. The recent restructure undertaken by HMT, one of the largest public sector corporations of India, is on the SBU lines.

Thirty-nine year old HMT has 24 divisions, four business groups, 16 production units, 35,000 employees and a motley basket of products—machine tools including computer numerically controlled machines, flexible manufacturing systems and factory automation, tractors, printing machines, diecasting and plastic injection moulding machines, dairy machinery, bearings, lamps and lampmaking machines and a wide range of quartz analogue and digital watches. The company had just 2 per cent profit before tax on a turnover of Rs 793 crore in '90-91.

A World Bank sponsored study recommended a restructure plan for HMT. Earlier, the company had four business groups—machine tools, watches, lamps and agricultural machinery. The mix of products within a business group had vastly different market and technology attributes. The machine tools group for example, included printing press and other general industrial machinery. In the reorganised set up, the SBUs are: machine tools, consumer products, tractors and engineering components, industrial machinery, technology and information systems.

Right now, more and more companies of India are taking to the SBU concept. The Kirloskars, the Thapar group of companies, Piramal enterprises, the Dalmia group of companies, Premier Auto, L&T, Mahindra and Mahindra, and Voltas are all experimenting with the idea. In multi-product companies with clearly demarcated product categories, identification of SBUs becomes fairly easy. But even here, things may be often deceptive. In Kirloskar Oil Engines, for instance, the management found that the market, selling strategies, and type of marketing for large engines, medium sized engines, and small engines were completely different. While the small ones go mainly to the small scale sector, the large ones are sold to large corporations. Even the sales pitch for different kinds of customers are different. Hence, Kirloskar Engines split its business into three SBUs on the basis of the size of the engines. Each SBU has its own marketing strategies based on the requirements of the segment. In Voltas too, while room airconditioners have gone into the domestic appliances division, central airconditioning has gone into the industrial machinery division. It seems Indian business is waking up to the efficacy of SBUs in strategic planning.

The concept of SBU gives practical direction to the strategic planning job in multi-business enterprises. It removes the vagueness and confusion with regard to strategic planning quite often experienced by such complex enterprises. Through the process of analysing, segregating and then regrouping a wide assortment of businesses into well defined, clearly demarcated and distinct categories or SBUs, a multi-business firm can lay the real foundation on which the strategy and structure of the corporation can rest.

FOR INDIAN FIRMS, DEVELOPING COMPETITIVE ADVANTAGE BECOMES THE PRIME CHALLENGE IN THE ALTERED SCENARIO

All the tasks thus far explained—defining one's business and mission, setting the priorities of the individual businesses and their objectives, environmental and internal scanning—are careful preludes to a crucial task—the task of building competitive advantage and developing strategies for the fight in the market place. These steps constitute a behind-the-curtain preparation aimed at protecting the competitive position of the firm in the market.

This is precisely the task facing the Indian companies today. As pointed out earlier, their search for strategies has just commenced. They will find that the age of easy profits is coming to a grinding halt; they will have to earn their profits the hard way; they will compete on price front as well as non-price front. New brand wars will commence. As Government driven business environment yields place to market driven environment, fortunes of many products and businesses will waver. Companies, caught as they are in the new heat of competition, will be compelled to seek lasting alternatives; that means their search for competitive advantage for the corporation will begin.

9

Gaining Competitive Advantage in the New Context

In chapter 7 we elaborately dealt with the nature and intensity of the business challenges emanating from the new economic policies and open regime. The intense competition that is going to set in and the vulnerability of the companies facing the competition, were the major points that emerged in those discussions. In chapter 8, we saw that the new challenges could be tackled through strategic planning. We also saw that every company in India is now called upon to reclarify its mission, reformulate its objectives and develop strategies that would work in the changed context. The subject of developing strategies had been reserved for an in-depth discussion.

Before we actually take up the subject of strategy development, it is essential to devote some attention to the subject of competitive advantage, a subject that is closely linked to strategy development and one that is not-so-well appreciated by most companies in India. Competitive advantage is in fact, the fit between an organisation and the strategy it decides to employ. They have to go hand in hand. And without a tangible competitive advantage, a company cannot put any worthwhile strategy into position.

We are devoting this whole chapter for discussing competitive advantage, since it is so basic to strategy formulation and only with a sound knowledge of the role of competitive advantage, can a meaningful discussion on developing strategies be carried out. The chapter will provide a detailed account of the role of competitive advantage, its particular relevance at this juncture to Indian industry and business and how it enlarges or delimits the strategic choices available to a firm. Competitive advantage is in fact the long term answer to vulnerability. And since vulnerability, whatever may be its underlying causes, is the major challenge facing the Indian corporations in the open regime, a detailed discussion of competitive advantage becomes particularly essential in this treatise.

THE NATURE AND SIGNIFICANCE OF COMPETITIVE ADVANTAGE

A competitive advantage is basically a position of superiority in relation to competition. And the superiority can be in any of the relevant functions performed by the firm and its competition. The extent of the superiority will decide the extent of competitive edge the firm can enjoy in the market. It is through this superiority that the firm attempts to have a comfortable position for itself in the relevant industry. The position can be had in different ways, using different attributes of superiority. No firm can be strong in all functions. Some may be strong in production, they may have flexible production systems and the benefit of variety; some may be strong in introducing new products; big firms can have benefits of size and small firms can have flexibility and speed of functioning. Superiority can also be derived by a firm from its distinctiveness in the performance of the functions concerned. The very fact that the same function can be performed in different ways, offers scope for distinctive performance and consequent distinctive advantage. *So, in developing a competitive advantage, a firm is basically trying to see how uniquely and how advantageously a particular function or a group of functions can be performed superior to competition.*

Competitive advantage, the heart of strategy

Analysis shows that most companies keep changing strategies frequently, the failure of one leading to the birth of another. They do so because they operate without a tangible competitive advantage to their credit.

Competitive advantage is the route to long term corporate success. Successful companies normally try to put into shape strategies which revolve around an area of distinctive competence or an area where the firm has built up a competitive advantage. Competitive advantage, therefore, is the heart of strategy. The need for securing a competitive advantage is demonstrated by the fact that some of the most imaginative and well written strategies fail in the market as the companies have not acquired the competitive advantage required to make the strategy work for the company. In other words, it is the acquisition of competitive advantage that takes a corporation closer to its objectives, whatever be its strategy. In the absence of such an advantage, objectives remain elusive and strategies remain hollow. And in actual practice, many corporations, big and small, are seen to fail mainly because they have not addressed themselves to this primary requirement of building a competitive advantage.

In a competitive market, all firms do have some strategy; it may be explicit and well formulated; or it may be implicit, manifesting itself only through the activities of the firm. In either case, as we shall illustrate subsequently, the successful strategy is always woven around the competitive advantage of the firm. Scoring over competition and defending against competition, both hinge on competitive advantage. The competitive strategy and the competitive advantage of the firm can be understood by examining the various activities of the firm, by seeing how differently the firm performs these activities, as compared with its competition.

SOURCES OF COMPETITIVE ADVANTAGE AND COMPETITIVE ADVANTAGE FACTORS

As mentioned earlier, competitive advantage can emanate from any of the several functions a corporation is called upon to perform. In fact, each of the functions carried out by the firm can generate a set of competitive advantage factors and each of these factors is a potential source of competitive advantage.

The competitive advantage factors of a firm can therefore be broadly grouped under the following categories:

Marketing factors
Production factors
R&D and engineering factors
Personnel and expertise factors
Corporate resource and finance factors

In the search for gaining competitive advantage, the strategist disaggregates the major functions of the corporation into several sub-factors and entities. Through this breaking down of the 'whole' into its many parts, the strategist isolates the particular function/factor where his corporation's potential advantage lies. He actually tries to zero down on that specific factor, a factor to which he can point out and say — here lies our company's strength, or here is our potential strength, and we can build it up into a competitive advantage.

A corporation taking to the strategic planning route invariably undertakes a competitive advantage factor analysis. The purpose of this analysis is to identify the extent of the firm's competence in the various advantage factors. Some companies have competence in the marketing area. And within the marketing area, the specific strength and competence may be in distribution. Hindustan Lever is one company that has built up over the years a distinctive competence in distribution. It has a distribution network reaching the remotest rural areas of India. It is a competence which many of its competitors in the soaps-detergents-shampoo market cannot match. Modi Xerox too, built up a distinctive advantage in marketing but its specific area of advantage was service. The company was trying to achieve the norm of 'within 24 hours service'. Reliance Industries exploited all the advantage factors and built up competitive advantages in most of them. For example, the company gave substantial importance to the corporate resource and finance factors.

Through its phenomenal growth in the early '80s, the company had earned the position of a hi-profit, hi-growth company with substantial corporate resources and expertise. It used this advantage to raise funds through mega issues, for its diversification and expansion. In the human resources factor too, the company gained substantial advantage. The company hired and retained a heavy pool of highly talented engineers-technicians-managers. In fact, the company even went to the extent of cornering and keeping highly qualified people when it embarked on its diversification programmes. In production factors too, the company built up its clout. The company exploited fully all its competitive advantage factors.

Gaining a competitive advantage and clout even in one of the generic advantage factors is a big victory for many companies. And gaining advantage in one factor by itself, vests a firm with a great capacity to score over competition. The phenomenal winners in any industry usually gather competitive advantages in several factors. No wonder they command unquestioned dominance in the respective industry. Reliance is an example.

Component elements of competitive advantage factors

From the foregoing description, it is easy to discern that each of the functions performed by the firm may give rise to a number of competitive advantage factors. Given below is a fairly exhausive list of competitive advantage factors, function wise.

Marketing

1. Product mix
2. Packaging
3. Service norms
4. New product leadership
5. Pricing
6. Strength of personal selling
7. Channel strength
8. Marketing communications
9. Brand dominance
10. Market share
11. Market research and market intelligence
12. Marketing organisation

Production

1. Scale economies
2. Production and post-production facilities
3. Locational advantage

4. Raw materials — cost, quality and delivery
5. Maintenance strength
6. Inventory norms

R&D and Engineering

1. Basic R&D capabilities
2. Advanced R&D capabilities
3. Speed of R&D
4. Development of intrinsically new products
5. Value engineering

Personnel/Expertise

1. High calibre employees
2. Motivation level
3. Lower costs of labour
4. Industrial peace
5. Training and development

Corporate resources and finance

1. Corporate image and prestige
2. The CEO
3. Company size
4. Corporate performance record
5. Assets, resources, financial clout
6. Structure and systems.

The above list of factors can of course be stretched further to help zero down on the advantage factor on a more micro level. The present picture however is enough to show the nature of the competitive advantage factors available in the various functional areas, the scope of these factors and their viability for manipulation.

In short, the various functional areas are the concrete sources of competitive advantage for the firm.

While sources of competitive advantage may be many, finally it amounts to a cost or a differentiation advantage

Whatever may be the sources from which a firm derives its competitive advantage and whatever may be the specific competitive advantage factors the given firm is credited with, ultimately, competitive advantage manifests itself in either a cost advantage or a differentiation advantage to the firm. To put it more elaborately, whether the competitive advantage emanates from production factors or marketing factors or any other factors the benefit results in the form of a cost or differentiation advantage and it invariably shows up as such to the firm. And that is precisely why strategies too finally fall under two broad categories—cost/price based strategies and differentiation based strategies. We shall see the ramifications relating to this subject in the succeeding chapter. Cost advantage for example, can emanate from unique production facilities, latest technologies, ingenious inventory handling, innovative use of raw materials, efficient distribution etc. Similarly, the differentiation advantage too, can come through any of the functions the company performs. The ability to introduce new products, attractive service guarantees and superior quality assurance, are all sources of competitive advantage. Similarly, having a complete product line, ensuring ready availability of spare parts, new channel practices like a door delivery system are all functions or factors of functions from which a differentiated advantage can accrue.

Individual firms have to carefully spot the competitive advantage factors

It is obvious that different firms will derive their competitive advantage from different competitive advantage factors. Individual firms have to carefully spot their competitive advantage factors and nurture them. By studying the competitive advantage factors and by isolating them and analysing them with respect to the firm's internal strength and weakness in the given area, the firm has to find out what its distinctive advantages are. The firm should also simultaneously address itself to the question whether it can develop new strengths in addition to the advantage it already possesses. The search is for a position and a package of advantages to protect the position.

It has to be pointed out that effective top managers and leaders of corporations will be aware of the competitive advantage their corporations enjoy and the factors that make up the competitive advantage. However, in a changing environment wherein ever new forces of competition keep coming up all the time, maintaining the competitive edge one enjoys, is a continuous task.

In locating the corporation's competitive advantages and competitive advantage factors, the basic questions raised are: which are the functions the firm does well, compared to competitors? Does the firm really excel in them? Is it substantial enough to form the nucleus of a competitive strategy for the firm? And, which are the functions where the firm is weak? To what extent does the weakness matter in the overall perfomance?

This, in effect, is the process of internal scanning of the firm. And this process has to be carried out in the context of the competition and the overall external environment of the firm. For, only then can the firm spot its competitive advantage correctly. For, the competitive advantage of a firm is always relative to competition. In other words, analysis of the firm's competition and the overall industry structure are vital steps in arriving at the competitive advantage factors of the firm. This will be elaborated in one of the subsequent sections.

COMPETITIVE ADVANTAGE PROFILE (CAP)

The competitive advantage profiles of a few companies are considered here as illustrative examples.

CAP of Reliance Textiles

Reliance Textiles, (now Reliance Industries) had strengths in several factors and had built up a powerful competitive advantage profile as shown below:

Competitive advantage factors	Nature of competitive strength/ weaknesses
Marketing factors	Access to latest DuPont technology for crimped yarn, leading to premium fabrics
	A vast chain of exclusive VIMAL showrooms in all the Metros and class I towns; jumbo show rooms in the metros; and strong state level stockists
Production factors	State-of-the-art factory for producing contemporary synthetic fibre fabrics
	Superior scale economies compared to competition
R&D and Engineering factors	Competence for designing and making unique fabrics/designs and creative dress combinations. Employed more than 200 designers; and released more than 10,000 distinct designs per year
Personnel and Expertise factors	Highly qualified, highly paid experts in each field
Corporate and Finance factors	Prestige in the capital market and ability to raise large equity. Successful past record— profit of Rs 96 crore in 1986—the highest achieved by any Indian company till then; dividend outflow of Rs 16.22 crore, also the highest by an Indian company

CAP of Bajaj Auto Limited

Marketing factors	Wide product line—full range of scooters, mobikes, mopeds and three wheelers; 76 per cent market share in scooters, 27 per cent in mobikes, 6 per cent in mopeds; overall 48 per cent in two wheelers.
	Did not have a full fledged marketing organisation till 1987
Production factors	World's third largest two wheeler manufacturer and the largest in India. Capacity 10 lakh vehicles per year. Strong in engineering. 400 strong quality assurance outfit. One of the finest automotive units in the world. Quality dominance over competition
R&D and Engineering factors	Strong in-house R&D facilities for consistent product augmentation. High budget.
Personnel and Expertise factors	Medium position
Corporate and Finance factors	High profit, cash rich company. One of the few potential global players of India

CAP of Asian Paints

Marketing factors	Market leader with 35 per cent share, the closest competitor not having even half of the company's turnover. Wide product line with more than 40 different decorative paints, and some of them offered in as many as 150 shades, most of the shades offered in eight different sizes of packing. High brand rating. Capability for accurate sales forecasting. Highly computerised MIS
Production factors	Enormous size advantage in relation to competition. Benefit of backward integration with the manufacture of paint inputs; finesse in production planning and scheduling, matching with marketing requirements.
R&D and Engineering factors	Medium position
Personnel and Expertise factors	High calibre human resource; employing the maximum number of MBAs

Corporate and Finance factors	Rs 70 crore reserves. High profile corporate image. Enviable track record in breaking the mighty position of MNCs in paint industry

It can be easily seen that the companies cited in the above examples display competitive advantage in more than one factor. These companies by virtue of their advantage in several factors have been in a position to forge a variety of strategies in the market place and command a position of eminence. In fact, the actual market positions of these companies substantiate this point. Some of the best run companies of India have been consciously selected here to drive home the points relating to competitive advantage. Many Indian companies will fall in the other extreme of the scale, displaying no worthwhile advantage at all to their credit, in any of the factors.

Analysing industry structure and competition helps sizing up of competitive advantage of the firm

A proper understanding of industry structure and competition is absolutely essential for sizing up the competitive advantage factors of a firm. The market share, brand dominance and company size are all competitive advantage factors for a firm. In order to assess to what extent the perceived advantages of a firm constitute a competitive advantage, it is essential to know where the firm stands in these respects, relative to competition. That is why analysis of industry structure and competition become relevant in sizing up the competitive advantage. Industry structure analysis will tell the firm, the number of players in the industry, their respective market shares, their installed capacities and their relative strengths within the industry and thereby help the process of advantage identification. The very manner in which the industry is structured and the players are distributed/located within the industry, would reveal to what extent perceived strength of a firm actually constitutes a competitive advantage.

Let us see a few examples:

In the cigarettes industry of India, there are nine players accounting for as much as 97 per cent of the aggregate sales. Of this, one contestant alone, i.e., ITC commands 56 per cent share. The next two players together, (Godfrey Philips and GTC) account for less than 20 per cent share. ITC secures a prominent competitive advantage in this business primarily through the more than half industry share enjoyed by it. If the number two in the industry could command say, a 40 per cent share, the structure of the industry as well as the composition of competition as such would have been different with the implication that the 56 per cent share of ITC would not constitute by itself into a distinct competitive advantage. Similar is the case with the toothpaste business of India. In the industry with seven major players, Colgate commands 53 per cent share. The number two has just a 15 per cent share.

In the textile industry on the other hand, there are 160 players and the top five, Bombay Dyeing, Reliance Industries, Garden Silk, Century Textiles, Mafatlal Fine, together account for only 2.5 per cent of the aggregate sales. There is also not much of variation in strength among the top five; they are all practically equals. It is very obvious that a new entrant aspiring for a place in this industry will not normally feel threatened by a predominantly high market share as a competitive advantage enjoyed by the existing players. Whereas anyone looking at the industry structure and the composition of competition in the cigarette business or toothpaste business will feel deterred by the overwhelming market shares enjoyed by the number one player.

In the sewing threads industry, there are five contestants. Here also two players—Madura Coats and Mahavir Spinning—together command 99 per cent of the business, the leader Madura Coats accounting for 74 per cent of the aggregate sales and Mahavir Spinning, 25 per cent. In this industry too, the high market share of 74 per cent is a distinct competitive advantage of the leader which can dissuade newcomers.

Quite contrary to the above position, is the nylon tyre chord industry. There is a more balanced distribution among the players, the total number of players being eight. The leader SRF accounts for 26 per cent of the aggregate sales; the next two BRC and NRC, 16 per cent each and the next two, J.K. Synthetics and Century Enka 15 and 12 per cent respectively.

In the nylon filament yarn industry, the picture is even more well balanced. Each of the top five, in an industry of nine players, has a market share of more than 10 per cent, with Modipon the leader holding 15.5 per cent.

The above examples illustrate that industry analysis is an essential step in locating the competitive advantages enjoyed by the already existing contestants in an industry. Similarly, in sizing up how certain competitive advantages enjoyed by the existing contestants display themselves as entry barriers to aspiring newcomers also, industry analysis is helpful. To locate these entry barriers and to size up the aspiring entrant's capacity to overcome these barriers, industry/competition analysis becomes essential. Here the main concern is understanding the competitive advantage enjoyed by existing competitors.

The test of competitive advantage

What exactly is the test of a competitive advantage? How does one conclude whether a particular factor cited as an advantage of the company really constitutes a competitive advantage to the firm in the market? Basically, a factor noted as a favourable factor can be counted as a distinct competitive advantage only if it is capable of influencing one or the other of the forces of competition, in the company's favour. Forces of competition are many and varied. Factors like number and character of existing competitors, likely new competitors, powerful suppliers, powerful buyers and substitute products and processes are some of the forces that shape the nature and intensity of competition in an industry. A competitive advantage should enable a company to influence any of these factors in the company's favour. It can be through controlling these competitive forces and gaining a substantial dominance over them, or through insulating the company from these forces and thereby reducing the company's vulnerability. The touchstone of competitive advantage is that it will either add to the competitive strength of the company or help reduce the company's existing level of vulnerability. When such a strength of the company actually accomplishes this, it becomes a competitive advantage to the firm.

For example, new entrants poised to enter a business are a source of direct competition to a firm already in the business. Entry can be prevented if there are sufficient barriers to entry, like say, economies of scale, brand dominance, absolute cost advantage, or Government policies against addition of capacity. By building up entry barriers, through any of these routes, the firm can block or at least delay the newcomer's entry. But, it can build such barriers, only if it possesses some distinct competitive advantage. This can be seen from the examples of CAPs furnished earlier. All the companies were leaders in their respective business and were barrier builders as well. They had their distinct competitive advantages; they had built up barriers in the form of scale economies as well as brand dominance.

HOW DO COMPANIES ACQUIRE COMPETITIVE ADVANTAGE?

While competitive advantage serves as the back up to strategy formulation, strategy is needed for building competitive advantage. The point is that while corporate level grand strategies take care of competitive advantage building, the business/market level strategies of the firm use the corporation's competitive advantage as the foundation to work on. Competitive advantage building is thus a conscious and strategic activity of the corporate management. And its decisions and actions, regarding acquisitions, mergers, divestment and technology and marketing tie ups come under competitive advantage building, and with these competitive advantages, the corporation can forge the business/market level strategies for the fight in the market.

Competitive advantage obviously cannot be gained overnight. The firm has to know the intricacies of the business it is in, the customer, the products, the technology, the processes and the competition. In the current context in particular, the firm must know the changing boundaries of competition, the new competition from products under evolution and the new competition from the process of globalisation and import liberalisation.

Some examples are cited here to show how corporate managements through their strategic decisions acquire or sharpen competitive advantages.

*Asian Paints acquires competitive advantage through
innovative marketing and efficient inventory control*

Asian Paints (AP), the leader in the Indian paint industry, has achieved the lowest cost as well as the highest differentiated position in the industry. Its 'Apcolite' is the largest selling brand of paint in the country. This brand alone is made available in 151 different shades. Most of them are available in eight different pack sizes. Being in the business of 'colours', the company has successfully utilised colour to achieve the highest intensity of product differentiation, which none of its competitors could match.

Simultaneously, Asian Paints also achieved the lowest cost position in the industry. Normally, the conscious option for the differentiated route with an ever widening product line points towards higher inventory levels and consequently higher inventory costs. But Asian Paints, through its innovative inventory management, managed to retain its inventory at the lowest possible levels. The company monitored its inventory through its extensive computer network. Its SKU (Stock Keeping Units) rates are the best in the industry. In 1991, AP's finished products inventory was 7 per cent of sales while for the competitors it was nearly twice that level. In fact, AP saved so much on the inventory carrying costs that it almost earned its promotion budget through the savings effected in inventory costs. AP actually spends 10 per cent of sales on promotion, the highest in the industry. It has to spend a great deal on promotion to maintain its differentiation advantage. But strikingly, it keeps its total costs the lowest, despite the heavy expenditure on promotion.

*Nestle's competitive advantage
through brand dominance*

The fact that strong competitive advantage can be acquired through brand dominance is demonstrated well by Nestle's Maggi noodles. When Brooke Bond's new food business venture Indo-Nissin Foods decided to launch its Top Ramen brand of noodles in the Indian market, they were entering a market dominated by the Maggi noodles for nearly 10 years. Nestle' had nurtured the brand in such a fine way that Maggi became a household name and noodles a favourite food of children and even adults. Maggi thrived on the assurance of 'quick food'. The welcome taste was the next winning point. Retail support built over ten years gave further strength to Maggi. Top Ramen entered with a powerful initial launching campaign, highlighting the Japanese connection for noodles as a food item and laying stress on Nissin strength. But the brand could not take off. The brand dominance of Maggi in the noodles market served as a powerful competitive advantage for Nestle.

*Videocon acquires competitive advantage
through integration*

When Videocon quoted a very high bid for the Uptron Colour Picture
Tubes, which the UP Government had decided to sell as part of their
privatisation plan, Videocon was trying to acquire a substantial competitive advantage. It was part of its integration plan. The company wanted
to become a totally integrated TV manufacturer. The take-over of Uptron
Colour Picture Tubes, would make Videocon the only company in the
country having an integrated manufacturing line for colour televisions —
from glass shells for picture tubes to the complete set. The integration
meant a distinct competitive advantage to Videocon.

*IDM acquires competitive advantage through
intensive R&D*

After several years of losses, International Data Management Ltd (IDM)
was coming out of the woods by the beginning of the '90s. The route
adopted was R&D. IDM's business was confined to setting up data
processing centres, making punch cards and printer ribbons. When the
needs of computer business changed rapidly in the early '80s, the
company found it difficult to cope with the new need and slid into a
period of losses. It learnt the hard way that with the growing standardisation of computer hardware, only software companies can be flexible
and also command a premium through human addition. It was however
not possible for the company to suddenly achieve distinction as a
software outfit. IDM laboured hard in that direction and through its in-
house R&D and assistance from a US research institute, developed certain
sophisticated techniques that conferred on it the much needed distinctive
edge. Geographical imaging systems became IDM's major innovation. It
developed the techniques to study geographical land mass. When clients
like the meteorological department, HAL and Hindustan Shipyard faced a
geographical problem, IDM sent application engineers to the site to
analyse and suggest solutions, i.e., tools and database to deal with the
requirement. Since each such problem is unique, the company gathered a
good deal of expertise in this sphere. Moreover, software dealing with
geographical problems is by its very nature impossible to import. With
the specialisation developed through R&D, IDM was able to practically
ride like a master in this particular field of application.

Competitive advantage through alliances

When a firm is unable to build a competitive advantage all by itself, it can
gain such an advantage through an alliance with another firm. The
plethora of strategic alliances taking place in recent times underscores the
importance of this route. Strategic alliances are in fact a common feature
the world over. For example, in the global electronics industry, several

strategic alliances have emerged—alliances between rivals to have better access in selected markets to the mutual advantage of the partners. Some of these alliances were IBM-Apple, IBM-Siemens, Motorola-Toshiba and Intel-NEC. This trend of corporate courtship is now spreading in India.

ICICI's strategic alliance with J.P Morgan

The Industrial Credit and Investment Corporation of India (ICICI) has taken J.P. Morgan (JPM), the international portfolio managers and investors, as its partner for its new venture. JPM has put in an equity of Rs 50 crore in the venture, forming 40 per cent of the total equity stake in the venture. The benefits to ICICI are obvious, they will have access to state-of-the art technology in merchant banking, portfolio management and trading.

Alliance of IL&FS with Orix Corporation

Infrastructure Leasing and Financial Service (IL&FS), has roped in Orix International of Japan. Orix has bought a 20 per cent stake in IL&FS paying Rs 29.50 crore at a premium of Rs 150 per share of Rs 100 face value. Orix is a leading financial service company with total assets exceeding $35 billion. The tie up is expected to benefit IL&FS in two ways. First, IL&FS would be able to cash in on the expertise of Orix in the leasing business. Second, with the tie up, it would be easier for IL&FS to tap the Japanese Samurai market.

Kotak Mahindra's alliance with Bank of Madura

Kotak Mahindra has struck a strategic alliance with Bank of Madura (BOM). Kotak Mahindra has been nursing for long, the ambition to takeover or start a private sector bank. It forged a strategic alliance with Bank of Madura (BOM), with a definite game plan. In the first place, it did not want to wait indefinitely for the day the RBI would permit setting up of new private banks; it went ahead striking an alliance with an existing private sector bank. Secondly, it wanted to be prepared and be ready to circumvent other possible barriers and enter the banking industry at all costs in the quickest possible time. It knew that private banks like the BOM, are well placed to emulate the foreign banks in pursuing most profitable lines of banking business. And by following this route it could also avoid the gestation period; a bank set up anew, will have to go through a long gestation period before it could produce results. As a part of the Kotak-BOM strategic alliance, four nominees of Kotak Mahindra joined the board of BOM. The expectation was that BOM would enter new businesses like mutual funds, asset securitisation and foreign loan syndication. Kotak Mahindra's expertise and contacts and BOM's inherent banking and organisational strength would make good synergy.

Through this move Kotak Mahindra was obviously trying to gain a powerful competitive advantage. In the coming years, competition in the banking business is bound to be tough, from foreign banks and newly set up Indian private banks. Kotak Mahindra was acting with forethought, gaining the advantage of earlier entry, in alliance with an existing bank.

Tatas' alliance with AT&T in switch gears

Tatas have recently forged an alliance with AT&T, world leader in Telecommunications for setting up a switching system unit in India. Together, they will set up a joint venture—AT&T Switching Systems (India) Pvt. Ltd., which will produce state-of-the-art central office switching equipment for use in India's telecommunications network. AT&T with a turnover of $65 billion has a special place in the telecommunications industry. It is noted for its technical leadership in the industry where it represents the highest standards. Its 5 ESS(R) Switching System is supposed to be a very versatile system. Through the partnership, the joint venture will produce the most technically advanced range of telecommunications equipment. Tatas have obviously acquired a substantial competitive advantage through the alliance.

Creating entry barriers will bring competitive advantage

Entry barriers are like walls built around the boundaries of an industry. The major barriers to entry are: economies of scale, cost advantage independent of size, brand dominance, channel clout and Government policies relating to the industry. All these are defences for the existing contestants and barricades to newcomers. While scale economies are the key barriers to entry in some industries, product differentiation and brand dominance are the key barriers in some other industries. Cost advantages that cannot be replicated by potential rivals is a common entry barrier in all industries. The cost advantage can emanate from ownership of technology, access to the best raw material sources, assets already purchased at lower prices, favourable location etc. It is obvious that while all these barriers act as hurdles to the new entrants, by the same token, they serve as competitive advantage to those who have already built them up.

FIRMS ACQUIRE HIGHER DEGREE OF COMPETITIVE ADVANTAGE ONLY BY BUILDING CORE COMPETENCIES

We have seen in the foregoing sections that firms develop competitive advantage by working with one or more of the various competitive advantage factors. Analysis shows that in many cases, companies and competition soon converge on product-price-differentiation-attributes. They reach a stage where there is little scope left to differentiate further, whether on product, service or any other conceivable attributes. At such a stage where there is a saturation, only corporations who enjoy core competencies in the root technology/process/expertise keep gaining. And, in today's technology driven world, technology is one main source of core competency. Through command over technologies and processes firms bring out proprietary products which lend competitive advantage to them.

Prof. C.K. Prahalad in his HBR article on *The Core Competence of the Corporation* knowledgeably discusses the concept of core competencies and its role in building long-term competitive advantage. Through an examination of a large bunch of internationally successful companies and their world famous products, Prof. Prahalad drives home the point that it is not a particular product as such that lends these corporations a world dominance. Behind the product, there is the core competency — the interwoven technology/process/expertise. For example, Sony has a core competence in miniaturisation; it can make any product tiny. Philip's has optical media expertise. It has achieved its competence in this field as a result of a decade long research and development. Honda has a core competence in engines which gives it a competitive advantage in diverse products like car, motorcycle, lawn mower and generator. Canon's core competence lie in optics, imaging and microprocessor controls that together lend Canon distinct competitive advantage in products as diverse as copiers, laser printers, cameras and image scanners. JVC built up core competence in video recording/video tape technology which finally gave JVC unique and novel products in these fields. Yamaha introduced the digital piano, Komatsu developed the underwater remote-controlled bulldozer and Casio brought the small-screen colour LCD television. Behind every one of these inventions, there lie the distinct core competencies of these corporations, which are built out of the corporations' command over several technologies.

Building core competence becomes essential to competitive advantage building because, advantages emanating from the product-price-performance-trade offs are almost always short term. Especially in an era where technologies are altering existing boundaries of businesses, advantage can last only through competence enjoyed at the very roots of products. And only through expertise over several technologies and a complete command in their infinite variety of uses, a company can occupy a highly advantageous position. DuPont's core competence in chemical technology, ITT's core competence in electronics and NEC's core competence in telecommunications, semiconductors and mainframes will see them through any exacting competitive situations.

To build core competencies, it is not necessary for companies to invest heavily in fundamental research. What is required is a corporation's commitment to look for relevant technologies in its field, harness them, develop the human expertise to understand them and work on them like building blocks, so that the corporation has the basic strength to push out any product based on demands of changing times and patterns. In fact, companies who always make it a policy to manufacture the crucial components of their products instead of outsourcing them quite often enjoy the scope for core competence building, while those who as a policy decide to source their crucial components from outside suppliers deny themselves the opportunity to build core competencies in their business. The latter, may enjoy some cost advantage, which may ultimately give them a competing edge in the price-marketing factors. But, in the long term, such a corporation could be foregoing an opportunity for core competence building in its chosen business. When the manufacture of crucial components are just seen as a cost centre, the chances of core competence building are getting lost. For example, the American Auto giant Chrysler tends to view engines as just one more component for its car assembly. But in the case of Honda, it would never give up the responsibility of manufacturing its engines. Honda has also centralised all its critical engine-related R&D in Japan, while it does not mind outsourcing body parts overseas and sharing responsibility for body design with its affiliates worldwide. No wonder, Honda could build up a core competence in engines, and use it as the back up for gaining competitive advantage in several product categories.

In the changed context of India today, the crucial task before corporate managements is just not to build some short term competitive advantage but to endow the organisation with a portfolio of core competencies. The batttle for global leadership is being waged on the strength of core competence and not on some brands as is being perceived by many. Behind the visible and apparent battle of the brands, there lies a substantive war between core competencies of corporations. The latter is always behind the scene.

Only by looking at the global corporations, can Indian companies get an idea of core competence building. Because, in the historic evolution of business, Indian business is only now reaching a stage where they can put into practice such an advanced concept. And the economic liberalisation has made the ground conducive to such an effort. Indian Companies must set themselves the task of core competence building.

COMPETITIVE ADVANTAGE BUILDING, A CONSCIOUS AND LONG TERM PROCESS REQUIRING COMMITMENT OF SIZEABLE RESOURCES

Developing and nurturing a durable competitive advantage involves a conscious choice of the management. It also involves a long term effort. And sizeable resources have to be committed for the effort to succeed. Even when the total resources available with the firm is relatively limited, the competitive advantage building firm will ensure that its competitive advantage factor, whether it is research and development, personal selling or brand dominance, gets its due share out of the limited resources. It will nourish the particular factors that bring the competitive advantage. In short, competitive advantage is always built with management's commitment, through time and resources.

10

Developing Strategies

The strength of the strategic planning process of a corporation is ultimately tested through the actual strategies forged by the corporation and the way the corporation protects its competitive position. The success or failure of all the tasks of strategic planning which we have discussed in detail in the previous two chapters, manifests through the strategy that is finally forged out by the firm. We shall now see how corporations handle this burden of developing strategies. Since the Indian companies will now find themselves neckdeep in competition and commence their search for strategies to suit the new situation, we shall try to enrich our discussion with illustrations/cases that are especially relevant to the new situation.

The purpose of strategy is to exploit the unique advantages of the firm in facing the challenges of the environment. A strategy begins with a concern and burden of how best to use the limited resources of the firm in realising the objectives, confronting successfully the environmental realities. The objectives will tell where the firm wants to go; the strategy will provide the design for getting there. Strategy is the opposite of ad hoc responses to the changes in competition, consumer tastes, technology and other environmental variables. It implies long term, well thought out and prepared responses to the various forces of competition and environment.

FUNDAMENTALLY, A FIRM HAS TO PUT STRATEGY IN OPERATION AT TWO DISTINCT LEVELS

Strategy has to operate at two distinct levels of a corporation, taking care of two distinct strategic requirements: the requirements at the corporate level of the firm and those at its individual business units level. These are distinct from one another and have to be tackled through distinct strategies. We shall examine in detail how these demands are to be met.

CORPORATE LEVEL STRATEGIES

A corporation during its course of growth is called upon to make certain corporate level strategic decisions regarding the nature and line of its growth. These decisions taken at the corporate level, normally come under one or the other of five broad generic categories of strategy. A corporation selects a particular generic strategy depending upon the unique realities facing the corporation.

The generic strategies available to a firm at the corporate level

The generic strategies a firm can adopt at the corporate level may belong to one or the other of the five categories: stability, expansion, diversification, retrenchment and combination.

Stability strategy

A corporation resorting to the route of stability stays with the same business. It will try to sharpen its existing strategies to bring about incremental improvements in the functioning of the corporation, maintaining its position in the existing products/business. Such a strategy stems from the corporation's faith that it enjoys a fairly comfortable and secure position in the existing industry, assured of a certain level of profits. And, it does not foresee any major threats to its industry which can hurt its secure position.

Expansion strategy

In the expansion strategy, the corporation meets its growth objective while staying with its existing business/products. Growth is brought about through size/capacity increase. The emphasis is on bigger size. It essentially means more of the same thing.

Diversification strategy

The corporation opting for the diversification strategy is eager to exploit possible opportunities arising in the environment. The corporation may also anticipate substantive changes in its existing business. It is not sure as to what extent it can secure its position in the context of the anticipated challenges. It is eager to spread its risks and vulnerability by diversifying into new business. To ward off potential dangers and also to harness the opportunities, the corporation mid way takes the crucial decision to diversify.

Retrenchment strategy

In retrenchment strategy, the decision is to altogether drop some of the unattractive businesses. Retrenchment/divestment is not necessarily to be seen as a matter of failure. It is a matter of conscious corporate judgement to get out as early as possible, from unattractive, unprofitable businesses.

For example, General Electric maintains as a policy that it should be either No.1 or at least No.2 in each of its business/market or else, it should get out. GE divested its computer business and air conditioning business as it could not achieve the desired positions in these businesses. Appropriate and timely retrenchment decisions are as crucial as the most vital expansion decisions.

Combination strategy

In the combination strategy, the corporation decides to avail of all the above mentioned strategic routes, stability, expansion, diversification and retrenchment, across its different businesses.

The decision regarding the adoption of these generic strategy routes will usually be influenced by the stage of development of the industry of which the corporation is a part. Each of these broad strategy routes demands distinctive handling by the corporate managements. The knowledge, expertise and skills required to handle these different strategy routes also vary. That is precisely why corporate managements who have successfully carried the organisation through a stability strategy quite often find the job difficult while taking their organisation through the expansion/diversification routes.

Diversification has come to be regarded as synonymous with strategy

While there is less risk associated with resorting to a stability strategy, the business rewards associated with such a strategy are also limited. Companies naturally feel that they are more vulnerable in pursuing a stability strategy, remaining with the same business. They also find that after a point, even expansion does not bring them the desired growth. No wonder, in their pursuit of growth, companies have come to regard the diversification strategy as synonymous with growth. It has also become synonymous with strategy per se.

Example of corporate strategy—Unilever

Unilever's corporate strategy covering its group of companies in India provides insight into the corporate strategy of a large, multi-business corporation. Primarily, it serves as an illustration of the expansion/diversification category of strategic option. At the same time, it also serves as an illustration of how a strategic organisation with global spread, responds to radical changes in the economic environment in a country in which it has vital stakes.

For a long time, Unilever has been on the look out for expansion/diversification opportunities for its group of companies in India. When the opportunities actually materialised following the liberalisation,

Unilever acted in a very strategic manner and managed two major acquisitions in quick succession—one each in soaps and detergents and food products, the two sectors where it wanted to expand and attain the position of mega business. Hindustan Lever, the group's flagship company, took over Tomco. Brooke Bond, the other major company in the group, took over Kissan Products of the UB group. Almost simultaneously, Unilever exploited the other opportunity provided by liberalisation, viz., the scope for parent company consolidation in its Indian companies.

HLL absorbs Tomco and becomes a mega business in soaps

Unilever knew that in the new environment of India, challenges of various kinds will crop up and size of operation would in itself be one of these challenges. Accordingly, Unilever chalked up strategies for size increase. Acquisition of Tomco was the outcome. Unilever felt that by taking over Tomco and merging it with HLL, the market share of HLL would go up significantly and the enlarged share could be better defended against possible onslaught of new competition. Unilever's thinking was on these lines: Tomco has some good brands; it has a lot of unutilised capacity and there are basic synergies to be derived from a merger; and Tomco's major brands are not in direct competition with HLL brands.

With the acquisition, HLL will corner around 60 per cent of the Indian market for soaps in the organised sector. At present, HLL accounts for 40 to 45 per cent of the market. Tomco's hold is about 15 per cent. The merger would thus lead to a total domination of HLL in the soaps market, on the lines of Colgate's hold over the toothpaste market. The turnover of the enlarged HLL would be in the order of Rs 2500 to Rs 3000 crore.

The clubbing together of HLL and Tomco will create tremendous manufacturing and marketing synergies. HLL which has 17 manufacturing facilities will gain an additional seven Tomco plants. HLL's network of stockists, will also double from the present 3000. HLL's production and marketing network in the South is weak, whereas Tomco has a strong marketing network in the South.

The principal attraction for Unilever/HLL in the acquisition of Tomco is that it brings a host of strong brands like Hamam, Moti, Jai, Revel and 501. The brands of the two companies complement each other. Tomco soaps have oriental brand names like Moti and Hamam, a segment in which HLL did not have any representation. HLL soaps have continental brand names. Moreover, HLL—which has targeted its products to the upper end of the market—will also gain from Tomco's ethnic appeal. It is acknowledged that Tomco brands understand local aspirations and needs very well. Moreover, Tomco's Hamam is the largest selling soap in the family soap segment in which HLL is unrepresented. The 501 laundry soap is a popular, medium priced bar, a comparable product of which is not available with HLL. So also the Revel Plus detergent used in washing machines. Instead of spending Rs 5 crore each to launch a new brand in any of these segments, HLL has adopted the strategy of buying out the competition.

HLL had, as a part of its strategy, also thought through what should be done with Tomco after the takeover. In HLL's view, what would be required was an upgradation of Tomco's production facilities and some support to Tomco's brands. The five major Tomco brands of soaps and detergents, namely, Hamam, Moti, Jai, Revel and 501, would need an immediate investment of about Rs 15 crore.

Absorption of Tomco by HLL is a counter thrust to P&G-Godrej tie-up. In fact, it actually upstages the P&G-Godrej tie-up. P&G and Godrej Soaps Limited are to set up a new venture, Procter&Gamble Godrej (PGG) with the American multinational holding 51 per cent equity and Godrej 49 per cent. PGG proposes to manufacture and market detergents, soaps and a whole range of toiletries. PGG has bought out two detergent brands of Godrej, Key and Trilo. Godrej has also transferred its new plant at Malanpur, Gwalior with an estimated capacity of 30,000 tonnes per annum to PGG. But estimates suggest that HLL, with the takeover of Tomco will have a massive manufacturing and marketing advantage over PGG. While HLL may have 60 per cent market share, PGG's share may be just 10 per cent to start with.

Brooke Bond absorbs Kissan Products

The motives of Unilever in the acquisition of Kissan Products are similar to those in the acquisition of Tomco. The group chose Brooke Bond as the vehicle for the absorption of Kissan, in view of the natural affinity of the businesses of Brooke Bond with those of Kissan. Along with Kissan, Brooke Bond managed to acquire Merryweather as well as the food division of Herbertsons India which became part of the amalgamated Kissan products. The Unilever group had already acquired 33 per cent of equity capital of Kissan Products from Cadbury Schweppes plc of the UK. The acquisition of the holding of UB in the two subsidiaries will enable Unilever group to secure an additional 35 per cent of equity capital. The reconstructed Kissan Products would merge with BBIL. Kissan currently has market shares of 65 per cent in jams, 39 per cent in sauces and a whopping 85 per cent in squashes. Brooke Bond is putting up a project for frozen foods with a capital outlay of Rs 56 crore to produce up to 8 million litre of frozen desserts every year. Brooke Bond has also identified five Indian vegetables which it plans to process and market; Rs 20 crore is likely to be invested in this project. And, besides the Kissan and Dipy's brands, Brooke Bond also has Kothari General Foods (acquired last year) in its stable.

*Consistently voting for a strategy of
growth through acquisitions*

An interesting feature in all these new strategic moves of Unilever is that
the group has stayed with its core strategy— the strategy of expansion
through the acquisition route. Between 1956 and 1973, Unilever had only
one company in India—Hindustan Lever. Acquisitions have played an
important part in the growth of the Unilever empire in India. In fact, the
world over Unilever has grown with such a strategy. In 1973, following
the worldwide takeover of Lipton by Unilever, Lipton India Ltd came into
its fold in India. And in 1984, Brooke Bond India Limited (BBIL) was
taken over following a similar worldwide takeover of Brooke Bond. In
1986, following the acquisition of Cheseborough Ponds Inc, the Indian
operations in the form of Pond's India Limited (PIL) came through too. In
the same year, the Dutch perfumery flavour company, Naarden, was also
taken over and the name of its Indian subsidiary was changed to Quest
India International Ltd, (QIL).

*Unilever, the parent company, acquires majority
equity in all its group companies in India*

Parent company consolidation was the other major part of Unilever's
corporate strategy in the aftermath of India's liberalisation and
deregulation. The MNC consolidated its position, acquiring 51 per cent
equity control in *each* of its companies in India, the moment 51 per cent
foreign equity holding was permitted under the new economic regime.
And it managed it at attractive prices and with minimal fresh investment,
through a smart three step move involving merger of companies in the
group and incremental fresh investment. In the first step, Unilever merged
two of its plantation companies—Doom Dooma Ltd., in Assam and Tea
Estates Ltd.,—with Brooke Bond India Ltd. Earlier, Unilever held a 74 per
cent stake each in Doom Dooma India Ltd, and Tea Estates Ltd. These
two companies were merged with BBIL to facilitate Unilever jack up its
stake in BBIL from 39.4 to 49.9 per cent. In the second step, Unilever
brought in Rs 37 crore to Lipton, to increase its stake in Lipton from 39.4
per cent to 51 per cent. In the third step, Quest India International
Ltd(QIL), a closely held company in which Unilever held a 73 per cent
stake, was merged with Ponds India Ltd (PIL) to take Unilever's stake in
the combined company to 51 per cent from 40 per cent in the pre-merger
Pond's.

With these moves, Unilever managed to take full advantage of the
relaxations in the FERA rules. It has also managed to restructure its
Indian businesses in the process. All the four companies—HLL, PIL, BBIL
and Lipton—will function as subsidiaries of the parent company; and will
together muster a Rs 4,000 crore to Rs 5,000 crore annual turnover in the
Indian market. And in each of them 51 per cent equity will be held by the

parent MNC. Unilever did not stop with these moves. When it took over Tomco through HLL, it still managed to have majority equity control in the enlarged HLL.

To sum up, the corporate strategy forged by Unilever at this juncture covers wide ranging corporate strategic considerations like expansion and growth in its varying businesses in India, partial elimination of competition through takeovers, achieving the benefits of synergy among businesses, parent company majority ownership and control and a profitable enlargement of stock for the parent company. It is difficult to think of a more shrewd corporate strategy in the Indian business scene.

DIVERSIFICATION RUSH IN THE OPEN REGIME

One of the significant developments in the industrial scene of India in the open regime is a big diversification rush on the part of a large number of companies. As pointed out earlier, companies resort to diversification due to two kinds of compulsions—to ward off the perceived vulnerability of being confined to the present business and to exploit the opportunities presented by the environment. While these are the normal commercial compulsions behind corporate diversifications, it has been different in the Indian context all these years. Diversification as a strategy was resorted to on the basis of a vastly different set of considerations peculiar to the economic climate that prevailed in the country. All these years, Government policies, more than commercial compulsions were the main driving force behind diversifications by Indian companies. Licensing rules, limits on capacity, regulations on expansions, preferential treatment for certain sectors and corporate size restrictions directed an organisation's decisions on diversification. For example, regulation on capacity limits forced the growth seeking companies to go for unrelated diversification. Similarly, import restrictions led many trading companies to enter some new businesses. The tax structure and the compulsion for a safe tax management was another major driving force behind the diversification of many companies, especially the family run businesses. The point to be noted is that while for the companies of the developed world, diversification as a growth strategy was an outcome of the opportunities displayed by the business situations, in India, till recently, the main motivation for diversification arose out of Government regulations. The Indian companies were either evading some Government restrictions or exploiting some Government incentives. When in the '70s and the '80s, the world over, more caution was being built into the diversification strategy, in India the opposite was the trend. A study conducted at the beginning of the '80s among 50 large corporations of India—the private firms, MNCs and public sector firms—showed that India had considerably more unrelated diversifications, compared with the West. The study also indicated that while companies merrily went ahead with diversification, their strategies and structure did not concurrently evolve to take care of the demands of such diversification.

Now, in the open regime, supported by the new optimism generated by the NEP, companies are again resorting to diversification. But the context as well as the compulsions have vastly changed. The new economic policies and the consequent changes in the structure of industries, massive entry of multinationals and the introduction of new products/new technology and the resultant impact of these factors on the mega business environment provide a new set of temptations as well as compulsions for corporations to diversify. As pointed out in the chapter on Business Challenges of the Open Regime, the new business environment is such that there are enough threats forcing the Indian companies to think of expansion/diversification. There are enough opportunities too in the new environment providing temptation for the companies to take to the diversification strategy. That means Indian companies today are placed in a naturally conducive setting to exploit the diversification strategy.

It is only natural therefore that we now see a rush towards diversification. Some of these companies resorted to acquisitions/mergers as the route for their diversification while others preferred joint ventures. A number of companies chose the start-up route and promoted new ventures in their chosen field of diversification. It is, however, essential for these companies to raise and answer certain basic questions and ensure that the diversification strategy is handled correctly.

Diversification requires careful pre-planning/pre-testing

A corporation taking to the diversification route, should first assess the interrelationships of its existing businesses. It should identify the core business that will lay the foundation for its corporate strategy. It has to then assess and find out whether it is safer to "stay close to the knittings" and go in for related diversification or whether it has the competence to manage unrelated diversification. Diversification often fails because of lack of competence on the part of the firm to manage the new business. There is a greater possibility of success when the diversification venture adds value/strength to the existing business. Similarly, diversification into related areas normally assures greater success. For, in related diversification, there is scope for sharing skills and combining activities at the business level. IBM for example, operates in around 20 related fields, each business deriving benefits from the other businesses. When companies resorting to diversification give weightage to the interrelationships and synergy among existing businesses and the new ones, chances of success of the diversification are seen to be greater.

One major reason for diversification failures is the lack of corporate concern for building core competencies and competitive advantage. When new businesses are congenially forged out of the core competencies nurtured and developed by the corporation over a period of time and supported by the competitive advantage enjoyed by the corporation in different factors, there is a greater assurance of success for the new business. On the contrary, when the new business is one of those acquisitions made to look fit through rationalisation rather than chosen on the strength of intrinsic synergy with the corporation, the efforts needed to make the new business win would be tremendous.

A study conducted by Porter analysing the diversification records of 33 large US corporations for the period 1950-1986 shows that diversification—whether through acquisition, joint venture or start-up—has not generally brought the profitability sought by these corporations. This was due to the fact that the companies undertaking diversification often failed in either assessing the attractiveness of the new industry or in ensuring some competitive advantage through the acquisition. In some cases they also failed to correctly estimate the cost of entry with respect to the long term rewards. The diversifiers were seen to be eager to somehow rationalise the diversification decision rather than analyse the pros and cons of diversification and the inter-business linkages resulting from the diversification. Subsequent studies and literature on the subject of corporate diversification that appeared in the late '80s also was pointing towards the need for more caution in taking up unrelated diversifications. The views generally converged on the idea that successful companies in undertaking diversifications generally ensure that such ventures result in transferring of skills and sharing of activities and facilities so that the organisation benefits from the already existing relationships among the various businesses.

The pre-testing yardsticks

Porter recommends three pre-testing measures for the diversifying corporation: the attractiveness test, the cost of entry test and the better-off test. The attractiveness test will ensure that the industries chosen for diversification will be structurally attractive or capable of being made attractive. The cost-of-entry test will ensure that the cost of entering the new business will not dissipate all the future profits of the corporation. And the better-off test will see to it that either the new unit gains competitive advantage from the new relationship or the parent company gains an addtional clout through the new business. In analysing diversification cases, it is often found that in most cases none of these advantages accrue to the firm and over a period of time the company is forced to divest the new venture, proving in retrospect, the decision for diversification a mistake.

Preplanning/Pretesting of diversification should find answers for questions like: what is the motive behind diversification? Is it going to be built around some core businesses and core competencies? Or, is the firm moving into totally unknown and unrelated areas? Where does the balance of advantage lie between investing in and developing the core business and diversifying into the new business? What organisational competence should be developed in managing the diversified firm? What are the inter-business linkages? Can the corporation benefit from say, common marketing facilities or process? Can there be a transferring of skills? Does the diversification add to the corporate fit? Or does it strain the corporate balance? Is it better to stay 'close to the knittings'? Since almost all the Indian companies in the present juncture are impatiently looking for growth through expansion/diversification, this would be a relevant exercise for all of them. They should find answers to these questions.

Assessing industry attractiveness, a major pre-test for diversification

Experience arising out of several diversification cases among Indian companies shows that there are plenty of instances where diversification was not successful. And a main reason for the misfiring of this effort was the lack of attention paid to the analysis of the attractiveness of the new industry they were entering. Most of the companies assumed that the new industries would fit their existing businesses well. In certain cases, the low cost of entry to the new industry tempted them. And in yet other cases the industries appeared to be on a growth trend. Whatever be the apparent attractions, unless the entrant is sure about the profitability of the industry, or confident of changing the industry structure to ensure profitability, the diversification strategy cannot succeed. The predicament in diversification is that when an industry displays substantial attractiveness for a firm to enter, concurrently the cost of entry into that industry is also high. The more attractive it is, the more difficult and costly it is to enter the industry. In some cases, the cost may be so high that the expected profit from the industry may not materialise. That is precisely why pre-testing of diversification becomes essential.

Of all the pre-testing measures, industry attractiveness test is the most crucial one. Usually, a number of factors in combination, render an industry attractive or unattractive. The important ones among these are: size, market growth, pricing, profitability, competitive structure, technology and environmental factors. Profitability of the industry is of course a major criterion. Industries vastly differ in their profitability and profit potential. To cite an example, the profitability of Indian tea and coffee industry is about 11 per cent (profit after tax as a percentage of gross capital employed), whereas that of the pharmaceutical industry is as low as 2.8 per cent. Soaps and detergents industry has a profitability of 8.2 per cent and food products 5 per cent. This was the position at the beginning of the nineties. Naturally, the position varies over time depending upon the evolution of the industry, the extent of new investment, competition, and Government regulations. For example, in the beginning of the eighties, the profitability of pharmaceutical industry, was more than 4 per cent. By the beginning of the '90s, it came down to 2.8

per cent. Price control was the major factor that affected the profitability in the intervening period. In fact, the profitability/attractiveness of several industries in India was substantially influenced by price controls by Government. It has of course worked both ways; sometimes eroding the profitability of an industry and in rare cases, making an industry more attractive for existing investors as well as new investors. The fertiliser industry was a case of the latter kind where the Government's pricing policy in the eighties, contributed a great deal to enhancing the industry attractiveness. And quite naturally, the industry attracted some of the major private corporations of India and big investment flowed into the industry. But now, a reversal is taking place. With the withdrawal of fertiliser subsidies and the Government administered retention pricing system, the industry is losing its attractiveness. So, industry attractiveness is a changing phenomenon and monitoring it and dovetailing the company's strategies to it, has to be an on-going task.

Industry attractiveness arises basically out of the rate of return on investment available by competing in the industry. And the rate of return is, as pointed out earlier, a function of the industry structure. The paradox for aspiring entrants is that often, an attractive industry with high average return on investment will have high entry barriers as well. Therefore, it is difficult to enter such industries. An entrant would like the industry to have a favourable structure—a structure that supports returns exceeding the cost of capital. If such a return is not readily assured, the entrant should be in a position to restructure the industry by its entry and position and enhance the industry attractiveness and gain a return above the industry average. In fact, many industries acquire and display their full potential when new entrants come with fresh investments and promotional strategies and change the very character of the industry.

Unrelated diversification—the example of Lan Eseda

The attempt of Lan Eseda, the computer software company to diversify into sponge iron provides an excellent illustration of the problems and risks in unrelated diversification. There is absolutely no guarantee that success in computer software business will ensure a company success in sponge iron business. There is no synergy; the advantage of related experience is also not there. In fact, if Lan Eseda had some experience in the sponge iron business, it would have got a signal against diversification into sponge iron, at least as far as the timing of the venture was concerned. Lan Eseda now jockeys for a position in the new field at a time when even units entrenched in the industry would think twice before embarking upon an expansion in their own business. Sponge iron has been facing a lot of problems in recent times. With the deregulation, overcrowding has added to the vulnerability of the business. The availability of substitute product—imported steel melting scrap—has also become very easy with the liberalisation of imports. In fact, it is available at lesser prices with the reduction in import tariffs. Moreover, demand recession has hit the industry and quite a few existing units in the industry like Sunflag Iron and Bihar Sponge are unable to market their sponge iron. Evidently, Lan Eseda has not seriously gone through the industry attractiveness test, discussed in detail in the earlier section, before embarking on its diversification. Again, Lan Eseda does not seem to have built up any managerial competence for managing successfully the sponge iron business. The expertise in the software business which Lan Eseda banks on is quite unrelated to the expertise needed for managing a sponge iron venture.

Related diversification—the example of Pond's India

Quest International India Ltd., (QIL), the perfumery, flavour and food ingredients company of the Unilever group merged with Pond's India Ltd., another Unilever company. On the business prospects front, the merger is in tune with the Unilever market strategy of having personal products as one of its core business and an area of future thrust. And for Pond's India the move is one of related diversification; QIL's expertise in the fine fragrance will help them to put world renowned perfumes in the market. Pond's India's thrust is to introduce strong brands on the prestigeous fine-fragrance market.

Diversification for countering vulnerability—the example of Eicher

Eicher's is an example of diversification for countering vulnerability. For many years Eicher remained a single product company, manufacturing tractors. In recent times, it has grown into a diversified group, with interests ranging from trucks and motorcycles to exports, management consultancy and financial services. Tractors, of course, continue as the major business. The group turnover has increased many times over and has crossed Rs 450 crore in 1991-92. In fact, the company is now on the global track.

Diversifying companies have to master entry strategies

Earlier it was mentioned that for a successful diversification into a new business, pretesting of the attractiveness of the new industry and other parameters would be helpful. Even after an effective pretesting, the actual job of entering the business/market remains to be handled. In fact, entry is a corporate burden and a corporate concern. Successful entry is a matter of great competitive skill demanding corporate clout and resource commitment. Because, in this attempt companies often encounter a head on collision with established firms having a strong foothold in the business concerned.

In any industry, existing players, especially the dominant ones among them, always seek ways and means of protecting their hard earned positions. And the main route they adopt is to build entry barriers in the industry so as to prevent the entry of new contestants. Entry barriers are like walls built around the boundaries of an industry. Aspiring new entrants have to break the barriers. And just as there are routes to building barriers there are routes to breaking the barriers, too.

Entry barriers normally emanate from five different sources: economies of scale, brand dominance, cost advantage independent of size, channel clout and in certain cases Government policies relating to the industry. All of them are defences for the existing contestants and barriers to newcomers. These barriers to entry, when attacked properly, become passages for entry into the industry for the aspiring new entrants.

Scale economies in production, marketing, R&D and service are used as barriers to entry in several industries, especially the high-technology industries. They dissuade entry of new contestants forcing them to either enter on a large scale or accept a cost disadvantage consequent to a smaller scale and then work their way up. The existing level of product differentiation and brand dominance in the market creates another entry barrier which forces the aspirant to invest heavily to overcome established and strongly rated brand loyalties. Absolute cost advantage that is not available to new entrants, is the next major entry barrier. Existing players derive cost advantage emanating from proprietory technology, access to the best raw material sources, assets already purchased at lower prices, favourable location etc. This means that the potential entrant will suffer cost disadvantages on several counts, independent of size of operation. Heavy investments and prolonged waiting for an average return on investment become essential to cross the barrier. Well established channel practices constitute yet another entry barrier. Either the new entrant should break the barrier by breaking the channel practices, or accept it at a disadvantage. Government too can limit or even foreclose entry to a given industry, with controls and licence requirements. For example, in India, several industries are reserved for the small scale sector where the big business houses are not allowed to enter and compete. The MRTP and FERA regulations have also served in the past as entry barriers in several industries.

Two broad routes for breaking entry barriers

Two strategic approaches are possible for breaking barriers and facilitating entry:

> to follow the strategy of existing players, and

> to go for an altogether different strategy

To cite an instance, the new entrant can offset the barrier of channel clout of existing players, either by following the same channel strategy or an altogether different channel strategy. In industries that have reached a certain stage of maturity, the channel practices and customer expectations display a certain set pattern. In such cases the new entrants normally find it advantageous to follow the existing channel strategies of the competitors.

At the same time some companies do consciously go in for an altogether different path, so as to demolish the barriers and derive an extra advantage. This is precisely what Reliance did. Reliance Textiles demolished the existing channel practices and set up its own nation-wide chain of retail show rooms. The barrier posed by the existing wholesale textile trade of India was overcome by Reliance by adopting a totally new channel policy and then entering the market in a big way.

Diversifying companies keen to enter an intrinsically new business have wider scope in the matter of entry. The strategies in such cases will revolve around exploiting technological and environmental changes. Intrinsically new products can serve as parachutes on which the new entrants can land right in the midst of the business, avoiding several barriers.

CORPORATE STRATEGY'S ROLE IN BUILDING CORE COMPETENCE AND COMPETITIVE ADVANTAGE

Companies often fail in their business level strategies mainly because they have not endowed their business units with any unique strategic support/ competitive advantage that can function as the real bulwark for the businesses. The corporate managements, whether they opt for stability, expansion or diversification should keep in focus the basic requirements of that decision. It should result in building long term competitive advantage for the firm. As elaborated in the chapter on competitive advantage, successful corporations make it their strategic priority to build their core competencies and long term competitive advantages, so that they will serve as the real back up for the business level strategies of the business units of the corporation.

From the Indian context too, some examples can be cited where corporations have taken to competitive advantage building through corporate strategies. Bajaj Auto is one company that has taken a real lead in competitive advantage building in its business of scooters. In the chapter on Gaining Competitive Advantage, we had provided a competitive advantage profile of Bajaj Auto. In the late '70s when several Indian companies expressed their intention to enter the two wheeler business, Bajaj Auto, so far the undisputed leader in the Indian two wheeler scene, sent out signals that it was planning to produce a million pieces, adequate enough to take care of the entire demand. When even this signal did not have the intended impact, Bajaj went all out to increase its capacity and ensured that its size was at least three to four times that of its nearest competitor. It also closed all niches by getting into every segment like the mopeds and motorcycles and also offered vehicles in various power categories. Bajaj also prudently used its relative strength in costs vis-a-vis the competition and launched an aggressive advertising campaign. Advertising is one cost where small players are no match for a giant. Service coverage was also increased considerably, again an avenue which smaller contenders cannot afford to imitate. In effect, Bajaj signalled at every stage that it was totally committed to maintaining its premier position. It can be seen that every decision taken by the top management of Bajaj Auto during this period went towards building long term competitive advantage for the corporation rather than helping it secure some short term business benefits. In fact, the benefit of these decisions were reaped by Bajaj Auto later in the mid '80s and the early '90s when the two wheeler scene was rocked by heavy competition.

It is high time top managements of Indian companies recognised the requirement of building long term competitive advantage. It is very much essential for supporting the business level strategies of the companies. They should also recognise the distinction between corporate level strategies and business level strategies. Corporate management should appreciate their responsibility to develop long term competitive advantage and core competencies. A corporation is not the sum total of a motley group of stand-alone businesses. On the contrary, the corporation as an entity provides the sap and succour by which the individual businesses and their strategies thrive. For Indian companies the time has now come when this new demand on corporate managements will be put to test. The difficulty will be all the more noticeable when it is recognised that even some of the best run companies of India have not used their corporate strategies to provide the required backup for their individual businesses and the business level strategies.

BUSINESS LEVEL STRATEGIES

As a firm grows and transforms itself into a multi-business entity, which is the emerging pattern in India today, corporate managements have to become increasingly aware of the vastly differing strategic requirements/strategic agenda at the corporate level and the individual business level. The previous section examined what these strategic demands are at the corporate level. At the individual business level, the managers are concerned with the life and death struggle of meeting competition in the concerned business, protecting their share, protecting their profits, keeping short term prosperity and ensuring long term health and viability of their business. Their job is forging the right competitive strategies in the market, as their fight is always in the market place. They have to win and retain customers. The kaleidoscopic variety of strategies and strategic stances that are being written about in volumes relate to competitive strategy played at the business level. On the other hand, the strategic demands at the corporate level revolve around the growth of the total corporation with the best utilisation of the corporate resources across existing businesses. Before going on to a discussion of competitive strategies at the business level it is essential to understand that the differences between the corporate level strategies and business level strategies are not subtle, but are very substantive. To put it differently, while the individual businesses and their strategies revolve around the task of smartly marketing their products and ensuring profits, the corporate managements' job is building long term competitive advantages and developing core competencies for the corporation.

Formulating business level/competitive strategy

It is common knowledge that one of the major tasks facing the strategist is to size up correctly the various competitive forces having a bearing on the functioning of the enterprise. All along, in their effort towards forging appropriate strategies for their businesses, the strategy formulators took cognizance of only the competitors, forgetting other forces shaping competition. And their strategies were accordingly aimed at checking the competitor, countering him through price cuts and channel incentives, launching a new advertisement campaign, introducing a new packaging and the like. In understanding the constituents that shaped competition in their respective industries, their view was not comprehensive enough. Even big corporations of the world suffered from such a myopic understanding of the various factors and forces that shape the total competition in their industry. This approach, as has been proved time and again, had its inherent limitations. Analysis shows that in addition to 'competition proper', there are several other competitive forces affecting the functioning of a business which need to be reckoned with in strategy formulation.

According to Michael E. Porter, "...There are five major and vital forces that decide the nature and intensity of competition—the threat of new entrants, bargaining power of customers, bargaining power of suppliers, threat of substitute products and the jockeying among the existing contestants... . The collective strength of these forces determine the ultimate profit potential of an industry. And the strategist's goal is to find a position in the industry where his company can best defend itself against these forces or can influence them in his company's favour... . Strategy can be viewed as building defences against the competitive forces." Porter emphasises that in the task of strategy formulation, strategists cannot stop with sizing up of 'competition proper', but have to size up the other forces that shape competition, forces that emanate from customers, new products, suppliers and new entrants. The strategy should be able to influence all these forces in favour of the business so that the business can secure for itself a position of superiority in the market in relation to competition. Later, when we analyse in detail the various kinds of strategies adopted by companies, we shall see how these strategies make an attempt to influence these forces of competition. We shall also see how strategies aimed at handling 'competitors' alone, ignoring the other competitive forces, prove inadequate in countering competition.

GENERIC APPROACHES TO BUSINESS LEVEL STRATEGIES — THE PRICE AND NON PRICE ROUTES

The burden of business level strategy is to decide how the firm should compete in the given industry/business. And an abundance of strategies and strategy options are available to business executives in chartering the fortunes of their business through the thick of competition. With the ever increasing demands from the markets, executives in charge of businesses keep on innovating new strategies and renovating existing ones. It is a relentless race to stay ahead of competition. And precisely because of this reality, a vast array of strategies as well as a kaleidoscopic variety of strategy stances have emerged, to be copied, modified upon and debated. Management literature handling the subject from different premises is also available in plenty. Some of the widely practised ones among these strategies will be discussed later in this chapter. But before delving deeper into this subject of competitive strategies, it has to be pointed out that basically there are only two broad routes available for forging competitive strategies at the business level. They are: the price route and the non-price route. Any strategy has to be ultimately either a price based strategy or a non-price strategy.

Companies taking to the price route compete on the strength of their pricing policy and the resultant price cushions they are able to enjoy. Normally those who decide to exploit the price route and thus compete on price will enjoy certain substantial cost advantage, giving them substantial flexibility in pricing and marketing.

The non-price route to strategy revolves around features other than price. The product with its innumerable features, the service and the various other functions performed by the corporation are all possible sources of non-price differentiation strategy. In fact, any of the ever so many activities performed by the business unit or the ever so many offerings made by it can constitute the nucleus for differentiation. We shall be taking up for a detailed discussion the differentiation route to strategy formulation later on in this chapter. At this point it is sufficient to point out that the major business battles are fought on the strength of the differentiation strategy rather than the price based route. In almost all product categories and almost all markets of the world, this is true. The major temptation and also the major benefits in resorting to the differentiation strategy is that it allows the firm to move away from the disadvantages of a wholly price based competition. In other words, differentiation allows the company the freedom and flexibility to fight on the non-price front. Differentiation therefore is a crucial option for a firm in its search for a rewarding strategy.

It has to be clarified that from the same aspect/activity, a cost advantage as well as a differentiation advantage can accrue. A corporation may decide to exploit the aspect/activity for either a cost advantage or a differentiation advantage, depending on the context. Aspects like scale, linkages, timing of entry, location, the extent of integration are all sources from which a corporation can bring forth the cost advantage as well as differentiation advantage. For example, in the matter of integration, the level of integration a firm seeks can give it a differentiation advantage or a cost advantage or both, depending on circumstances. It can confer on the firm a uniqueness in its product offering and provide access to more activities which can be further sources of differentiation. It will enable the firm to exercise control over the performance of that activity. The cost, reliability and quality of the activities can be controlled by the firm, which in a de-integrated set up are mostly left to the supplier of these activities. In this way, integration can bring in a differentiation advantage. There are also several instances when integration can lower the costs and bring in substantive cost advantage to the firm. The point to be noted is that the extent of cost advantage arising out of integration will depend on the behaviour of cost in the particular industry and the trade off between doing the activity in house vis-a-vis buying it.

THE PRICE ROUTE TO STRATEGY

The corporation that opts for the price route in its competitive battle will enjoy certain flexibilities in the matter of pricing of its products, and can use price as the main competitive lever. It will juggle the price of its products to suit the varying competitive demands, as it will be enjoying certain inherent cost advantages. Such advantages may emanate from several activities/areas of operation, finally resulting in substantial cost advantage to the corporation. The major areas from where such cost advantages can accrue are: scale economies, absolute cost advantages, benefits of early entry, a large market share built over a period of time, corporate synergy in major activities like production and marketing of the different business etc. Such benefits provide the firm vast freedom in the matter of pricing—it may go in for a pro-active pricing, a reactive pricing, product bundling or unbundled pricing or a product line pricing or it may even go to the extent of pricing across businesses and markets where the fights are global in character. Since the entire stake is built around pricing, the corporation opting for this route, is ever vigilant to exploit every opportunity to extract a cost advantage.

A corporation resorting to the price route to competitive strategy should be enjoying in the overall sense, a cost leadership within its industry. Such a firm will enjoy a low cost position which yields above average returns in its industry, in spite of strong competition. The corporation will have efficient scale economies, it will always be looking for cost reduction through different routes: experience curve effects, cost control, dropping unprofitable customers/segments, minimal cost in R&D, just in time inventory etc. And with the cumulative support of all these factors, it fights on the cost/price front.

To resort to price led strategies a firm should have consciously taken to that route fairly early in its evolutionary process. After producing a particular product and getting stuck in the face of competition one cannot successfully opt for a price led strategy. Conscious cost reduction programmes, a steady pursuit of automation, a constant vigil to exploit learning curve effects, search for cost effective technologies/processes as well as a corporation-wide commitment to cost reduction are essential pre-requisites for a price led strategy to succeed. Without obtaining a cost leadership in the concerned industry through resorting to such steps early on, it is difficult to compete on the basis of price. The point to be highlighted is that for opting for the price route a firm should have built up sustainable and long term sources of cost advantage.

The example of Siva PC

Sterling Computers's Siva PC is an apt example of price based strategy. The company has been active for many years now, in the PC segment of the computer market in India. It has been consistently following a strategy based on price. It promises reasonable quality at a very competitive price which the other units in the industry find difficult to match. During 1987-89 Sterling managed to hit the competitors hard through the price route. In the NEP era, especially after the 1993 budget, the company struck even more strongly at the competitors through the price route. It offered the Siva 386 DX system operating at 40 MHZ with a 40 MB Hard disk and a one year warranty at a price of Rs 29,970/-. The competitors in the industry were almost dazed with this price based strategy of Siva PC. Some of them claimed that the price was 40 per cent below average industry price and was also below the raw material cost of most players in the industry! Some others went round saying that the Siva product was absolutely shoddy and that was how it could afford to sell at such low prices. But in an industry like the PC, it is difficult for any player to make big sales without an acceptable quality. Evidently Sterling operates with certain cost advantages and also with wafer thin margins. The strategy is heavily dependent on price and the unit is prepared for price cuts to hit the competitors and gain market share.

De-integration for cost advantage

De-integration or out sourcing is a method normally resorted to, for obtaining cost advantage. In de-integration, companies normally exploit the capabilities of suppliers/channels. Companies opting for cost advantage may opt for different levels of de-integration.

In the modern world, where the latest information technology/ transportation facilities can eliminate or reduce the delay associated with distance and time, several activities/functions of the firm can be ideally de-integrated, resulting in substantial cost advantage. In fact, today many leading corporations of the world are seeking substantial cost advantage through out-sourcing several of their activities. They can buy supplies/ components from anywhere at the shortest possible time using the best logistic capabilities and they can coordinate these activities through modern communication systems. Such companies maintain a lean organisation, undertaking only those core activities where the company wants to maintain its own standards and uniqueness. Then they aggressively seek ways to eliminate, limit, or outsource the other activities to the maximum extent possible. Finally, only those activities that are essential to its chosen areas of strategic focus are retained in-house. Some of them go to the maximum possible extent of de-integration as a contrast to the highly integrated companies who own large raw material bases, factories, research laboratories, warehouses, transport systems and marketing offices. In the international scene, Apple computer and Honda Motor company are two ideal cases of extreme de-integration.

De-integration for cost advantage—Apple Computer: Taking the cue from many other successful companies, Apple Computer initially succeeded by organising itself as a lean company that purposely manufactured as little as possible in-house. Since its business strength lay in creating the friendly look and feel of its software and hardware, Apple's management concentrated on designing and controlling its product concepts, especially Apple DOS, which was not even made available for licence. Other components and activities were outsourced wherever possible. Apple bought microprocessors from Synertek, other chips from Hitachi, Texas Instruments, and Motorola, video monitors from Hitachi, power supplies from Astec, and printers from Tokyo Electric and Qume. Similarly, Apple kept its internal service activities and investments to a minimum by outsourcing application software development to Microsoft, promotion to Regis McKenna, product styling to Frogdesign, and distribution to ITT and Computer Land. When it came to the Apple II, it was estimated to cost less than $500 to build, of which $350 was for purchased components.

THE NON-PRICE ROUTE/DIFFERENTIATION ROUTE TO STRATEGY

Differentiation as a strategic weapon works on the principle that any activity or entity can be made distinctive from competing offers through certain strategic approaches. It is this possibility that is exploited by the business firms voting for differentiation strategy. From the simplest of commodities to the most sophisticated of products and services, the scope for differentiation is tremendous.

The most stimulating idea on differentiation was put forward by Levitt in one of his HBR classics, *Marketing Success, through Differentiation of Anything*. He elaborated that in the business scene, there is no such thing as a commodity. All goods and services are differentiable. In the market place differentiation is everywhere. Everybody — producer, fabricator, seller, broker, the agent and the merchant tries constantly to distinguish his offer from that of his competitors. This is true even of those who produce and deal in primary metals, grains, chemicals, plastics and money. After explaining how, from the simplest of commodities to the most complicated of products, differentiation can be put to use, Levitt goes on to show how "the way in which the manager operates becomes an extention of product differentiation".

Companies can differentiate their offers in many ways. Right from collaboration, plant location to post-sales service, a company can perceptibly differentiate and add buyer value. Companies can differentiate through every activity that they perform and they should choose those functions which give them the greatest relative advantage. A mango fruit juice manufacturing company may differentiate itself by using only the choicest fruit such as Alphonso mangoes. A furniture manufacturer can stay with the best Burma teak and command a premium. Modi's collaboration with Rank Xerox is a classic example of how collaboration can provide effective differentiation. In the case of Garden Silks, emphasis on design has given the company the advantage of differentiation. A firm can as a matter of policy, employ only technically qualified workers or professionally qualified sales force and thereby differentiate and add value. Even in operations with massive automation, a firm can ensure it is technologically superior and there by command a premium in the market place. A strategically designed manufacturing system may promise a lower delivery time and a wide product range which can be a sustainable ground for differentiation. A company can also differentiate by its channel. Eureka Forbes has successfully used personal selling as the sole means of reaching the customer. If we draw examples from the international scene, IBM in Computers differentiated along technology and service, Caterpillar Tractor differentiated through its global dealer network, Coca Cola and Pepsi Cola differentiated through brand image and Rolls Royce in automobiles differentiated on superior quality.

'The Product' offers infinite scope for pursuing the differentiation strategy

All along, the marketing men of India carried the idea that successful strategy revolves around advertising and sales promotion. A critical examination of the various marketing campaigns run by the Indian companies in the '80s, which by itself is considered as the decade that ushered in 'marketing' in India, will show that there was a preoccupation with advertising, trade promotions and a personal selling push in the strategy basket. It looked as though a business is made through advertising campaigns and innovative sales promotions. This preoccupation with advertising and sales promotion blurred their visions about 'Product' and the ultimate potential it holds in forging a successful competitive strategy. In this section we will analyse in some depth the strategic potential of Product. Even the firms operating on price realise that price wars are both expensive as well as dangerous as they often result in diminishing the returns to the firms and also in the deterioration of quality standards of the products. Firms operating on price led strategies, therefore, are finally tempted to strengthen their position in areas other than price, create brand preference, attract floating customers and brand switchers through the differentiation route.

Product is also the No 1 entity in the 4 Ps of marketing. While all the 4 Ps are important elements, from the point of view of strategy, normally the other Ps go as elaborations of the offer, the chief part of which is the product. In a natural way, the marketing strategy revolves around the product.

Product differentiation can be achieved through multiple sources and in multiple ways

Whatever may be the source and the route, in order to be meaningful or useful, the differentiation should create buyer value that is unique as well as sustainable. A few examples of such differentiation from the Indian business experience are provided here.

Differentiation through product convenience—Kinetic Honda

Countering the effect of recession and scoring over competition have been the twin challenges in the two wheeler industry in the liberalised regime. Kinetic Honda admirably demonstrated how the twin tasks could be accomplished through the differentiation strategy. In an year ('91-92) that was characterised by a slump in the industry (growth rate, minus 14 per cent), it registered a growth rate of plus 14 per cent. Production in the year was over 87,000 units.

Kinetic Honda's market research revealed that most of the existing two wheeler models were not user-friendly. Starting the two wheeler was always a problem to the user. Kinetic Honda brought in the new-wave scooter which had an electronic ignition and could do away with the painful kick-start routine. In addition, the new model contained a whole range of features including automatic gear shifting, choke, built-in indicators and a streamlined aerodynamic design.

Not only did the company succeed in marketing its two wheeler in the years of recession, it also embarked upon a programme to consolidate its market position. It planned to introduce new models and to increase the production to 10,000 units per month in 1994-95 and 25,000 per month in the subsequent two years. On the anvil are four new models to be rolled out in phases over the next four years, with doubling of capacity.

Toothpaste with Gel—Differentiation by HLL

In the toothpaste business, HLL has achieved differentiation by introducing the Gel based toothpaste. And HLL's Close-up has carved out a niche in the toothpaste market. Gel is not just a gimmick. It makes the toothpaste quite different. It creates a buyer value that is unique and sustainable. While the ordinary toothpastes use calcium carbonate as carrier, the Gel pastes use glycerine, which is capable of improving the flavour. Moreover, the paste with glycerine as base can be coloured nicely. During the four year period 1988-92, HLL was able to increase its market share through this differentiation, by nearly four times, from less than 4 per cent to over 15 per cent. Colgate was compelled to copy this differentiation as its market share fell from 57 per cent to 52 per cent during the same period.

Differentiation by Indecor Paints with addition of insecticide

Indecor Paints brought in a new paint product, Vinycide, the single coat plastic emulsion paint for 'insect free interiors'. It was a paint with an insecticide built in. It was claimed that the paint was an innovation with a unique formula from ARTLIN of France, a paint that had already turned interiors in Europe beautiful and insect free. And since it comes in white, it lets you create colours of your choice by adding stainers. An attempt was also made to make star hotels and lodging houses the special market segment for the product by suggesting that their guests deserved to stay in insect free rooms! Like the Gel toothpaste, this paint product too did offer something new to the users.

Differentiation by Dunlop tyres with end-use in mind

Dunlop differentiated its tyres for different cars, keeping the end use in mind, when it introduced its range of Dunlop—OLYMPUS Nylon car tyres. The differentiation brought about by the company is explained below in its own words.

"Most tyres don't recognise the fact that every car is different and needs its own special kind of tyre. So, when we designed the Olympus range, we studied each car separately. For the Maruti, we designed a tyre specially for its front wheel drive. We built an extra-wide tyre for Premier, because it goes through a lot of wear and tear on city roads. And for the Ambassador, we reinforced the tyre walls with extra rubber to take the extra weight. Because we see the Maruti, Premier and Ambassador as three different cars—not the same car in three different sizes."

Competitive benefit will arise only if differentiation creates buyer value. The major task involved, therefore in differentiating a product is to identify certain product attributes that can attract differential responses from the buyers.

Product customisation

Product customisation is a commonly resorted method for differentiating products from that of competition. In product customisation, the customer's specific requirements are taken into account while developing the product. This is a frequent practice in industrial products marketing, where the manufacturer and the user are in closer contact and the product gets customised to the requirements of the customer. Through customisation, the firm makes the offer distinctive and acceptable to the customer.

In product augmentation, voluntary improvements are brought about by the manufacturer in order to enhance the value of the product. These improvements are neither suggested by the customers, as in product customisation, nor even expected by them. The firm on its own, augments the product, by adding an extra facility or an extra feature to it. For example, when the manufacturers of Aristocrat moulded luggage introduced luggage cases with wheels, it was a case of product augmentation. The wheel was an extra facility the manufacturer thought of and added to the luggage. Instead of lifting and carrying the suitcase, the users could now pull it along the ground on its wheels. The feature provided a distinctiveness to the Aristocrat luggage.

INVENTION/INNOVATION/NEW PRODUCT DEVELOPMENT

Aiming at inventing an intrinsically new product and skimming the market is an excellent strategy companies with resources can employ. Japanese companies have been excelling this way.

Big corporations who wage their business wars on the strength of their products, are keeping an eye always on the potential products/ intrinsically new products in their chosen line. Such corporations who have heavy resources and organisational clout to their support are in search of tomorrow's products—the potential products. To make tomorrow's product today is their aim. There are no limits to the 'potential product'. The limit is set only by the technological and economic resources of the firm. Big corporations operating in modern fields like electronics, both consumer electronics and industrial electronics, computers, chemicals, bio-engineering etc., are investing heavily to invent new products and reap the benefits of innovation and early entry into so far non-existent markets. Theirs is the route of innovation and new products.

**Companies take to product innovation to meet
changes in demand, to make new profits and
to combat environmental threats**

In an age of scientific and technological advancement, change in customer
requirements is a natural outcome—change in food habits, change in
comforts and conveniences of life and change in social habits. Any
business has to be vigilant to these changes taking place in its environment. People always seek better and better products—more convenience
in products, more fashion and more value for the money they part with.
A business firm has to respond to these dynamic requirements of its
clientele—and these responses take the shape of product innovation. And
through such a response, the firm reaps substantial benefits.

Companies take to new products from growth and profit angles too.
Products that are already established, often have their limitations in
enhancing the profit level of the firm. Quite often, profits from products
decline as they reach the maturity stage of their life cycle and the profits
vanish, as they glide into the next stage of decline. It thus becomes
essential for business firms to bring in new products to replace old,
declining and losing products. New products become part and parcel of
the growth requirements of the firm and in many cases, new profits come
to the firm only through new products.

The need for responding to change and the need for new profits are
not the only factors that persuade business firms to go in for the
innovation based strategy. There is a more compelling factor, the need to
counter the threats arising from the environment. A business firm is
vulnerable to many factors, such as changes in general economic
conditions, social/political/legal pressures, technological changes and
supply problems. This is in addition to the ever present vulnerability from
competition. Changes in the fiscal and monetary policies of the country
affect the companies and their businesses seriously. Social and political
pressures and international economic trends also contribute to the
vulnerability of businesses. In the '70s IBM and Coca Cola had to leave
the Indian market on political rather than economic considerations. Social
demands on environmental protection often pose new problems to several
companies, especially in industries like chemicals. Legal restrictions
prevent several companies from expanding their capacities in their
existing product lines. Technological changes make several products
suddenly obsolete. Problems of supply of raw materials, utilities, etc., also
render existing businesses/products risk prone. For example, scarcity and
high cost of oil and electricity force some companies to take a second look
at their existing products and businesses.

Such threats make some of the current products of the firm highly
vulnerable. And to reduce the vulnerability of their business as a whole,
companies seek out new products. New products offer new avenues of
growth and thus help secure the overall viability of the firm. The risk also

gets spread over several products, existing ones and totally new ones. Thus, for many firms, product innovation/invention/new product development become an unavoidable weapon against environmental threats. It is always safer not to put all the eggs in one basket.

Product invention normally remains the forte of big firms

Though new products can bring new profits to firms, product innovation as a strategic weapon normally cannot be adopted by small companies, as substantial resources are required for making the strategy work. That is why bringing out intrinsically new products and services in the market place remains the forte of giant corporations, mostly in the economically advanced countries. And even within the developed world only giant corporations like Du Pont, or IBM, or General Electric, or General Foods or Sony are pioneering such efforts.

Innovation/invention carries huge rewards for the risk taker

The innovators invest heavily in research and development and often have several new product ideas lined up, each in different stages of formulation. While such firms remain leaders in their chosen markets, enjoying all the attendant advantages of being a leader, the vast majority of the companies prefer to be followers, entering with similar products after the pioneer establishes his new product. Majority of the firms shy away from new product development, because new products normally suffer from high attrition rate as well as a high rate of market failure. Even those products which reach the market after years of preparation and work, often fail miserably. Many of them suddenly die out after the initial boom. Innovation has thus remained the forte of big companies who can absorb the cost and fatigue of such failures. They believe in reaping big profits through entering totally new areas of business with totally new products. They can enter totally new territories, win over new customers, establish new channels and ride comfortably on the back of the new product. It is evident that bringing out totally new products and getting them established in the market as successful products is time consuming, investment heavy, risk laden and difficult tasks. But the innovation hungry company does not mind all these hassles. Even the craziest of new product ideas holds attraction for them.

New Product Idea—The Walkman story

The Walkman story is an apt illustration of how development of new products is often the forte of companies with enormous resources and great thirst for new products. Walkman, the personalised stereo cassette player brought out by Sony would not have seen the light of day but for Sony's resources and the thirst of Akio Morita, and Masaru Ibuka for product innovation.

Sony had introduced in the late seventies a compact, portable, small, tape recorder, 'Pressman' which sold very well. Sony wanted to introduce stereo facilities in the 'Pressman', but found that the stereo recording machine could not be fitted in the limited space available in the unit.

When Ibuka the honorary chairman of Sony was shown the failed Pressman stereo system, he immediately remembered another project being conducted by another department in Sony in developing light-weight headphones. Instantly, the new product idea flashed across Ibuka's mind — Why not combine these two? He sensed that the essence of the new product job was to reduce the weight of the stereo unit to the barest minimum. Akio Morita, chairman of Sony, endorsed the idea. Being a marketing genius, he fully grasped the potential of the new product with teenagers as the target market. He knew any expenditure on this new product would be worthwhile. He ordered his engineers to strip out the heavy speaker from it and replace it with a lightweight amplifier plus lightweight head phones. Walkman was the outcome.

The lesson to be learnt is that it needs an organisation like Sony and men like Ibuka and Morita to nurture such a new product idea and translate it into a reality. New product development needs the kind of environment and people which have been the hallmarks of corporations like Sony. "Do what others have not done", has been one of the mottoes of Sony and the genesis of Walkman is a testimony to the creativity of Sony.

Positioning strategy

The significance of product positioning in the full exploitation of the strategic potential of the product can be easily understood from David Ogilvy's assertion, "The result of your campaign depends less on how we write your advertising than on how your product is positioned."

Positioning is the outcome of a conscious strategy of marketing. Some unique feature of the product, some unique feature of the market or some unique feature of the competition is normally isolated and around that feature the product is placed in the market. Positioning comes out of the marketing man's awareness that a product cannot be 'everything to everyone'; it can only be something to someone; and hence the need for careful product positioning. Identifying these features imaginatively and using it as the 'plank' on which to pedestal the product is the essence of positioning. So, the product can be positioned against a competing brand, it can be positioned for an exclusive well-to-do segment of the market, it can be positioned for men, it can be positioned for children, it can be positioned for the fun-loving youth, it can be positioned for a health-conscious market, it can be positioned on a claim of luxury, a claim of distinctiveness, a claim of convenience, novelty, usage.

The strategist has to formulate his positioning theme right from the product idea stage. He cannot suddenly invent a positioning theme when he is ready to enter the market with his product. He should have already decided what his 'cash on' point should be, where he should introduce his product and for whom, and on what distinctive claim he should go around and promote his product. Positioning is essentially a battle for capturing a place in the mind of the prospect. As Al Ries and Jack Trout put it, "Positioning is what you do to the mind of the prospect. That is, you position the product in the mind of the prospect."

Obviously, positioning is a technique which the strategist has to employ with a lot of care and pre-planning. By positioning a product in a particular way, the marketing man is committing the product to the particular decision and situation. If the positioning decision is faulty, the product suffers heavy damages. It may take a long time and enormous effort to retrieve a wrongly positioned product. Though repositioning a successful product later in its life-cycle to take care of the new requirement may be easy, it is not at all easy to retrieve and reposition a wrongly positioned product.

INTEGRATION STRATEGY

Analysis shows that companies with long term intention on building differentiation advantage go in for integration opting to manufacture all their products and components and own as many facilities and services as possible, in-house. Though, initially, building up such facilities is investment intensive these corporations opt for such investment as they feel this is the surest route to finally control these activities in their favour and thereby derive the best of differentiation benefit.

In the Indian context, Reliance Textiles and Videocon Industries can be cited as examples of companies which have consciously opted for a strategy of high integration with the long term view of securing a significant differentiation advantage for themselves.

Reliance Textiles—High degree of integration

Reliance Textiles provides an apt example of vertical integration. While several of India's textile companies operated by purchasing grey cloth and doing the printing, Reliance went in for the highest degree of vertical integration in the textile industry and Reliance Textiles became India's largest and most modern, vertically integrated composite textile plant.

It has a spinning division set up at a cost of Rs 18.5 crore. It has 12,500 spindles turning out myriad varieties of yarn spun on the Worsted System, for worsted and other blended suitings. This is one of the most modern worsted spinning yarn plant in Asia.

In the yarn division, hundreds of tonnes of yarn is crimped, texturised, twisted, coned, rewound, doubled, dyed and reeled.

In the knitting division, the two departments—circular and warp knitting—produce 50 lakh metres of dress material and shirting annually.

The weaving division, considered the most modern division of its kind in the country, has an installation of 154 ultra modern shuttleless Sulzer machines among others; it produces more than one crore metres of Vimal Suitings in over 15,000 designs and colour combinations annually.

In the design studio, more than 250 artists apply their skills to create a dazzling array of over 10,000 original designs annually.

The printing department houses some of the most modern Rotary and Flat-Bed printing machinery, with an installed capacity of 4 crore metres per annum.

The processing department ensures exclusive excellence in finishing. This is done on the most sophisticated machinery—the Smith SD-28 Relaxing and Washing Machines, in synchronisation with a Hirano-4 Suction Dryer and ATYC Suplex Jet Dyeing machines.

In the research and development wing, new yarn counts and fabric manufacture are innovated each season, and sophisticated machinery probes other areas of fabric manufacture. The facilities include colour-matching computers and a quality control department.

Videocon, another case of high integration

Videocon has given high emphasis to establishing very high capacities, in-house, in all its businesses, TVs, audios, VCRs/VCP, washing machines, air conditioners and refrigerators. The firm's intention was to achieve command over all its manufacturing activities. To achieve this the company resorted to backward integration. It invested Rs 52 crore in moulding shops to meet their entire requirements of cabinets for TVs, audios, VCRs/VCP and tubs for its washing machines. It invested Rs 22 crore in component manufacturing facilities, to make flyback transformers and tuners and another Rs 16 crore to manufacture Black and White picture tubes. It also acquired the Uptron colour picture tube manufacturing facility. In addition, the company also promoted a glass shells project in collaboration with GNVFC. And, Videocon emerged as the fully integrated entertainment electronics group in the country. The fact that it was in a number of related industries enabled Videocon to fully utilise common shop and assembly facilities, in addition to substantially gaining the benefit of common expertise. The vertical integration was carried to such an extent that in respect of the TV business the company could virtually claim "We can make TV sets virtually from sand".

The company also has gone in for the best technologies of the world. For its refrigerators and washing machines it has Matsushitas' technologies; for audio and VCRs it has Toshiba technology. Videocon recognises that for an ultimate differentiation advantage in the industry, substantial investment is called for supported by the right technologies.

Flexible Manufacturing Systems (FMS), another route to differentiation

While the advantages associated with mass production and large volume runs and the resultant cost advantages are being successfully used by companies in marketing their products, at the opposite end of the spectrum are to be seen another group of companies who go in for the more modern idea of flexible manufacturing, small lot runs and the resultant variety in production. Today this has become the competing edge for many Japanese companies in their life and death fight with American companies.

Through the FMS route the corporation manufactures many different products/varieties of same products in the same assembly line, switches from one to another instantly as well as at low cost, makes profits on short volume runs and brings out new offerings much faster than competition. The advantage is that FMS offers a quicker and a more versatile response to consumers. The focus is on flexibility instead of standardisation. At Japan's Toshiba for example, flexibility in manufacturing is an explicit goal. Its computer factory at Ome, for example, assembles nine different word processors on the same line and on an adjacent line assembles 20 varieties of laptop computers. The factory makes them in batches of 20; in fact, the line can accommodate lot sizes as small as 10. The flexible lines allow the company to guard against running short of a hot selling model or over producing those models which are slowing down. The net impact is that the company's response to the market is faster and it cashes in on the varying demand patterns ahead of competition.

In the auto industry, while many American companies still devote a production line to a single model, Japan's Toyota started installing flexible lines in the mid '80s. At Toyota a line can weld a Camry one minute, a Lexus the next, then a Crown, with no pause whatsoever.

Of course, investment in flexible manufacturing systems is not cheap. In fact, it requires enormous investment. But the benefit is reaped elsewhere—through exploiting the economies of scope, the ability to spread costs across many products and through realisation of quicker sales and a large product base. The profits are made through variety and speed and quicker responses to the market. It is found that when the typical American company with an FMS used it to turn out 10 different items, Japanese companies turned out as many as 93 items. Obviously, flexibility in manufacturing and the consequent benefits in marketing is becoming a strategic asset.

The globalised product offer

We have seen in detail that product differentiation is a major route to strategically managing one's products and markets. As a total contrast to this route, there are some companies practising what Theodore Levitt calls the globalised product offer. Quite a few Japanese firms in consumer electronics, for example, offer a globalised product rather than a differentiated product. Companies going in for the global product consciously ignore the differences among the various markets and they opt for treating the entire market as if it were one single homogeneous entity. They serve the whole market—and often several nations of the world together constitute their market—with the same product, without any differentiation whatsoever either in the product or the other elements of the marketing mix. They focus their attention on the commonalities of the market rather than on its subtle differences, and satisfy the entire market with the same product offer. Products like Coca Cola, Pond's Cold Cream, Walkman etc., are instances of global products.

In offering a global product, the firm derives the benefit of low relative cost. It sells the same thing, the same way all over the globe. And the two parameters that make global product possible are technology and the commonalities in consumer preferences. The firms offering global products unrelentingly push for economy and value enhancement that translate into a standardisation at high quality levels, resulting in globally acceptable products.

Quality as the centre-piece of strategies

Several companies have reaped substantial business success through bankng on the quality route. In the international scene several of the well known multinational companies like Siemens, ITT, Honda etc., have taken to the quality route in making their product offers distinct from that of competition. For example, Honda Motor Co. has the following item as a guiding principle: Don't accept bad parts, don't make bad parts, don't ship bad parts. Such a directive sends corporate wide cautioning on the quality standards expected of every department/function.

In fact, countries like Japan and Germany have built their reputation on quality. And many of the products emerging from these countries have become globally acceptable. When several of the American companies gave extra focus on sales oriented innovations, the West German companies gave extra focus to ensuring that they produce a well engineered product. They believed that product quality can be an unmistakable weapon in the market. They went to the extent of proving that the customer will even wait for the well made product. They also believe that quality is a feature that produces a self perpetuating reputation.

Internationally many corporations today have moved up to the 'zero defect' level in their products. Such corporations are aware that the rewards coming through the quality route are lasting and substantial. And on the other extreme, there are many companies especially in the developing countries, who feel that the cost of ensuring quality is too high and therefore they make do without this yardstick. In fact, quality has a cost but it is a cost that can be realised back in terms of reputation and business prosperity.

Quality as a route to successful strategy is not confined to the manufactured product. In fact quality is equally relevant, to the services group. The product of the service sector may be intangibles. It is also not possible to test service through the yardsticks of quality-testing in manufactured products. And because of this reason the main test in the quality of services can be only to find out whether the consumer is totally satisfied or not. Whether it is a travel agency, a beauty parlour, or a portfolio investor firm, the final quality test can only be through the customer. Pure service businesses like airlines, banks, transport, insurance, computer services, management consultancy, etc., evaluate the quality of their offers by evaluating the customer responses. Because of the fact that service quality is more elusive than product quality, managements have to apply more time to think in this direction. Organisations make use of focus groups and customer surveys to really understand the customer's version of the quality of their service. Organisations like McDonalds have found that an effective strategy will aim at a precise statement of what the customer wants, and then ensure a system to measure whether the customer's perceptions and requirements are met.

DRAWING FROM BOTH PRICE AND DIFFERENTIATION ROUTES, COMPANIES FORGE A VARIETY OF STRATEGIES TO SUIT THEIR UNIQUE SITUATIONAL DESIGNS

In actual practice, companies draw relevant elements from both price and differentiation routes and forge unique strategies to suit their unique situational design and relative position in the industry. There are strategies for the leader, strategies for the challenger, strategies for specialisers. This is but natural. As long as their situational designs and consequently their specific requirements of strategy differ from each other firms will evidently follow different strategies. One firm may find it appropriate to have a direct confrontation with the market leader; another may find it appropriate to keep aloof for some time from the heat of competition; the third may find it relevant to chalk out a strategy of sheer survival.

Offensive strategy

Offensive strategy, as the name indicates, is a strategy of aggression/ confrontation. An offensive strategy is usually employed by a firm that is not presently the leader, but aspires to leadership position in the industry. It is normally the No 2 or No 3 or any other strong contestant in the industry that resorts to such a strategy. An ambitious newcomer to the industry too can employ the strategy to advantage. In either case, the firm that adopts the offensive strategy assumes the position of the challenger.

The challenger aggressively tries to expand his market share; the leader mostly is the target of attack. The challenger utilises all the elements of the marketing mix in attacking the leader. He can be offensive in price with daring price cuts; he can be offensive in product, by supplying superior products or enlarging the variety of products supplied. He may opt to provide superior service and better channel motivation. He may also be aggressive in advertising and sales promotion. Usually, a strong offensive strategy has all these elements blended suitably.

A firm must have some strong and sustainable competitive advantage to be an effective challenger. It must also have the capability to neutralise the leader's competitive advantages. A challenger can attack the leader either by being 'same as the leader' or by being 'radically different from the leader'.

Defensive strategy

A defensive strategy is usually employed by the leader who has the compulsion to defend his leadership position against the onslaught of powerful existing competitors or strong new entrants with the ambition to dislodge the leader from his No 1 position. The leader's concern is: how best can I defend my position? The leader cannot assume that its position in the industry is safe and its job, easy. It has to maintain constant vigilance and defend its position against the attack of the challengers; because in any industry challengers keep appearing. In the moulded luggage market VIP had to defend itself against Aristocrat; in the detergents market Surf had to defend its position against Nirma; in the toothpaste market Colgate had to defend itself against Promise.

A leader trying to defend his leadership must have a strategy that helps expansion of the total demand of the industry so that he can keep growing despite the challengers nibbling his market share continuously. Market expansion can be achieved by finding more users or new users or by increasing the usage. The leader should also try to increase its market share even when industry demand remains at a constant level. Continuous innovation is another element of the defensive strategy of a leader. The leader leads through innovation; the challengers would need time to catch up. The leader also defends by ensuring that all his flanks are well covered and the challenger does not easily attack him from the sides, unawares.

As in warfare, in business too, the best way to defend is through building an impregnable fort around one's territory. The best defensive strategy, is the one that banks on continuous gaining of competitive advantage so that the challenger is frustrated and constrained. The leader can gain his continuous competitive advantage by continuously improving his relative cost position or his differentiation position or both. Such a strategy would reduce the very probability of being challenged. It makes challenging more difficult, or less attractive or both. A leader can work out a strong defensive strategy by the very way in which he chooses to compete in the industry. By creating structural barriers he can make entry/mobility difficult for the challenger. He can also make challenging unattractive by lowering his prices and reducing his own profits.

Niche strategy

In this case, the firm neither confronts others nor defends itself. It cultivates a small market segment for itself with unique products/ services, supported by a unique marketing mix. These segments will be too small to attract big competitors. Normally, smaller firms with distinctive capabilities adopt niche strategy.

In niche strategy, specialisation is the key. A nicher, being a relatively smaller firm in the industry, finds it advantageous to serve a part of the market, specialised in some way. A nicher may serve some specific customers or some specific uses; he may carve out his niche on territorial basis; he may achieve his distinction through his one-up service; or he may specialise in one or two products and concentrate his efforts on them unlike the larger player who gives attention to a large variety of products.

A market niche to be worthwhile, must have characteristics such as reasonable size, reasonable profit potential and reasonable growth potential. The firm must have the capabilities to serve the niche effectively and profitably. After a while, even niches get attacked by other players including other nichers.

Many tea companies adopt niche strategy

In recent times, a number of small tea gardens of India have created their own niches in the world markets. Today, instead of asking for Assam tea or Darjeeling tea, tea lovers in several parts of Europe have started asking for Castleton, Jungpana, Seeyok, Selimbong, Margaret's Hope, Goomtea, Chamong, Namring or Lingia. They have become well known names in the speciality tea markets of the world. The small tea companies devote their attention to growing the finest teas and sell the limited production overseas at a very attractive price and profit. They have not even invested in creating fresh brand names for their teas. Instead they have capitalised on the names of their estates. Darjeeling based Castleton Tea Estates promoted Castleton tea. And now in Europe, especially in Germany, these small Indian tea estates with exotic names have become synonymous with the most sought after teas in the world. A good part of the credit for this niche development no doubt goes to the Castleton Tea Estates which was the first to reposition its teas as an up market high priced speciality. And other small tea estates in and around soon followed Castleton. At a time when Indian tea has been made to compete with cheap soft drinks, these estates are introducing 'designer teas' and winning international customers. Typical of niche marketing, economics shows that only small estates can specialise in these super teas; for the big tea companies volume is very important.

11

Strategies for Going Global

The enormous protection that was available to Indian industry and business all these years had given them the feeling that in their business pursuit, they do not have to go beyond their home market. With the New Economic Policy, the situation has been radically altered. The new policy simultaneously compels and entices Indian industry and business into entering world markets. Tracing the business challenges of the open regime, we had indicated in chapter 7 that in the new context, many Indian companies have already made their first forays into the world markets. Going global has actually become an inescapable requirement for them. Indian companies who could all these years enjoy the smug comfort of an assured domestic market have been suddenly stirred and shaken up by the forces of change unleashed by the NEP.

THE COMPULSIONS FOR INDIAN COMPANIES TO GO GLOBAL

A variety of compulsions now drive Indian industry and business towards exports and global business. It would be useful to assess these objective conditions that drive them towards globalisation, before taking up for discussion the strategies they may adopt in their globalisation endeavour.

The NTP and the efforts at integrating India's economy with the world economy: the first compulsion

In the first place, the new trade policy, especially the linking of import to export and the market determined exchange rate system, has compelled practically every business organisation to try its hand at exports. For instance, it is only after the trade policy reforms that the Thapar group decided to seriously take to exports. Says group chairman, L.M.Thapar, "We started exports only when it became certain that companies will have to generate their own forex outgo. Before that exports were negligible. But exports are being paid a lot of attention at present." The average import intensity for Indian manufacturing is more than 30 per cent. No wonder, for Indian industry, enhancement of exports and a viable global strategy in business have become realities that can no longer be postponed. The new trade policy has also made exports an attractive proposition, increasing the motivation of organisations to play the export game. As India's economy gets integrated further with the world economy, the need as well as the attraction for going global will also increase. Industry and business will inevitably have to adapt themselves to the new realities of Indian economy. They will rethink their strategy in the light of the changes and this will naturally lead them to the idea of going global.

The heat of competition at home will compel many companies to turn to world markets

The very fact that global operators from various countries will now freely enter the Indian market with their wide range of products, is a compulsion for companies hitherto dependent on the internal market to turn to the international market. As the new players with their large output and aggressive promotion may take away a big slice of the available demand for several products, the domestic companies in their struggle for survival will naturally be looking to other markets. Similarly, import liberalisation has also created marketing problems for a number of companies. Their customers are being weaned away by the competi- tiveness of the imported products. These companies will naturally turn to outside markets and try to overcome their new vulnerability. Though the fight outside India is not going to be any less difficult, the markets outside India will for the first time become a temptation to several companies in India. There is yet another dimension to the new search for outside markets under competitive pressure. In the new context, the MNCs can freely expand their capacities and market their products with full freedom. Consequently, the Indian companies will feel the disadvantages of size. They may look minuscule vis-a-vis the giants. In fact, the mergers and acquisitions going on in the Indian scene to which reference has been made elsewhere in this book, are an attempt to overcome quickly this size disadvantage. More of this phenomenon is bound to be witnessed in the coming days. The interesting fact is that while such capacity additions/product line extensions through mergers and acquisitions are envisaged to fight the opponents at the domestic front, the very enlargement of capacity and volume of production will serve as a compulsion to turn to export markets.

For many firms, the very ambition to be world players will be the driving force for going global

For a number of firms, their very ambition to become global operators may egg them on to look to the world markets. Already, several firms, many of them units of the big industrial houses of the country, are quite active on the export scene. These firms have already realised through experience that for reaping the full benefit of the high potential of world markets, they must become global operators, with manufacturing and supply bases across countries. In several cases, the firms also feel the compulsion to develop their own brands for the global markets. Naturally, for these companies, 'going global' means going far beyond just having an export target for a part of their production. Their sights are set on becoming a truly global company. In fact, when ITC says that "we want to buy a global brand", it is this aspiration of becoming a full fledged global operator, that is getting spelt out. The opening up of the economy and its integration with the global economy have provided a conducive setting for these companies to vigorously pursue their global ambitions.

The fact that different companies are driven by different compulsions in their new search for exports and globalisation can be easily discerned. Companies like TISCO need a great deal of foreign exchange for importing their requirements of raw materials, spares and components. Their eagerness to earn on their own, as much of their foreign exchange requirements as possible, drives them towards exports. By this strategy, they can reduce their vulnerability as well as cost of operations. If they were to depend totally on the market for their exchange requirements, their vulnerability as well as costs will soar to a prohibitive level. In the case of MRF, the leader in tyre industry, the long glut in the industry and the new compulsion to buy from the market the foreign exchange required for its essential imports, pushed the company towards exports. Already, MRF is the largest exporter of tyres, having stepped up the exports to Rs 85 crore in 1992-93. Its new subsidiary, MRF International Ltd., has begun the process of going global. It has started tapping export possibilities in other areas like leather. The objective is to earn Rs 500 crore from exports within the next two or three years. DCM Data Products turned to export as a forced turnaround option. When the company found the going tough in the domestic computer market, it started exporting printed circuit boards. DCM has now plans for exporting entire computer systems under its own brand name. W.S. Industries, manufacturers of electrical equipments for power transmission and distribution, went global for countering its vulnerability in the domestic market. Its main customer was the Government and its fortunes dwindled with the downtrend in Government run power projects. The company is now planning to set up plants in Canada, Malaysia, Egypt and Australia for the manufacture of electrical equipment.

Firms like Parle Agro and Sundaram Fasteners go for exports as they are keen to gain a degree of international presence, keeping long term benefits in mind. And firms like ITC, Reliance Industries, Hindujas, Hindustan Lever, Birla International, Raunaq International, Essar World Trade, Eicher, Ceat, Videocon and SRF have taken to exports in a big way with the larger objective of becoming true multinationals.

THREE BASIC FACTORS INDIAN FIRMS HAVE TO RECKON WITH WHILE FORMULATING GLOBAL STRATEGIES

While formulating their globalisation strategy, Indian companies must consider three basic factors: (i) the global business environment and the opportunities available in the global market; (ii) India's competitive advantage as a nation; and (iii) the competitive advantage of the individual company concerned. Only by dovetailing these three determinants, can any company put into operation a successful strategy for going global.

THE GLOBAL BUSINESS ENVIRONMENT AND THE OPPORTUNITIES AVAILABLE IN WORLD MARKETS

In chapter 7, discussing the business challenges arising from the open regime, it was mentioned that India's liberalisation has coincided with all round changes in the global business scene. The emergence of US as the arbiter of world affairs in the new unipolar world, the resurgence of Germany, the break-up of USSR and the demise of Comecon, China's fusion into market economy, the formation of the new European Commission (EC) and the emergence of Japan as the new monitor of international business were highlighted as the major episodes shaping the world business scene of the 1990s. In this chapter, we shall go a little deeper into the subject of international environmental dynamics, before taking up for discussion, possible globalisation strategies for Indian firms.

Multinational market groups

The emergence of multinational market groups in world trade is an important issue facing Indian companies on the globalisation track. These market groups have already exercised great impact on the pattern and style of international trade and the impact is bound to be stronger in the coming years. National markets of many nations have merged into a huge unified market as a result of such multinational grouping. Bilateral and multilateral trade agreements are also taking place today in an extensive manner among the various countries of the world. The political alignments and groupings among the various countries of the world naturally influence to a significant extent the pattern of world trade and business. But more than politics or security/military considerations, economic interests have weighed the maximum in most of these groupings. In addition to these groupings, in recent years, exporting nations and importing nations have formed powerful cartels among themselves for various commodities.

The economic integration of the 12 European nations into a single, unified trading bloc, the EC, is the most important development in world trade in recent times. With one of the highest per capita incomes and a massive 38 per cent share of world business, EC is literally a big factor influencing the course of global trade. Not only will the 12 member States of the EC be part of this bloc, the arrangement is to be extended to cover the markets of Austria, Sweden, Finland, Norway, Iceland, and Switzerland as well. This one market, envisaging the free flow of capital, labour, goods and services, will span Europe from the Arctic to the Mediterranean, and be larger than the US and Japanese markets put together, commanding a consumer strength of over 380 million. In due course, the East European economies of Hungary, Czechoslovakia and Poland may also seek entry into the EC. With the US, Canada and Mexico signing the North American Free Trade Agreement (NAFTA), another huge unified trading bloc with a $6,500 billion output has been formed. And the six countries of the Association of South East Asian Nations (ASEAN) have already decided to start a round of tariff cuts creating a free market in 15 products.

The share of these major trading blocs in world trade and the percentage of India's total exports accounted for by each of them are as follows:

Trading Bloc	% share of the bloc in world trade	% share of India's exports accounted by the bloc
EC (European Commission)	38.62	27.05
NAFTA (North American Free Trade Agreement)	16.52	17.64
Japan	9.03	9.24
EFTA (European Free Trade Association)	6.22	2.61
East Europe and Former USSR	5.07	10.62
ASEAN (Association of South East Asian Nations)	4.62	5.67

It can be seen that the EC, NAFTA, Japan and Russia are the most vital export markets for India. They are big markets and they also account for two-thirds of India's exports at present.

Recent trends in global trade

Overall, world trade grew by three per cent in 1991-92 as against five per cent in 1990-91 and seven to nine per cent in the 1980s. For North America and Asia, exports grew by 11 per cent in 1991-92; Latin American exports grew by just four per cent; exports from the Gulf countries and East Europe sharply declined by 15 per cent; and Japan's exports grew by just three per cent. However, with a modest recovery expected in the economies of the US, UK, France, Germany and Japan, world trade is expected to pick up in the 1990s, though modestly. One major stumbling block in the possible predictions, arises from the delay in the GATT negotiations. With GATT negotiations dragging for more than six years now, the hopes of an open world trading system governed by GATT is fast giving way to a system of protected regional trade blocs and preferential trading arrangements.

The increasing complexity of global trade makes Indian firms' task daunting

Thus, Indian companies have to reckon with a combination of challenges such as the formulation of exclusive trading blocs by the major trading nations of the world and the increasing protectionism of practically all countries and trade blocs. All hopes of a fair multilateral trading system too have almost been belied. Indian industry and business have to necessarily adapt to this difficult global environmental dynamics. Weighing the pros and cons of these economic groupings of the world, commentators predict that things are not going to be easy for India and the Indian business firms.

Country-to-country relations between India and other nations will also influence the prospects

On top of the general scenario of world trade described above, India's relations with individual countries will also have an impact on the business of Indian firms. Indian firms must take this factor into consideration in their global strategies. We shall illustrate this point with the Indo-US situation of recent times.

For quite sometime now, the US has been toughening its stand on several issues of concern to India. It has been insisting that India should sign the Nuclear Nonproliferation Treaty and India has been refusing to do so. On trade matters, the US has been threatening to retaliate against India, under its 301, Special 301 and super 301 provisions for not having taken adequate steps to protect US patents. And finally, it did implement the threat by withdrawing tariff concessions India enjoyed till then under the Generalised System of Preferences (GSP) in pharmaceutical and chemical exports to the United States. Subsequently, it also blacklisted India's Space Research Organisation, ISRO, on the issue of import of cryogenic engines from Russia. The US has also been at loggerheads with India on India's negotiating position at GATT.

What can Indian companies looking for business in the US do under these circumstances? It is precisely a situation where economic diplomacy must be brought into full play. India must formulate a strategy specifically covering her trade relations with the US. India can possibly utilise her current economic reforms as a strategic tool and try to reshape

Indo-US trade relations. She can also utilise the fact that India and the United States are the world's largest democracies, and bring about a commonality of approach between the two countries in the emerging international order. Again, by deflecting excessive focus from the mutual differences for some time, the medium term prospects can be improved. And individual Indian companies can employ similar economic diplomacy at micro level, utilising their relations and goodwill among their US customers and by lobbying with the government, trade and business of that country. They can also readjust their strategies for the interim period. Even if the Government is unable to resolve the political dilemmas, the firms should be in a position to resolve them in the specific context of their business. In this attempt, they can draw useful lessons from the MNCs of the world who survive and grow even in hostile environments. As explained earlier, these global companies win through the strength of their products which hold attraction for all countries, including those where governments and political processes are not all that helpful to them. The pull of their products on the people of those countries is so tremendous that political/government pressures cannot damage them.

Host governments becoming bargainers

Apart from the country-to-country relations aspect, even in a general sense, global companies have to deal tactfully with the governments of the countries where they have substantial business interests. In particular, in nations undergoing political and economic transformations, the governments become powerful bargainers vis-a-vis foreign firms who desire access to the markets of these nations. The governments demand a number of things such as local equity participation, technology transfer, local manufacturing facility, local employment, research facilities and export obligations. These demands quite often affect not only the financial operations of the MNCs but also their strategic freedom and managerial autonomy. They may have to make changes even in their core strategies and policies for remaining in these markets. More than handling the forces of international competition, managing the governments of the host countries thus becomes their crucial function. The success of the MNCs depends on striking a healthy balance between the demands of the host government and its own business interests. If the company has a unique technology with it or if it enjoys a great consumer pull for its products, or if it has already built a participant image in the life of the local people, its bargaining power may be larger. The entry of Pepsi into the Indian market is a good example of an MNC strategically unifying its interests with the demands of the host government. Indian companies will come across several such instances when they go global. Some of the host governments may not be warm to them. Some of them may be even hostile. Indian firms must learn the art of tactfully managing the host governments. However, sometimes, it may become absolutely impossible to adjust to the demands of the host government. For example, Mahindra & Mahindra, who set up a jeep assembly plant in Greece in 1986 was constantly under trouble due to changes in Government policy in that country. After a long time the company found that the particular investment in Greece was a mistake and decided to write it off as a cost for gaining experience for the group!

Companies going global have to understand the cultural dynamics of global markets

Besides dealing with the emerging global trade scenario, companies going global must be able to tackle the cultural dynamics of global societies and markets. When the business crosses the national borders of a country, it becomes enormously more complex. While a variety of factors, economic, legal and political, contribute to the complexity of international business, the one that contributes the utmost to the complexity is the cultural dynamics of the global markets.

Endel J. Kolde has eloquently described the cultural dynamics of the world markets in the following words:

> Multinational enterprises must function in a world of contrasts: old and new, primitive and modern, pious and agnostic, unutterably beautiful and sickeningly squalid, educated and ignorant, progressive and stagnant, sophisticated and naive—all in constant agitation. To interpret this volatile diversity, to make sense out of this apparent chaos, we must try to identify the underlying forces....

Indian companies with global ambitions must understand the cultural dynamics of the diverse markets by studying the people, their life styles, their social interactions, their sensibilities, their faiths and fancies. In other words, the companies must become a native in the foreign land and communicate with the people of the land in their lingo and idiom. Cultural diversity continues despite the world getting closer. Understanding these cultural variances and nuances and responding to them in a manner and style appealing to the foreign buyer is no easy task. A nation's history, its social and religious heritage, the value system of its people, the code of conduct handed down through generations—all these are components of a nation's culture. With painstaking efforts, Indian companies must size up the cultural dynamics of the different world markets.

The fact that the task of understanding and correctly responding to the cultural dynamics of global markets is not easy even for the world's veteran MNCs, clearly emerges from the words of Jack Welch, the CEO of General Electric when he says, "For US companies, globalisation is getting increasingly difficult. The expansion into Europe was comparatively easy from a cultural standpoint. When Japan developed, the cultural differences were larger, and US business has had more difficulties there. Looking ahead, the cultural challenges will be larger still in the rest of Asia—from China to Indonesia to Thailand to India—where more than half the world lives. US companies will have to adapt to those cultures if they are to succeed in the 21st century."

INDIA'S COMPETITIVE ADVANTAGE AS A NATION

Just as individual industrial and business units have their competitive advantage, entire nations also have their competitive or comparative advantage in the global business context. And companies going global must size up their national competitive advantage and develop their strategies on the strength of this competitive advantage. It would be useful to capture briefly the fundamentals of the concept of competitive advantage of nations before going into a specific discussion of India's competitive advantage.

The concept of competitive advantage of nations

Michael Porter, in his book, *Competitive Advantage of Nations*, deals extensively with this concept. Different countries have competitive advantage in different industries. As in the case of enterprises, nations too build competitive advantage through a planned process and effort spread over time. Endowment of natural resources by itself, does not confer any significant competitive advantage, though natural resources are facilitating factors in the process. When a whole industry in a country operates on a higher plane of performance, the country acquires a competitive advantage in that field. This position is normally acquired through the capacity of the whole industry in the country for innovation and technology upgradation. A favourable and supportive home environment created by the government, people and institutions of the country add further strength to the nation's competitive advantage building. Nations acquire competitive advantage in particular industries because it is in those industries that their home environment is strong in terms of industry competitiveness and innovation.

Competitive advantage of nations is not a vague idea. Nations do demonstrate in concrete terms their superiority in selected industries which are readily discernible. For example, we think of Germany for high-performance autos, Japan for consumer electronics, Switzerland for banking and pharmaceuticals, Italy for footwear and the US for commercial aircraft. Their competitive advantage in the respective industries is transparent; they are better than their best worldwide competitors.

Probing into the mechanics of building a nation's competitive advantage, we find four or five specific factors that account for it. In the first place, the nation's position in factors of production, such as skilled labour and infrastructure that are basic for competing in an industry, influences the nation's competitive advantage. The nature of home market demand for the relevant product is another determinant. The presence of related industries with high degree of competitiveness also influences a nation's competitive advantage in the specific industries. Structure of firms and rivalry among firms within the home country also determine national competitive advantage, since these factors create the national environment in which domestic companies learn to compete. Similarly, when a national environment permits and supports the accumulation of specialised assets and skills, companies in the country and the nation as a whole, gain a competitive advantage in the concerned field. Moreover, when a national environment encourages flow of information about products and processes and also puts pressure on companies to innovate and invest, the country gains a competitive advantage. Domestic rivalry usually creates such pressures on companies to innovate and improve. The rivals push each other to lower the costs, improve quality and service, and create new products and processes, taking the country as a whole to higher planes of competitive advantage.

Where does India as a nation, stand in competitive advantage

Viewed against the above mentioned ideas of competitive advantage of nations, it is a painful fact that India cannot claim much of competitive advantage in the world context. While in some of the factors like endowment of natural resources and availability of labour, India has an edge, as we shall elaborate later, in several of the other, more important determinants of national competitive advantage, India miserably lags behind.

India lacks competitiveness

There are in fact several inhibiting factors relating to technology, productivity, quality and discipline which hamper India's exports. Put bluntly, India, her industry and her products, are just not competitive, compared not only to the developed countries but even to some of the newly industrialised countries. Wrong policies, paucity of resources, poor technology base and lack of international marketing competence had left India for years an exporter of mere commodities, leaving the benefits of value addition to other countries. And India's potential to become a global shop floor for many products could not be exploited at all. Indian products rank low in the global market. Indian brand names are not recognised and the image of India's after sales service is quite low. In terms of overall international orientation too, India has to be rated low.

On the subject of domestic rivalry among firms too, the Indian reality has not been favourable to competitive advantage building. Too much of protection, licensing and capacity regulations over a long period has perpetuated a situation of complacency among Indian companies. Instead of rivalry and healthy competition leading to new products, new processes and high quality, several Indian firms have been competing with one another in compromising the quality.

While the fact that India as a nation, lacks competitiveness is well known, the gravity of the weakness is not often grasped fully. Among the market economies of the world, India is practically at the bottom in competitiveness as rated by the World Economic Forum and IMD, in their latest study report on World Competitiveness. The study covers 20 industrial countries (Group I) which are members of the Organisation for Economic Cooperation and Development and ten others (Group II) selected on the basis of their impact on world trade. India finds a place in the second group, and appears lowest in rank in the group in international competitiveness, coming below Singapore, Hong Kong, Korea, Taiwan, Malaysia, Thailand, Mexico, Indonesia and Brazil. The study assesses a country's competitiveness on the basis of certain relevant factors. The countries are ranked under each of the factors and then given an overall face. It is only in science and technology that India achieves a reasonable placing, coming fourth. In all the other factors, the country is placed between the seventh and tenth positions.

The poor industrial competitiveness of India is the cumulative effect of gaps in a variety of vital areas—technology, productivity, quality and infrastructure. Poor productivity is the principal drawback. To cite one instance, in the computer software business, the revenue productivity per person in the US is $86,000 compared to $21,000 in India. How do then, Indian firms compete with the US? It is an indicator of the distance Indian businessmen have to cover in their emerging competition with the global· players.

Economic policies followed over the years, have denied India the competitive advantage that was her due

It was mentioned earlier that government policy packages play a substantial role in building competitive advantages of nations. In the case of India, the policy packages followed by the Government over the past four decades have, instead of conferring competitive advantages on the country, deprived her of all avenues for competitive advantage building. India has remained a closed economy for far too long a period. The opening up of the economy attempted in the new economic programme is behind schedule by at least two decades. The course correction that is now on, will no doubt, help the country to acquire some competitive advantage, but the process will take its own time.

In industries such as steel, cement, fertiliser, paper and petrochemicals, Indian costs are very high for two main reasons: the capital (fixed asset) costs are very high due to the hitherto high import duties on capital goods and (ii) the cost of money in India has traditionally been more than double of international level. For years, Government has been appropriating at a very low interest, a major part of the bank deposits to finance its own deficits, thereby forcing much higher interest rates on the residual finance available for investment in industry and commerce. Indian industry has, therefore, had a significant built-in "structural cost disadvantage", as compared to its international competitors. However, most companies did not even realise this because they were not exposed to competition from abroad. Licensing reservations and MRTP restrictions prevented them from building up sufficiently large businesses (by international standards) in related areas. That is why Indian units are not significant in any particular industry by world standards and do not enjoy the advantages of scale. With the relaxation of licensing and MRTP, companies in India do not any longer have the compulsion to diversify in order to grow. They can enjoy the benefits of large size and specialisation in any particular industry. But it will need a great effort to overcome the ill effects of the past policies.

Even now, many areas where India has a competitive advantage are reserved for the small scale sector. Such policy-induced bias often turns out to be counter productive. For example, such a policy encourages the small-scale sector to venture out into exports. But, the sector does not have the resources required for global marketing and forming strategic alliances. It is also unable to make a thrust in non-traditional exports. Such policy drawbacks serve as major handicaps in India's present efforts at globalisation. India is yet to work out a strategy of globalisation wherein her domestic industry fast acquires the capability to be competitive worldwide instead of remaining content with a mere domestic survival objective.

Poor track record in exports

Since independence, India's economy has been mostly inward looking, with exports never moving above 7 per cent of GDP. Moreover, India's exports have always constituted a negligible part of world trade. The volume of world trade in 1991 is estimated by GATT at $3,500 billion. India's exports amounted to less than $10 billion, constituting less than 0.3 per cent of world trade. Worse still, India's share has been declining steadily over the years. It seems that India is pretty close to being marginalised by the technology-led changes in the developed countries.

Way back in 1948, India's share in world exports was 2.41 per cent; by 1958, it fell to 1.13 per cent; by 1968 it fell still further to 0.7 per cent; by 1978 to 0.53 per cent; by 1985, it reached the level of 0.39 per cent and by 1991, it nosedived to less than 0.3 per cent. The message is obvious—throughout, the rate of growth of India's exports has been far below the rate of growth of world exports. World exports grew at an annual compound rate of 14.4 per cent between 1970 and 1985. The corresponding figure for India is only 11.5 per cent. Again, in 1950, India ranked 16th in exports among the countries of the world. It got pushed to the 21st position in 1960; to the 31st position in 1970; to the 41st position in 1980; and now, it is oscillating between the 40th and 45th positions. For a country of India's size, potential, capabilities and needs, her exports should have been much higher.

Furthermore, imports have all along been outpacing exports, creating frequent balance of payments problems. In recent years, India's foreign trade deficit has been constantly going up on account of her imports outstripping exports. By the end of 1990-91, the foreign trade deficit of India stood as high as Rs 10,800 crore. It was just Rs 99 crore in 1970-71. It mounted particularly steeply in the '80s and reached the peak by 1990-91.

In recent times, India's problems on the export front have intensified

India's exports in recent years, have been facing a host of new problems. The first year of the liberalisation era, 1991-92 saw a negative growth in India's exports. The drop was 1.9 per cent in dollar terms. There were of course some extenuating circumstances. The unprecedented import compression had denied exporters critical imported inputs. Many countries in the world were going through a period of recession. And the unforeseen disintegration of the Soviet Union added to India's woes on the export front during '91-92. Even after giving due allowance to these extenuating circumstances, there has been cause for much worry. In recent years, India has found it difficult to push exports of traditional items. In fact, exports of certain traditional items have received a setback. Plantation crops like tea and coffee are one example. The attempts at boosting exports through the multinationals have also not helped India much. The export performance of the multinationals operating in India has been quite tardy; even the meagre exports that had been achieved, had come through traditional products and products of the SSI sector which India could have exported even without the participation of the MNCs.

A few favourable aspects

Notwithstanding the above observations regarding the poor position of India's competitive advantage, the country does have a few favourable points in this matter:

  Availability of natural resources in select fields

  A reasonably strong and diversified industrial base

  Abundance of skilled manpower at relatively low cost

  Capacity of the people to learn fast and adapt

  Expertise in software in various fields including computer, medical science and engineering

Widespread use of and familiarity with English language and the resulting facility of international communication

Resilience as a nation

These are fairly substantial national advantages, which if exploited well, can make India a global production centre in respect of quite a few products/services. In the matter of human resources in particular, India's position is quite enviable. For several years now, the country has been a supplier of doctors, engineers and technicians, not only to the expertise-scarce countries of the middle east and Africa, but even to the most demanding countries like the US. Even a modern discipline like management education has become widespread in India and there is a fairly good supply of management graduates. In other words, in practically all modern branches of learning, India has an abundance of high calibre people. Secondly, this human resource is available at a relatively low price. For example, according to World Bank estimates, average monthly wages for a computer programmer in India is just $225. In Philippines, it is $450, in Singapore $600, Malaysia, $800, UK $2,000 and USA, $2,500.

Considering specific industries/product categories, India has strong competitive advantage in leather, textiles, gems and jewellery, software, fine chemicals, auto parts, machine tools, light engineering products, two-wheelers, engineering services, agri products and tourism.

COMPETITIVE ADVANTAGE OF THE INDIVIDUAL FIRMS: AN IMPORTANT CONSIDERATION

It is the competitive advantage of the individual companies concerned, that will finally decide the choice of strategies for global business. For, as already seen in chapters 8, 9 and 10 the competitive advantage of the companies often delimits the choice of strategies. The competitive advantage has to serve as the back up for strategy formulation and its successful execution. Competitive advantage of the individual companies is as significant to global business as it is to domestic business. Since the ramifications of the subject of competitive advantage have already been analysed threadbare, they are not being dealt with at length here. Suffice to state here that in global business, competitive advantage of firms and competitive advantage of nations must go as a package.

STRATEGIES FOR GOING GLOBAL

Let us now consider the different strategy options available for global business. Business firms enter global markets through one or the other of the following routes: Exports; Licensing of technology and knowhow; Multinational trading; Joint ventures; and Full fledged global operations with production/supply bases across countries. Of these, licensing of knowhow is of low relevance to Indian firms at present because of the low technology base of the country. We shall discuss all the other routes in detail.

THE EXPORT ROUTE

Export is the primary route to global business. And as far as India is concerned, a majority of the Indian firms with international business aspirations, stop with the export route. That means by and large Indian companies have remained with the most primary endeavour at globalisation. And even here, as we saw earlier, while discussing the contemporary status of India's exports, the performance is nowhere near the desired level. And today when more and more companies are taking to the export route, it is essential that the pursuit becomes more systematic with more thought given to India's comparative advantage as a nation and the distinctive competence of the firms.

THRUST PRODUCTS FOR EXPORTS—SELECT EXAMPLES

In view of the contextual setting in which India is placed at the moment, Indian exporters would benefit by concentrating their efforts on the traditional products which are assured winners and a few select modern items. There is, indeed, a lot of wisdom in adopting such an export basket. For, in recent years, the bulk of India's export is accounted for by traditional products like agri-products including plantation products, marine products and extraction items and the three star business, gems/jewellery, leather and textiles/garments. Computer software is showing signs of becoming another high potential item. In other words, the contextual realities and the dictates of current competitive advantage indicate that in the short term, Indian firms may have to concentrate on traditional and relatively low value added products, including in particular, items like leather, textiles and gems and jewellery, which have registered high growth during the last decade. Modern/industrial products cannot be expected to perform a sudden miracle. They have to go through major modernisation/efficiency improvement before they can contribute substantially to exports. Such an emphasis on relatively low value added items for the present, can provide the required breathing space for Indian industry to bring its technology, quality and competitiveness up to world standards.

The Government has identified 34 products as high focus export items: agricultural products, agro chemicals, auto components, bicycles, automobiles, cement, drugs and pharmaceuticals, dyes and intermediates, electric power generation and distribution equipment, floriculture, footwear, fresh fruits, gold jewellery, handtools, I.C. engines, industrial castings, tomato paste, tropical fruit juices, pulp and concentrates, preserved mushrooms, readymade garments, rice, software packages, systems software, CAD/CAM, spices, sugar, molasses, alcohol, sugar machinery, synthetic textiles and tyres. Products like automobiles and capital equipments, figuring in the list, may be difficult to push in the immediate future. A lot more effort over a longer term may be required to make such modern/industrial items export winners.

We are discussing below a few items which can form part of thrust products for export by Indian firms in the short/medium term.

Tobacco

India has a strong competitive advantage in tobacco production. The country is already the world's third largest producer of tobacco. Today, the world's major cigarette manufacturers, especially those owning the superior brands, are looking for low cost production areas around the world, for growing high quality Virginia and Burley tobaccos. India's major advantage in this context is that India ranks first among the low-cost producers. Obviously, the country is ideally suited to become a big player in the tobacco market of the world. But India so far could not assume such a role, mainly because the globally preferred varieties, Virginia and Burley tobaccos, form only a limited part of Indian production. India can encourage these varieties and Indian companies can line up with world producers. Through such a strategy, Indian companies can corner a good chunk of the $250 billion world market for tobacco. And there are companies in India, led by the ITC, with versatile experience in the tobacco business. Even other companies in related fields can enter this line with their transferable expertise. In other words, for Indian entrepreneurs, the scenario offers an ideal opportunity. They can become the best sources of the required grades of tobacco for the foreign cigaratte makers.

Spices

Spices can be another thrust sector though at present India's share in the global spices trade is not all that commendable. In terms of volume, India's share in the global spices trade of four lakh tonnes, has been in the range of 25-30 per cent. In value terms it is just around 10 per cent. Competition from emerging producers has removed India from her pedestal. Now, more than 50 countries of the world are growing different spices and offering them at competitive prices. In fact, India has already lost considerable ground to Guatemala in cardamom trade. In black pepper too, the country is facing a threat, not only from traditional suppliers like Brazil, Indonesia and Malaysia, but also from new entrants like Vietnam, Thailand and Madagascar. Despite these discouraging features, spices can be a thrust sector for Indian export as India is a major producer of spices. The country already exports around 1,30,000 tonnes of spices valued at Rs 362 crore. Sixty-three varieties of spices are grown in

India on one million hectares with a total output of 20 lakh tonnes a year valued at over Rs 4,200 crore. Out of this, only a small quantity is exported at present. Given the extensive natural advantages enjoyed by India in spices and its centuries old reputation as the 'land of spices', the country can do much better in exports.

Already there is one welcome trend. In items like chillies, ginger and turmeric, India seems to be doing well. Thirty-three thousand four hundred tonnes of chillies valued at Rs 100 crore were exported in 1991-92 as compared to 24,500 tonnes valued at Rs 27.56 crore in the previous year. The export of ginger went up from 6,555 tonnes valued at Rs 11.96 crore in 1990-91 to 13,396 tonnes valued at Rs 20 crore in 1991-92 and that of turmeric from 13,600 tonnes valued at Rs 16 crore to 16,600 tonnes valued at Rs 32 crore. Chillies, the most pungent spice, has already overtaken the king of spices, black pepper, in 1991-92. Of course, during the year, China and Mexico, the major suppliers of chillies, could not meet demands as their chilli crop was damaged during the year. This provided an opportunity to India to step in. However, as the largest producer of chillies in the world, India need not be content with the position of a last resort supplier in the global market. Indian production of chillies now exceeds nine lakh tonnes providing sizeable export surplus. And 'Sannam chilli', a variety grown extensively by India, is known the world over. All that India has to do is to offer the variety at competitive prices. This can be done by raising the productivity to 1200 to 1500 kg per hectare from the present level of 900 kg per hectare. The cultivation of other export oriented varieties, 'Paprika' and 'Bird eye' could also be popularised.

Another category in which India has performed well in recent times is spice oils and oleoresins. The exports went up from 892 tonnes valued at Rs 32 crore in 1990-91 to 1,132 tonnes valued at Rs 56 crore in 1991-92. With this, the share of these value added items went up to 15.2 per cent from 8.3 per cent. The export of spice oil and oleoresins now ranks high, next to chilli and black pepper.

The real boost to India's spices export can come from black pepper, which has all along been the mainstay of India's spices export. Indian black pepper known as 'Malabar Black Pepper'and 'King of Indian spices' is popular in the international market; and India accounts for over one-third of world production of black pepper.

The Spices Board had constituted an expert panel—the Forum for increasing exports of spices, under the Chairmanship of Dr. M.S. Swaminathan. The Forum, in its report, has suggested a package of measures for doubling India's spices exports by 2001 AD. The measures include time bound intervention on planting, quality improvement, value addition, packaging, market promotion and marketing. Already the Union Commerce Ministry and the Spices Board have designated spices as one of the extreme focus areas for export promotion.

Replacing existing low yielding varieties with high yielding ones alone will improve productivity. Such new varieties with the desired market qualities can be evolved. The next focus must be on marketing by promoting Indian brands. Targetting the retail trade and consumers directly has to be an integral part of the new marketing strategy for spices. There is a large sales potential in the world market for branded consumer packs. The main retail outlets such as supermarkets and chain stores are also happy with branded packs. The branded consumer packs also enjoy a considerable mark-up, with a 500 to 1,000 per cent difference between landed bulk price and retail sale price. Evidently, branded spices would provide higher value and returns.

A conscious effort to build confidence among consumers is also essential. An effective post-export follow up and adherence to the latest standards in processing technology as well as attractive packaging are the other requisites. Once they are ensured the 'land of spices' can stage a comeback.

Marine Products

India is emerging as a major force in the international markets for marine products. India's exports of marine products amounted to Rs 1,743 crore in 1992-93. In dollar terms it was $588 million. The target for 1993-94 is Rs 2,080 crore or $615 million. It is particularly significant that most of these exports are to developed countries like Japan, USA, UK and Europe.

An increasing number of large industrial houses have been venturing into the fisheries sector in recent years. A major attraction for them is the high prices of shrimp, tuna and other marine foods in the international market. In fact, the scope for earning sizeable foreign exchange from the export of shrimps has been a significant factor in the development of deep sea fishing in India. With the liberalisation of foreign collaborations, there has been a rush for promoting deep sea fishing projects. Advanced fishing nations such as Japan, Korea, Philippines, USA and France, who have hitherto been shying away from Indian waters, are showing keen interest and have already joined hands with the Indian entrepreneurs for development of deep sea fishing in the Indian waters. The Government has cleared as many as 17 such projects, all of them 100 per cent export oriented units. Most of them have foreign equity participation. The proposed total investment in all these projects put together is around Rs 900 crore.

Within the marine products range, Shrimp offers very high scope for India. Already, shrimps constitute about half in terms of volume and three fourth in terms of value of all marine foods exported by India. In the $40 billion world market for sea foods, India has just one per cent share. By concentrating on shrimps, India can tap a good portion of the world market for sea foods. With the long coast line and with coastal areas abounding in saline soil, the natural facilities for shrimp cultivation is ideally set. But only a few Indian companies have entered the business of shrimp exports. And 90 per cent of the existing exports is in the form of commodity, not in the form of branded and packaged shrimps. Branded sea foods can easily earn a 25 per cent premium over commodity sea foods.

India's present handicap is that the number of firms operating in this business is too small and each of them is a very small player by international standards. The largest shrimp exporter of India, Cham Ice and Cold Storage, Porbundar, earns only Rs 70 crore per year compared to the turnover of Rs 1,800 crore of the C.P. group, the largest exporter from Thailand. Large scale exploitation of the market requires large scale farming and modern facilities for preservation and processing. This, in turn requires heavy investment at home, in equipments and technology. For example, manufacturers may have to shift from block-freezing of entire consignments to individual quick freezing method, for switching over to branded and packaged marketing of shrimps. Development of infrastructure relating to mechanised vessels, strengthening of harbours, setting up of aqua-culture and prawn hatcheries and reprocessing facilities are also essential for a large scale entry into the world markets.

Leather

Leather and leather products constitute an expanding category in India's exports. Export of leather totalled Rs 3,692 crore in 1992-93. The target for 1993-94 is Rs 4,768 crore, indicating a growth of 17 per cent. Leather exports is expected to cross the Rs 10,000 crore mark by 1995-96.

Leather is an item in which India has a durable competitive advantage. India produces the best quality raw hides and skins. Abundant availability of inexpensive labour is her other major advantage. The negative aspect is that the country lacks processing and manufacturing facilities and marketing expertise compared to world leaders. The inadequacies are however not insurmountable. The leading leather goods manufacturers like Italy, South Korea and Taiwan will soon be forced to slow down their production due to rising cost of production. A bright future, therefore, awaits countries like China, India, Indonesia, and Thailand, where labour is comparatively cheaper. The major user countries—the developed countries—no longer produce any leather goods. Strict pollution control measures and rising labour charges have already forced them to curtail or stop production. India can increase its market share in the global business for leather and leather products from the present meagre 2.5 per cent to over 10 per cent within this decade. And that means a great deal of gain, as the size of the world market is $40 billion.

For several years, India had been exporting her leather in raw form, with very little value addition. India is now consciously attempting a shift from the export of raw hides and skins to finished leather products, adding considerable value to the commodity. And the efforts at value addition have already rewarded the leather industry to some extent. But, the scope for further value addition is immense. Out of a global trade of $30 billion in leather shoes, leather garments and other leather products, India accounts for just $1 billion or 3.3 per cent. With a proper exploitation of natural advantages, India can take a leap forward.

In the global markets, big profits are made through branded products. India, which exports more than Rs 200 crore worth of footwear a year, is not exporting branded shoes. A shoe exported at $20 per pair from India is sold in Europe and the US under some well known international brand at $80 to $100 at the retail level. It is evident that India should concentrate on the export of finished leather goods with her own brand names. As long as India sells without brand, she is exporting just a commodity.

It is in the premium segment of leather footwear and leather products that the country is particularly weak. Inadequacies in product design, quality of craftsmanship and inadequacy of supply base for handling large volumes are the handicaps. Technological upgradation, better material processing and automation are needed for increasing India's share of this large and growing market. India needs well-produced leather to produce marketable leather products. While Indian companies have access to leather and skilled people, they lack designing capability and access to channels of marketing. The establishment of the Footwear Design and Development Institute at Noida is expected to help improve to an extent the technological base of Indian footwear exports.

Only through increased emphasis on finished products, can India increase substantially her export earnings from this sector. Moreover, it is bad business sense on India's part to export her raw materials to her very competitors who can make finished products out of them and beat her in the finished product business.

Indian firms in the leather business should also try to enlarge their operations to global size. And in this endeavour, the Government must come to their rescue by dereserving the business from the SSI sector. A committee appointed recently by the Government has in its report contrasted the small production scale of the Indian leather units with the large facilities in other leather exporting countries including the Asian Tigers.

The committee report has also suggested that one way to increase realisation from the exports is to have tie-ups with global footwear marketing companies and to own some brand names. Today, several footwear manufacturing companies are closing down in Europe and the US. They have well known brands, designing and marketing infrastructure. India can tie up with them. The committee report recommended that the Indian leather industry be permitted to lease brand names, as establishing a new brand is prohibitive, cost wise.

The global trade in leather products is expected to grow to $50 billion during this decade. Indian firms should strive for at least a 10 per cent share of it so as to achieve exports earnings of at least $5 billion a year from this line.

Textiles

Textiles constitute another strong area in India's exports. In recent times in particular, it has been doing exceedingly well. Textiles and garments are the single largest category of products exported from India, accounting for about 25 per cent of India's total exports. The category includes cotton fabrics, made-ups and cotton yarn, readymade garments, silk, man-made textiles, wool and woollens and coir. Of these, the cotton sector is the leader, though in some years, the export of cotton products has suffered to some extent, mostly due to quota restrictions imposed by several importing countries. Textile exports touched a record level of $6,590 million in 1992-93 compared with $5,797 million in the previous year, showing an increase of 13.7 per cent. The export target for 1993-94 would amount to a further increase of 12 per cent over the performance in 1992-93. One welcome feature is that in recent years some value addition is taking place in textile exports. Of the $6,590 million worth of exports in 1992-93, textiles and clothing accounted for as much as $5,616 million. Readymade garments alone accounted for $3,052 million. Recently, a spate of 100 per cent EOUs to manufacture denim and terry towels has come into existence adding a new dimension to the traditional export segment. Arvind Mills, Mafatlals and Bhilwara are among the big players. Arvind's exports are in the order of Rs 200 crore.The Mafatlal group has accounted for Rs 170 crore in value added items in 1992-93. They have set up marketing offices in the UK and Switzerland.

India is a signatory to the multi-fibre agreement (MFA) which governs the major part of world trade in textiles and clothing. Under MFA, India has negotiated bilateral textile agreements with European community, the United States, Canada, Norway, Austria, Finland and Sweden.

As far as India is concerned textiles form a crucial part of the GATT negotiations. But for today's quota restrictions, textile exports which already happen to be the country's single largest export item, would have boomed by now. As far as cotton textile exports are concerned, 50 per cent of the exports are for quota countries and the remaining 50 per cent go to the non-quota countries. If the Dunkel Draft proposals for a 10 year phase-out period for textile quotas are accepted, India can make substantial headway into the world textile markets.

Garments is one area where the country has a natural competitive advantage because of cheap labour. In India, labour cost constitues only five per cent of the total cost of production of readymade, compared with as much as 50 per cent in Europe. Moreover,the new economic policy has allowed large firms to set up garment manufacturing units, provided they exported 50 per cent of their production. Many large business houses are now entering the business; a number of them are securing collaborations with well-known foreign garment firms and are setting up large scale manufacturing units; others are trying to secure well known foreign labels and marketing collaborations.

Mafatlals have plans to export readymade garments under their own brand names. Some of the world's most famous garment sellers like Mark and Spencer of London are already sourcing the cloth for their garments from Mafatlals. Now, Mafatlals want to graduate to export of fabrics and garments. Arvind Mills who have already become a major global player in denim, have also turned to export of readymade garments. In fact, they have already established an international network for marketing shirtings and readymade garments, besides denim. We shall be discussing the global business efforts of Arvind Mills in greater detail later in this chapter. DCM and Morarjee Mills also have set their sights firmly on export of readymade garments. The latest in the series of textile companies to go international is the Bhilwara group. The group has recently set up an overseas company named Bhilwara Overseas Ltd, headquartered in Douglas, UK, and is keen to market its products in Europe. The company is also planning to develop sourcing points for readymade garments in various Asian countries to ease the pressure on its Indian operations.

The rush into the readymade garments is not limited to textile firms like the Mafatlals, the Bhilwara Group, Arvind Mills, DCM and Morarjee Mills. Many non-textile firms have also turned towards export of readymade garments. ITC, Eicher, Triveni Engineering and Vam Organics are the striking examples of this category. In fact, all these companies have tied up with well known international brands and are poised to market their readymade garments globally and at home. Eicher has gone with SamSung of S. Korea, Triveni with Esprit of France and ITC has tied up with three different brands, one each from Germany, US and Italy.

Zodiac is trying to market Indian brands such as Globe Trotter and Mark Gibaldi abroad. It plans to set up exclusive shops in Dubai and Doha. It has also tied up with wholesalers in Europe.

NF Corp of the US is planning to set up a 100 per cent export-oriented unit in association with Du Pont Sportswear (manufacturers of Wrangler jeans in India). Italian lace maker Italiano is planning to source supplies from India. It plans to invest 50 per cent equity in a joint venture with the Tatia group, and provide the latest lace designs as well.

The strategy required for the future is three fold: development of production base; improvement of quality; and evolving of a marketing strategy that will help exploit untapped and non-traditional products and markets. In particular, the steps should include development of non-quota markets, product development for catering to up-market segments and product diversification into items like swimwear, beachwear, institutional/industrial clothing, defence and para-military clothing etc.

Quality is of utmost importance. According to a market survey conducted by the Japan Apparel Manufacturers Association in consultation with 18 Japanese trading firms, Indian garment exporters pay very little attention to quality. While the average defect rate in the case of Japan's domestic products is 3 to 5 per cent, the rate is 15 to 25 per cent for Indian garments. Examples of defects pointed out include: "needles found in garments", "mismatch of sleeves and bodies", etc. The survey has also indicated that there is fundamental difference in perception of what constitutes quality. To quote from the report, "Apparel firms in India believe that the quality of fabric determines the quality of the garment but the Japanese think that every aspect from sewing to packaging, decides quality." The Japanese importers expect the Indian exporters to exercise quality control starting from source and quality checks at each stage of production rather than merely inspecting sample lots of finished products.

Gems and jewellery

Over the years, gems and jewellery has emerged as a very major foreign exchange earner for India. Polished diamonds constitute the main item in this group. During 1992-93 earnings from the export of gems and jewellery totalled Rs 9,404 crore. Diamond accounted for Rs 8,313 crore. An export target of Rs 11,408 crore or $3.5 billion has been envisaged for gems and jewellery for 1993-94 with a net value addition of $1 billion. The net value addition is around 30 per cent.

India has a great deal of competitive advantage in the export of polished diamonds. India has been processing more than 60 per cent of the diamonds mined in the world. Basically it is the skill of her artisans that has earned her this predominant position. There are more than five lakh skilled diamond artisans in India. An additional plus point is that the artisans are available at low wages. This abundant availability of inexpensive skilled artisans works out as an unbeatable competitive advantage for India, especially in the small diamond segment. Indian artisans are noted for their special skill in working with small diamonds and in producing the brilliant cut in them. This unique human expertise coupled with the presence of 35,000 cutting factories and 2600 active exporters has helped India become a global force in this business.

All over the world, lovers of diamond prefer the brilliant cut, which means the diamond is given 58 facets as a result of cutting. In fact 80 per cent of all diamonds sold in the world have a brilliant cut. And brilliant cut involves great skill, when the diamonds are small.

India however suffers from two major weaknesses in this business. It has a very low market share in the larger diamond segment. Higher profits lie in working with larger diamonds. Though in terms of volume, India is world No 1 in the export of polished diamonds, with a 62 per cent share of world trade, in value terms, India's share is much lower. For Indian export to increase in value terms, a shift would be required from smaller to larger and more valuable stones. Israel and Belgium dominate this segment at present. Indian diamond exporters must grab a good share of this segment from them. The second major weakness is that India's share in jewellery is quite low, though her share in polished stones is very high. The benefit of value addition now goes to other countries who use the diamonds cut by India. For India, it makes sense to embed the diamonds in jewellery and then export them. Moreover, with 62 per cent of the stones market already in India's bag, further growth has to come from the jewellery market. India has no doubt made an entry into this market. Out of Rs 7,222 crore of exports in '92-93, Rs 739 crore came from jewellery (both diamond and gold). But, it has constituted a mere 0.33 per cent of the world trade in jewellery.

Indian exporters will have to cross a number of hurdles before they become a force in global jewellery market. Unlike diamond stones, jewellery is sold on the strength of brand names which customers recognise and demand. Indian exporters have no brands of their own. Moreover, jewellery needs a higher technology compared to diamond cutting and India lacks such technology. In addition, internationally sought fashion designers are a must for promoting jewellery. India is still to catch up in this respect. And finally Indian exporters also lack the needed marketing network. Indian exporters can in the first stage collaborate with jewellery marketers of the world and promote Indian jewellery. In the next stage, they can go for direct marketing in various parts of the world .

It is esential for India's gems and jewellery industry to chalk out strategies to shift from export of smaller diamonds to bigger ones and from export of cut and polished diamonds to export of diamond-studded jewellery. Moreover, for India, the future does not lie in 22 carat hand made jewellery; the real market is in 14 or 18 carat machine made jewellery and especially diamond studded jewellery. The world market for gold jewellery is $60 billion of which $40 billion is in diamond jewellery. Indian exporters have to work towards higher value added, creatively designed, diamond studded, fashion jewellery exports so as to enhance the net value addition. Through apt promotional strategies they must also promote their jewellery among different cultures across the world markets.

Two wheelers

Two wheelers is another industry in which India has strong competitive advantages. The industry is labour intensive and India has an abundance of low cost labour. The raw materials needed for the industry are also available in India in abundance. India already supports a large internal demand base for two wheelers. Two wheeler is an industry where the major companies of India can legitimately claim global scale status. The country is also the third largest producer of two wheelers in the world. And, India's Bajaj Auto Limited is the second largest firm in two wheelers in the world. All these are features favouring an Indian lead in this business. In fact, Rahul Bajaj, chairman of Bajaj Auto, is correctly sizing up this position, when he says "...to face the challenge of global competitiveness, Indian companies would have to go in for labour-intensive products and at the same time put up plants which are global in their economies of scale. They should choose products which would command a chunk of the huge domestic market. Two wheelers ideally meet these prescriptions."

Global opportunities in two wheeler business are also growing, making it an attractive business for Indian companies to participate. The size of world market of two wheelers is upwards of $22 billion. It should not be difficult for the Indian companies to exploit the comparative advantages of India in this field combining it with their own competitive advantages as a company, and build new openings in the world market.

Indian companies can design two wheelers specifically suited to the different segments of the global market. Products of Hero Honda and Bajaj Auto are already familiar brands outside India. Indian companies can also plan to export components and knocked-down kits to multinational two wheeler manufacturers in countries, where Indian brands cannot effectively compete. The companies also can concentrate on selected geographical segments of world markets. For example, they can attempt to develop markets in Latin American countries. They can also concentrate on the fast growing Chinese market for scooters. The ASEAN is another promising segment. And there are countries like Thailand and Malaysia with import barriers which could also be penetrated through appropriate strategies. Entry into these protected markets is possible through setting up joint ventures there.

Electronics

Electronics is another sector with high export potential. In fact, the Government and the industry have identified it as a promising export sector. Availability of technically qualified manpower and an already developed domestic industry are factors in favour of electronics exports. Another substantial attraction is the new Electronic Park scheme introduced by the Government. The scheme is designed to serve as a back up for electronics exports.

The Electronic Parks

In the chapter on the New Industrial Policy, discussing the liberalisation in Foreign Direct Investment (FDI), we had mentioned that the eletronics sector has been a special beneficiary of the liberalisation package and the Government has been very keen to attract FDI in the electronics sector. The Government extended a number of incentives for FDI in the sector and also helped the sector through the formation of Electronic Hardware Technology Parks (EHTP). The EHTP scheme is as much an export promotion device, as it is an FDI promotion device.

Having identified strengthening of the electronic component industry as the key to increased electronic exports and having realised that attracting electronic MNCs into India is the best way to step up the production of electronic components in the country in the shortest possible time, the Government took several steps to attract electronic multinationals into India. And launching of the Electronic Hardware Technology Parks (EHTP) scheme, was the most significant of all these steps. Besides serving as catalysts of electronics exports, the EHTPs can also enhance the prospects of foreign investment in India in this sector. Already, Goldstar of South Korea, Motorola of the USA and leading Japanese companies have demonstrated their interest in investing in electronics in India. The scheme envisages duty-free imports of capital goods to keep the production costs at the minimum. By giving liberal access to domestic market the scheme encourages foreign companies to shift their manufacturing units to India. The multinationals are expected to strengthen the electronic component base within India in a big way. The scheme would be very attractive to the multinationals on account of the cost advantage which India offers to components meant for export production. Added to this, a part of the domestic market for electronics is also thrown open to the MNCs under the EHTP scheme. These facilities should make the MNCs' production in Indian EHTP far more competitive than in any of the other newly industrialised countries. The Indian electronics industry too would benefit from this production base, by getting an assured supply of the vitally needed components at attractive prices. This, in turn, would help the industry boost exports.

The production target for the electronics sector in the Eighth Plan envisages a big increase from Rs 9,540 crore in 1990-91 to Rs 30,000 crore by 1996-97. The export target by 1996-97 is Rs 6,500 crore. Government's expectation is that the EHTPs may help achieve such a level of performance.

Computer software

Computer software is eminently suited to be another thrust area in India's export efforts. And Indian companies are already doing reasonably well in the field. Between 1985-86 and 1991-92, India's software exports recorded a compound annual growth rate of 57 per cent, rendering it the second fastest growing Indian export product. India's current export earnings through software is around at Rs 675 crore. It is expected to cross Rs 900 crore in 1993-94. According to National Association of Software and Service Companies (NASSCOM), India can easily achieve an export of Rs 2,000 crore by 1994-95. In fact, expert studies indicate that India can reach a figure of Rs 10,000 crore by the end of the decade.

A field in which India has a major competitive advantage

Software export is a field in which India has a strong competitive advantage. India's manpower is her first advantage, since the business is highly manpower intensive and knowledge intensive. India's knowledge rich manpower provides her a real competitive advantage in this field and renders her a strong contender in the global software market. Widespread computer education has given the required edge to the manpower. The fact that supply of software professionals is quite limited in countries like the US, Germany, Russia, Australia, New Zealand, France and Japan, compared to the mountains of software needed by them, is in India's favour. This, coupled with the price competitiveness of India, throws up tremendous possibilities for India in software export. The low capital requirement of the business is another attraction for India, a capital scarce country. The country is able to make competitive offers in terms of price and quality; it already enjoys 12 per cent market share of the overall world export opportunity and 20 per cent of the professional service market. As the exports are growing year by year, the confidence of the Indian professionals is also getting strengthened. The country has already built up a good image and reputation internationally in the field.

India's software export is characterised by yet another favourable factor—plenty of players are already operating in it and many more are poised to enter. The business obviously holds attraction to a large number of entrepreneurs and business houses in the country. The multitude of players in the field has ensured the presence of robust competition in the business.

There are already more than 200 firms in the country engaged in software export. And practically all the big corporations of India are making a beeline to enter the business: Reliance, ITC, Mahindra & Mahindra, L&T, SRF, JK, the Oberoi group, Sundaram Fasteners, Ramco and several others. Even the State Trading Corporation (STC) which witnessed a massive drop in its turnover from Rs 3,000 crore to Rs 1,000 crore on account of decanalisation of foreign trade—has identified computer software as a thrust area for its various counter trade deals.

At present Tata Consultancy Service (TCS) is the largest software exporter in the country with an export of Rs 142 crore in 1991-92. Several other companies like Tata Unisys, Citi Corp, Digital, Patni Computers and Wipro Systems are in the Rs 10 crore to Rs 40 crore bracket. Companies like Wipro, Digital, PSI, TCS and TUL have planned to double their export earnings in a single year. Companies like Wipro Systems (WSL), are setting up a dedicated Software Technology Park (STP) at Bangalore in collaboration with Bell Northern Research of the US. Prospects for PSI-Bull too have brightened up with IBM buying Groupe Bull, the parent company of PSI-Bull. Infosys has plans to enhance its offshore capabilities to employ as many as 1,000 software professionals and to open up new offices in San Francisco and Paris.

World Bank funded, Maxi-Micro/IDC survey

In 1992, a study was conducted by IDC (India) and Maxi-Micro/IDC (US), on the possibilities of software export by India. The study which was funded by the World Bank also devoted its attention to the strategies that should be adopted to make Indian software export competitive in the global market.

The study identified six target countries—US, Japan, Germany, UK, France and Italy—for Indian software exporters to concentrate on, as they account for 78 per cent of the worldwide external spending on information technology and 83 per cent of India's software exports. The investigation covered six competing countries—Ireland, Israel, Singapore, Philippines, China and Hungary—besides India as the sources of supply. The six target countries presently source $1.45 billion worth of software products and services from outside.

According to the study, the total foreign opportunity available in 1996 will be about $7.4 billion, up by $6 billion from $1.4 billion in 1991. Of this, professional services will have a share of 54 per cent at $4.0 billion, packaged software will have a 34 per cent market share at $2.5 billion and support services 12 per cent at $0.9 billion. The study suggests that if the action programme, as defined in the study, is undertaken, India should be able to capture a 13.5 per cent share of the total opportunity. And that means an export earning of $1 billion.

The first issue tackled by the study was awareness about Indian software capabilities. In a country like the US, which is still very much the international software bastion, software vendors were not only very well aware of India's software capability, but also chose India as the first option. At the actual user level, India figured third in the awareness list, after Israel and Ireland. The study established acceptance of India as a source of cost effective software by vendors as well as actual users.

The study then looked at the five strategic areas of marketing and distribution; productivity, costs and standards; education and training; financing; and infrastructure. It is of the view that India needs to strengthen itself in each of these areas if it desires to capture a larger slice of the global software business.

The study has suggested forming a government-industry Software Development Board (SDB)—on the lines of the existing software export promotion body in Singapore. The SDB will iron out the overall strategy and coordinate the strategies and activities of all the players. It will have overall responsibility for marketing. It will open liaison offices in target countries, attract development/service centres to India, and assist the players by providing market information and counsel.

Strategy options

One option that can be seriously considered by the software exporters of India is to shift the product mix to off-shore projects and products. Reducing the dependence on body-shopping, they should establish joint venture partnerships and alliances and develop multinational business relations. They should also tap the huge potential that exists in the packaged software products market and leverage existing distribution channels. There are indications that the opportunity for software professional services worldwide may shift in favour of off-shore from 39 per cent in 1991 to 54 per cent in 1996.

The big profits in the business of course lie in new products or innovative products. But launching a new product is very expensive: typically $5 million to $10 million (Rs 15 crore to Rs 30 crore) for an application package. And to successfully launch one, Indian companies must be organically linked to the world market so that they can anticipate the demand for it. If the demand becomes obvious, there will be a plethora of products launched to meet it by competing countries/ companies. The competitive advantage of India in terms of cheaper computer professionals alone is not of much use in tapping the profit opportunities in new products. The country has to acquire a set of other relevant competitive advantages for an effective presence in this segment.

One ideal option is to launch high-priced, top-of-the-line products which have an element of customisation. This way, they can compete on the strength of lower cost of customisation and make handsome profits. Tata Unisys Ltd (TUL) did that fairly successfully with its financial accounting package Easydeal, which was provided for a licence fee of $3,00,000.

Indian software firms should also focus on contract software rather than packages. Packaged software is not something one can produce overnight and it is not a field where India has any distinctive expertise. In fact, India is a novice in the field of testing and packaging software. Indian firms normally do not know the base requirement, the need behind the package. Today, some foreign company indicates the need and India does the development and again the foreign companies do the packaging.

Indian companies can also tie up with overseas dealers for marketing support.The advantage, especially the cost advantage of doing the design work in India, can be exploited and marketing left to the clout of the overseas partner. Companies like Intec Systems and Wipro Infotech are already trying such a strategy.

A strategy must be devised for capturing and sustaining a good share of the world demand

The present position is that although India's software export earnings are rising, India is still losing ground in the total foreign opportunity. India's share of foreign opportunity slipped to 11.7 per cent in 1990-91, from 19.9 per cent in 1989-90, although in absolute terms export revenues increased from $120 million to $164 million. If India continues this trend, by 1995-96, its share of foreign opportunity would have slipped to 9 per cent. On the other hand, if the weaknesses and inadequacies are removed and right strategies are followed, it is envisaged that the Indian sotfware exports will be able to capture 13.5 per cent share of the foreign opportunity in

1995-96. That means India's software export revenues can touch $1 billion in 1995-96.

Problems of low productivity and low value addition have to be tackled

India has to overcome several shortcomings, if she desires to capture and sustain a good share of the world demand. In the first place, the problems of low productivity and low value addition have to be tackled. The revenue productivity per person in the US, Ireland and Singapore is $ 86,000, $42,000 and $31,000 respectively. As against the above levels of productivity of other countries, India's productivity is only $21,000. By 1996, the figure in the US is likely to go up to $181,000 and in Singapore, to $112,000. According to the World Bank study, referred to elsewhere in this section, India's productivity should increase at least to $58,000 by 1996 if India has to remain a major player in the world software market. Restricted access to hardware platforms is another hurdle to be overcome.

Domestic computer base has to be strengthened

A well-developed software business within the country is an essential requirement for carving out a solid base for India's computer software in the world export market. But domestic computerisation has been rather weak in India. Many industrial undertakings in India are not very keen to computerise; and sectors like transportation, which has a lot of potential, lack plans to improve their computerisation.

In India, in the software business, exports have been consistently larger than domestic business. In 1991-92, the share has become 5:3 in favour of exports. Had the domestic base been stronger, Indian firms would have fared much better in exports.

A large pool of trained personnel must be developed rapidly

Availability of the right kind of manpower must also be ensured. Boosting software export on a large scale depends on the availability of ample personnel. It is not manpower per se, that matters but export oriented manpower. At present there are only about 7,000 trained computer software personnel in India involved in software exports. At the current manpower growth rate, India will have 13,000 trained software professionals by 1995-96. But to realise the target of software exports of $1 billion by that year, India will need 17,000 trained professionals with an individual productivity of $58,200 a year. That means a crash programme for generating computer professionals at a much faster rate than at present is called for. Substantial enhancement in training facilities and infrastructure in terms of quality as well as quantity is needed. There is a mismatch between the training imparted by India to her software professionals and the skills required in international markets. This short-coming has to be rectified.

Quality control systems needs to be strengthened

There are also significant shortcomings in quality control systems. Sometimes quality standards are diluted beyond acceptable levels. The penetration of modern technologies like Computer Aided Software Engineering (CASE) which gives a big fillip to quality and productivity, is less than one per cent in India. Software engineering techniques, project management skills, capacity for handling huge projects and capacity for making requirement analysis are also inadequate.

Telecom/Datacom facilities need enlargement

And finally, there is the inadequacy of Telecom and Datacom facilities so essential for providing a fillip to software exports. Off-shore projects in particular require sophisticated telecom infrastructure. While India is way ahead of others in OEM professional services and software for parallel processing, it lacks in infrastructure. A comparison with the competing countries indicates that while the telecom infrastructure in India is above average, that of Ireland, Israel and Singapore is much stronger. If India wants to improve its ranking, it has to improve its telecom facilities. Once this basic infrastructure of telecom is strengthened, India would be the leader among the eight developing countries covered by the world bank study. This would require the provision of high speed datacom links by the Government at internationally competitive prices throughout the major metros in the country.

The Videsh Sanchar Nigam Ltd (VSNL) has recently provided the much-needed 64 kbps point-to-point links to as many as 21 companies including TCS, American Express, Mico, Tata Unisys, Hewlett-Packard and Digital Equipment. Moreover, the various software technology parks would also begin installing their earth stations.

The conclusions are obvious. With proper strategies, it is possible for Indian firms to become major global players in this business.

SETTING UP JOINT VENTURES ABROAD

In the present-day world, joint ventures are an important part of globalisation strategies. As Kenichi Ohmae says in *The Borderless World:* Globalisation mandates alliances, makes them absolutely essential to strategy. In recent years, India has set up a number of joint ventures in a number of countries. These joint ventures cover a wide field like iron and steel, metal products, machinery and appliances, automobiles and ancillaries, light engineering products, sugar and textiles, chemicals and pharmaceuticals, pulp and paper, food products, leather and rubber products, construction jobs, transport services and trade and consultancy services. The total number of Indian joint ventures abroad by the beginning of 1990 was 193. Over 80 per cent of such projects are concentrated in Malaysia, Singapore, Nigeria, Indonesia, Thailand, Nepal and Kenya. A few are in UK, USA, Russia and the UAE. India has also established a few multilateral joint ventures, in which apart from India and the concerned importing country, a third country from the industrially advanced world also participates. The total equity participation in all these joint ventures was around Rs 100 crore. These joint ventures abroad have been conceived primarily as a vehicle of export promotion. To a small extent, they were also to serve the purpose of internationalising their operations. It has to be admitted that so far, barring a few exceptions, these joint ventures have neither earned a significant quantum of foreign exchange nor boosted the Indian image substantially.

Setting up joint ventures in foreign markets is certainly a useful strategy for gaining entry and access to global markets. The firm gets literally close to the market, thereby ensuring for itself substantial benefits which can be ultimately utilised for competitive thrust in the market. The next major benefit of joint ventures, a more lasting benefit for that matter, is that with a joint venture, the consumers in the foreign market start perceiving the Indian firm as a firm of their own land and start building an identification with the firm and its products. In other words, through a joint venture, the Indian firm becomes a native in the foreign land. And that is the best forerunner to the birth of an acceptable multinational. As mentioned already, quite a few Indian companies have already taken to the route of joint ventures and set up such ventures in a number of countries. While this attempt of Indian companies to go global through joint ventures may not be comparable to the activities of the multinationals of the developed world, the fact that a beginning has been made by Indian companies in going global through this strategy is significant. In recent years, the joint venture concept has taken firmer roots; more companies have picked it up as the strategy for realising their globalisation ambitions; not only has the number of joint ventures grown, the size of investment in individual ventures has also increased considerably. While a large number of these joint ventures are still in third world countries, the advanced countries too account for a few.

Speaking specifically of the NEP era, as many as 45 joint ventures abroad have been approved by the Government of India, for 1991-92 and 1992-93 with equity participation ranging from seven per cent to hundred per cent. The biggest is by Tata Chemicals which has put up an aluminium smelter in Venezuela with an equity of $140 million making up 40 per cent of the stake. Aditya Birla group has planned a Rs 100 crore aluminium fluoride project in Austraila and two carbon black projects in Poland and Egypt at a combined cost of Rs 140 crore.

Getting right partners for joint ventures abroad

How to get hold or acquire a sound foreign partner for one's joint venture abroad is the real issue. Because, an essential condition for a joint venture to materialise is that, the Indian company concerned should be able to attract a sound foreign company as partner. And to facilitate such a partnership the Indian side should possess certain basic strengths like: (i) substantial capital to invest, (ii) some attractive products/product idea; and (iii) the expertise required to make the product tick. If the joint venture is proposed in a developing country, all the three ingredients may have to be offered by the promoter of the joint venture, whereas in the case of ventures in the advanced world, the capital part may come from local sources. The point is that to get a proper partner, the Indian companies should be seen as candidates with some substantial competitive strength at their disposal. For example, when a joint venture between Toyota Motor company of Japan and General Motors of the US was mooted, Toyota was in a better position to negotiate as it had a good product idea with it—the small front wheel drive Toyota model. Toyota could also secure the right to appoint the President and CEO of the joint venture, which was to be based at the GM site in California.

Fortunately, at least some companies of India are already in a position to demonstrate these strengths and gain right partners for their joint ventures abroad. Blowplast for example, in its bid to add thrust to its exports of moulded luggage, is setting up joint ventures in partnership with major distribution companies in Europe. The first of these ventures is expected to take off in September 1993. Blowplast will go into a 50:50 equity partnership with one of the largest distributors in the line in UK. A similar tie-up with a company in Germany is on the anvil. Blowplast is already the second largest manufacturer of moulded luggage in the world with sales of about 3.6 million pieces annually, next only to Samsonite which sells about 11 million pieces. Blowplast in other words, is able to provide capital, product idea and expertise. Naturally, it is able to promote joint ventures with considerable ease with the best possible foreign partners.

Similarly, HMT is setting up a foundry in Dubai in a joint venture with the Easa Saleh Al Gurg Group of Dubai for the manufacture of castings, a line in which HMT has expertise. The Indian partners in the joint venture will hold about 40 per cent of the equity. Piramal group is planning a venture in Indonesia. NDI (Ispat) has taken over steel plants in Mexico and Trinidad. The Munjals of the Hero group, are going to Mauritius and also to Central American countries. Dalmia has set up a textile weaving and finishing plant in Hungary, acquired a viscose factory in Germany and set up a cotton weaving mill in Turkey and a palmoil refinery in Malaysia. Dalmia has also plans to tie up with Hungarian garment makers. The Mahindras have set up Mahindras Hellenic in Greece, to assemble jeeps. Telco is setting up a plant in Portugal to assemble trucks. Tatas and the Mahindras have plans to move to Europe and the integrated EC market. Reliance Industries has already formed Reliance Europe headquartered in London. Ballarpur Industries is working out a $850 million venture in Indonesia for paper and rayon grade pulp.

And now that technical expertise and labour is no longer as cheap in the ASEAN countries as it was earlier, new opportunities for joint ventures will arise for Indian companies. With India open for business, Indian firms will now be in an advantageous position in the matter of building alliances.

Buying out popular, on-going brands in different countries of the world

The process of establishing a new brand in a foreign country, is very expensive; worse still, it is enormously time consuming. Indian companies can consider the option of buying out on-going brands in different parts of the world market. There are always firms all over the world, looking for divestment and sale of their firms/brands. Of course, strong brands will demand their due price. It may be worthwhile to pay the due price and buy out the firm/brand. Indian companies can use acquisitions of firms and buying out of brands as the device to enter the world markets at a lesser cost and with practically no gestation period.

Using middlemen's brands

Many Indian products, especially agro-based products, are still going to the world markets as commodities. The value addition goes to the credit of the foreign distributors. Indian companies can at least share the benefit of value addition by having tie-ups with foreign distributors and super markets and sell the products using their brand names. This strategy of using middlemen brands is the opposite extreme of the one adopted by some of the Assam Tea estates who sell their tea to niche markets abroad under their own Indian brand names.

BECOMING A MULTINATIONAL TRADER

Another way to get access to world markets is to become a multinational trader. In fact, it is a field in which Indian companies can shine because, traditionally, India had been a good trading nation. In modern times she has been cut off from world markets for a variety of reasons which are well known. The time is now ripe for Indian companies to sharpen their traditional skills in trading, making available to the global markets the products on demand at an acceptable price. And in the changed world context where communication as well as transportation have compressed distances, products on demand can be sourced from anywhere, not necessarily from one's home country, and supplied to any market. Some of the big business houses of India like the ITC are already in this field of multinational trading and are realising the high rewards associated with the new business proposition.

ITC Global, already entrenched as a multinational trader

The Singapore-based ITC Global is a two-year old wholly-owned subsidiary of ITC and is primarily a trading company. It has targetted a $250 million turnover from multinational trading in 1993. The Singapore Government is in the process of granting ITC Global, the Approved International Trader status. It is selling Indian cement, sea food, leather products, match box, cashew and cigarettes in the Far Eastern markets. It purchases pulses and sesame seeds from Burma and cashew and black pepper from Vietnam for sale in the same region. It purchases tea from Indonesia for sales in Egypt. Such multinational trading can lead ITC to the launching of manufacturing enterprises, in different countries. The trading gives the company a feel of the different markets, the pattern of demand, the behaviour of countries and markets and an idea of the rules and regulations peculiar to the countries; on the whole, it affords the enterprise an on-the-job training facility without the risk of capital investment. For enhancing the export of agricultural and other products, the company is also negotiating with private labels which have a large chunk of the market in such goods in the US and Europe. Private labels are brands owned by stores or the ones that dominate a particular region within the country. For example, in toothpaste, private labels hold 18 per cent of the market in the US and in cigarettes 36 per cent.

BECOMING A FULL FLEDGED GLOBAL CORPORATION

Becoming full fledged MNCs in their own right, is no doubt the most difficult and the most rewarding of all strategies of globalisation for Indian companies. Efforts in this direction have obviously to start from scratch as at present there is not even a single Indian MNC in the international business scene. There is no Indian Siemens or Unilever or P&G or Suzuki or Honda. Nor is there a single Indian brand that can claim international presence and recognition. Moreover, past efforts by Indian companies in acquiring MNC connections through joint ventures in India have seldom put them on the path of becoming MNCs themselves. The connections in fact benefitted the MNCs more than the Indian partners. As a matter of fact, with the current liberalisation, chances are that the Indian partner loses its identity and the MNC partner becomes the symbol as well as substance of the venture. In the joint venture of Godrej and P&G for example, Godrej may be gobbled up by P&G; in Maruti-Suzuki, Suzuki may render Maruti inconsequential and in Hero-Honda, Honda can do the same thing to Hero. And even in a relatively weaker tie up like the one between Isuzu and Hindustan Motors (HM), the same phenomenon can happen. Isuzu can take the stronger position vis-a-vis HM. The fight between Maruti and HM, itself may turn out to be a direct fight between Suzuki and Isuzu. Because in all these cases, the market/consumers recognise only the foreign suffix and not the Indian prefix in the ventures! And this would seem quite natural and justified.

After all, the brand strength as well as the technology strength come from the foreign suffix and not from the Indian prefix in these ventures. The sum and substance of all this is that Indian companies cannot become global businesses just by having a connection with an MNC. The connection will not help Indian firms to achieve globalisation unless there is a relationship of reasonable equality between the Indian and the overseas partners. Rahul Bajaj puts it succinctly, when he says, "Indian licensees of foreign firms or junior partners in alliances would not be able to fulfil the objective. The partners must be 'reasonably equal' in their strength. Even the case of Maruti Udyog did not fully meet this criterion." The point is that the initiative has to originate from the Indian firm and the task and burden of establishing the product/brand must remain with it always. The Indian firms must travel the route which the MNCs of the world have travelled in becoming global enterprises. They have to build their product clout, technology clout and brand clout.

Indian companies must venture out on their own, into world markets with select Indian products and Indian brands putting up their own production/marketing bases across countries. They can certainly take whatever useful help and partnerships that can be spotted and obtained along their route, from local firms or MNCs as the case may be. Those with relatively larger resources, larger capabilities and greater ambition can certainly aspire to become full fledged MNCs in their own right with their own manufacturing facilities across countries and win markets on a global basis.

In fact, manufacturing/marketing bases across the world become essential for a global corporation for a number of reasons. In the case of most products, such dispersal of manufacturing facilities would be essential for timely and cost-effective supply to the various markets of the world. Dispersal would also be essential for manufacturing the products with market specific features and adaptations. In the context of increasing protectionism practised by several countries/trade blocs, establishment of production bases within the country/trade bloc would help overcome the hurdle of protectionism. For example, the EC has emerged not only as the largest trade bloc in the world, but also as the market with unique protectionism. The context demands that foreign companies should set up production bases within the EC countries if they want to do business with the EC market. The local presence of the companies would give them the advantage of operating in that market without let or hindrance. This is what the main competitiors of the EC—Japan and the US—have done. They have bought up the existing companies within the EC member states so that any future protectionist regulations can be countered by them effectively. Indian firms must emulate them and establish their companies within the EC countries. They must do the same in the Japanese market as well. The import laws of Japan are among the most stringent in the world. The best way to get into the Japanese market is to set up a plant within Japan. They do not raise much objection to other countries setting shop in Japan; their resistance is concentrated on the actual flow of goods into their country from outside.

ITC, an apt example of globalisation endeavour

ITC is one Indian company which serves as an apt example of a stage-by-stage progression in globalisation strategy. ITC started with the primary route, 'exporting from home base'. It enlarged its position by becoming an MNC trader. It then explored the joint venture route; it has plans for joint ventures as well as outright purchase of some going concerns abroad. It has also plans to buy out some on-going multinational brands. And finally, it has also chalked out plans for becoming a full fledged MNC.

ITC has been one of the earliest companies to become a Star Trading House. Today, it exports 40 different products to nearly 50 countries, earning an annual export turnover of Rs 500 crore.

'Exporting from home base' was to be the strategy to start with. There were three parts to this strategy: In respect of products like handicrafts, and gems and jewellery, ITC would try to exploit export opportunities by adopting on licence/lease basis, small scale units producing these items. In respect of granite products, leather and leather products, and readymade garments, ITC would spot companies engaged in these businesses and would invest up to 24 per cent in the equity of the companies and secure management control of the companies. In processed foods, frozen foods, fatty chemicals and derivatives and electronics, ITC would set up its own export units in free trade zones with foreign collaborations, with buyback arrangements. The three pronged approach aims at expanding ITC's export-basket in the shortest time and increasing its export turnover with the minimum capital investment.

Initially, the export thrust was to be on agricultural products. ITC wanted to harness the country's natural advantages as an agricultural nation and its own competitive advantage in the agro-based business. Its agricultural export basket was to include tobacco, spices, prawns, cashew, fruit pulp, sun flower oil, oil seeds and tea. The growth of ITC in the oils and seeds business at home was expected to propel the exports of these products. With the launch of ITC Agro Tech, seeds already constitute a major business of ITC. In edible oil, ITC's Sundrop, Sudham, Crystal and other brands have given it a leading 10 per cent share in the Indian market.

ITC soon became an MNC trader. As already mentioned, it set up ITC Global with Singapore as headquarters. It has set a target of $1 billion international trading turnover to be achieved in a span of 7 years. Initially, ITC Global depended on ITC's own products. Later on, it added purchased products and services to its list. For the next stage ITC has plans to set up manufacturing bases abroad. ITC's aim is to become the first Indian multinational.

ITC floated another foreign subsidiary—ITC Infotech Ltd—with headquarters in the UK. It is a software company and will spearhead ITC's software exports, especially to the EC and US markets. It is planning an export turnover of Rs 50 crore initially.

Subsequently, ITC also developed a joint venture, ITC Scotts Land Ltd, in partnership with the Singapore based conglomerate, the Scotts Holding Ltd. ITC Scotts Land Ltd, will focus on property development and management of hotels, tourism and recreation related activities as well as conference facilities and condominiums. Scotts Holding has diversified interests in various business concerns in the hospitality, leisure and lifestyle, and fast food industries. The Scotts group of companies is one of Singapore's best known enterprises with operations also in the highly competitive Asia-Pacific region. It also owns and manages Scotts Shopping Centre and has developed Singapore's first festival market, Law Pa Sat.

ITC's globalisation relied on three principles. (i) It is preferable that exports maintain an organic link with the company's domestic business; the growth abroad has to be facilitated by the company's operations back home. (ii) The process of promoting the corporate name of the company abroad is very important for a company with true global ambitions. (iii) International competitiveness is a must for any firm with global aspirations. ITC proudly proclaims, "Whatever we produce will be globally competitive in terms of cost and quality." And in tobacco and other agri-products with which ITC has made its impact on the world markets, the company has lived up to its claim.

Arvind Mills

In textiles, Arvind Mills has emerged as a forceful exporter. It seems that what ITC has done in agri products, Arvind can accomplish in textiles. As per its corporate plan, the Arvind group will achieve an export turnover of Rs 600 crore, over the next three years. And exports would form as much as 60 per cent of its total turnover.

Between 1987 and 1993 Arvind's primary emphasis in export has been on denim. Having achieved considerable success in denim, the company started developing the technology and market for value added cottons, shirtings and bottoms. Its plan is to achieve a well balanced mix comprising a variety of cotton rich fabrics, yarn and readymade garments which are highly profitable and which can also provide large volumes. Arvind already accounts for a major share of USA's total import of denim.

The group's aim is to be among the top five companies in the world in high value cotton shirting. And it is in the process of becoming a truly multinational corporation from India with strong manufacturing, distribution and marketing infrastructure globally. By 1994, the company would have set up plants to weave Arvind fabrics in at least five centres abroad, in Asia, Europe and South Asia. The group has established an international network for marketing denim, cotton shirting, readymade garments and yarn, establishing its own offices and warehouses in the Middle East, South East Asia and North America.

Initially however, Arvind's sales did not pick up fast in the market of the developed countries. Arvind probed why its sales did not catch up even though its quality compared well with the best in the world. And soon discovered that it was distribution that needed improving. Across the world, a new way of distribution was gaining force at that time. Buyers wanted just-in-time delivery. It meant buyers would order only as much cloth as they wanted, precisely when they wanted it. It also meant that there was no time for inspection. So the denim had to be of 'inspection-free' quality. Since this helped buyers cut inventory costs, they were willing to pay a higher price when such a service was provided . Moreover, a company could increase its market share in those markets, only by providing the 'just-in-time' service. Arvind fully appreciated the market requirement and came closer to its international clients in three steps. First, it tied up with some of the world's largest trading houses to market its denim in Europe. Then it set up subsidiaries in a few key markets abroad and also a global network of offices and warehouses. As for countries with import restrictions, it planned overseas manufacturing facilties. The strategy paid off. Arvind is now the world's eighth largest supplier of denim. And is set to move higher, with production slated to touch 50 million meters per annum.

Arvind has succeeded in its globalisation venture by understanding and relating correctly to changes in the textile industry in USA, EC, Japan and the Far East. It has clearly identified its core strengths—the capability to manufacuture and market value added cotton textiles based on its rich experience of last five decades. It has also made the necessary changes in its strategy in the globalisation context with the right sense of timing.

Becoming a global corporation is no easy task

While the rewards of operating globally are great, the risks involved are also proportionately large. Competing globally puts many strange and unconventional demands on the firm. Usually, resources of a high order are needed for global operations. Sometimes major investments may have to be made with zero or even negative ROI. Products may have to be severely underpriced in some national markets seeking compensation in some other nations. In several instances, construction of production facilities in high labour-cost countries may have to be undertaken, quite contrary to the common perception that MNCs always operate from low cost bases. For example, Honda invested heavily in its motorcycle venture in Europe and waited for seven full years for profits. It financed the effort from cash flows earned from home and the US. Companies opting for global business have to tolerate many such adverse situations.

Another point is that all businesses do not lend themselves for global operations. And all of them may not have the potential to become global. The company has to ascertain the position before opting for the risk of heavy investment that a global competition entails.

Going global is not going to be an easy exercise for the Indian firms. Globalisation implies that individual Indian companies have to achieve a global presence by getting access to markets throughout the world and by matching their global competitors. Indian companies with global ambitions must consciously decide that they will take on the world's best; be as good as the best company in the world operating in the field. They must benchmark the best company and try to emulate it and become one better than it in course of time.

Indian companies can join together and tap world markets

In the new context, Indian companies would do well to form partnerships among themselves to fight in the global arena. To fight transnational companies like GE, Siemens, or Philips, which can offer broader product lines from worldwide sources, Indian companies like L&T, Telco, Bhel, Tata Electric and Reliance can team up, pooling their resources and expertise and sharing the burden of hefty investment. Such corporate courtship is one strategy through which at least some truly global corporations can emerge from India.

The basic requirement is that Indian companies must enjoy size advantage. They have to become internally big, through acquisitions, mergers and expansions and be assured of large supply, so that they can play the global game. Using the domestic market and high production capacity as the leverage, the battle can be launched. They also have to build internal infrastructure, in tune with the latest trends. In addition they must also be in a position to invest in infrastructure in the foreign markets.

Such a coming together of Indian companies would be essential not only for investing abroad on a big scale and carrying on as a global corporation, but even for exporting from the home base. For, in the emerging global scenario, size would be of crucial importance in winning export orders. A trade bloc like EC would not like to deal with pigmy suppliers. It may need millions of pieces of a given product at a time. It would go through large trading giants who will make bulk procurement to cater to the large unified market. The Indian companies, being of the size they are, will hardly be in a position to cater to orders of that magnitude.

'INDIA' MUST BE MARKETED TO THE WORLD BEFORE MARKETING INDIAN PRODUCTS

If Indian products, especially manufactured and branded products, have to gain ready acceptance in the markets of the world, the image of India as a slip-shod producer has to be erased from the collective memory of these countries. India should make a mammoth effort to sell 'Product India' as such before selling the nation's products to them. That is, how many countries have become big exporters in the world markets. West Germany and Japan are the best examples of this phenomenon. They promoted a good image of themselves among the countries of the world; several of their products that were introduced in other countries came to be identified as zero-defect products. In due course of time, any product from these countries became acceptable to other nations. India should follow this example and market herself as a nation worth doing business with. India can also utilise the foreign tourists coming here, to promote India and Indian products. The multitude of tourists coming to India can be a 'medium' for communicating to the global markets about India and her products. India should be in a position to demonstrate to the tourists that she produces high quality products. And some of these products must be used as carriers of a good Indian image. A product from a country will experience a demand pull from another country only if the former has already built up a good image.

If a country is able to export its values and tastes besides its products, it has an added advantage. The success of US companies in fast food and credit cards, for example, reflects the spread of the American tastes and American concepts into the rest of the world. Nations export their values and tastes through tourists, through media, through political influence and through the foreign activities of their citizens and companies.

ACHIEVING INDUSTRIAL COMPETITIVENESS, A TOP PRIORITY TASK

Indian companies have to make their products internationally competitive—in quality, price and other parameters—if they have to succeed in their international business ventures. Achieving industrial competitiveness essentially involves bridging the gaps in technology, productivity, quality and infrastructure. While some of these factors are the responsibility of the country as a whole some of them are the responsibility of individual companies. First and foremost, it is essential for the companies to bridge the technology gap. Without upgrading their technology, Indian companies cannot produce what the overseas markets need. The companies must adopt international technological specifications and standards as their own. It is the only dependable route for quality and price competitiveness. Improvement in productivity is another major condition along with technology upgradation for achieving industrial competitiveness. Indian companies must exploit their advantages in natural resources and labour and employ the best technology and ensure higher productivity.

HIGH CONCERN FOR QUALITY A MUST FOR FIRMS WITH GLOBAL AMBITIONS

Historically, quality assurance has remained a low priority with Indian industry. Even now several Indian producers are lax, when it comes to quality. Poor quality has been identified as the single most important hindrance to India's exports. As this reality is universally known, the image of Indian products barring a few exceptions, is quite poor in the world markets. Indian firms with global ambition have to unfortunately start with this handicap.

The keen interest Indian companies are showing in recent times in quality related matters including ISO 9000 certification, is largely traceable to the economic liberalisation and the new compulsions for going global. Of course, the coincidental development of tightening up of quality requirements by several countries/markets, especially the EC has also been a contributing factor. In 1989, there was only one firm in India with the ISO certification; 1990 saw the addition of just one company to the list. But since 1991, the story has been different. Nearly 70 firms have qualified in 1992-93.

ISO 9000 and its associated series is now the minimum international quality standards mandatory for any industry wishing to enter the European markets. The EC has stipulated that from January 1993 onwards, only companies with the ISO quality certification will be allowed to have trade links with the twelve European countries who are members of EC. The EC has also laid new norms on product liability; it is not enough if a supplier demonstrates that his product is well designed, he must also demonstrate that the product is manufactured within a system that conforms to internationally accepted norms. While most quality standards relate to the product, ISO 9000 prescribes the quality standards for the manufacturing system/organisation as a whole. Following this development Indian manufacturers and entrepreneurs with vital export interests have suddenly started concentrating on quality. And sensing the new interest shown by Indian companies in ISO certification, international agencies like Bureau Veritas Quality International (BVQI) of Britain, the main agency for providing ISO 9000 certification, the German certification agency, RW-TUV-SN Ltd., and the Dutch Council for Certification Bodies, RvC, have opened their offices in India. Even Bureau of Indian Standards (BIS) has formulated IS 14000 which is an equivalent to ISO 9000. The very effort involved in obtaining the ISO certification and in adhering to it, will make the Indian firms understand the distance they have to travel in achieving global competitiveness on the quality plank. Often Indian companies which join the select band of ISO certificate holders, realise to their surprise that 1000 odd German and 600 odd Japanese firms already have the ISO certification.

Besides product quality, packaging and delivery standards would also call for substantial improvement. They are related issues. Weakness in any one of them is sufficient to make a company's position in world markets vulnerable. In the case of Indian companies, unfortunately, weaknesses in all these factors exist simultaneously.

ORGANISATION STRUCTURE FOR INTERNATIONAL BUSINESS

The change over from domestic to international business involves a great deal of organisational adjustments. And devising an effective organisation structure capable of handling the unique problems and tasks involved is a major concern in international business. Many of the established MNCs, in their earlier years, have been going on organising and reorganising their outfits in their eagerness to meet the everchanging scenario of world markets. From division structure, companies have changed over to a global product structure or area-division structure and then to a global matrix or grid structure. Then most of them reversed the steps. They changed the global matrix structure and went back to the simpler international division structure. For example, Dow Chemicals which served as a case study of the global matrix finally returned to a conventional structure with geographically based managers. Citibank too adopted the matrix organisation and then retreated from the matrix structure. The experiences of several companies point towards the futility of frequently changing the organisation structure for handling the diverse demands of international business. In fact, several MNCs stayed with a simple divisional structure and demonstrated that with such a simple structure they could tide over any difficult situation. It has been by and large accepted that there is no such thing as the ideal organisation structure that will totally take care of the problems faced in international business. What really matters is right strategies and competent executives who can give fast and right decisions to local problems. Flexibility is the key requirement. And that is precisely why the Indian public sector companies, all along used to rigidity of procedure and centralised decision making, feel handicapped while venturing into foreign markets. The Indian private sector corporations, on the other hand, are in a better position to switch over to the new requirements of global operations.

12

Creating and Sustaining a Strategic Organisation

Strategic planning cannot and does not stop with the development of strategies and plans. To be meaningful and complete, strategic planning must take care of implementation as well. Strategic organisations are always involved in putting strategy into practice. For example, when the Honda Motor company gives a one-line direction to its employees, "Don't buy bad parts, Don't make bad parts, Don't ship bad parts" the company is putting into practice one particular element of its strategy—strict adherence to quality. The company is also effectively bridging its strategy-performance gap by translating the strategy into easily assimilable practice by all its employees. It needs the meticulous execution of a thousand small things for even a superb strategy to succeed. When Buck Rodgers says about IBM "...Above all, we want a reputation for doing the little things well...", he is actually letting us into the secrets of strategic performance of his company. Similarly, when Jan Carlzon, who championed the successful turnaround of Scandinavian Air System (SAS) says about his strategy, "...the SAS strategy was to become the premier airline of business people...it was every airliner's aspiration...the difference is we executed it... . Rather than doing one thing a thousand per cent better, we wish to do a thousand things one per cent better", he is just talking about his company's way of implementing strategy. When several American companies admit that to copy the '3M way' is a virtual impossibility, they mean that it is extremely difficult to copy the way 3M implements its strategy.

Strategic organisations around the world achieve growth and success by doing several known things and by doing them better, every time. They look around, observe what their competitors and peers are doing, copy them and then improve upon them. Among great achievers of the corporate world, there goes on a constant benchmarking of not only products and product features, but a higher order benchmarking of practices, faiths, values and skills. Their doors are open to the best ideas around in any area of their activity. They are committed to bridging the strategy-execution gap, narrowing it down to the maximum extent possible.

CONTEMPORARY IDEAS ON CORPORATE SUCCESS

There is an on going search for identifying strategic factors responsible for corporate success. As a result, there is a rapidly growing volume of literature on the subject of corporate success and corporate excellence. The 1980s especially witnessed several such studies. And the management world has received a great deal of insight into the theme—what constitutes excellence, what the routes to excellence are and how the great corporations have achieved excellence. Indian companies, placed as they are in the unique predicament of having to compress their learning time, can benefit utmost by a study of the practices of successful corporations.

The Peters-Waterman thesis

Peters and Waterman came up with plenty of lessons from America's best run companies, in their classic *In Search of Excellence*. They have identified eight attributes that characterise the well run companies. These companies have a bias for action, they remain close to the customer, they believe in autonomy and entrepreneurship, they have a great respect for their people, they remain conscious of their values, they stay with businesses they really know, they have simple structure, forms and systems, they practise simultaneously loose-tight properties—loose in giving freedom to the shop floor man, tight in maintaining core values.

A close scrutiny of the Peters-Waterman thesis reveals that ultimately it is leadership that matters most. To quote from the treatise, "Many of the excellent companies—IBM, P&G, Emerson, J&J and Dana—seem to have taken their basic character under the tutelege of a very special leader. They seem to have developed cultures that have incorporated the values and practices of the great leader, the shared values surviving long after the passing of the original Guru." The book abounds in references to such men—Bill, Dave, Johnson, Watson—the leaders of America's great corporations. It explains how these leaders cast a spell over every nerve of their organisation, literally becoming living legends. A simple but noble deed of the founder, an act performed a generation ago, is remembered in the corridors of the corporation through the ripple effect of culture. Stories of small but moving incidents, permeate the corporate climate of such organisations. Peters and Waterman give an endless list of such events and such people who worked magic in their factories.

The Hickman-Silva prescription

Closely following *In Search of Excellence* came the other scholarly work *Creating Excellence* by Craig Hickman and Michael Silva. If Peters and Waterman drew their clues to corporate success and eminence from live research, going to every simple detail of management practice, Hickman and Silva brought in some scintillating ideas on excellence, through theory, pure and simple. They identify six key components that lead a corporation to excellence—*vision, insight, focus, patience, strategy* and *culture. Vision* helps to move from the present to the future; *insight* helps to search into the heart of a problem; *vision* needs to be backed by *focus.* And any programme of action needs *patience* too, especially when the goal is big and the activity strenuous and time consuming. And *strategy* is the heart of any great project. Finally, excellence is impossible without a corporate *culture* that evokes pride, confidence and a sense of elation among the workforce of the corporation.

The Iacocca experience

The autobiography of Lee Iacocca, the man who took Chrysler to the heights of excellence from the brink of liquidation was the next in the series. Iacocca vividly talks about the sacrifice made by the entire workforce of Chrysler. Of course Iacocca, the leader, set a personal example, volunteering to work on a token salary of $1 a month; the leader's sincerity was felt by everyone, and there was no propaganda about it. It was "a shared perception, an awareness that everybody was bleeding equally of the sacrifice made, the sacrifice acceptable and noble". The Iacocca story is a classic example of the leader's potential to move his men, emotionally and physically, to achieve what looked impossible.

The Matsushita classic

Next in the series was the Matsushita story, *Not for Bread Alone.* When Matsushita himself let out his open secrets about his world famous enterprise—how the three member Matsushita Electric Company consisting of Matsushita, his wife and his brother-in-law, grew into a global corporation with more than 1,60,000 employees engaged in 193 enterprises throughout the world—the management world was learning about another classic experience in organisation building. And building it the typical Japanese way—through productivity and self-induced strict work ethics, through a transparent management, through a life long relationship between the employee and his company, and above all through Matsushita's pet theme of the Sunao mind—the open mind. Yes, it was not for bread alone—from both the employees' side and from the organisation's side.

Fortune parameters

The *Fortune* magazine, for its selection of the top 500 companies in the USA, bases its evaluation on eight factors: 1) Quality of management; 2) Quality of product/services; 3) Innovativeness; 4) Long-term investment value; 5) Financial soundness; 6) Ability to attract, develop and retain talented people; 7) Community and environmental responsibility; and 8) Use of corporate assets.

For ranking the world's 50 biggest industrial leaders, *Fortune* goes by four principal factors—emphasis on delegation, positive communication; planning (long range and global) and restructuring.

Other studies

Many other well researched works/literary contributions have also come out in recent times on the subject of corporate success and excellence. Charles Garfield, President of the Peak Performance Center, California, and a researcher in human performance, conducted a research on the characteristics of management effectiveness and found that team building and the ability to develop people were the fundamentals of management excellence.

It is remarkable that all these works, written from different experience profiles and different stand points, are congruent in the basic ideas on excellence in management.

These classic experiences from the management world are cited here with a purpose. For Indian companies one good way to learn is to learn from the experiences of best companies of the world and biographies of men who created such companies. These companies have reached a state of eminence, obviously, by going through tough times. And they have become the models for strategic organisations, capable of withstanding any traumatic experience in their fields. They are protected by a strategic architecture built assiduously over the years. A peep into their history, their motifs and their way of doing things, gives a lot of clues about the shaping of such strategic organisations.

THE STRATEGIC ORGANISATION

Strategy, after all, is an extension of a company's capabilities. Its people, its style of functioning, its structure and systems will set the limits to the strategy it can put into practice. The strategy a Reliance Industries can put through, an HMT may not be able to. The strategy a Tata Steel can put through, a SAIL may not be able to. Behind a vibrant strategy, there is a vibrant team, a vibrant organisation, a vibrant structure; otherwise the strategy is a cracker that cannot fire and burst. So, it is easy to conclude that behind a farsighted strategy, there is, or ought to be, an ever vigilant organisation, with a committed leadership and a competent team.

The guiding principles of a strategic organisation cannot be fitted into a formula or an equation; they only lend for description. All that is possible is to trace the characteristics of such an organisation. It is also feasible to look around for corporations who by and large display these characteristics and then try to identify how they are able to attain these characteristics and attain their present positions. Just as ideas like corporate success and corporate excellence are universally understood without a tight definition of it, it is possible to understand the broad features of a strategic organisation and to identify organisations worthy of emulation by virtue of their strategic character. The features of a strategic organisation are highlighted here by means of some illustrative examples.

Lessons from Intel

The remarkable turnaround of Intel became possible because of the inherent strategic strength of the organisation. The company transformed itself from the position of a heavily losing producer of commodity memory chips to the world's largest semiconductor manufacturer. It repositioned itself in the best manner possible to exploit the enormous increase taking place in the Personal Computer business around the world. Intel had to reorient its very mission. The fact that Intel could successfully do it, is proof of the strategic strength it carried.

In the strategic repositioning, Intel's main theme worked around the principle—invest and lead. The company was not only committing itself to research for the most novel product in its field, it also believed in exploiting the product idea commercially. Intel realised that in its business, a leading edge can come only through investing in a leading manufacturing capacity which in turn required heavy investment. Obviously, this was a context where the Intel management had to take heavy risks on investing for building the company's future. Intel did take the decision in favour of such heavy investment for R&D and new product commercialisation facilities. In 1993 the company is investing $2.5 billion, equal to 43 per cent of the company's total annual income of the previous year, into R&D and capital outlays.

And this is but one part of the corporate transformation Intel is undergoing to keep it strategically fit for tomorrow's fight. The very business mission at Intel is changing; the methods and systems are also fast changing. The company which till now saw itself as a supplier of computer chips to a few industrial customers, now considers itself a firm having 100 million consumers, all users of PCs round the world. Intel is no longer catering merely to a few industrial buyers making computers; the entire lot of PC users are now seen as the direct customers of Intel and that makes a hell of a lot of difference in the way Intel will command the market in future. To quote Andrew Grove, Intel CEO, "For us, the turning point was around 1985, when we decided to get completely out of DRAMS (dynamic random access memories), the product our company was created to make. To take advantage of some of the opportunities I see ahead, we are going to have to transform ourselves again. The time to do it is while our core business is still so strong... . We have got to become more than a micro processor company... . Our corporate mission is to be the pre-eminent supplier of building blocks to the new computing industry... . If we develop the right building blocks, we will win... . There is no competitor around who can do as much damage to us as we can do to ourselves... ."

Lessons from General Electric

America's General Electric (GE) is known not only as a leader in its business, but also as a corporation pioneering new management ideas and practices. And through that pursuit, GE has been emerging stronger. And the management experiment under the dynamic captaincy of Jack Welch proves that GE carries the strong will typical of a strategic organisation, that has the readiness to change and the capability to change and thereby stay ahead. How does GE perceive the hard time ahead for all global players? And how does it respond? To quote Jack Welch, "Trying to define what will happen three to five years out, in specific quantitative terms, is a futile excercise. The world is moving too fast for that. What should a company do instead? First of all, define its vision and its destiny in broad but clear terms. Second, maximise its own productivity. Finally, be organisationally and culturally flexible enough to meet massive change."

And GE can simultaneously be 'hard and soft', hard in its core decisions like closing down plants, divesting and cutting layers; and still practise candour, fairness, fun around work, trust and openness. The most distinguishing of all changes taking place in GE is the drive towards openness. At GE it amounts to boundarylessness, at least that is what GE is striving for in its pursuit of becoming a totally flexible and capable organisation. To quote Welch again, "If the company is to achieve its goals, we have all got to become boundaryless. Boundaries are crazy... . The union is just another boundary and you have to reach across the same way you want to reach across the boundaries separating you from your customers and your suppliers and your colleagues overseas."

Lessons from GM

In the '80s General Motors of America took to radical changes in its functioning. Till then, GM was the symbol of 20th century American eminence in manufacturing. GM was also the representative of the typical 20th century hierarchical organisation, domineering and authoritarian. But, GM in the last lap of the 20th century is shaping itself into a different organisation. It recognises that it was too complacent with its eminent position, to take note of what was happening in its industry globally. When the American customers switched over to Japanese cars, superior in quality and convenience with a cost advantage of $1500 to $2200 per car compared to those of GM, GM's eminence in cars was becoming a story of the past. But GM and GM's leadership had the grit to take GM to not only new businesses but to totally new ways of running the company. Roger Smith, in the '80s, made it his mission to change GM, from its mission and grand strategies down to its day to day way of doing things. In fact, GM's Saturn project, designed to overtake the Japanese super eminence in cars, was in essence a symbol of GM's total restructuring and learning. And the rules of the Saturn team were something like this—an autoworker, an automobile engineer, a shopfloor manager and a union shop steward may sit together and decide the best way to produce the best car; they may have the freedom to look for the best technologies. GM Vice Chairman Howard Kehrl said about Saturn project "...it is not a car, it is a process.... And the process in this case is a re-evaluation of all we thought was correct..." The strategic strength of GM is that it can rededicate itself to 'reinventing the wheel'.

Lessons from Ford

Ford Motor Company as part of its rejuvenation programme had to lay emphasis on corporate values. After spelling out the corporate mission Ford unambiguously clarifies the values the organisation holds important. Let us see the corporate statement at Ford on its organisational values:

> "...How we accomplish our mission is as important as the mission itself. Fundamental to success for the company are these basic values.

VALUES

> People — Our people are the source of our strength. They provide our corporate intelligence and determine our reputation and vitality. Involvement and teamwork are our core human values.

> Products — Our products are the end result of our efforts, and they should be the best in serving customers worldwide. As our products are viewed, so are we viewed.

> Profits — Profits are the ultimate measure of how efficiently we provide customers with the best products for their needs. Profits are required to survive and grow..."

Lessons from AT&T

AT&T is still managing its transition from a mere telephone company to a high-technology information company. When more than three quarters of a century ago, Theodore Vail, the founder, laid down the mission, "...we will give a telephone to every American at a low price...that is our mission..." the all powerful telephone monopoly of America was getting formed. But, the last lap of the century is witnessing AT&T managing its challenging transition from a telephone monopoly to an aggressive leader in the overarching businesses of computers, telecommunications and electronic information. And in managing this change, AT&T's formidable challenge was from within, to develop a competitive culture for the people of the company, who have always enjoyed the stability of a monopoly business. From total stability AT&T was learning to live with uncertainties. The biggest problems in the transition were the AT&T

managers, who were all along used to taking decisions, with full information, going through all possible analysis and satisfying several of the written down instructions and practices. AT&T's main job was to instill into these managers, risk taking, innovating and entrepreneurial skills. AT&T initiated programmes to change its bureaucratic culture and to make people work it out in the thick of ambiguity and uncertainty, with common sense and executive judgement guiding them. From the quiet world of the telephone business they had to now come out and develop a highly competent organisation, which could master the new technologies, invent new products and compete with well settled giants in new fields.

Many Indian companies too provide valuable insights on the subject

There are several Indian companies, which really qualify for being classified as strategic organisations. Companies like TISCO, TELCO, Asian Paints, Bajaj Auto, Hindustan Lever, ITC, Reliance Industries, L&T and Amul are fine examples of this group. Just like their counterparts in the developed world, these organisations too provide equally valuable insights on the way strategic organisations are run. We shall be drawing profusely from them in the sections that follow.

WHAT DISTINGUISHES A STRATEGIC ORGANISATION FROM THE OTHERS

Strategically agile organisations, wherever they are, and whatever be the business they are in, share certain commonalities in their approaches to certain key factors relating to the organisation.

With strategic organisations, planning is practical; they believe 'execution is strategy'

Strategic organisations are guided by a strategic architecture that is pragmatic and practical. In such organisations, strategic planning is not a centralised, dreamy, board room activity. Planning is part and parcel of executive responsibility. The very same people who are responsible for the success of strategies will have a substantive role in the process of planning and shaping of strategies. And execution is emphasised all the time, at all the levels. The strategic planning process usually achieves a high success rate in these organisations. On the contrary, strategic planning comes a cropper in organisations which are ignorant of the practical nature of the strategic planning task and are lacking in execution capability. In fact the importance of execution capability can never be over emphasised. Indian firms seem to be particularly weak in execution of plans. And as a nation, India gets poor credit for execution of plans. Bhoothalingam highlights this fact nicely when he says "We developed the illusion that whatever is written is as good as done." The reference, obviously is to the great skill displayed by the country in making the plan, juxtaposed to poor execution. In fact, even some of those large corporations of the West who had long back taken to formal strategic planning, found that the process did not help them when their corporations were faced with all round economic decline. The very subject of long term planning attracted criticism on the ground that the external environment was too volatile to be well captured in a set of predetermined findings. Subsequent studies however proved that the defaulter was not the process. Poor execution was the problem. Those companies who had built up the organisation edifice to pragmatically handle strategic planning and strategies, could stay ahead even in declining and difficult times. The difference obviously was between the corporation who could only plan strategies and those who could plan and execute strategies. Execution requires an organisational competence, which is the forte of strategic organisations. The test of a strategic organisation is that it can take on problems as it has the strength of choices and the organisational grit to exercise those choices, changing even the very nature and business of the organisation if warranted. Such organisations retain command over situations, however exacting the situation might be.

STRATEGIC ORGANISATIONS ARE FLEXIBLE, ADAPTING AND OPEN IN THEIR STRUCTURE

It is seen that with well run companies, structure is one distinctive component of strategic strength. And their search for a more effective structure is an on going one. The hallmark of their practices in structure by and large centres around these features: rigidities of hierarchy are becoming less and less; more de-layering is taking place which means people are coming closer; instead of long winding chains, people work in cohesive teams; the structure means flexibility; it ensures accessibility. And the unique feature is that such principles and patterns of structure could work because in these organisations there exists a mutual trust and openness among the so called rank and file, among middle management and top management, among trade unions and management. The rigid structure of the olden days was fast yielding to an adaptive structure in these organisations.

The continuous search for more efficient organisational structure

Many of these companies mid course find their organisational structure and systems inadequate or inappropriate to take them through their changing objectives and programmes. And they are ready to change their structure and systems, though changing them is no easy task. And such companies who are determined to fight it out are seen taking to radical changes in their structure and systems. For example, GE is on the path of a major organisational restructuring; making the organisation structure thinner through a substantial de-layering is one of the features of the GE restructure. In fact, GE from its traditional 'big bureaucratic organisation' is trying to move to the other extreme of 'boundarylessness'. It is opting for 'the direct, personal two way communication' and trying to 'expose its people without the protection of title or position to ideas from everywhere'. It is seen that such organisations in their quest to remain competent are looking for more and more of simplicity in their structure and systems. Their goal is speed and efficiency of operations. For example, to ensure speed of action and thus improve the efficiency in the final market response, GE is going to extreme degrees of delegation of powers to the subordinate levels. By delegating powers down the line, GE is finding time for its top management to do more precious jobs for the corporation.

In most of the leading corporations of India too, like the ITC, L&T and Hindustan Lever to whom we had made a reference earlier, structures and systems have become less and less complex over a period of time. There is increasing emphasis on one to one interaction among managers and an on the spot resolution of problems. Many of them have dispensed with formal note writing for solving day-to-day problems. And these organisations ensure high degree of delegation of powers to functional managers down the line. This pattern has in turn significantly contributed to development of a highly capable middle manager group with these companies. These organisations are also action oriented. And some of them display a high degree of openness within the organisation. Their structure is also conducive to promoting team work of people from different disciplines. Management training is another major concern for them. Some of them ensure that at least once in two years their key managers are exposed to training.

In fact, experimentation on structure and systems in itself makes some of these companies unique.

ITC's organisation structure based on product group operations has substantially contributed to the ease and agility of its functioning. It has not only demarcated its total business into specific product groups, but has also ensured that the structure enables the managers within a product group to function, as if it is a distinct corporate enterprise with its own mission, targets and strategy. A remarkable innovation of ITC is the creation of notional boards of directors for its various product groups for giving near autonomy to the different businesses. There is a board for the hotel group, a board for leaf tobacco and a board for cigarettes. These boards function as if they are managing separate companies. It is ensured that all the heads of these product groups also serve on the corporate ITC board. The level of managerial autonomy within these distinctive product groups is also outstanding.

In systems too, these companies have used modern ideas and gained the benefits thereof. Hindustan Lever is a particularly good example of systems-based company. The management system at HLL has reached an outstanding level of effectiveness. Through emphasis on systems, HLL has attained sophistication and effectiveness in corporate planning, budgeting, performance reporting, marketing information processing, personnel administration and management training. The objective of the system is not to perpetuate bureaucracy in management decision-making but to work toward effective management. There are many management experts who believe that a substantial part of HLL's success emanates from its outstanding systems. Similarly, the Amul system for collection and transmission of milk is another example of a successful system. In the perfection of its details, the system at Amul is comparable to Coca Cola's world famous franchise system. Similarly, Asian Paints' computer-based distribution planning system, and production planning system are unique in the paint industry. The nation wide network of branches and hundreds of depots of Asian Paints are computer linked; and with up to date information on sales and stock, the company does a perfect inventory control and keeps its costs lowest in the industry. ITC's marketing information system is considered to be one of the finest among Indian companies, well designed for the collection and analysis of data on customers, dealers and competitors.

Emphasis on 'team' seems to be another characteristic of strategic organisations. They get work done more and more by teams rather than by individuals. The management of work too is by teams rather than by individuals. The teams, not individuals, are made the building blocks of organisational performance in these companies. These organisations recognise that in today's highly advanced scientific world, more than individuals, teams of individuals, have to work towards creating something special. Tools of modern science are being best exploited and competent teams are put on work. Cross-disciplinary team work is becoming a pattern for strategic advantage building. There is an increasing trend towards simplifying the very work culture, showing greater reliance on group activity.

These organisations also combine managerial and non-managerial activities as often as possible. They also encourage multiple competencies in each individual. They are moving away from the traditional concept of work. The trend now seems to be to organise work around a 'business process' rather than a task. A 'work flow' takes care of an identified business process. And a number of such work flows link the internal activities of the firm to the requirements of the customers and markets. People conveniently and comfortably move along this chain, taking care of the work involved.

In structure, most Indian companies suffer handicaps

In the unique context of management transition now prevailing in India, organisational structure will have a very special relevance in the successful rendering of corporate strategies. Because, historically the organisational structure in many Indian companies has been an inhibitor, rather than a facilitator of efficiency and growth. The Indian management scene all along has witnessed extremes of management structure in different sectors of the corporate world, given their different ownership/ management patterns. At one extreme are the public sector corporations with their time old rigidities of corporate structure; at the other extreme are the family run companies with a total centralisation of power in a few hands and in between the two have been the MNCs with a fairly good degree of professionalisation, in structure and systems. The MNCs have used their world connections and benefitted by imbibing new ideas on structure. The most handicapped were the public sector corporations. Structure, systems and methods in the public sector companies were designed basically to oversee, to caution and to control rather than to perform, to expedite or to motivate. Structure served as a direct impediment to performance. The way it was organised, it gave rise to an impasse; it did not lead to performance. The very purpose of an organisational structure which is to provide the frame and facility to get work done was ignored. An overdose of caution in a general atmosphere of external control and mistrust was becoming the all pervasive feature of the public sector companies of India. An impersonal and notional ownership of the public sector among other things, contributed largely to such an organisational atmosphere.

Many Indian companies are initiating changes in structure and systems

However, in recent times many Indian companies have started redesigning their structure and systems. The new momentum towards a market driven economy is the major driving force for the structural changes in the Indian corporations. The main issue here is that the new demand for customer satisfaction calls for an agile organisation. The fact that Indian companies are now graduating from a single product/single business company to a multi-business, diversified corporation, lends an additional dimension to the importance of structure. But for the new situation, most of them might have found their existing structure and systems sufficient to take care of their requirements. In the new context of a diversification spree with acquisitions and takeovers as the major growth strategy, they will be meeting a different set of demands in structure and systems. In other words, the Indian companies have entered a totally different stage in their life cycle calling for greater speed, agility and efficiency of operation, calling for new structures and systems.

In addition to the forces of economic liberalisation, the on going break up of big family businesses and the transition from family management to professional management has also been contributing to organisational restructuring in several companies. Moreover, the new information technology with its grand facilities renders a de-layering of organisational structure feasible. In short, the new environment brought about by deregulation, intensification of competitive forces, globalisation and the facilities provided by the new information technology are all important factors demanding India's corporate managements to go in for a structure that will lead to superior performance.

To cite some instances, Escorts is fast moving toward a total change of its structure and systems. Escorts was all along a highly labour intensive organisation. It now opts to become technology intensive. It is reducing labour and moving towards automation; Escorts is actually hunting for the latest technology; it is also computerising extensively. Larsen and Toubro, on the advice of the US consultancy firm McKinsey, is considering reorganising its 14 business groups into five compact divisions, each a profit centre. The company may also move out of areas like food processing, prawn farming, leather and trading; it also has plans for strategic alliances with key global players in certain priority areas; all these in turn may involve further restructuring. Greaves Cotton's 14 business divisions too have been restructured into five compact groups, each a profit centre. And some of the subsidiaries and associate companies are being merged into the parent company, to take advantage of manufacturing synergies; in the process, several of the existing structural patterns in the company are likely to get reorganised.

The Tata group is also adopting structural changes. It is, in fact, an instance of a big industrial empire with a high degree of diversification throwing up pressures that the existing structure cannot handle. Though it is part and parcel of the growth process, what is required is timely intervention and reshaping of the structure to take care of the continuing growth requirements. Otherwise structure by itself becomes a handicap to management. The various businesses of the Tata group, ranging from tea to computer and cars, are organised into separate companies with Tata Sons functioning as the holding company. Though for decades, the structure supported business growth, with every business drawing from the corporate image of Tata, the '80s witnessed instances where Tata Sons, the holding company, could not intervene on crucial business decisions affecting some of the companies. For the first time, it was felt that the holding company did not have enough hold, and restructure plans were essential. The merit of Tata organisation is that the need for change was well appreciated by the corporate management and timely intervention was made towards restructure.

STRATEGIC ORGANISATIONS ARE LEARNING ORGANISATIONS

Strategic organisations are seen to be learning organisations. The capacity for continuous learning and adapting is a vital characteristic with them. By being learning organisations, they are able to deal with the changes in the environment, society, competition and technology much better than the other players. They continuously build up a knowledge base and through this learning process keep creating their own future; they never stop with the current position even when the current position is in itself an eminent one. It is seen that when organisations currently in eminent positions, stop learning, cease to be vigilant and forget to be competitive, they lose their position of eminence.

Organisational and managerial obsolescence is one major hurdle faced by modern enterprise, and for achieving success, it is very essential for the enterprises to prevent this obsolescence. Strategic organisations spot the symptoms of obsolescence at an early stage and develop and implement appropriate remedies. They improve the changeability of the organisation and prepare the people for change.

WITH STRATEGIC ORGANISATIONS, PEOPLE ARE THE PRIME ASSET AND PEOPLE MAKE A DYNAMIC DIFFERENCE

The leading companies of the world today, are seen to believe that people or human resources are their most precious asset. For these organisations, everything boils down to people and they do believe that their people can work wonders. The success of their strategy is ensured through the skills of their people—people who formulate strategies and people who implement them. Focussing on the ever-increasing value and significance of the people in an organisation, Jack Welch, CEO of General Electric says "... we are trying to differentiate GE competitively by raising as much intellectual and creative capital from our workforce as we possibly can. That's lot tougher than raising financial capital, which a strong company can find in any market anywhere in the world... ."

These organisations believe that their route to excellence is their people. These companies may be technology driven companies or market driven companies, but their mainstay is 'people'. For them, their people constitute the crew in the voyage to excellence.

At different points of time in the evolution of the 'Business Corporation,' different factors have received greater weightage as contributors to corporate growth. Till the '70s, ideas like experience curve, portfolio manipulation, competitive cost position analysis and the several quantitative techniques dominated the scene. The '80s marked a difference in orientation. The 'soft values' entered the scene. People, and the new terminology of HRD became the new focus; ideas like corporate culture, corporate values and business ethics came to the front row. A change in orientation was obvious—from hard rules about span of control, hierarchy, authority and accountability, companies moved towards the softer ideas like trust, openness and fairplay, ideas which of course were more difficult to practise. Companies bent on success took to the difficult route.

In the Indian context, ITC is a company attributing great significance to its people. It is interesting to listen to ITC, "... the company's two supreme tenets are (1) People are its most valuable asset and (2) The best means of growth come from within...It is ITC's firm conviction that with physical resources and technology either commonly available to or purchasable by any organisation, the quality and effectiveness of knowledge-based managers of an enterprise individually and collectively represent a "Dynamic Difference" which is the sole cause of difference between success and failure..."

Tata Consultancy Services (TCS), provides another example. TCS is one company that meticulously builds up its people-asset and through that distinction, stays ahead in business. TCS pioneered computer software exports from India in the late '60s. And today TCS is the biggest and the most successful software exporter in India. The route to TCS success in the highly competitive computer software market lies in the high-quality workforce it has developed over the years. According to TCS, "Software business is a people business. There is no other investment". Out of TCS's staff strength of 2800, 2400 people are B.Techs, M.Techs or Ph.Ds. And the new recruits go through an 18 months long specially tailored training programme. TCS today has the expertise to undertake highly demanding software contracts on site anywhere in the world. And it invests heavily to keep the 'people strength' up to date and fit. The company spends 7 per cent of its annual turnover on training. TCS is also one of the best pay masters in the industry in India. TELCO, another Tata company, has over the years developed efficient workers and managers, who remain loyal to the company. This 'people strength' has been built into a competitive advantage by the company through investing in people and training them. While a normal company always goes on "recruiting" its key people, a company like TELCO seeking a competitive advantage in its people, always 'retains' them. In fact, the Tata group as a whole is known for its reliance on people. They have around their empire some of the best talents in the world in their respective fields. In fact, no other Indian company has gone to the extent of openly declaring that it will suffer the idiosyncracies of its best people and get the benefit of their brains and talents.

Motivation, the key factor

Motivation is perhaps the most important condition that builds a working bond between the people and their organisation. Managers can seldom succeed in an environment of low motivation or de-motivation. To quote Jack Welch once again, "We have got to take the punitive aspect out of the management process in order to get enough bubbling up of ideas, because the bubbling up is in fact the only way for us to make it, to win..." And one has to remember that Jack Welch is known to be one of America's toughest corporate bosses!

And motivation is not always directly related to a monetary benefit. Motivation can spring from the very presence of a great leader, motivation can come out of a great company culture, motivation can come out of the very sense of participation in a great project. How to motivate the people, how to involve them consciously in the process of growth and development of the unit in which they work, how to make them respond favourably and positively to the changing needs and demands of their organisation—this is one of the main challenges the Indian companies have to encounter in their new environment.

Success should earn rewards and rewards in turn should motivate success; this is the simple principle on which motivation works. A high performer expects rewards. The pre NEP trends in man management in Indian companies, especially in the public sector, were towards treating the performer and non-performer alike. No wonder these organisations could not attain a higher order performance. Only a few corporations in the private sector worked on the slogan 'Spot merit, use merit, reward merit' as the basic philosophy of their reward system and motivation plans. And these organisations generally came to be identified as companies with top-class manager performance.

L&T is one company keen to preserve an excellent workforce, by providing proper motivation. Holck-Larsen, the founder of L&T is reported to have said, when he was asked to explain the factor contributing to the outstanding success of L&T, "We have always recruited the best engineers and professionals without paying any attention whatsoever to extraneous social or political considerations." The company is equally noted for its merit based promotion policy. Through these policies, L&T today has one of the best qualified managerial staff in the country selected and promoted on the sole criterion of merit. And L&T is conspicuous for its highly committed manager community.

With Hindustan Lever, its very recruitment and development programmes serve as sources of motivation. The company is known throughout the country for its professionalism and the care and concern with which its managers are selected. The quality, depth and frequency of Hindustan Lever's training programmes is also found to be the envy of the managerial community. Hindustan Lever has earned the prestige of being cited as a managerial model for the country. The company also believes in encouraging its outstanding managers, without being bothered by hierarchical levels or channels. It is common at HLL to see young managers being provided challenging managerial opportunities.

Asian Paints, in its historic fight against the multinational companies solely relied on the management competence of its people. It kept ready an army of management graduates and other technically qualified workforce, motivated them well and waged a successful battle.

What makes companies like L&T, Asian Paints and Hindustan Lever stand head-and-shoulders above others is their human resources policies which places a heavy emphasis on motivation and continuous managerial training and upgradation of skills.

Explaining the challenges facing the corporations in the '90s, Peter

Drucker makes the poignant observation in his recent book, *Managing for the Future: The 1990s and Beyond*, that the greatest challenge for corporations will be its people, especially the middle management people. Drucker points out that the very structure of management will undergo a sharp change. There will be a drastic reduction of management layers as well as number of managers in the organisation. And one of the more demanding tasks of corporate managements will be to retain the middle manager loyalty. As the managerial layers get compressed and the opportunities of growth for the people get narrowed, the worst affected group happens to be the middle level manager. An important challenge therefore is to still motivate him and retain him with the corporation. Companies who have a variety of means of motivating their people alone can stand up to the new task.

ORGANISATIONAL CULTURE PROVIDES HIGHER ORDER SUSTENANCE TO THE STRATEGIC ORGANISATION

An organisational culture is a set of deep formed and embedded, deep felt, shared values among the people of the organisation. Such a set of values that govern the broad behaviour of a corporation is also found to influence its ultimate performance. It may be an unwritten code, communicated through the past and present practices of the organisation. Just as a society cannot function without a set of values, a business enterprise which is an organ of society cannot function without its own set of values and ethics. It is seen that the enterprise which always adheres to its well established business ethics and values attracts and retains people, whereas the 'hire and fire' enterprise always keeps recruiting people.

An ennobling culture —The Matsushita example

The world famous Matsushita Electric Company provides an all time valid case on the significance of an effective organisational culture in the growth and success of business corporations. The company today has more than 1,60,000 employees engaged in 193 enterprises throughout the world. To the straight and simple question, "What is the key to Matsushita Corporation's success in management?", Matsushita gives a straight and simple answer:

a) He had a good staff.
b) His policies were clear.
c) He upheld ideas to be striven for.
d) His chosen field of electrical appliances was appropriate at the time.
e) He did not allow factions to form within his company.
f) He followed a policy of open management.
g) He worked towards a system of 'management by all employees'.
h) He regarded the company as a Public Institution.

Clearly, concern for its people, has made a contribution to Matsushita's excellence. The Matsushita philosophy on effective management, centres around developing and retaining good people with the corporation. To quote Matsushita: 1) "We make people before we make products." This 'people first' philosophy is fundamental to the corporation's entire activities. And it forms the foundation of the organisational culture. 2) "We use the collective wisdom of all employees of the corporation." Every employee in Matsushita learns to think like a business manager and every one has to share knowledge with others while striving to explore new and better ways of performing his duties. 3) "The Company is a training centre for life." It is a place where employees can give full play to their personality, skills and talents; it is not just a place for earning one's bread. The corporation fulfils a very important educational function. 4) The corporation makes extra efforts to motivate those who are given more responsibility. The corporate faith is that "every ordinary employee is capable of doing extraordinary things" and therefore the company strives to create a condition wherein an employee can realise self fulfilment by achieving extraordinary results.

Matsushita is an organisation famous for its practice of 'open management'. The company from its very inception gave full account of its balance sheet every month to the employees, to keep them informed of the company's month to month sales and profits. The individual worker was simply thrilled to see how he and his colleagues were faring and how they collectively contributed to the growth of the corporation. And as mentioned earlier, the company encouraged the 'SUNAO' mind—an open and adaptable mind throughout the organisation. At Matsushita, the SUNAO mind is a fundamental driving force for successful management.

SUPERIOR LEADERSHIP, A HALLMARK OF STRATEGIC ORGANISATIONS

The best way to understand the characterstic features of good corporate leaderhip, is to really look at corporate leaders who have built up successful corporations. In several cases, corporations owe their success to a couple of leaders who have remained at the helm of affairs during the crucial times in the history of these corporations.

Corporate leadership essentially emanates from the chief executive and the top management team of an enterprise. It is seen that where the chief executive is an outstanding leader and team builder, the environment in the organisation offers tremendous scope for superior performance. Corporate leadership is found to have great 'trickling down effect' on the various levels in the organisation. Personal qualities of the chief executive form an integral part of his management style and are seen to influence the organisational environment. In organisations where the chief executive is known for his concern for human dignity and involvement in human problems, the managers are seen to be more secure, enjoying favourable work environment. In such organisations, people are seen to give their best to the organisation.

A good corporate image which is a prerequisite for success is also largely shaped by the company's leadership. Even a very efficient, dynamic and highly motivated workforce may fail if the corporate image of the organisation is poor. The corporate image is a reservoir of various plus points the organisation has gained over a long period of time through the programmes and policies of a succession of chief executives. A consistently good leadership and a good corporate image are seen to be substantial competitive advantages with the strategic organisation.

The new leadership role

It is seen that the leaders of strategic organisations are subjected continuously to new leadership demands. And they are measuring up to the demands. It appears that the leader of the future cannot be on top of the organisation pyramid. With several of these organisations, the pyramid is seen to be turning upside down. And in this inverted pyramid, the leader is at the bottom, carrying the entire weight and reponsibility of the organisation. He has to keep the organisation vibrant and maintain a dynamic balance, even as things outside are fast changing. It is seen that in these organisations the authority of the leader does not flow from status, but from his commitment to the corporation and his concern for its future. One of the most outstanding examples cited in recent times of lifting up a corporation by its bootlaces, is that of Lee Iacocca. Iacocca accepted a fresh agenda and a bold new vision for the sinking Chrysler. He translated his vision, made his people realise the objectives each one had to achieve. He combined the task approach beautifully with people orientation. His people orientation permitted his subordinates to be their own boss and to set their own goals which made them more productive and better motivated.

Corporate leadership, the Indian context

For many Indian companies in their present predicament of total change, half the problem will be solved with the right leadership. Because, one of the main tasks in front of them is to take certain crucial decisions regarding their future—regarding products, businesses, expansions, diversifications and big investment. The altered situation displays the need for a highly competent, dynamic leadership. Fortunately there is no dearth of business leaders in India. If one has to cite instances, the first reference of course must be made to JRD Tata. JRD symbolises most of the distinguishing features of an ideal corporate leader—vision, strategic foresight, daring, higher order knowledge, grit, sacrifice, above board personal qualities, commitment to superior cause and finally ethics of a high order. In an environment of economic freedom, JRD could have created and led several GEs and GMs. Many other Indian corporations too have had the privilege of getting nurtured by outstanding corporate leaders. L&T owes its eminence to its founder leader Holck-Larsen. C.H. Choksey's Asian Paints has become the envy of the paint industry, all along dominated by multinationals. ITC's growth from a cigarette company to today's multi-business organisation is a direct consequence of A.N. Haksar's business leadership. In the case of HLL too, though it had the support of an MNC parent, T.Thomas gave the new contours for growth and diversification. Reliance's Dhirubhai Ambani, who had to start from small beginnings is an example of vision and strategy achieving phenomenal success. Rahul Bajaj of Bajaj Auto and Kurian of Amul are also examples of outstanding leadership. Each one of these leaders has displayed a sense of purpose and mission that has filtered down the entire organisation. And each one of them has demonstrated a remarkable business leadership that converted the mission into a reality.

The discussions in this chapter have been oriented towards providing a glimpse of the substantive changes taking place in the organisational sphere. As far as India is concerned, right now, far reaching changes are taking place in the economic, and marketing environments of the country. Corporate growth in the emerging context would evidently demand bold and strategic response to the sweeping changes. The Indian companies have to equip themselves to squarely face the era of change that is setting in. From the crucible of management wisdom to which ever so many management authors, business leaders and organisations have contributed Indian companies obviously have to borrow and adopt the appropriate lessons.

References

Abell, Derek, *Strategic Market Planning: Problems and Analytical Perspectives*, Prentice Hall, New Jersey, 1979.

Abell, Derek, *Defining the Business: The Starting Point of Strategic Planning*, Prentice Hall, Englewood Cliffs, N.J., 1980.

Ansoff, H. Igor, *Corporate Strategy*, McGraw Hill, New York, 1965.

Ansoff, H. Igor, *Strategies for Diversification*, Harvard Business Review, September-October 1957.

Bhattacharyya, S.K, *Achieving Managerial Excellence*, Macmillan India Limited, 1989.

Budget 1991-92, Government of India, July '91.

Budget 1992-93, Government of India, February '92.

Budget 1993-94, Government of India, February '93.

Chandler, A.D., *Strategy and Structure*, Garden City, Double-day, New York, 1962.

Doz, Yves L. and Prahlad, C.K., *How MNCs cope with host government intervention*, Harvard Business Review, March-April 1980.

Drucker, Peter F., *Management: Tasks, Responsibilities, Practices*, Harper & Row, New York, 1973.

Drucker, Peter F., *Managing for the future: the 1990s and Beyond*.

Economic Intelligence Service, Various Volumes, Centre for Monitoring Indian Economy, Bombay.

Economic Survey 1990-91, Government of India, New Delhi, July 1991.

Economic Survey 1991-92, Government of India, New Delhi, Feb 1992.

Economic Survey 1992-93, Government of India, New Delhi, Feb 1993.

Ghosh, Arun, *India in Transition: Economic Policy Options*, Wheeler Publishing Co., Allahabad, 1993.

Glueck, W.F. and Jauch, L.R., *Business Policy and Strategic Management*, McGraw-Hill International Book Company, 1984.

Grove, Andrew S., *High Output Management*, Souvenir Press, London, 1984.

Gupta, S.P., *Liberalisation: Its Impact on the Indian Economy*, Macmillan India Limited, New Delhi, 1993.

Hickman, Craig R. and Silva, Michael A, *Creating Excellence*, New American Library, New York, 1984.

Iacocca, Lee, *An autobiography*, Bantam Books, New York, 1984.

Jha, L.K., *Economic Strategy for the '80s*, Allied Publishers Private Limited, 1980.

Kilmann, Ralph, *Beyond the quick fix*, Jossey-Bass Inc, San Francisco, 1985.

Kolde, Endel J., *International Business Enterprises*, Prentice Hall, N. Jersey, 1968.

Kotter, John P, *What effective General Managers really do*, Harvard Business Review, November-December 1982.

Levitt, Theodore, *Marketing success through differentiation of anything*, Harvard Business Review, Jan-Feb 1980.

Levitt, Theodore, *Marketing Intangible Products and Product Intangibles*, Harvard Business Review, May-June 1981.

Levitt, Theodore, *The Globalisation of Markets*, Harvard Business Review, May-June 1983.

Matsushita, Konosuke, *Not For Bread Alone.*

Newman, William H, (Ed) *Managers for the Year 2000*, Prentice Hall Inc.

Peters, Thomas J. and Waterman, Robert H. Jr, *In Search of Excellence*, Harper & Row, New York, 1982.

Porter, Michael E., *How Competitive Forces Shape Strategy*, Harvard Business Review, March-April 1979.

Porter, Michael E., *Competitive Strategy: Techniques for Analyzing Industries and Competitors*, The Free Press, New York, 1980.

Porter, Michael E., *Competitive Advantage: Creating and sustaining superior performance*, The Free Press, New York, 1985.

Porter, Michael E., *The Competitive Advantage of Nations*, The Free Press, New York, 1990.

Potts, Marks and Behr, Peter, *The Leading Edge*, Tata McGraw-Hill Publishing Company Limited, 1989.

Prahalad, C.K. and Hamel, Gary, *The Core Competence of the Corporation*, Harvard Business Review, May-June 1990.

Quinn, James Brian, et. al, *Beyond Products:Services-Based Strategy*, Harvard Business Review, March-April 1990.

Ramaswamy, V.S. and Namakumari, S., *Marketing Management—Planning, Implementation and Control; The Indian Context*, Macmillan India Ltd., New Delhi, 1990.

Rao, S.L., *Economic Reforms and Indian Markets*, Wheeler Publishing Co., Allahabad, 1993.

Ries, Al. and Trout, Jack, *Positioning: The Battle for Your Mind*, Warner Books, New York, 1982.

Robertson, Thomas S. and Wind, Yoram, *Marketing Strategy* in Strategic Management Handbook, (ed) Kennath J. Albert, McGraw Hill, 1983.

Steiner, G. and Miner, J. *Management Policy and Strategy*, Macmillan, New York, 1982.

Tichy, Noel M. and Sherman, Stratford, *Control Your Destiny or Someone Else Will*, Doubleday.

Wargo, Robert J.J. *Konosuke Matsushita and Human Resource Development*, PHP INSTITUTE INC., Japan, Unpublished Paper.

Subject Index